THRICE GREATEST HERMES

VOLUME III – EXCERPTS AND FRAGMENTS

THRICE GREATEST HERMES

VOLUME III – EXCERPTS AND FRAGMENTS

BY
G.R.S. MEAD

Athens ✠ Manchester

Thrice Greatest Hermes, Volume III – Excerpts and Fragments

Published by: Old Book Publishing Ltd

Book Cover Design: Old Book Publishing Ltd

Copyright © 2012 Old Book Publishing Ltd
All rights reserved.

Title of original: Thrice Greatest Hermes
Volume III – Excerpts and Fragments

Originally published in 1906 by The Theosophical Publishing Society

Cover image: The Emerald Tablet of Hermes Trismegistus

ISBN–10: 1-78107-127-6 Volume I
ISBN–10: 1-78107-128-4 Volume II
ISBN–10: 1-78107-129-2 **Volume III**
ISBN–10: 1-78107-130-6 Set

ISBN–13: 978-1-78107-127-4 Volume I
ISBN–13: 978-1-78107-128-1 Volume II
ISBN–13: 978-1-78107-129-8 **Volume III**
ISBN–13: 978-1-78107-130-4 Set

EDITOR'S NOTE

Old Book Publishing Ltd takes care in preserving the wording and images of the original books. For this reason we have invested in technology that enables us to enhance the quality of such reproduction. This investment helps overcome problems encountered when reproducing old books, such as stains, coloured paper, discolouration of ink, yellowed pages, see-through and onion skin type paper.

This reproduction book, produced from digital images of the original, may contain occasional defects such as missing pages or blemishes due to the original source content or were introduced by the scanning process.

These are scanned pages and the quality of print represents accurately the print quality of the original book, though we may have been able to enhance it.

As this book has been scanned and/or reformatted from the original we cannot guarantee that it is error-free or contains the full content of the original.

However, we believe that this work is culturally important, and despite its imperfections, have elected to bring it back into print as part of our commitment to the preservation of printed works.

Old Book Publishing

Thrice-Greatest Hermes

Studies in Hellenistic Theosophy and Gnosis

Being a Translation of the Extant Sermons and
Fragments of the Trismegistic Literature, with
Prolegomena, Commentaries, and Notes

By
G. R. S. Mead

Volume III.—Excerpts and Fragments

London and Benares
The Theosophical Publishing Society
1906

Contents

I. EXCERPTS BY STOBÆUS

	PAGE
Ex. I. OF PIETY AND TRUE PHILOSOPHY	3
Commentary	12
Ex. II. OF THE INEFFABILITY OF GOD	14
Commentary	15
Ex. III. OF TRUTH	17
Commentary	23
Ex. IV. GOD, NATURE AND THE GODS	24
Commentary	25
Ex. V. OF MATTER	26
Ex. VI. OF TIME	28
Ex. VII. OF BODIES EVERLASTING AND BODIES PERISHABLE	30
Commentary	33
Ex. VIII. OF ENERGY AND FEELING	34
Commentary	43
Ex. IX. OF THE DECANS AND THE STARS	45
Commentary	54
Ex. X. CONCERNING THE RULE OF PROVIDENCE, NECESSITY AND FATE	55
Commentary	57

CONTENTS

	PAGE
Ex. XI. OF JUSTICE	58
Commentary	59
Ex. XII. OF PROVIDENCE AND FATE	60
Ex. XIII. OF THE WHOLE ECONOMY	61
Ex. XIV. OF SOUL, I.	63
Ex. XV. OF SOUL, II.	65
The Embryonic Stages of Incarnation	68
Ex. XVI. OF SOUL, III.	72
Ex. XVII. OF SOUL, IV.	75
Ex. XVIII. OF SOUL, V.	77
Commentary	79
Ex. XIX. OF SOUL, VI.	80
Commentary	82
Ex. XX. THE POWER OF CHOICE	84
Commentary	86
Ex. XXI. OF ISIS TO HORUS	87
Commentary	87
Ex. XXII. AN APOPHTHEGM	88
Ex. XXIII. FROM "APHRODITE"	89
Commentary	90
Ex. XXIV. A HYMN OF THE GODS	91
Commentary	92
Ex. XXV. THE VIRGIN OF THE WORLD, I.	93
Ex. XXVI. THE VIRGIN OF THE WORLD, II.	125

COMMENTARY

Argument	134
Sources?	146
The Direct Voice and the Books of Hermes	147

CONTENTS

	PAGE
Kamephis and the Dark Mystery	149
Kneph-Kamephis	151
Hermes I. and Hermes II.	152
The Black Rite	155
Black Land	158
The Pupil of the World's Eye	159
The Son of the Virgin	160
The Mystery of the Birth of Horus	162
"Ishon"	165
The Sixty Soul-Regions	168
Plutarch's Yogin	169
The Plain of Truth	171
The Boundaries of the Numbers which Pre-exist in the Soul	173
The Mysterious "Cylinder"	175
The Eagle, Lion, Dragon and Dolphin	180
Momus	182
The Mystic Geography of Sacred Lands	184

Ex. XXVII. From the Sermon of Isis to Horus . 188

COMMENTARY

Argument	204
Title and Ordering	206
The Books of Isis and Horus	207
The Watery Sphere and Subtle Body	209
The Habitat of Encarnate Souls	210

II. REFERENCES AND FRAGMENTS IN THE FATHERS

I. JUSTIN MARTYR

i. The Most Ancient of Philosophers	215
The "Words of Ammon"	215
The Ineffability of God	216
ii. Hermes and Asclepius Sons of God	217
iii. Hermes the Word who brings Tidings from God	217
The Sons of God in Hellenistic Theology	218
An Unverifiable Quotation	218
II. ATHENAGORAS	220

III. CLEMENT OF ALEXANDRIA

	PAGE
i. Many Hermeses and Asclepiuses	221
ii. The Apotheosis of Hermes and Asclepius	222
iii. The Books of Hermes	222
The General Catalogue of the Egyptian Priestly Library	225

IV. TERTULLIAN

i. Hermes the Master of all Physics	226
ii. Hermes the Writer of Scripture	227
iii. Hermes the First Preacher of Reincarnation	227
iv. Hermes on Metempsychosis	
FRAG. I.	228

V. CYPRIAN

God is beyond all Understanding	229

VI. ARNOBIUS

The School of Hermes	230

VII. LACTANTIUS

i. Thoyth-Hermes and his Books on the Gnosis	231
FRAG. II.	233
The Historical Origin of the Hermetic Tradition	233
ii. Uranus, Cronus and Hermes, Adepts of the Perfect Science	234
iii. Divine Providence	235
iv. On Mortal and Immortal Sight	
FRAG. III.	235
v. Man made after the Image of God	236
vi. Hermes the First Natural Philosopher	237
vii. The Daimon-Chief	237
viii. Devotion in God-Gnosis	
FRAG. IV.	238
ix. The Cosmic Son of God	
FRAG. V.	239

CONTENTS

	PAGE
x. The Demiurge of God	240
xi. The Name of God	
FRAG. VI.	241
xii. The Holy Word about the Lord of All	
FRAG. VII.	241
xiii. His Own Father and Own Mother	242
xiv. The Power and Greatness of the Word	242
xv. The Fatherless and Motherless	242
xvi. Piety the Gnosis of God	243
xvii. The Only Way to Worship God	243
xviii. The Worthiest Sacrifice to God	
FRAG. VIII.	244
xix. Man made in the Image of God	244
xx. Contemplation	245
xxi. The Dual Nature of Man	
FRAG. IX.	245
Wonder the Beginning of Philosophy	246
xxii. The Cosmic Restoration	
FRAG. X.	247
xxiii. Of Hermes and his Doctrine Concerning God	247
xxiv. A Repetition	248
xxv. Plato as Prophet follows Trismegistus	248

VIII. AUGUSTINE

i.–iii. Three Quotations from the Old Latin Version of the "Perfect Sermon"	249

IX. CYRIL OF ALEXANDRIA

i. Cyril's Corpus of XV. Books	251
ii. The Incorporeal Eye	
FRAG. XI.	253
iii. The Heavenly Word Proceeding Forth	
FRAG. XII.	254
The Pyramid	
FRAG. XIII.	254

x   CONTENTS

	PAGE
The Nature of God's Intellectual Word	
FRAG. XIV.	255
The Word of the Creator	
FRAG. XV.	256
iv. Mind of Mind	
FRAG. XVI.	257
He is All	
FRAG. XVII.	258
Concerning Spirit	
FRAG. XVIII.	258
The "To Asclepius" of Cyril's Corpus	259
v. From "The Mind"	260
vi. Osiris and Thrice-greatest Agathodaimon	
FRAG. XIX.	261
"Let there be Earth!"	
FRAG. XX	262
The Generation of the Sun	
FRAG. XXI.	262
"Let the Sun be!"	
FRAG. XXII.	263
vii. The Firmament	
FRAG. XXIII.	263
viii. From the "To Asclepius"	264
ix. The Sole Protection	265
x. The Supreme Artist	
FRAG. XXIV.	266
xi. An Unreferenced Quotation	
FRAG. XXV.	266

X. SUIDAS

Hermes speaks of the Trinity	268
An Orphic Hymn	269

XI. ANONYMOUS 270

III. REFERENCES AND FRAGMENTS IN THE PHILOSOPHERS

I. ZOSIMUS

	PAGE
On the Anthrōpos-Doctrine	273
The Processions of Fate	273
"The Inner Door"	274
Against Magic	
Frag. XXVI.	275
Thoth the First Man	276
The Libraries of the Ptolemies	277
Nikotheos	278
From the Books of the Chaldæans	279
Man the Mind	
Frag. XXVII.	280
The Counterfeit Daimon	281
His Advice to Theosebeia	283

II. JAMBLICHUS

Abammon the Teacher	285
Hermes the Inspirer	286
Those of the Hermaïc Nature	288
The Books of Hermes	289
The Monad from the One	291
The Tradition of the Trismegistic Literature	291
Bitys	294
Ostanes-Asclepius	296
From the Hermaïc Workings	297
The Cosmic Spheres	299

III. JULIAN THE EMPEROR

The Disciples of Wisdom	303

IV. FULGENTIUS THE MYTHOGRAPHER

Frag. XXVIII.	305

IV. CONCLUSION

	PAGE
An Attempt at Classifying the Extant Literature	306
Of Hermes	306
To Tat	308
To Asclepius	310
To Ammon	311
Of Asclepius	312
Of Isis	312
From the Agathodaimon Literature	313
Of Judgments of Value	314
The Sons of God	316
Concerning Dates	319
The Blend of Traditions	321
Of Initiation	323
A Last Word	325

V. INDEX

I

Excerpts by Stobæus

EXCERPT I.

OF PIETY AND [TRUE] PHILOSOPHY

(Title from Patrizzi (p. 4); preceded by "Of Thrice-greatest Hermes."

Text: Stobæus, *Phys.*, xxxv. 1, under heading: "Of Hermes—from the [Book] to Tat"; G. pp. 273–278; M. i. 190–194; W. i. 273–278.[1]

Ménard, Livre IV., No. i. of "Fragments from the Books of Hermes to his Son Tat," pp. 225–230.)

1.[2] *Her.* Both for the sake of love to man, and piety[3] to God, I [now], my son, for the first time take pen in hand.[4]

---

[1] G. = Gaisford (T.), *Joannis Stobæi Florilegium* (Oxford, 1822), 4 vols.; *Io. Stob. Ec. Phys. et Ethic. Libri Duo* (Oxford, 1850), 2 vols.

M. = Meineke (A.), *Joh. Stob. Flor.* (Leipzig, 1855, 1856), 3 vols.; *Joh. Stob. Ec. Phys. et Ethic. Lib. Duo* (Leipzig, 1860), 2 vols.

W. = Wachsmuth (C.), *Io. Stob. Anthologii Lib. Duo Priores . . . Ec. Phys. et Ethic.* (Berlin, 1884), 2 vols.

H. = Hense (O.), *I. Stob. Anth. Lib. Tert.* (Berlin, 1894), 1 vol., incomplete.

[2] I have numbered the paragraphs in all the excerpts for convenience of reference.

[3] εὐσεβείας,—it might also be rendered by worship.

[4] τόδε συγγράφω.

For there can be no piety more righteous than to know the things that are, and to give thanks for these to Him who made them,—which I will never cease to do.

2. *Tat.* By doing what, O father, then, if naught be true down here, may one live wisely?

Her. Be pious,[1] son! Who pious is, doth reach the height of [all] philosophy[2]; without philosophy the height of piety cannot be scaled.

But he who learns what are existent things, and how they have been ordered, and by whom, and for whose sake,—he will give thanks for all unto the Demiurge, as unto a good sire, a nurse [most] excellent, a steward who doth never break his trust.[3]

3. Who giveth thanks, he will be pious; and he who pious is, will [get to] know both where is Truth, and what it is.

And as he learns, he will more and more pious grow.

For never, son, can an embodied soul that has once leaped aloft, so as to get a hold upon the truly Good and True, slip back again into the contrary.

For when the soul [once] knows the Author of its Peace,[4] 'tis filled with wondrous love,[5] and

---

[1] Or give worship unto God,—εὐσέβει.
[2] In its true sense of wisdom-loving.   [3] ἐπιτρόπῳ πιστῷ.
[4] *Cf. C. H.*, xiii. (xiv.) 3, Comment.
[5] *Cf. P. S. A.*, ix. 1; xii. 3.

OF PIETY AND TRUE PHILOSOPHY

with forgetfulness[1] of every ill, and can no more keep from the Good.

4. Let this be, O [my] son, the goal of piety;—to which if thou attain, thou shalt both nobly live, and happily depart from life, for that thy soul no longer will be ignorant of whither it should wing its flight again.

This is the only [Way], my son,—the Path [that leads] to Truth, [the Path] on which our forebears,[2] too, did set their feet, and, setting them, did find the Good.[3]

Solemn and smooth this Path, yet difficult to tread for soul while still in body.

5. For first it hath to fight against itself, and make a great dissension, and manage that the victory should rest with the one part [of its own self].

For that there is a contest of the one against the two,[4]—the former trying to flee, the latter dragging down.

---

[1] Where λήθη (forgetfulness) is opposed to ἔρως (love),—that is to say, reminiscence, the secret of the μάθησις (*mathēsis*) of the Pythagoreans, the knowledge of the Author of our being or of our "race" within,—ψυχὴ μαθοῦσα ἑαυτῆς τὸν προπάτορα (*cf.* Ex. iii. 6).

[2] *Cf. C. H.*, x. (xi.) 5; *P. S. A.*, xi. 4; xxxvii. 3; Lact., *D. I.*, i. 11.

[3] *Cf. C. H.*, xi. (xii.) 21.

[4] The "one" is the rational element (τὸ λογικόν) and the "two" are the passional (τὸ θυμικόν) and desiderative (τὸ ἐπιθυμητικόν) elements of the irrational nature (τὸ ἄλογον, or τὸ αἰσθητὸν as below), the "heart" and the "appetite." *Cf.* Ex. xvii.; see also "Orphic Psychology" in my *Orpheus* (London, 1896), pp. 273-275.

And there's great strife and battle [dire] of these with one another,—the one desiring to escape, the others striving to detain.

6. The victory, moreover, of the one or of the others[1] is not resemblant.

For that the one doth hasten [upwards] to the Good, the others settle [downwards] to the bad.

The one longs to be freed; the others love their slavery.

If [now] the two be vanquished, they remain deprived of their own selves and of their ruler[2]; but if the one be worsted, 'tis harried by the two, and driven about, being tortured by the life down here.

This[3] is, [my] son, the one who leadeth thee upon the Thither[4] Path.

Thou must, [my] son, first leave behind thy body,[5] before the end [of it[6] is reached], and come out victor in the life of conflict, and thus as victor wend thy way towards home.

7. And now, [my] son, I will go through the things that are by heads[7]; for thou wilt understand the things that will be said, if thou remember what thy ears have heard.

All things that are, are [then] in motion; alone the that which is not, is exempt from it.

---

[1] Lit. of the two.   [2] That is, the one.   [3] Sc. the one.
[4] ἐκεῖσε—that is, to the Good and True, or God.
[5] Cf. Ex. ix. 12.   [6] Sc. the Path.
[7] Or summarily; cf. § 16 below.

OF PIETY AND TRUE PHILOSOPHY

Every body is in a state of change; [but] all bodies are not dissolvable; some bodies [only] are dissolvable.

Not every animal is mortal; not every animal, immortal.

That which can be dissolved, can [also] be destroyed; the permanent [is] the unchangeable; the that which doth not change, [is] the eternal.

What doth become[1] for ever, for ever also is destroyed[2]; what once for all becomes, is never more destroyed, nor does it [ever more] become some other thing.

8. First God; second the Cosmos; third [is] man.[3]

The Cosmos, for man's sake; and man, for God's.

The soul's irrational part[4] is mortal; its rational part, immortal.

All essence [is] immortal; all essence, free from change.

All that exists[5] [is] twofold; naught of existing things remains.

Not all are moved by soul; the soul moves all that doth exist.[6]

---

[1] Or is born. [2] Or dies.

[3] πρῶτον ὁ θεὸς, δεύτερον ὁ κόσμος, τρίτον ὁ ἄνθρωπος. *Cf. P. S. A.*, x.: "The Lord of the Eternity (Æon) is the first God; second is Cosmos; man's the third."

[4] Lit. sensible part,—τὸ αἰσθητόν.

[5] πᾶν τὸ ὄν,—as opposed to οὐσία (essence).

[6] The meaning of *ex*-istence, being the coming out of pure being into the state of becoming.

9. All that suffereth [is] sensible; not all that's sensible, doth suffer.

All that feels pain, doth also have experience of pleasure,—a mortal life[1]; not all that doth experience pleasure, feeleth [also] pain,—a life immortal.

Not every body's subject to disease; all bodies subject to disease are subject [too] to dissolution.

10. The mind's in God; the reasoning faculty's[2] in man.

The reason's in the mind; the mind's above all suffering.

Nothing in body's true[3]; all in the bodiless is free from what's untrue.

All that becomes, [is] subject unto change; not all that doth become, need be dissolved.

Naught['s] good upon the earth; naught['s] bad in heaven.

11. God['s] good; [and] man [is] bad.[4]

Good [is] free-willed; bad is against the will.

The gods do choose what things *are* good, as good; . . .

The good law of the mighty [One][5] is *the* good law; good law's *the* law.

[1] Or animal; perhaps this and the following interjection are glosses.

[2] ὁ λογισμός,—perhaps a mistake for λόγος, as Patrizzi has it.

[3] Or real.

[4] But see § 15 below; and *cf. C. H.*, x. (xi.) 12.

[5] The text is faulty; as is also apparently that of the following sentence. None of the conjectures yet put forward are satisfactory.

OF PIETY AND TRUE PHILOSOPHY

Time's for the gods; the law for men.[1]

Bad is the stuff that feeds the world; time is the thing that brings man to an end.

12. All in the heaven is free from change; all on the earth is subject unto it.

Naught in the heaven's a slave; naught on the earth is free.

Nothing can *not* be known in heaven; naught can be known on earth.

The things on earth do not consort with things in heaven.[2]

All things in heaven are free from blame; all on the earth are blameworthy.

The immortal is not mortal; the mortal, not immortal.

That which is sown, is not invariably brought forth; but that which is brought forth, must have invariably been sown.

13. [Now] for a body that can be dissolved, [there are] two "times":—[the period] from its sowing till its birth, and from its birth until its death; but for an everlasting body, the time from birth alone.[3]

Things subject unto dissolution wax and wane.

The matter that's dissolved, doth undergo two

[1] Or time is divine, the law is man's.

[2] I have not adopted W.'s lengthy emendations.

[3] This is the idea of sempiternity—of things which have a beginning but no end.

contrary transformings:—death and birth; but everlasting [matter], doth change either to its own self, or into things like to itself.

The birth of man [is] the beginning of his dissolution; man's dissolution the beginning of his birth.

That which departs,[1] [returns; and what returns] departs [again].[2]

14. Of things existent, some are in bodies, some in forms, and some [are] in activities.[3]

Body['s] in forms; and form and energy in body.

The deathless shares not in the mortal [part]; the mortal shares in the immortal.

The mortal body doth not mount[4] into the deathless one; the deathless one descends[5] into the mortal frame.

Activities do not ascend, but they descend.

15. The things on earth bestow no benefit on things in heaven; the things in heaven shower every benefit on things on earth.

Of bodies everlasting heaven is the container; of those corruptible, the earth.

Earth [is] irrational; the heaven [is] rational.

The things in heaven [are] under it; the things on earth above the earth.

---

[1] Or dies.
[2] There is a lacuna in the text.
[3] Or energies.
[4] Lit. go.
[5] Lit. comes.

Heaven['s] the first element; earth['s] the last element.

Fore-knowledge[1] [is] God's Order; Necessity['s] handmaiden to Fore-knowledge.

Fortune['s][2] the course of the disorderly,—the image of activity,[3] untrue opinion.

What, [then] is God? The Good that naught can change.

What, man? The bad that can be changed.[4]

16. If thou rememberest these heads,[5] thou wilt remember also what I have already set forth for thee with greater wealth of words. For these are summaries[6] of those.

Avoid, however, converse with the many [on these things]; not that I would that thou shouldst keep them selfishly unto thyself, but rather that thou shouldst not seem ridiculous unto the multitude.[7]

For that the like's acceptable unto the like; the unlike's never friend to the unlike.

Such words as these have very very few to give them ear; nay, probably, they will not even have the few.[8]

They have, moreover, some [strange force]

[1] Or Providence. *Cf. P. S. A.*, xxxix. 2; § 17 below; and Ex. xi. 1.
[2] τύχη.   [3] Or energy.
[4] Reading τρεπτὸν for the hopeless ἄτρεπτον of the text. *Cf.* § 11 above.
[5] *Cf.* § 7 above.   [6] περιοχαί.
[7] *Cf. C. H.*, xiii. (xiv.) 13 and 22.   [8] *Cf. P. S. A.*, xxii. 1.

peculiar unto themselves; for they provoke the evil all the more to bad.

Wherefore thou shouldst protect the many [from themselves], for they ignore the power of what's been said.

17. *Tat.* What meanest thou, O father?

Her. This, [my] son! All that in man is animal, is proner unto bad [than unto good]; nay, it doth cohabit with it, because it is in love with it.

Now if this animal should learn that Cosmos is subject to genesis, and all things come and go according to Fore-knowledge [1] and by Necessity, Fate ruling all,—in no long time it would grow worse than it is now,[2] [and] thinking scorn of the whole [universe] as being subject unto genesis, and unto Fate referring [all] the causes of the bad, would never cease from every evil deed.

Wherefore, care should be taken of them, in order that being [left] in ignorance, they may become less bad through fear of the unknown.

COMMENTARY

Patrizzi thought so highly of this excerpt that he chose it for Book I. of his collection. He, however, erroneously made the persons of the dialogue Asclepius and Tat, instead of Hermes and Tat—an unaccountable

[1] Or Providence; *cf.* § 15 above.   [2] Lit. than itself.

OF PIETY AND TRUE PHILOSOPHY 13

mistake, in which he has been followed by all the editors of Stobæus except Wachsmuth.

In the introduction the treatise purports to be a letter written to Tat,—a new departure, for it is "for the first time"; on the other hand the form of the treatise is the usual one of oral instruction, of question and answer (§ 2). Nevertheless in § 16 we learn that the definitions given in §§ 7–15 are intended as heads or summaries of previous sermons.

But already in *C. H.*, x. (xi.) 1, we have an abridgment or epitome (or rather a summation) of the General Sermons delivered to Tat, just as we have in *C. H.*, xvi., "the summing up and digest, as it were, of all the rest" of the Sermons of Asclepius to the King, under the traditional title, "The Definitions of Asclepius." The headings in our sermon, then, may probably have been intended for the summary of the teaching of the Expository Sermons to Tat (see in Cyril, Frag. xv.). Some of our definitions, however, are strikingly similar to those in *C. H.*, x. (xi.), but this may be accounted for by supposing that "The Key" itself was one of, or rather the continuation of, the Expository Sermons.[1]

The warning to use great discretion in communicating the instruction to the "many," because of the danger of teaching the Gnosis to the morally unfit, seems to be an appropriate ending to the sermon; we may then be fairly confident that we have in the above a complete tractate of "The [? Expository] Sermons to Tat"; the title, however, is the invention of Patrizzi, and not original.

[1] *Cf.* R. (p. 128), who calls them a "Collection of Sayings of Hermes."

EXCERPT II.

[OF THE INEFFABILITY OF GOD]

(I have added the title, the excerpt not being found in Patrizzi.

Text: Stob., *Flor.*, lxxx. [lxxviii.] 9, under the heading: "Of Hermes from the [Book] to Tat"; G. iii. 135; M. iii. 104, 105.[1]

Ménard, Livre IV., No. x. of "Fragments from the Books of Hermes to his Son Tat," p. 256.)

[*Her.*] To understand[2] God is difficult, to speak [of Him] impossible.

For that the Bodiless can never be expressed in body, the Perfect never can be comprehended by that which is imperfect, and that 'tis difficult for the Eternal to company with the ephemeral.

The one is for ever, the other doth pass; the one is in [the clarity of] Truth, the other in the shadow of appearance.

So far off from the stronger [is] the weaker,

[1] Hense's text ends with xlii. 17; the second part has apparently never been published.
[2] Or think of.

OF THE INEFFABILITY OF GOD 15

the lesser from the greater [is so far], as [is] the mortal [far] from the Divine.

It is the distance, then, between the two that dims the Vision of the Beautiful.

For 'tis with eyes that bodies can be seen, with tongue that things seen can be spoken of; but That which hath no body, that is unmanifest, and figureless, and is not made objective [to us] out of matter,—cannot be comprehended by our sense.

I have it in my mind, O Tat, I have it in my mind, that what cannot be spoken of, is God.

COMMENTARY

Justin Martyr quotes these opening words of our excerpt *verbatim*, assigning them to Hermes (*Cohort.*, 38; Otto, ii. 122).[1]

The substance of the second sentence is given twice by Lactantius in Latin (*Div. Institt.*, ii. 8; Ep. 4); in the second passage the Church Father also quotes *verbatim* the first sentence of our excerpt, and from his introductory words we learn that they were the *beginning* of a written sermon from Hermes to his son (Tat).

The first four sentences are also quoted in almost identical words (there being two variants of reading and two slight additions) by Cyril,—*Contra Julianum*, i. 31 (Migne, col. 549 B),—who, moreover, gives some additional lines, beginning (Frag. xi.): "If, then, there be an incorporeal eye," etc.

[1] Which see for Commentary under "Fragments."

If, furthermore, we are right in supposing that Frag. xv. (Cyril, *ibid.*, i. 33) is from the same sermon, then this sermon is the "First Sermon of the Expository [Sermons] to Tat," and the Stobæan heading, "From the [Book] to Tat," will mean the collection of Expository Sermons (see Comment. on Frag. xv.).

EXCERPT III.

OF TRUTH

(Title from Patrizzi (p. 46b), preceded by: "Of Thrice-greatest Hermes to Tat."

Text: Stob., *Flor.*, xi. 23, under heading: "Of Hermes from the [Sermons] to Tat"; G. i. 307–311; M. i. 248–251; H. iii. 436–441.

Ménard, Livre IV., No. ix. of "Fragments from the Books of Hermes to his Son Tat," pp. 251–255.)

1. [*Her.*] Concerning Truth, O Tat, it is not possible that man should dare to speak, for man's an animal imperfect, composed out of imperfect members, his tabernacle[1] patched together from many bodies strange [to him].

But what is possible and right, this do I say, —that Truth is [to be found] in the eternal bodies only, [those things] of which the bodies in themselves are true,[2]—fire very fire and nothing else, earth very earth and nothing else, air very air and nothing else, and water very water and naught else.

[1] σκῆνος. *Cf.* Ex. vii. 3 note, and also § 5 below. [2] Or real.

Our frames, however, are a compound of all these. For they have [in them] fire, and they have also earth, they've water, too, and air; but they are neither fire, nor earth, nor water, nor air,[1] nor any [element that's] true.

And if our composition has not had Truth for its beginning, how can it either see or speak the Truth?

Nay, it can only have a notion of it,—[and that too] if God will.

2. All things, accordingly, that are on earth, O Tat, are not the Truth; they're copies [only] of the True.

And these are not all things, but few [of them]; the rest consist of falsity and error, Tat, and shows of seeming like unto images.

Whenever the appearance doth receive the influx from above, it turns into a copy of the Truth; without its[2] energizing from above, it is left false.

Just as the portrait also indicates the body in the picture, but in itself is not a body, in spite of the appearance of the thing that's seen.

'Tis seen as having eyes; but it sees naught, hears naught at all.

The picture, too, has all the other things, but they are false, tricking the sight of the beholders,

[1] Compare Lact., *D. I.*, ii. 12.   [2] That is, Truth's.

OF TRUTH

—these thinking that they see what's true, while what they see is really false.

All, then, who do not see what's false see truth.

If, then, we thus do comprehend, or see, each one of these[1] just as it really is, we really comprehend and see.

But if [we comprehend, or see, things] contrary to that which is, we shall not comprehend, nor shall we know aught true.

3. [*Tat.*] There is, then, father, Truth e'en on the earth?

[*Her.*] Not inconsiderably, O son, art thou at fault.

Truth is in no wise, Tat, upon the earth, nor can it be.

But some men can, [I say,] have an idea of it, —should God grant them the power of godly vision.[2]

Thus there is nothing true on earth,—[so much] I know and say. All are appearances and shows,—I know and speak true [things]. We ought not, surely, though, to call the knowing and the speaking of true things the Truth?

4. [*Tat.*] Why, how on earth ought we to know and speak of things being true,—yet nothing's true on earth?

[1] This presumably refers to the simple elements of things in themselves.

[2] τὴν θεοπτικὴν ... δύναμιν.

[*Her.*] This [much] is true,—that we do not know aught that's true down here.[1] How could it be, O son?

For Truth is the most perfect virtue, the very highest Good, by matter undisturbed, uncircumscribed by body,—naked, [and] evident, changeless, august, unalterable Good.

But things down here, O son, thou seest what they are,—not able to receive this Good, corruptible, [and] passible, dissolvable, changeful, and ever altering, being born from one another.

Things, then, that are not true even to their own selves, how can they [possibly] be true?

For all that alters is untrue; it does not stay in what it is, but shows itself to us by changing into one another its appearances.

5. [*Tat.*] And even man,—is he not true, O father?

[*Her.*] As man,—he is not true, O son. For that the True is that which has its composition from itself alone, and in itself stays as it is.

But man has been composed of many things, and does not stay in his own self.

He changes and he alters, from age to age, from form to form, and that too, even while he's still in [one and] the [same] tent.[2]

Nay, many fail to recognize their children,

---

[1] Taking ἐνθάδε with the preceding clause.
[2] *Cf.* § 1 above.

when a brief space of time comes in between ; and so again of children with their parents.

That, then, which changes so that it's no longer recognized,—can that be true, O Tat?

Is it not, rather, false, coming and going,[1] in the [all] varied shows of its [continual] changes?

But do thou have it in thy mind that a true thing is that which stays and lasts for aye.

But "man" is not for ever; wherefore it [2] is not true. "Man's" an appearance. And appearance is extreme untruth.

6. [*Tat.*] But these external bodies,[3] father, too, in that they change, are they not true?

[*Her.*] All that is subject unto genesis and change, is verily not true; but in as much as they are brought to being by the Forefather [4] [of them all], they have their matter true.

But even they have something false in that they change; for naught that doth not stay with its own self is true.

[*Tat.*] True, father [mine]! Is one to say, then, that the Sun alone,—in that in greater measure than the rest of them he doth not change but stayeth with himself,—is Truth?

[*Her.*] [Nay, rather, but] because he, and

[1] Lit. becoming.
[2] Neuter, that is, the series of temporary appearances of the true man.
[3] The heavenly bodies presumably.
[4] τοῦ προπάτορος; *cf.* Ex. i. 3.

he only, hath entrusted unto him the making of all things in cosmos,[1] ruling all and making all;—to whom I reverence give, and worship pay unto his Truth, and recognise him as the Demiurge after the One and First.

[*Tat.*] What then, O father, should'st thou say is the first Truth?

[*Her.*] The One and Only, Tat,—He who is not of matter, or in body, the colourless, the figureless, the changeless [One], He who doth alter not, who ever is.

But the untrue, O son, doth perish. All things, however, on the earth that perish,—the Forethought of the True hath comprehended [them], and doth and will encompass [them].

For birth without corruption[2] cannot be; corruption followeth on every birth, in order that it may be born again.

For that things that are born, must of necessity be born from things that are destroyed[3]; and things that have been born, must of necessity be [once again] destroyed, in order that the genesis of things existent may not stop.

First, [then], see that thou recognize him[4] as the Demiurge for birth-and-death[5] of [all] existent things.

[1] *Cf.* Ex. vii. 2, and § 7 below.   [2] Or perishing.
[3] Or are corrupted, or perish.
[4] That is, the Sun; *cf.* § 6 above.   [5] Lit. genesis.

8. Things that are born out of destruction, then, must of necessity be false,—in that they are becoming now these things, now those. For 'tis impossible they should *become* the same.

But that which is not "same,"—how can it possibly be true?

Such things we should, then, call appearances, [my] son; for instance, if we give the man his proper designation, [we ought to designate him] a man's[1] appearance;—[and so] the child a child's appearance, the youth a youth's appearance, the man a man's appearance, the old man an appearance of the same.

For man is not a man, nor child a child, nor youth a youth, nor grown up man a grown up man, nor aged man a [single] aged man.

But as they change they are untrue,—both pre-existent things and things existent.

But thus think of them, son,—as even these untruths being energies dependent from above from Truth itself.

And this being so, I say untruth is Truth's in-working.[2]

COMMENT

The excerpt seems complete in itself, but whether it lay before Stobæus as a single sermon or as a part of a sermon it is impossible to say.

[1] Lit. manhood's.   [2] Or operation; ἐνέργημα.

EXCERPT IV.

[GOD, NATURE AND THE GODS]

(Patrizzi (p. 51b) gives no title; but simply the heading "In Another [Book]."

Text: Stob., *Phys.*, xxxv. 11, under the heading: "Of Hermes"; G. pp. 295, 296; M. i. 206; W. i. 293.

Ménard, Livre IV., No. iv. of "Fragments Divers," p. 274).

1. [*Her.*] There is, then, That which transcends being,[1]—beyond all things existent, and all that really are.

For That-transcending-being is [that mystery] because of which exists that being-ness[2] which is called universal, common unto intelligibles that really are, and to those beings which are thought of according to the law of sameness.

Those which are contrary to these, according to the law of otherness, are again themselves according to themselves.[3]

[1] Or the pre-existent; τὸ πρὸ ὄν, or τὸ προόν.

[2] οὐσιότης; or essentiality.

[3] This seems to refer to the seven spheres of difference or otherness (κατὰ τὸ ἕτερον) moving symbolically against, or "crosswise with," the all-embracing sphere of sameness (καθ' ἑαυτό); or it may mean that they have a sameness in the fact that their motions enter into themselves "again."

And Nature is an essence which the senses can perceive, containing in itself all sensibles.

2. Between these [1] are the intelligible [2] and the sensible gods.

Things that pertain to the intelligence, share in [the nature of] the Gods that are intelligible only; while things pertaining to opinion, have their part with those that are the sensible.

These latter are the images of the intelligences [3]; the Sun, for instance, is the image of the Demiurgic God above the Heaven.

For just as He hath made the universe, so doth Sun make the animals, and generate the plants, and regulate the breaths. [4]

COMMENT

I have supplied the title for the sake of uniformity. If we compare our extract with Ex. vii., and especially the last sentence of the former with the first sentence of § 2 of the latter, and note that in Stobæus the one excerpt follows almost immediately on the other, we shall be fairly well persuaded that they both come from the same collection—namely, the Sermons to Tat.

[1] Presumably God and Nature.

[2] νοηματικοί,—a very rare form, and may possibly mean perceptible.

[3] νοημάτων.

[4] Or spirits. The last clause, "and regulates," etc., is absent from some MSS., and is, therefore, considered spurious by some editors; but its unexpectedness is a strong guarantee of its genuineness. The "spirits" are the prāṇa's of Hindu physiological psychology; cf. C. H., x. (xi.) 13, Comment., and Exs. xv. 2, xix. 3.

EXCERPT V

[OF MATTER]

(I have added the title, it being the same as that of the main section of Stobæus, Patrizzi (p. 51) giving only the simple heading " From the [Sermons] to Tat."

Text: Stobæus, *Phys.*, xi. 2, under the heading: " Of Hermes from the [Sermons] to Tat "; G. p. 121 ; M. i. 84, 85; W. i. 131.

Ménard, Livre IV., No. viii. of "Fragments from the Books of Hermes to his son Tat," p. 250.)

Her. Matter both has been born, O son, and it has been [before it came into existence]; for Matter is the vase of genesis,[1] and genesis, the mode of energy of God, who's free from all necessity of genesis, and pre-exists.

[Matter], accordingly, by its reception of the seed of genesis, did come [herself] to birth, and [so] became subject to change, and, being shaped,

[1] Or receptacle or field of genesis, or birth (ἀγγεῖον γενέσεως). The idea of a vessel or vase of birth was a familiar symbol with the Pythagoreans ; μεταγγισμός (from the simile of pouring water out of one vessel into another) being one of their synonyms for metempsychosis.

took forms; for she, contriving the forms of her [own] changing, presided over her own changing self.

The unborn state[1] of Matter, then, was formlessness[2]; its genesis is its being brought into activity.

[1] ἀγεννησία.

[2] ἀμορφία. Compare this with the Christian Gnostic commentator of the Naassene Document, quoted by Hippolytus (*Philos.* v. 7), and the comment of Hippolytus on him: "Their first and Blessed Formless Essence (ἀσχημάτιστος οὐσία), the cause of all forms" ("Myth of Man," § 7).

EXCERPT VI.

OF TIME

(Title from Patrizzi (p. 38b); followed by: "To the Same Tat."

Text: Stob., *Phys.*, viii. 41, under heading: "Of Hermes from the [Sermons] to Tat"; G. p. 93; M. i. 64.

Ménard, Livre IV., No. v. of "Fragments from the Books of Hermes to his Son Tat," p. 241.)

1. Now to find out concerning the three times; for they are neither by themselves, nor [yet] are they at-oned; and [yet] again they are at-oned, and by themselves [as well].

For should'st thou think the present is without the past, it can't be present unless it has become already past.[1]

For from the past the present comes, and from the present future goes.

But if we have to scrutinize more closely, thus let us argue:

2. Past time doth pass into no longer being

[1] That is, apparently, you cannot *think* of the present until it is already past.

this,[1] and future [time] doth not exist, in its not being present; nay, present even is not present, in its continuing.

Time, then, which *stands* not [steady] (ἕστηκε), but which is on the turn, without a central point at which to stop,—how can it be called *in-stant* (ἐνεστώς),[2] seeing even that it hath no power to *stand* (ἑστάναι)?

Again, past joining present, and present [joining] future, they [thus] are one; for they are not without them[3] in their sameness, and their oneness, and their continuity.

Thus, [then], time's both continuous and discontinuous, though one and the same [time].

[1] That is, apparently, "present."

[2] The usual term in Greek for "present," but I have here translated it by "instant" in order to keep the word-play, which would otherwise entirely vanish in translation.

[3] That is, apparently, any one without the other two, or any two without the other one.

EXCERPT VII.

OF BODIES EVERLASTING [AND BODIES PERISHABLE]

(Title (first half) from Patrizzi (p. 45b), followed by "To the Same Tat."

Text: Stob., *Phys.*, xxxv. 8, under the curious heading: "Of Hermes—From the [Sermons] to Ammon to Tat"; where "to Tat" is evidently a marginal correction for an erroneous "to Ammon." G. pp. 292-294; M. i. 204, 205; W. i. 290-292.

Ménard, Livre IV., No. iii. of "Fragments from the Books of Hermes to his Son Tat," pp. 238, 239.)

1. [*Her.*] The Lord and Demiurge of all eternal bodies, Tat, when He had made them once for all, made them no more, nor doth He make them [now].

Committing them unto themselves, and co-uniting them with one another, He let them go, in want of naught, as everlasting things.

If they have want of any, it will be want of one another and not of any increase to their number from without, in that they are immortal.

BODIES EVERLASTING AND BODIES PERISHABLE

For that it needs must be that bodies made by Him should have their nature of this kind.

2. Our Demiurge,[1] however, who is [himself already] in a body,[2] hath made us,—he makes for ever, and will [ever] make, bodies corruptible and under sway of death.

For 'twere not law that he should imitate the Maker of himself,—all the more so as 'tis impossible.

For that the latter did create from the first essence which is bodiless; the former made as from the bodying[3] brought into existence [by his Lord].

3. It follows, then, according to right reason, that while those bodies, since they are brought into existence from incorporal essence, are free from death, ours are corruptible and under sway of death,—in that our matter is composed of bodies,[4] as may be seen from their being weak and needing much assistance.

For how would it be possible our bodies' continuity should last, unless it had some nutriment imported [into it] from similar elements, and [so] renewed our bodies day by day?

For that we have a stream of earth, and water,

---

[1] That is, the Demiurge of our bodies, which are not everlasting.
[2] The Sun, perhaps; *cf. C. H.*, xvi. 18; and Ex., iii. 6 and iv. 2; and Lact., *D. I.*, iv. 6.
[3] σωματώσεως,—*cf.* Ex. viii. 5.
[4] *Sc.* the elements.

fire, and air, flowing into us, which renovates our bodies, and keeps our tent [1] together.

We are too weak to bear the motions [of our frames], enduring them not even for one single day.

For know, [my] son, that if our bodies did not rest at night, we should not last a single day.

4. Wherefore, our Maker, being good, and with foreknowledge of all things, in order that the animal may last, hath given sleep, the greatest [calm [2]] of the fatigue of motion, and hath appointed equal time to each, or rather more, for rest.

Ponder well, son, the mightiest energy of sleep,—the opposite to the soul's [energy], but not inferior to it.

For that just as the soul is motion's energy, so bodies also cannot live without [the help of] sleep.

For 'tis the relaxation and the recreation of the jointed limbs; it also operates within,

[1] σκῆνος,—used by Plato (*ap.* Clem. Alex., 703), and the Pythagoreans (Timæus Locr., 100 A, 101, c, E), and the Later Platonists, for the body as the tabernacle of the soul. See especially the response of the Oracle at Delphi, when consulted concerning the state of the soul of Plotinus after death, as quoted by Porphyry in his *Life of Plotinus* : " But now since thou hast struck thy tent, and left the tomb of thy angelic soul" (see my " Lives of the Later Platonists" in *The Theosophical Review* (July, 1896), xviii. 372. *Cf.* Ex. iii. 1 and 5 ; and *C. H.*, xiii. (xiv.) 12 and 15.

[2] Added by Heeren to complete the sense.

BODIES EVERLASTING AND BODIES PERISHABLE 33

converting into body the fresh supply of matter that flows in, apportioning to each its proper [kind],—the water to the blood, the earth to bones and marrow, the air to nerves and veins, the fire to sight.[1]

Wherefore the body, too, feels keen delight in sleep, for it is sleep that brings this [feeling of] delight into activity.

COMMENT

Patrizzi's title is by no means descriptive of the main contents of the excerpt, which is evidently from the Sermons of Hermes to Tat, and from the same collection of these from which Stobæus has taken the previous two extracts,—that is, presumably, the Expository Sermons.

[1] *Cf. C. H.*, xvi. 7, note.

EXCERPT VIII.

OF ENERGY AND FEELING

(Title from Patrizzi (p. 44); preceded by "Of Thrice-greatest Hermes."

Text: Stob., *Phys.*, xxxv. 6, under the heading: "From the [Sermons] to Tat"; G. pp. 284–291; M. i. 198–203; W. i. 284–289.

Ménard, Livre IV., No. ii. of "Fragments from the Books of Hermes to his Son Tat," pp. 231–237.)

1. *Tat.* Rightly hast thou explained these things, O father [mine]. Now give me further teaching as to those.

For thou hast said somewhere[1] that science and that art do constitute the rational's energy.[2]

But now thou say'st that the irrational lives,[3] through deprivation of the rational, are and are called *ir*-rational.

According to this reasoning, [therefore], it follows of necessity that the irrational lives are

[1] That is in some previous sermon.

[2] Action or operation,—ἐνέργειαν εἶναι τοῦ λογικοῦ. *Cf.* § 11 below.

[3] Or animals.

without any share in science or in art, through deprivation of the rational.

2. *Her.* [It follows] of necessity, [my] son.

Tat. How, then, O father, do we see some of irrational [creatures] using [both] intelligence, and art?—the ants, for instance, storing their food for winter, and in like fashion, [too,] the creatures of the air building their nests, and the four-footed beasts [each] knowing their own holes.[1]

Her. These things they do, O son, neither by science nor by art, but by [the force of] nature.

Science and art are teachable; but none of these irrationals is taught a thing.

Things done by nature are [so] done by reason of the general energy of things.

Things [done] by art and science are achieved by those who know, [and] not by all.

Things done by all are brought into activity[2] by nature.

3. For instance, all look up [to heaven]; but all [are] not musicians, or [are] all archers, or hunters, or the rest.

But some of them have learned one thing,

---

[1] καὶ τὰ ἀέρια ζῶα ὁμοίως καλιὰς ἑαυτοῖς συντιθέντα, τὰ δὲ τετράποδα γνωρίζοντα τοὺς φωλεοὺς τοὺς ἰδίους. Compare Matt. viii. 20 = Luke ix. 58 (word for word): αἱ ἀλώπεκες φωλεοὺς ἔχουσιν καὶ τὰ πετεινὰ τοῦ οὐρανοῦ κατασχηνώσεις—"The foxes have holes and the birds of the air nests." The first and third Evangelists here copy verbally from their "Logia" source.

[2] Or energized.

[others another thing], science and art being active[1] [in them].

In the same way, if some ants only did this thing, and others not, thou would'st have rightly said they acted by [the light] of science, and stored their food by means of art.

But if they all without distinction are driven by their nature to [do] this, though [it may be] against their will,—'tis plain they do not do it or by science or by art.

4. For Tat, these energies, though [in themselves] they are incorporal, are [found] in bodies, and act through bodies.

Wherefore, O Tat, in that they are incorporal, thou sayest that they are immortal; but, in so far as without bodies they cannot manifest activity,[2] I say that they are ever in a body.

Things once called into being for some purpose, or some cause, things that come under Providence and Fate, can never stay inactive of their proper energy.

For that which is, shall ever be; for that this [being] is [the very] body and the life of it.

5. It follows from this reason, [then,] that these are always bodies.

Wherefore I say that "bodying"[3] itself is an eternal [exercise of] energy.

---

[1] Or energizing. [2] Lit. energize.

[3] σωμάτωσιν,—cf. Ex. vii. 2 ; cf. also the ψύχωσις of K. K., 9.

OF ENERGY AND FEELING

If bodies are on earth, they're subject unto dissolution; yet must these [ever] be [on earth to serve] as places and as organs for the energies.

The energies, however, [are] immortal, and the immortal is eternally,—[that is, that] body-making, if it ever is,[1] is energy.

6. [The energies] accompany the soul, though not appearing all at once.

Some of them energize the man the moment that he's born, united with the soul round its irrational [parts]; whereas the purer ones, with change of age,[2] co-operate with the soul's rational part.

But all these energies depend on bodies. From godly[3] bodies they descend to mortal [frames], these body-making [energies]; each one of them is [ever] active, either around the body or the soul.

Yea, they are active with the soul itself without a body. They are for ever in activity.

The soul, however, is not for ever in a *mortal* body, for it can be without the *body*; whereas the energies can never be without the *bodies*.

[1] That is, if it goes on continually.

[2] κατὰ μεταβολὴν τῆς ἡλικίας,—generally supposed to be the seventh year. Compare the apocryphal *logos*: "He who seeks me shall find me in children from the age of seven years"—quoted by the Christian Overwriter of the Naassene Document from the *Gospel according to Thomas* (Hipp., *Philos.*, v. 7; § 7 in "Myth of Man").

[3] Or divine,—the bodies of the Gods, the heavenly bodies, or the spiritual and immortal bodies of the soul.

This is a sacred saying (*logos*), son : Body apart from soul cannot persist ; its being can.[1]

7. *Tat.* What dost thou mean, O father [mine]?

Her. Thus understand it, Tat! When soul leaves body, body itself remains.

But [even] the body so abandoned,[2] as long as it remains, is in activity, being broken up and made to disappear.

For body without [the exercise of] energy could not experience these things.[3]

This energy, accordingly, continues with the body when the soul has gone.

This, therefore, is the difference of an immortal body and a mortal one,—that the immortal doth consist of a one single matter, but this [body does] not.

The former's active, and the latter's passive.

For every thing that maketh active is the stronger ; and [every thing] that is made active is the weaker.

The stronger, too, being in authority and free, doth lead ; the [weaker] follows [as] a slave.

8. The energies, then, energize not only bodies that are ensouled, but also [bodies] unensouled,

---

[1] συνεστάναι μὲν σῶμα χωρὶς ψυχῆς οὐ δύναται, τὸ δὲ εἶναι δύναται,— "its being" presumably refers to the abstract "bodying" (σωμάτωσις) referred to above.

[2] Lit. this body.   [3] *Sc.* dissolution and disappearance.

—stocks, stones,[1] and all such things;—both making [them] to grow, and to bear fruits, and ripening [them], dissolving, melting, rotting and crumbling [them], and setting up [in them] all like activities which bodies without souls can undergo.

For energy's[2] the name, O son, for just the thing that's going on,—that is becoming.

And many things needs must for ever be becoming; nay, rather, all things [must].

For never is Cosmos bereft of any of existent things, but being borne[3] for aye in its own self, it bears existent things,—[things] that shall never cease from being destroyed again.[4]

9. Know, then, that energy of every kind is ever free from death,—no matter what it is, or in what body.

And of the energies, some are of godly bodies, and some of those which are corruptible; some [are] general, and some special. Some [are] of genera, and some are of the parts of every genus.

The godly ones, [accordingly], are those that exercise their energies through everlasting bodies. And these are perfect [energies], in that [they energize] through perfect bodies.

But partial [energies are] those [that energize] through each one of the [single] living things.

---

[1] *Cf.* Naassene Document, § 4, and § 13 below. [2] Or activity.
[3] Or conceived. Reading αὖθις for αὐτοῦ, with Heeren.

And special [energies are those that energize] through each one of existent things.

10. This argument, accordingly, O son, deduces that all things are full of energies.

For though it needs must be that energies should be in bodies,—and there be many bodies in the Cosmos,—I say that energies are many more than bodies.

For often in one body there is [found] one, and a second and a third [activity],—not counting in the general ones that come with it.

By general ones I mean the purely corporal ones, that exercise themselves through the sensations[1] and the motions [of the body].

For that without these energies the body [of an animal] can not persist.

11. The souls of men, however, have a second class of energies,—the special ones [that exercise themselves] through arts, and sciences, and practices, and [purposed] doings.[2]

For that the feelings[3] follow on the energies or rather are completions[4] of the energies.

Know, then, O son, the difference of energy and of sensation.

[Thus] energy is sent down from above; whereas sensation, being in the body and having its existence from it, receives the energy

---

[1] Or feelings.
[2] $ἐνεργημάτων$,—cf. § 1 above.
[3] Or sensations.
[4] Or effects—$ἀποτελέσματα$.

and makes it manifest, as though it did embody it.

Wherefore I say sensations are both corporal and mortal, and last as long as doth the body [only].

Nay, rather, its sensations are born together with the body, and they die with it.

12. But the immortal bodies in themselves have no sensation,—[not even an] immortal [one], as though they were composed out of some essence of some kind.

For that sensation doth arise entirely from naught else than either from the bad or else the good that's added to the body, or that is, on the contrary, taken [from it] again.

But with eternal bodies there is no adding to nor taking from.

Wherefore, sensation doth not occur in them.

13. *Tat.* Is, then, sensation felt in every body?

Her. In every body, son; and energies are active in all [bodies, too].

Tat. Even in bodies without souls, O father [mine]?

Her. Even in them, O son. There are, however, differences in the sensations.

The feelings of the rationals occur with reason; those of irrationals are simply corporal; as for the things that have no soul, they [also] have sensations, but passive ones,—experience of increase [only] and decrease.[1]

Moreover, passion and sensation depend from one [same] head,[2] and they are gathered up again into the same, and that, too, by the energies.

14. Of lives[3] with souls there are two other energies which go with the sensations and the passions,—grief and joy.

And without these, an ensouled life, and most of all a rational one, could not experience sensation.

Wherefore, I say that there are forms of passions, — [and] forms that dominate the rational lives more [than the rest].

The energies, then, are the active forces [in sensations], while the sensations are the indications of the energies.

15. Further, as these[4] are corporal, they're set in motion by the irrational parts of [a man's] soul; wherefore, I say that both of them are mischievous.

For that both joy, though [for the moment] it provides sensation joined with pleasure, immediately becomes a cause of many ills[5] to

---

[1] *Cf.* § 8 above, and note.

[2] ἀπὸ μιᾶς κορυφῆς ἤρτηνται. Compare this with Plato, *Phædo*, i. 60 B, where Socrates speaks of the pleasant and the painful as "two (bodies) hanging from one head" (ἐκ μιᾶς κορυφῆς συνημμένω).

[3] Or animals.

[4] That is, the sensation of pleasure and pain.

[5] *Sc.* by contrast.

him who feeleth it; while grief [itself] provides [still] greater pains and suffering.

Wherefore, they both would seem [most] mischievous.

16. *Tat.* Can, then, sensation be the same in soul and body, father [mine]?

Her. How dost thou mean,—sensation in the soul, [my] son?

Tat. Surely it cannot be that soul's incorporal, and that sensation is a body, father,—sensation which is sometimes in a body and sometimes not, [just as the soul]?

Her. If we should put it *in* a body, son, we should [then] represent it as like the soul or [like] the energies. For that we say these[1] are incorporals in bodies.

But [as] sensation's neither energy nor soul, nor any other thing than body, according to what has been said above, it cannot, therefore, be incorporal.

And if it's not incorporal, it must be body.

For of existing things some must be bodies and the rest incorporal.

COMMENT

Again, as with the last excerpt, the earlier editions of Stobæus have Asclepius and Tat as the persons of

[1] That is, soul and energies.

the dialogue instead of Hermes and Tat. Wachsmuth gives them correctly.

The second sentence is of great interest, for it refers us presumably to *C. H.*, x. (xi.), 22: "God's rays, to use a figure, are his energies; the Cosmos's are natures; the arts and sciences are man's." Seeing, however, that "The Key" is an Epitome of the General Sermons to Tat, the statement may also have been made in one of these sermons.

In either case the existence of these General Sermons is presupposed, and, therefore, it may be that our excerpt is, again, one of the Expository Sermons to Tat.

The beginning of the Sermon has clearly been omitted by Stobæus, and apparently the end also.

EXCERPT IX.

OF [THE DECANS AND] THE STARS

(Patrizzi (p. 38b) does not give the first third of the text (§§ 1–5), and his title, "Of the Stars," is evidently incomplete; it is followed by "To the Same [*i.e.* Tat]."

Text: Stob., *Phys.*, xxi. 9, under the heading: "Of Hermes from the [Sermon] to Tat," pp. 184–190; M. i. 129–133; W. i. 189–194.

Ménard, Livre IV., No. vi. of "Fragments from the Books of Hermes to his Son Tat," pp. 242–247, under the sub-heading, "Of the Decans and the Stars.")

1. *Tat.* Since in thy former General Sermons (*Logoi*[1]), [father,] thou didst promise me an explanation of the Six-and-thirty Decans,[2] explain, I prithee, now concerning them and their activity.[3]

Her. There's not the slightest wish in me not to do so, O Tat, and this should prove the

---

[1] ἐν τοῖς ἔμπροσθεν γενικοῖς λόγοις. *Cf. C. H.*, x. (xi.) 1 and 7; xiii. (xiv.) 1; and Ex. xviii. 1.

[2] These are the "Horoscopes" of *P. S. A.*, xix. 3. *Cf.* also Origen, *C. Cels.*, viii. 58; R. 225, n. 1.

[3] Or energy.

most authoritative sermon (*logos*) and the chiefest of them all. So ponder on it well.

We have already spoken unto thee about the Circle of the Animals, or the Life-giving one,[1] of the Five Planets, and of Sun and Moon, and of the Circle [2] of each one of these.

2. *Tat.* Thou hast done so, Thrice-greatest one.

Her. Thus would I have thee understand as well about the Six-and-thirty Decans,—calling the former things to mind, in order that the sermon on the latter may also be well understood by thee.

Tat. I have recalled them, father, [to my mind].

Her. We said, [my] son, there is a Body which encompasses all things.

Conceive it, then, as being in itself a kind of figure of a sphere-like shape; so is the universe conformed.

Tat. I've thought of such a figure in my mind, just as thou dost describe, O father [mine].

3. *Her.* Beneath the Circle of this [all-embracing] frame [3] are ranged the Six-and-thirty Decans, between this Circle of the Universe and that one of the Animals, determining the boundaries of both these Circles, and, as it were,

---

[1] The zodiac; περὶ τοῦ ζωδιακοῦ κύκλου ἢ τοῦ ζωοφόρου,—of which the second member is probably a gloss; but see § 8 below.
[2] Or sphere. [3] Or body.

OF THE DECANS AND THE STARS

holding that of the Animals aloft up in the air, and [so] defining it.

They[1] share the motion of the Planetary Spheres, and [yet] have equal powers with the [main] motion of the Whole,[2] crosswise[3] the Seven.

They're[4] checked by nothing but the All-encircling Body, for this must be the final thing in the [whole grades of] motion,—itself by its own self.

But they speed on the Seven other Circles, because they[5] move with a less rapid motion than the [Circle] of the All.

Let us, then, think of them as though of Watchers stationed round [and watching] over both the Seven themselves and o'er the Circle of the All,—or rather over all things in the World,

---

[1] That is, the Decans.   [2] Or Universe.

[3] This refers to the astronomical system underlying the Pythagoreo-Platonic tradition, as, for instance, set forth allegorically and symbolically by Plato in the famous passage in *The Timæus* (36 B, c). "The entire compound he (the Demiurge) divided lengthways into two parts, which he joined to one another at the centre like the letter X, and bent them into a circular form, connecting them with themselves and each other at the point opposite to their original meeting point; and, comprehending them in a uniform revolution upon the same axis, he made the one the outer and the other the inner circle. Now the motion of the outer circle he called the motion of the same, and the motion of the inner circle the motion of the other or diverse" (Jowett's Translation, iii. 454, 455). The X symbolizes the "crosswise," which in terms of motion may be translated as "inverse to."

[4] *Sc.* the Decans.   [5] The Decans.

—holding together all, and keeping the good order of all things.

4. *Tat.* Thus do I have it, father, in my mind, from what thou say'st.

Her. Moreover, Tat, thou should'st have in thy mind that they are also free from the necessities laid on the other Stars.

They are not checked and settled in their course, nor are they [further] hindered and made to tread in their own steps again [1]; nor are they kept away from [2] the Sun's light,—[all of] which things the other Stars endure.

But free, above them all, as though they were inerrant Guards and Overseers of the whole, they night and day surround the universe.

5. *Tat.* Do these, then, also, further exercise an influence [3] upon us?

Her. The greatest, O [my] son. For if they act in [4] them,[5] how should they fail to act on us as well,—both on each one of us and generally? [6]

Thus, O [my] son, of all those things that happen generally, the bringing into action [7] is from these [8]; as for example,—and ponder what I say,—downfalls of kingdoms, states' rebellions,

[1] Referring, presumably, to the fixed stars and the planets.
[2] Reading ἀπὸ for ὑπὸ,—referring to eclipses.
[3] Or energy.   [4] Or energize.
[5] That is, the Seven Spheres.
[6] The rest of the fragment is also found in Patrizzi (p. 38b), under the title "Of the Stars."
[7] Or energy.   [8] *Sc.* the Decans.

plagues [and] famines, tidal waves [and] quakings of the earth; no one of these, O son, takes place without their action.[1]

Nay, further still, bear this in mind. If they rule over them, and we are in our turn beneath the Seven, dost thou not think that some of their activity extends to us as well,—[who are] assuredly their sons, or [come into existence] by their means?

6. *Tat.* What, [then,] may be the type[2] of body that they have, O father [mine]?

Her. The many call them daimones; but they are not some special class of daimones, for they have not some other kind of bodies made of some special kind of matter, nor are they moved by means of soul, as we [are moved], but they are [simple] operations[3] of these Six-and-thirty Gods.

Nay, further, still, have in thy mind, O Tat, their operations,—that they cast in the earth the seed of those whom [men] call Tanĕs, some playing the part of saviours, others being most destructive.[4]

[1] *Cf. C. H.*, xvi. 10.

[2] τύπος. The question concerning the spiritual and other spaces and their inhabitants, "Of what type are they?"—occurs with great frequency in the Bruce and Askew Gnostic Codices.

[3] Or energies.

[4] ὅτι καὶ εἰς τὴν γῆν σπερματίζουσιν ἃς καλοῦσί τάνας, τὰς μὲν σωτηρίους, τὰς δὲ ὀλεθριωτάτας. Neither Patrizzi nor Gaisford, nor Meineke, nor Wachsmuth, nor Ménard, has a word to say on this most interesting passage. I would suggest in the first place that

7. Further the Stars[1] in heaven as well do in their several [courses] bear them [2] underworkers[3]; and they[4] have ministers and warriors[5] too.

And they[6] in [everlasting] congress with them[7] speed on their course in æther floating, fullfilling [all] its[8] space, so that there is no space above empty of stars.

They are the cosmic engine of the universe,[9] having their own peculiar action, which is subordinate, however, to the action of the Thirty-six,—from whom throughout [all] lands arise the deaths of [all] the other lives[10] with souls, and hosts of [lesser] lives that spoil the fruit.

8. And under them[11] is what is called the

the text is faulty, and that we should read "οὓς καλοῦσι Τάνας, τοὺς μὲν σωτηρίους, τοὺς δὲ ὀλεθριωτάτους"; and in the second that Τάνας is a shortened form of Τιτᾶνας or Titans. Τάνας (? from Τᾶν) is connected with ταναός, "stretched out," from √ταν, just as Τιτὰν is connected with τιταίνω,—Τιτᾶνες thus signifying the Stretchers or Strivers. It may, however, also be connected with τίτας (τίτης) from τίνω, and so mean Avengers. *Cf.* J. Laurent. Lydus, *De Mensibus*, iv. 31 (W. 90, 24), as given in note to *P. S. A.*, xxviii. 1.

[1] The planetary spheres, presumably.

[2] *Sc.* the Decans.

[3] ὑπολειτουργούς—a ἅπαξ λεγόμενον. The term λειτουργοί, however, is of frequent occurrence in the Askew and Bruce Codices. See, for instance, *Pistis Sophia* (Schwartze's Trans.), p. 10: "*Atque decanoi archonton eorumque leitourgoi.*"

[4] The Decans.

[5] στρατιώτας—soldiers; one of the most famous of the degrees of the Mithriac mysteries was that of the Soldier. See Cumont (F.), *Textes et Monuments Figurés relatifs aux Mystères de Mithra* (Bruxelles; 1899), i. 315, and especially 317, n. 1.

[6] The Star-spheres. [7] The Decans.
[8] Æther's. [9] συγκοσμοῦντες τὸ πᾶν.
[10] Or animals. [11] The Decans.

OF THE DECANS AND THE STARS 51

Bear,[1]—just in the middle of the Circle of the Animals,[2] composed of seven stars, and with another corresponding [Bear][3] above its head.

Its energy is as it were an axle's, setting nowhere and nowhere rising, but stopping [ever] in the self-same space, and turning round the same, giving its proper motion[4] to the Life-producing Circle,[5] and handing over this whole universe from night to day, from day to night.

And after this[6] there is another choir of stars, to which we have not thought it proper to give names; but they who will come after us,[7] in imitation, will give them names themselves.[8]

9. Again, below the Moon, are other stars,[9] corruptible, deprived of energy, which hold together for a little while, in that they've been exhaled out of the earth itself into the air above the earth,—which ever are being broken up, in that they have a nature like unto [that of] useless lives on earth, which come into existence for no other purpose than to die,— such as the tribe of flies, and fleas, and worms, and other things like them.

---

[1] The Great Bear. Compare "Behold the Bear up there that circles round the Pole."
[2] The zodiac.
[3] The Little Bear.
[4] Lit. energy.
[5] *Cf.* § 1 above.
[6] *Sc.* the Bear.
[7] *Cf. P. S. A.*, xii. 3 ; xiv. 1.
[8] That is, apparently, invent them out of their own heads haphazard.
[9] Referring, presumably, to the phenomena of "shooting stars."

For these are useful, Tat, neither to us nor to the world; but, on the contrary, they trouble and annoy, being nature's by-products,[1] which owe their birth to her extravagance.[2]

Just in the same way, too, the stars exhaled from earth do not attain the upper space.

They cannot do so, since they are sent forth from below; and, owing to the greatness of their weight, dragged down by their own matter, they quickly are dispersed, and, breaking up, fall back again on earth, affecting nothing but the mere disturbance of the air about the earth.

10. There is another class, O Tat, that of the so-called long-haired [stars],[3] appearing at their proper times, and after a short time, becoming once again invisible;—they neither rise nor set nor are they broken up.

These are the brilliant messengers and heralds of the general destinies of things[4] that are to be.

They occupy the space below the Circle of the Sun.

When, then, some chance is going to happen to the world, [comets] appear, and, shining for some days, again return behind[5] the Circle of the Sun, and stay invisible,—some showing in

---

[1] παρακολουθήματα—*sequellæ*.

[2] See the same idea in Plutarch, *De Is. et Os.*, iv. 5, concerning lice.

[3] The comets—τῶν καλουμένων κομετῶν.

[4] ἀποτελεσμάτων.

[5] Lit. below.

OF THE DECANS AND THE STARS

the east, some in the north, some in the west, and others in the south. We call them Prophets.[1]

11. Such is the nature of the stars. The stars, however, differ from the star-groups.[2]

The stars are they which sail[3] in heaven; the star-groups, on the contrary, are fixed in heaven's frame,[4] and they are borne along together with the heaven,—Twelve out of which we call the Zōdia.[5]

He who knows these can form some notion clearly of [what] God is; and, if one should dare say so, becoming [thus] a seer for himself, [so] contemplate Him, and, contemplating Him, be blessed.

12. *Tat.* Blessèd, in truth, is he, O father [mine], who contemplateth Him.

Her. But 'tis impossible, O son, that one in body[6] should have this good chance.

Moreover, he should train his soul beforehand, here and now, that when it reacheth there, [the space] where it is possible for it to contemplate, it may not miss its way.

But men who love their bodies,—such men will never contemplate the Vision of the Beautiful and Good.

---

[1] μάντεις, seers or diviners.

[2] ἀστέρες δὲ ἄστρων διαφορὰν ἔχουσιν. The ἀστέρες are the planets, aerolites and comets; the ἄστρα are the *sidera*, signs of the fixed stars or constellations.

[3] Or float (αἰωρούμενοι), lit. are raised aloft. [4] Or body.

[5] The zodiac; lit. the animal signs, or signs of lives.

[6] *Cf.* Ex. i. 6.

For what, O son, is that [fair] Beauty which hath no form nor any colour, nor any mass?[1]

Tat. Can there be aught that's beautiful apart from these?

Her. God only, O [my] son; or rather that which is still greater,—the [proper] name of God.

COMMENTARY

The earlier editors of Stobæus (apparently following the mistake of Patrizzi) have Asclepius instead of Tat as the second person of the dialogue, which is clearly wrong according to the text itself (see the first sentence given to Hermes, and §§ 9 and 10).[2]

The excerpt is from a sermon in the Collection to Tat. It belongs to the further explanation of things referred to only generally in the General Sermons; it is, therefore, again probably from one of the Expository Sermons, in which series already a sermon has been given on the Zodiacal Twelve and on the Seven Spheres.

Seeing also that it is stated that this sermon is "most authoritative and the chiefest of them all," we must suppose that it came at the end of one of the Books of the Expository Sermons.

We seem to have the beginning of the sermon, but not the end, for Stobæus breaks off in an aimless and provoking fashion in the midst of a subject.

For a list of the Egyptian names of the Decans, with their Greek transcriptions and symbols, see Budge, *Gods of the Egyptians*, ii. 304-308.

[1] Or body.

[2] Ménard and Wachsmuth have Tat. For other changes of a similar nature *cf.* Exx. i. and viii., and *C. H.*, ii. (iii.), and xvii.

EXCERPT X.

[CONCERNING THE RULE OF PROVIDENCE, NECESSITY AND FATE]

(Title in Patrizzi (p. 38), "Of Fate," simply; followed by 'From the [Sermons] to Tat."

Text: Stob., *Phys.*, iv. 8, under heading: "Of Hermes to his Son"; G. pp. 61, 62; M. i. 42, 43; W. i. 73, 74.

Ménard, Livre IV., No. vii. of "Fragments from the Books of Hermes to his Son Tat," pp. 248, 249.)

1. [*Tat.*] Rightly, O father, hast thou told me all; now further, [pray,] recall unto my mind what are the things that Providence doth rule, and what the things ruled by Necessity, and in like fashion also [those] under Fate.

[*Her.*] I said there were in us, O Tat, three species of incorporals.

The first's a thing the mind alone can grasp[1]; it thus is colourless, figureless, massless,[2] proceeding out of the First Essence in itself, sensed by the mind alone.[3]

And there are also, [secondly,] in us, opposed

---
[1] Or an intelligible something.   [2] Or bodiless.
[3] That is, the intelligible essence.

to this,[1] configurings,[2]—of which this serves as the receptacle.[3]

But what has once been set in motion by the Primal[4] Essence for some [set] purpose of the Reason (*Logos*), and that has been conceived[5] [by it], straightway doth change into another form of motion; this is the image of the Demiurgic Thought.[6]

2. And there is [also] a third species of incorporals, which doth eventuate round bodies,— space, time, [and] motion, figure, surface,[7] size, [and] species.

Of these there are two [sets of] differences.

The first [lies] in the quality pertaining specially unto themselves; the second [set is] of the body.

The special qualities are figure, colour, species, space, time, movement.

[The differences] peculiar to body are figure

---

[1] *Sc.* of opposite nature to the first incorporal, as negative to positive, say.

[2] σχηματότητες—that is, the "somethings" more subtle or ideal than figures or shapes,— types, or prototypes, or paradigms of some kind.

[3] That is, plays the part of matter, "womb," or "nurse" to these.

[4] Lit. intelligible. [5] Or received.

[6] Or Mind. Heeren (as also all editors subsequent to him) thinks that something has here fallen out of the text, because he finds no *second* incorporal specifically mentioned; but the duality of the demiurgic thought, active and passive, creative and conceptive, will do very well for the second.

[7] Or appearance.

configured, and colour coloured; there's also form conformed, surface and size.[1]

The latter with the former have no part.

3. The Intelligible Essence, then, in company with God,[2] has power o'er its own self, and [power] to keep[3] another, in that it keeps itself, since Essence in itself is not under Necessity.

But when 'tis left by God, it takes unto itself the corporal nature; its choice of it being ruled by Providence,—that is, its choosing of the world.[4]

All the irrational is moved to-wards some reason.

Reason [comes] under Providence; unreason [falls] under Necessity; the things that happen in the corporal [fall] under Fate.

Such is the Sermon on the rule of Providence, Necessity and Fate.

COMMENT

I have taken the title from the concluding words, which are evidently the end of the sermon. Stobæus thus seems to have reproduced the whole of this little tractate, which should be read in connection with Exx. xi., xii. and xiii. *C. H.*, xii. (xiii.) 6 (see Commentary), seems to presuppose this sermon.

[1] The distinction seems to be between colour, form, etc., "in itself," and differentiated colours, forms, etc.

[2] πρὸς τῷ θεῷ γενομένη.   [3] Or save, preserve.

[4] This sentence seems to be corrupt.

EXCERPT XI.

[OF JUSTICE]

(I have added the title, the excerpt not being found in Patrizzi.

Text: Stob., *Phys.*, iii. 52, under the vague heading: "Of Hermes"; G. p. 50; M. i. 33, 34; W. i. 62, 63.

Ménard, Livre IV., No. iv. of "Fragments from the Books of Hermes to his Son Tat," p. 240.)

1. [*Her.*] For there hath been appointed, O [my] son, a very mighty Daimon turning in the universe's midst, that sees all things that men do on the earth.

Just as Foreknowledge[1] and Necessity have been set o'er the Order of the gods, in the same way is Justice set o'er men, causing the same to act on them.

For they rule o'er the order of the things existing as divine, which have no will, nor any power, to err.

For the Divine cannot be made to wander; from which the incapacity to err accrues [to it].

[1] Or Providence. *Cf.* Ex. i. 15, note.

OF JUSTICE

But Justice is appointed to correct the errors men commit on earth.

2. For, seeing that their race is under sway of death, and made out of bad matter, [it naturally errs], and failure is the natural thing, especially to those who are without the power of seeing the Divine.[1]

'Tis over these that Justice doth have special sway. They're subject both to Fate through the activities of birth,[2] and unto Justice through the mistakes [they make] in life.[3]

COMMENT

The title and place of this excerpt has been discussed in the Commentary on *C. H.*, xii. (xiii.) 6. It belongs to the Tat-Sermons, and in the collection of Lactantius probably stood prior to the Sermon of Hermes to Tat, "About the General Mind."[4]

[1] This recalls Philo's description of the Therapeuts, who were "taught ever more and more to see," and strive for the "intuition" or "sight of that which is,"—τῆς τοῦ ὄντος θέας (Philo, *D. V. C.*, 891 P., 473 M.).

[2] That is, through the natural accidents that attend life in a body.

[3] That is, in their way of living—ἐν τῷ βίῳ.

[4] Compare with it Exx. x., xii., xiii.

EXCERPT XII.

OF PROVIDENCE AND FATE

(Title from Patrizzi (p. 38); followed by: "From the [Sermons] to Ammon."

Text: Stob., *Phys.*, v. 20, under heading: "Of Hermes from the [Sermons] to Ammon"; G. p. 70; M. i. 48, 49; W. i. 82.

Ménard, Livre IV., No. ii. of "Fragments of the Books of Hermes to Ammon," p. 258.)

ALL things are born by Nature and by Fate, and there is not a [single] space bereft of Providence.

Now Providence is the Self-perfect[1] Reason.

And of this [Reason] there are two spontaneous powers,—Necessity and Fate.

And Fate doth minister to Providence and to Necessity; while unto Fate the Stars[2] do minister.

For Fate no one is able to escape, nor keep himself from their[3] shrewd scrutiny.[4]

For that the Stars are instruments of Fate; it is at its behest that they effect all things for nature and for men.[5]

---

[1] αὐτοτελὴς λόγος,— complete in itself.
[2] That is, the Seven Spheres. [3] *Sc.* of the Stars.
[4] δεινότητος. [5] With this extract compare Exx. x., xi., xiii.

EXCERPT XIII.

OF THE WHOLE ECONOMY

(Patrizzi (p. 38) gives no title, but only the heading: "To the Same Ammon (Ἄμμωνα)."

Text: Stob., *Phys.*, v. 16, under sub-heading: "Of the Whole Economy," followed by: "Of Hermes from the [Sermons] to Ammon (Ἀμοῦν[1])"; G. p. 68; M. i. 47; W. i. 79, 80.

Ménard, Livre IV., No. i. of "Fragments of the Books of Hermes to Ammon").

Now what supporteth the whole World,[2] is Providence; what holdeth it together and encircleth it about, is [called] Necessity; what drives all on and drives them round,[3] is Fate, bringing Necessity to bear on them (for that its nature is the bringing into play of [this] Necessity); [it[4] is] the cause of birth and death[5] of life.

So, then, the Cosmos is beneath the sway of

---

[1] The only place in which this form occurs in Stobæus; *cf.* v. 20, and xxxv. 4, 7, 8.
[2] Or Cosmos.
[3] Or makes them to revolve
[4] Fate—εἱμαρμένη.
[5] Or destruction.

Providence[1] (for 'tis the first to meet with it); but Providence [itself][2] extends itself to Heaven.

For which cause,[3] too, the Gods revolve, and speed round [Heaven],[4] possessed of tireless, never-ceasing motion.

But Fate [extends itself in Cosmos]; for which cause, too, Necessity [encompasses the Cosmos].[5]

And Providence foreknows; but Fate's the reason of the disposition of the Stars.[6]

Such is the law that no one can escape, by which all things are ordered.[7]

[1] Lit. "first has Providence." The following words in parentheses seem to be the gloss of a scribe who was puzzled by the sentence. Usener, however, would detect a lacuna after the parentheses and the beginning of a new excerpt after that, and Wachsmuth agrees with him. This seems to me to be unnecessary.

[2] That is, pure Providence unmixed with Necessity and Fate.

[3] That is, because of Providence, the law of heaven.

[4] αὐτόν.

[5] The text is hopeless, being simply: εἱμαρμένη δὲ, διότι καὶ ἀνάγκη.

[6] That is, the Seven Spheres.   [7] Cf. Exx. x., xi., xii.

EXCERPT XIV.

OF SOUL [I.]

(Title from Patrizzi (p. 40) ; preceded by "Of Thrice-greatest Hermes," and followed by "To the Same Ammon."

Text: Stob., *Phys.*, xxxv. 9, under heading: "Of Hermes from the [Sermons] to Ammon"; G. pp. 282, 283; M. i. 196, 197; W. 281, 282.

Ménard, Livre IV., No. iii. of "Fragments of the Books of Hermes to Ammon," pp. 259, 260.)

1. THE Soul is further [in itself] incorporal essence, and even when in body it by no means doth depart from the essentiality peculiar to itself.

Its nature is, according to its essence to be for ever moving, according to its thought [to be] self-motive [purely], not moved in something, nor towards something, nor [yet] because of something.

For it is prior [to them] in power, and prior stands not in any need of consequents.

"In something," furthermore,—means space, and time, and nature; "towards something,"— [this] means harmony, and form, and figure; "because of something,"—[this] means body, for 'tis because of body that there is time, and space, and nature.

Now all these things are in connection with each other by means of a congenital relationship.

2. For instance, now, the body must have space, for it would be past all contriving that a body should exist without a space.

It changes, too, in nature, and 'tis impossible for change to be apart from time, and from the movement nature makes; nor is it further possible for there to be composing of a body apart from harmony.

It is because of body, then, that space exists; for that by its reception of the changes of the body, it does not let a thing that's changing pass away.

But, changing, it doth alternate from one thing to another, and is deprived of being in a permanent condition, but not of being body.

For body, *quâ* body, remains body; but any special moment of its state does not remain.

The body, then, keeps changing in its states.

3. And so, space is incorporal, and time, and natural motion; but each of these has naturally its own peculiar property.

The property of space is receptivity; of time ['tis] interval and number; of nature [it is] motion; of harmony ['tis] love; of body, change.

The special nature of the Soul, however, is essential thought.[1]

[1] Or thinking according to essence,—ἡ κατ' οὐσίαν νόησις.

EXCERPT XV.

[OF SOUL, II.]

(Patrizzi (p. 40) runs this on to the preceding without a break.

Text: Stob., *Phys.*, xxxv. 7, under heading : "Of Hermes from the [Sermons] to Ammon"; G. pp. 291, 292; M. i. 203, 204; W. i. 289, 290.

Ménard, Livre IV., No. iv. of "Fragments of the Books of Hermes to Ammon," pp. 261, 262.)

1. THAT which is moved is moved according to the operation of the motion that doth move the all.

For that the Nature of the all supplies the all with motion,—one [motion being] the [one] according to its[1] Power, the other that according to [its] Operation.[2]

The former doth extend itself throughout the whole of Cosmos, and holdeth it together from within; the latter doth extend itself [around it], and encompasseth it from without. And these go everywhere together through all things.

[1] *Sc.* Nature's.
[2] Or energy.

Now the [Productive] Nature[1] of all things supplies the things produced with [power of re-] production, sowing the seeds of its own self, [and] having its becomings[2] by means of moving matter.

2. And Matter being moved was heated and did turn to Fire and Water,—the one [being] strong and active, and the other passive.

And Fire opposed by Water was dried up by it, and did become Earth borne on Water.

And when it[3] was excessively dried up,[4] a vapour rose from out the three,—from Water, Earth and Fire,—and became Air.

The [Four] came into congress, [then,] according to the reason of the Harmony,[5]—hot with cold, [and] dry with moist.

And from the union[6] of these [four] is spirit born, and seed proportionate to the surrounding Spirit.

This [spirit] falling in the womb does not remain inactive in the seed, but being active it transforms the seed, and [this] being [thus] transformed, develops growth and size.

---

[1] φύσις simply; but as there is a play in the original on the words φύσις, φύουσα, φυήν, and φυομένοις, I have tried to retain it in translation by a series of allied words.

[2] γενέσεις. [3] *Sc.* Fire. [4] περιξηραινομένου.

[5] Or law of Harmony,—κατὰ τὸν τῆς ἁρμονίας λόγον.

[6] Lit. "breathing with one breath,"—ἐκ τῆς συμπνοίας—a word-play on πνεῦμα (spirit). For "spirit," *cf. C. H.*, x. (xi.) 13, Comment., and Exx. xix. 3; iv. 2.

And as it grows in size, it draws unto itself a copy of a model,[1] and is modelled.

3. And on the model is the form supported,—by means of which that which is represented by an image is so represented.

Now, since the spirit in the womb had not the motion that maintaineth life, but that which causeth fermentation[2] [only], the Harmony composed the latter as the receptacle[3] of rational life.[4]

This [life] is indivisible and changeless; it never changes from its changelessness.

It[5] ruleth the conception of the thing within the womb, by means of numbers, delivereth it, and bringeth it into the outer air.

The Soul[6] dwells very near to it[7];—not owing to some common property, but under the constraint of Fate; for that it has no love to be with body.[8]

Wherefore, [the Harmony[9]] according unto Fate doth furnish to the thing that's born [its][10]

---

[1] Or image of a figure,—εἴδωλον ... σχήματος.

[2] τὴν δὲ βραστικήν.   [3] Or vehicle,—ὑποδοχήν.

[4] τῆς διανοητικῆς ζωῆς,—of the purposive rational life, otherwise called the Harmony.

[5] Sc. the Harmony.   [6] Reading ψυχὴ for ψυχῇ.

[7] The new-born babe.

[8] Compare Plutarch, *Frag.*, v. 9 (ed. Didot): "For you should know the intercourse and the conjunction of the soul with body is contrary to nature."

[9] It is not easy to disentangle the subjects of some of the above clauses.

[10] Sc. the thing's.

rational motion, and the intellectual essence of the life itself.

For that [this[1]] doth insinuate itself into the spirit, and set it moving with the motion of the life.[2]

COMMENTARY

Patrizzi is evidently at fault in running this on to Ex. xiv. without a break. The subject again is not so much "Of Soul" as "Of Conception and Birth," but as the general exposition falls in very well with the nature of the subjects treated in Exx. xiv. and xvi., we may keep the same general title, though we may be quite certain that it was not that of the original.

The exposition in § 2 is reminiscent of an apocalyptic style, and seems to be a Greek overworking of Egyptian ideas; for though the details are different and the precise meaning difficult to disentangle, the general point of view may be compared with the embryonic stages of incarnation given in the *Pistis Sophia* (pp. 344 ff.).

THE EMBRYONIC STAGES OF INCARNATION

"Then the Rulers summon the workmen of their æons, to the number of three hundred and sixty-five, and hand over to them the soul and the counterfeit of the spirit bound together, the one to the other, the counterfeit of the spirit being outside the soul, and the

[1] *Sc.* the rational movement.

[2] ζωτικῶς,—this may perhaps have some reference to the circle of lives, or the zodiac.

compound of the power within the soul being inside both, that they may hold together.

"(345) And the Rulers give commandment to the workmen, saying: 'This is the type which ye shall set in the body of the matter of the world. Set ye the compound of the power which is in the soul within all of them, that they may hold together, for it is their support, and outside the soul place the counterfeit of the spirit.' This is the order which they have given to their workmen, that they may set the antitypes in bodies.

"Following this plan the workmen of the Rulers bring the power, the soul and the counterfeit of the spirit, and pour them all three into the world, passing through the world of the Rulers of the Midst.

"The Rulers of the Midst also inspect the counterfeit of the spirit and also the destiny. The latter, whose name is the destiny, leadeth on a man until it hath him killed by the death which is destined for him. This the Rulers of the Great Fate have bound to the soul.

"And the workmen of the Sphere bind the soul with the power, with the counterfeit of the spirit and with the destiny. And the whole is divided so as to form two parts, to surround the man and also the woman in the world, in whom the sign hath been set for them to be sent unto them. (346) And they give one part to the man and the other to the woman in the food of the world, either in the aery, or watery, or etheric substance which they imbibe. . . .

"Now, therefore, when the workmen of the Rulers have cast one part into the woman and the other into the man in the manner which I have just related, even though [the pair] be removed to a great distance from one another, the workmen compel them secretly to be united together in the union of the world. Then the counterfeit of the spirit which is in the male cometh unto the part [of itself] which hath been sent into the world in the matter of the body [of the man], and sacrificeth it and casteth it into the womb of the woman, a deposit of the seed of iniquity. And forthwith the three hundred and sixty-five workmen of the Rulers enter into her, to take up their abode in her. The workmen of the two parts are all there together.

"(347) And the workmen check the blood that cometh from all the nourishment that the woman eateth or drinketh, and keep it in the womb of the woman for forty days. And after forty days, they work the blood [that cometh] from the essence of all the nourishment, and work it together carefully in the woman's womb.

"After forty days they spend another thirty days in building its members in the likeness of the body of a man; each buildeth a member. I will tell you of the decans who thus build [the body] . . . when I explain the emanation of the plērōma.

"Afterwards, when the workmen have completed the body entirely with all its members in seventy days, they summon into the body which they have builded, first the counterfeit of the spirit, next they summon the soul within those, and finally they summon the compound of the power within the soul, and the destiny they place outside all, for it is not blended with them, but followeth after and accompanieth them."

(An elaborate account of the "sealing" of the members of the plasm is then given.)

"And when the number of the months of the child's conception is full, the babe is born, the compound of the power being small in it, the soul being small in it, and the counterfeit of the spirit being small in it;

whereas the destiny, being vast, is not mingled with the body, according to the regulation of the three (350), but followeth after the soul, the body and the counterfeit of the spirit, until the soul passeth from the body according to the type of death whereby he shall die according to what hath been decreed unto him by the Rulers of the Great Fate."

EXCERPT XVI.

[OF SOUL, III.]

(I have added the title, Patrizzi (p. 40b) having only the heading: "To the Same Ammon."

Text: Stob., *Phys.*, xli. 3, under the simple heading: "Of Hermes"; G. pp. 323, 324; M. i. 227, 228; W. i. 320, 321.

Méuard, Livre IV., No. v. of "Fragments of the Books of Hermes to Ammon," pp. 263, 264.)

1. THE Soul is, then, incorporal essence; for if it should have body, it would no longer have the power of being self-maintained.[1]

For every body needeth being; it needeth also ordered life[2] as well.

For that for every thing that comes to birth,[3] change also must succeed.[4]

For that which doth become,[5] becomes in size; for in becoming it hath increase.

[1] Or of saving itself.
[2] ζωῆς τῆς ἐν τάξει κειμένης,—lit. life set, or placed, in order (as distinguished from intellectual life), that is, presumably, sensible or cosmic life.
[3] Or has becoming, or genesis
[4] Or follow.
[5] Or is born.

Again, for every thing that doth increase, decrease succeedeth; and on increase destruction.

For, sharing in the form of life,[1] it[2] lives; it shares, also, in being through the Soul.

2. But that which is the cause of being to another, is being first itself.

And by [this] "being" I now mean becoming in reason, and taking part in intellectual life.

It is the Soul that doth supply this intellectual life.

It is called living[3] through the life, and rational through the intellect, and mortal through the body.

Soul is, accordingly, a thing incorporal, possessing [in itself] the power of freedom from all change.

For how would it be possible to talk about an intellectual living thing,[4] if that there were no [living] essence to furnish life?

Nor, any more, would it be possible to say a rational [living] thing, were there no ratiocinative essence to furnish intellectual life.

3. It is not to all [lives] that intellect extends; [it doth depend] on the relationship of body's composition to the Harmony.

---

[1] εἴδους ζωῆς,—that is, formal life, or life set in order.

[2] *Sc.* body, or that which comes to birth.

[3] ζῶον (subs.) according to Gaisford,—that is, an animal; but I prefer ζωόν (adj.), taking it with the following λογικὸν and θνητόν.

[4] Or animal.

For if the hot in the compost be in excess, he's light[1] and fervid; but if the cold, he's heavy and he's dull.

For Nature makes the composition fit the Harmony.

There are three forms of the becoming,—the hot, the cold, and medium.

It[2] makes it fit according to the ruling Star[3] in the star-mixture.

And Soul receiving it,[4] as Fate decrees, supplies this work of Nature with [the proper kind of] life.

Nature, accordingly, assimilates the body's harmony unto the mixture of the Stars, and co-unites its complex mixtures with their Harmony, so that they are in mutual sympathy.

For that the end of the Stars' Harmony is to give birth to sympathy according to their Fate.

[1] κοῦφος (mas.),—the subject is, therefore, man, the rational animal.
[2] *Sc.* Nature.   [3] Or, presumably, planetary sphere.
[4] *Sc.* the body-compost.

EXCERPT XVII.

[OF SOUL, IV.]

(Patrizzi (p. 41) runs this on to the preceding without a break.

Text: Stob., *Phys.*, xli. 4, under heading: "Of the Same" —that is, "Of Hermes"; G. pp. 324, 325; M. i. 228, 229; W. i. 321, 322.

Ménard, Livre IV., No. vi. of "Fragments of the Book of Hermes to Ammon," pp. 265, 266.)

1. Soul, Ammon, then, is essence containing its own end within itself; in [its] beginning taking to itself the way of life allotted it by Fate, it draws also unto itself a reason like to matter, possessing "heart" and "appetite."[1]

"Heart," too, is matter; if it doth make its state accordant with the Soul's intelligence, it, [then,] becometh courage, and is not led away by cowardice.

And "appetite" is matter, too; if it doth make its state accord with the Soul's rational power, it [then] becometh temperance, and is not

[1] In a metaphorical sense,—θυμὸν καὶ ἐπιθυμία; terms originally belonging to a primitive stage of culture, and often translated "anger and concupiscence"—positive and negative, denoting the "too much" and the "too little" of the animal nature, and to be paralleled with the νοῦς and ἐπίνοια of the rational nature. *Cf.* Ex. i. 5 and xviii. 3.

moved by pleasure, for reasoning fills up the "appetite's" deficiency.

2. And when both [these][1] are harmonized, and equalized, and both are made subordinate to the Soul's rational power, justice is born.

For that their state of equilibrium doth take away the "heart's" excess, and equalizes the deficiency of "appetite."

The source of these,[2] however, is the penetrating essence of all thought,[3] its self by its own self, [working] in its own reason that doth think round everything,[4] with its own reason as its rule.[5]

It is the essence that doth lead and guide as ruler; its reason is as 'twere its counsellor who thinks about all things.[6]

3. The reason of the essence, then, is gnosis of those reasonings which furnish the irrational [part] with reasoning's conjecturing,[7]—a faint thing as compared with reasoning [itself], but reasoning as compared with the irrational, as echo unto voice, and moonlight to the sun.

And "heart" and "appetite" are harmonized upon a rational plan; they pull the one against the other, and [so] they learn to know in their own selves a circular intent.[8]

[1] Sc. virtues,—courage and temperance. [2] Sc. two virtues.
[3] ἡ διανοητικὴ οὐσία,—that is, the essence which penetrates, or pervades, all things by means of thought.
[4] ἐν τῷ αὐτῆς περινοητικῷ λόγῳ.
[5] Or power, or ruling principle.
[6] ὁ περινοητικός. [7] εἰκασμόν [8] διάνοια.

EXCERPT XVIII.

[OF SOUL, V.]

(Patrizzi (p. 41) runs this on to the last without a break.

Text: Stob., *Phys.*, xli. 5, under heading: "Of the Same"—that is, "Of Hermes"; G. pp. 325-327; M. i. 229, 230; W. i. 322-324.

Ménard, Livre IV., No. vii. of "Fragments of the Books of Hermes to Ammon," pp. 267, 268.)

1. [Now], every Soul is free from death and in perpetual motion.

For in the General Sermons[1] we have said some motions are by means of the activities,[2] others are owing to the bodies.

We say, moreover, that the Soul's produced out of a certain essence,—not a matter,—incorporal itself, just as its essence is.

Now every thing that's born, must of necessity be born from something.

All things, moreover, in which destruction followeth on birth, must of necessity have two kinds of motion with them:—the [motion] of

[1] *Cf. C. H.*, x. (xi.) 1 and 7; xiii. (xiv.) 1; and Ex. ix. 1.
[2] Or energies.

the Soul, by which they're moved; and body's [motion], by which they wax and wane.

Moreover, also, on the former's dissolution, the latter[1] is dissolved.

This I define, [then,] as the motion of bodies corruptible.

2. The Soul, however, is in perpetual motion,—in that perpetually it moves itself, and makes [its] motion active [too] in other things.

And so, according to this reason, every Soul is free from death, having for motion the making active of itself.

The kinds of Souls are three :—divine, [and] human, [and] irrational.

Now the divine [is that] of its divine body, in which there is the making active of itself. For it is moved in it, and moves itself.

For when it is set free from mortal lives, it separates itself from the irrational portions of itself, departs unto the godlike body, and as 'tis in perpetual motion, is moved in its own self, with the same motion as the universe.

3. The human [kind] has also something of the godlike [body], but it has joined to it as well the [parts] irrational,—the appetite and heart.[2]

These latter also are immortal, in that they

[1] The former is here the body; the latter, the motion of waxing and waning.
[2] *Cf.* Ex. xvii.

happen also in themselves to be activities; but [they are] the activities of mortal bodies.

Wherefore, they are removed far from the godlike portion of the Soul, when it is in its godlike body; but when this[1] enters in a mortal frame, they[2] also cling to it, and by the presence [of these elements] it keeps on being a human Soul.

But that of the irrationals consists of heart and appetite. And for this cause these lives are also called irrational, through deprivation of the reason of the Soul.

4. You may consider, too, as a fourth [kind] that of the soulless, which from without[3] the bodies operates in them, and sets them moving.

But this should [really] be the moving of itself within its godlike body, and the moving of these [other] things as it were by the way.

COMMENT

The mention of the General Sermons (§ 1) raises the question as to whether or no our extract may not be from one of the Sermons to Tat, for in all other cases these General Sermons are referred to in the Tat-literature. The contents, however, are so similar to the extracts from the Sermons to Ammon that we keep this excerpt with them.

[1] *Sc.* the divine part. [2] The irrational parts.
[3] The other kinds presumably operating in bodies from within.

EXCERPT XIX.

[OF SOUL, VI.]

(Patrizzi (p. 41b) runs this on to the last without a break.

Text: Stob., *Phys.*, xli. 6, under heading: "Of the Same"—that is, "Of Hermes"; G. pp. 327, 328; M. i. 229, 230; W. i. 324, 325.

Ménard, Livre IV., No. viii. of "Fragments of the Books of Hermes to Ammon," pp. 269, 270.)

1. SOUL, then, is an eternal intellectual essence, having for purpose[1] the reason of itself; and when it thinks with[2] [it,][3] it doth attract [unto itself] the Harmony's intention.[4]

But when it leaves behind the body Nature makes,[5] it bideth in and by itself,—the maker of itself in the noëtic[6] world.

It ruleth its own reason, bearing in its own thought[7] a motion (called by the name of life)

[1] νόημα.
[2] συννοοῦσα.
[3] Sc. the reason.
[4] διάνοιαν.
[5] Lit. the physical body.
[6] This might here be translated "the self-purposive," to pick up the word-play on νόημα and διάνοια.
[7] Or purpose,—νοήματι.

like unto [that of] that which cometh into life.[1]

2. For that the thing peculiar to the Soul [is this],—to furnish other things with what is like its own peculiarity.

There are, accordingly, two lives, two motions:
—one, that according to the essence of the Soul; the other, that according to the nature of the body.

The former [is] more general, [the latter is more partial]; the [life] that is according unto essence has no authority but its own self, the other [is] under necessity.

For every thing that's moved, is under the necessity of that which moveth [it].

The motion that doth move, however, is in close union with the love of the noëtic essence.

For Soul must be incorporal,—essence that hath no share in any body Nature makes.

For were it corporal, it would have neither reason nor intelligence.[2]

For every body is without intelligence; but when it doth receive of essence, it doth obtain the power of being a breathing animal.

3. The spirit [3] [hath the power to contemplate] the body; the reason of the essence hath the power to contemplate the Beautiful.

[1] That is, presumably, of the same nature as the motion of the soul in incarnation or perhaps of the animal soul.

[2] νόησιν.

[3] *Cf. C. H.*, x. (xi.) 13, Comment.; and Exx. xv. 2, iv. 2.

The sensible—the spirit—is that which can discern appearances. It is distributed into the various sense-organs[1]; a part of it becometh spirit by means of which we see,[2] [a part] by means of which we hear, [a part] by means of which we smell, [a part] by means of which we taste, [a part] by means of which we touch.

This spirit, when it is led upwards by the understanding, discerns that which is sensible[3]; but if 'tis not, it only maketh pictures for itself.

For it is of the body, and that, too, receptible of all [impressions].

4. The reason of the essence, on the other hand, is that which is possessed of judgment.[4]

The knowledge of things worthy [to be known] is co-existent with the reason; [that which is co-existent] with the spirit [is] opinion.

The latter has its operation from the surrounding world; the former, from itself.

COMMENT

As Exx. xvi.–xix. follow one another in Stobæus, it is highly probable that they are all taken from the same group of sermons, and as their contents are so similar to those of Exx. xiv. and xv., and these are stated by

[1] Lit. organic senses; *cf. C. H.*, x. (xi.) 17.
[2] Lit. spirituous sight.
[3] That is, the sensible or phenomenal world. [4] τὸ φρονοῦν.

Stobæus to be from the "Sermons to Ammon," we are fairly justified in grouping them all together. How many Sermons to Ammon there may have been in the collection used by Stobæus we have no means of knowing; they may also perhaps have had no distinctive title; but as Stobæus usually leaves out the titles in quoting, even when we know them from other sources, there is no definite conclusion to be drawn from his silence.

EXCERPT XX.

[THE POWER OF CHOICE]

(Patrizzi (p. 42) runs this on to Ex. xix. without a break.

Text: Stob., *Ethica*, vii. 31, under heading: "Of Hermes"; G. (ii.) pp. 654, 655; M. ii. 100, 101; W. ii. 160, 161.

Ménard, Livre IV., No. i. of "Fragments Divers," pp. 271, 272.)

THERE is, then, essence, reason, thought,[1] perception.[2]

Opinion and sensation move towards perception; reason directs itself towards essence; and thought sends itself forth through its own self.

And thought is interwoven with perception, and entering into one another they become one form,—which is that of the Soul [itself].

Opinion and sensation move towards the Soul's perception; but they do not remain in the same state. Hence is there excess, and falling short, and difference with them.

[1] νόημα.   [2] διάνοια.

When they are drawn away from the perception, they deteriorate; but when they follow it and are obedient, they share in the perceptive reason through the sciences.[1]

2. We have the power to choose; it is within our power to choose the better, and in like way [to choose] the worse, according to our will.[2]

And if [our] choice clings to the evil things, it doth consort with the corporeal nature; [and] for this cause Fate rules o'er him who makes this choice.

Since, then, the intellectual essence[3] in us is absolutely free, — [namely] the reason that embraces all in thought,—and that it ever is a law unto itself and self-identical, on this account Fate does not reach it.[4]

Thus furnishing it first from the First God, it[5] sent forth the perceptive reason, and the whole reason which Nature hath appointed unto them that come to birth.

With these the Soul consorting, consorteth with their fates, though [in herself] she hath no part [or lot] in their fates' nature.

[1] διὰ τῶν μαθημάτων.

[2] Reading ἑκουσίως for the meaningless ἀκουσίως of the text.

[3] Reading νοηματική with Patrizzi, instead of σωματική as with G. W. prefers ἀσώματος (incorporal).

[4] Sc. the reason.

[5] The Soul, or intellectual essence. The text is very obscure, and Wachsmuth does not seem to have improved it. Cf. C. H., xii. (xiii.) 8.

(Patrizzi (p. 42) adds the following to the preceding; it is not found in Stobæus, and appears to be a scholium.)

What is necessitated by the interwoven harmony [1] of [all] the parts, in no way differs from that which is fated.

COMMENT

I have supplied a temporary heading for the sake of uniformity. Our extract, however, seems to be taken from a lengthy treatise, and was probably one of the Sermons to Tat.

[1] Lit. interweaving.

EXCERPT XXI.

OF ISIS TO HORUS

(Title in Patrizzi (p. 45) is "From Isis."

Text: Stob., *Flor.*, xiii. 50, under the heading: "Of Hermes from the [Sermon] of Isis to Horus"; G. i. 328; M. i. 265; H. iii. 467.

Schow gives another heading, which Gaisford (in a note) thinks is from the Vienna codex, namely: "Of Hermes from the Intercession (or Supplication,—Πρεσβείας) of Isis."[1]

Ménard, Livre IV., No. ii. of "Fragments Divers," p. 272.)

A REFUTATION, when it is recognized, O greatest King, carries the man who is refuted towards the desire of things he did not know before.

COMMENT

This fragment is clearly not in the style of the excerpt from the "Sermon of Isis to Hermes" (Ex. xxvii.); it is far more closely reminiscent of *C. H.*, xvi. or xvii., and is, therefore, probably from the Sermon of Asclepius to the King.

[1] R. (p. 134, n. 3) says simply that the last word ("Horus") is missing in the Vindobonensis, and finds no difficulty in recognizing a type of literature in which King (Ammon) is a pupil of Isis.

EXCERPT XXII.

[AN APOPHTHEGM]

(Text: W., i. 34, 5.)

HERMES on being asked, What is God?—replied: The Demiurge of wholes,—the Mind most wise and everlasting.

EXCERPT XXIII.

FROM "APHRODITE"

(Title in Patrizzi (p. 45) is "The Likeness of Children," followed by: "From Aphrodite."

Text: Stob., *Phys.*, xxxvi. 2, under heading: "Of Hermes from 'Aphrodite'"; G. pp. 297, 298; M. i. 207, 208; W. i. 295, 296.

Ménard, Livre IV., No. iii. of "Fragments Divers," p. 273.)

[——] How, [then,] are offspring born like to their parents? Or how are they returned[1] to [their own] species[2]?

[*Aphrodite.*] I will set forth the reason. When generation stores up seed from the ripe blood being sweated forth,[3] it comes to pass that somehow there's exhaled from the whole mass[4] of limbs a certain essence, following the

[1] ἀποδίδοται,—referring, presumably, to the idea of metempsychosis.

[2] Or families.

[3] ἐξαφεδρουμένου. But W. has ἐξαφρουμένου (turned into foam), following the emendation of Usener, based on Clem. Al. *Pædagog.*, I. vi. 48.

[4] Lit. body.

law of a divine activity, as though the man himself were being born; the same thing also in the woman's case apparently takes place.

When, then, what floweth from the man hath the ascendancy, and keeps intact, the young one's brought to light resembling its sire; contrary wise, in the same way, [resembling] its dam.

Moreover, if there should be ascendancy of any part, [then] the resemblance [of the young] will favour that [especial] part.

But sometimes also for long generations the offspring favoureth the husband's form, because his decan has the greater influence[1] at that [particular] moment when the wife conceives.

COMMENT

This fragment belongs to a type of Hermetic literature of which it is the sole surviving specimen. It is in form identical with the Isis and Horus type; but what the name of the questioner of Aphrodite could have been is difficult to say.

[1] λόγον.

EXCERPT XXIV.

[A HYMN OF THE GODS]

(Text: Stob., *Phys.*, v. 14, under the simple heading: "Of Hermes"; G. p. 65; M. i. 45; W. i. 77. The same verses are read in the appendix to the *Anthologia Palatina*, p. 768, n. 40.)

SEVEN Stars far varied in their course revolved upon the [wide] Olympian plain; with them for ever will Eternity[1] spin [fate][2]:—Mēnē that shines by night, [and] gloomy Kronos, [and] sweet Hēlios, and Paphiē who's carried in the shrine,[3] courageous Arēs, fair-wingèd Hermēs, and Zeus the primal source[4] from whom Nature doth come.

Now they themselves have had the race of

[1] Or Æon.

[2] ἐπινήσεται. But the *Anthology* reads "καὶ τοῖσιν ἀεὶ κανονίζεται" —that is to say, Eternity or Æon is for ever regulated or measured by the Seven; which seems to have no sense unless it means that the Seven are the instruments, whereby Eternity is divided into time.

[3] That is, Venus, the image of whom was, presumably, carried in a small shrine in processions.

[4] ἀρχιγένεθλος.

men entrusted to their care; so that in us there is a Mēnē, Zeus, an Arēs, Paphiē, a Kronos, Hēlios and Hermēs.

Wherefore we are divided up [so as] to draw from the ætherial spirit,[1] tears, laughter, anger, birth, reason, sleep, desire.

Tears are Kronos, birth Zeus, reason [is] Hermēs, courage Mars, and Mēnē sleep, in sooth, and Cytherēa desire, and Hēlios [is] laughter—for 'tis because of him that justly every mortal thinking thing doth laugh and the immortal world.

COMMENT

This is the only known specimen of verses attributed to the Trismegistic tradition. Liddell and Scott, however, under "νυκτιφανής," do not question this attribution, while Clement of Alexandria (*Strom.*, vi. p. 633 [this is a reference of Wachsmuth's which I cannot verify]) praises the "Hymns of the Gods" of Hermes. On the contrary, in *Anthol. Palat.*, p. 442, n. 491, the seventh verse is ascribed to Theon of Alexandria.

[1] Meaning the one element or ether simply.

EXCERPT XXV.

THE VIRGIN OF THE WORLD [I.][1]

(Title in Patrizzi (p. 27b), in the Latin translation, "Minerva Mundi."[2]

Text: Stob., *Phys.*, xli. 44, under heading: "From Thrice-Greatest Hermes' Sacred Book 'The Virgin of the World'"; G. pp. 395-419; M. i. 281-298; W. i. 385-407.

Ménard, Livre III., No. i. of "Fragments of the Sacred Book entitled 'The Virgin of the World,'" pp. 177-200.)

1.[3] So speaking Isis doth pour forth for Horus the sweet draught (the first) of deathless-

[1] Or "Apple of the Eye of the World"—see Commentary. Referred to as K. K.,—*i.e.* Κόρη Κόσμου.

[2] Curiously enough, though the page-headings throughout have "Minerva Mundi," the heading of p. 28 still stands "Pupilla Mundi"—showing that Patrizzi himself was puzzled how to translate the Greek, and had probably in the first place translated it throughout "Pupilla Mundi," or "Apple of the Eye of the World." In his Introduction (p. 3), however, Patrizzi writes: "But there is extant also another [book of Hermes] with the title of 'The Sacred Book,' which we found in Cyprus, in a monastery called Enclistra, at the same time as the rest of the books, and which John Stobæus has inserted in his Physical Eclogues together with other fragments." This would seem to suggest that Patrizzi had seen the original Sermon, and that its main title was "The Sacred Book."

[3] I have numbered the paragraphs for convenience of reference.

ness[1] which souls have custom to receive from Gods, and thus begins her holiest discourse (*logos*):

Seeing that, Son Horus, Heaven, adorned with many a wreath [of starry crowns], is set o'er every nature of [all] things beneath, and that nowhere it lacketh aught of anything which the whole cosmos now doth hold,—in every way it needs must be that every nature which lies underneath, should be co-ordered and full-filled by those that lie above; for things below cannot of course give order to the ordering above.

It needs must, therefore, be the less should give place to the greater mysteries. The ordinance of the sublimer things transcends the lower; it is both sure in every way and falleth 'neath no mortal's thought. Wherefore the [mysteries] below did sigh, fearing the wondrous beauty and the everlasting durance of the ones above.

'Twas worth the gazing[2] and the pains to see Heaven's beauty, beauty that seemed like God, —God who was yet unknown, and the rich majesty of Night, who weaves her web with rapid light,[3] though it be less than Sun's, and of the other mysteries[4] in turn that move in Heaven, with ordered motions and with periods

[1] τὸ πρῶτον ἀμβροσίας.
[2] Or contemplation, θεωρίας.
[3] *Sc.* The weft and warp of stars.
[4] The planetary spheres.

of times, with certain hidden influences[1] bestowing order on the things below and co-increasing them.

2. Thus fear succeeded fear, and searching search incessant, and for so long as the Creator of the universals willed, did ignorance retain its grip on all. But when He judged it fit to manifest Him who He is, He breathed into the Gods the Loves, and freely poured the splendour[2] which He had within His heart, into their minds, in ever greater and still greater measure; that firstly they might have the wish to seek, next they might yearn to find, and finally have power to win success as well. But this, my Horus, wonder-worthy son, could never have been done had that seed[3] been subject to death, for *that* as yet had no existence, but only with a soul that could vibrate responsive to the mysteries of Heaven.

3. Such was all-knowing Hermes, who saw all things, and seeing understood, and understanding had the power both to disclose and to give explanation. For what he knew, he graved on stone; yet though he graved them onto stone he hid them mostly, keeping sure silence though in speech, that every younger age of cosmic time

---

[1] ἀπόροιαι, or emanations. *Cf.* R. 16, n. 4, for the conflation of the pure Egyptian emanation doctrine with astrological considerations.
[2] Radiance or light.
[3] *Sc.* the race of the Gods.

might seek for them. And thus, with charge unto his kinsmen of the Gods to keep sure watch, he mounted to the Stars.

To him succeeded Tat, who was at once his son and heir unto these knowledges; and not long afterwards Asclepius-Imuth, according to the will of Ptah who is Hephæstus,[1] and all the rest who were to make enquiry of the faithful certitude of heavenly contemplation, as Foreknowledge[2] willed, Foreknowledge queen of all.

4. Hermes, however, made explanation to surrounding [space], how that not even to his son (because of the yet newness of his youth) had he been able to hand on the Perfect Vision. But when the Sun did rise for me, and with all-seeing eyes I[3] gazed upon the hidden [mysteries] of that New Dawn, and contemplated them, slowly there came to me—but it was sure—conviction that the sacred symbols of the cosmic elements were hid away hard by the secrets of Osiris.

5. [Hermes], ere he returned to Heaven, invoked a spell on them, and spake these words. (For 'tis not meet, my son, that I should leave this proclamation ineffectual, but [rather] should speak forth what words [our] Hermes uttered

[1] For the restored text, see R. 122.
[2] Or Providence, πρόνοια.
[3] The masculine is here used, the writer forgetting for the moment that he had assumed the person of Isis.

when he hid his books away.) Thus then he said :

"O holy books, who have been made by my immortal hands, by incorruption's magic spells, . . .[1] free from decay throughout eternity remain and incorrupt from time ! Become unseeable, unfindable, for every one whose foot shall tread the plains of this [our] land, until old Heaven doth bring forth meet instruments for you, whom the Creator shall call souls."

Thus spake he; and, laying spells on them by means of his own works, he shuts them safe away in their own zones. And long enough the time has been since they were hid away.[2]

6. And Nature, O my son, was barren, till they who then were under orders to patrol the Heaven, approaching to the God of all, their King, reported on the lethargy of things. The time was come for cosmos to awake, and this was no one's task but His alone.

"We pray Thee, then," they said, "direct Thy thought to things which now exist and to what things the future needs."

7. When they spake thus, God smiled and said : "Nature, arise!" And from His word

[1] The text is here again hopeless. Meineke's emendation (*Adnot.*, p. cxxx.) ἃς . . . φαρμάκῳ χρίσας ἐπικρατῷ—which makes Hermes smear the books with some magical ointment—is ingenious, but hardly satisfactory, though Wachsmuth adopts it.

[2] This is purely conjectural ; the text is utterly corrupt.

there came a marvel, feminine, possessed of perfect beauty, gazing at which the Gods stood all-amazed. And God the Fore-father, with name of Nature, honoured her, and bade her be prolific.

Then gazing fixedly on the surrounding space, He spake these words as well : " Let Heaven be filled with all things full, and Air, and Æther too!" God spake and it was so. And Nature with herself communing knew she must not disregard the Sire's command ; so with the help of Toil she made a daughter fair, whom she did call Invention. And on her [1] God bestowed the gift of being, and with His gift He set apart all them that had been so-far made, filled them with mysteries, and to Invention gave the power of ruling them.

8. But He, no longer willing that the world above should be inert, but thinking good to fill it full of breaths, so that its parts should not remain immotive and inert, He thus began on these [2] with use of holy arts as proper for the bringing forth of His own special work.

For taking breath from His own Breath and blending this with knowing Fire,[3] He mingled them with certain other substances which have

[1] *Sc.* Invention.

[2] *Sc.* the breaths or spirits.

[3] πῦρ νοερόν—a term in frequent use subsequently among the Later Platonists ; *cf.* Porphyry, *ap.* Euseb., *Præp. Ev.*, XV. xi. 16

no power to know; and having made the two [1]—
either with other—one, with certain hidden words
of power, He thus set all the mixture going
thoroughly; until out of the compost smiled a
substance, as it were, far subtler, purer far, and
more translucent than the things from which it
came; it was so clear that no one but the Artist
could detect it.

9. And since it neither thawed when fire was
set unto it (for it was made of Fire), nor yet did
freeze when it had once been properly produced
(for it was made of Breath), but kept its mixture's
composition a certain special kind, peculiar to
itself, of special type and special blend,—(which
composition, you must know, God called Psychōsis, after the more auspicious meaning of the
name and from the similarity of its behaviour [2])

[1] Sc. the knowing and unknowing primal elements. Cf. P.S. A., vi.

[2] The text is very involved and obscure, and the meaning of the writer is by no means clear. Psychōsis (ψύχωσις) means either animation (quickening) or "making cold" (cf. ψύχω and ψυχόω); the name Psychōsis is thus apparently supposed by the writer to have some connection with the term ἔψυχε ("freeze," or grow cold), which he has just employed in his description of the behaviour of the mixture. In its less auspicious sense ἔψυχε meant "grow cold"; in its more auspicious meaning it signified "breathe." But even so it must be said that the further reason (viz., similarity of behaviour) given for the choice of the term Psychōsis is the exact opposite of what is stated in the description of the soul-stuff's nature; and this is all the more puzzling when we recall the theory of Origen and his predecessors that the soul (ψυχή) was so-called precisely because it *had* grown cold and fallen away from the Divine heat and life. With the term cf. the σωμάτωσις of Exx. viii. 5, vii. 2.

—it was from this coagulate He fashioned souls enough in myriads,[1] moulding with order and with measure the efflorescent product of the mixture for what He willed, with skilled experience and fitting reason, so that they should not be compelled to differ any way one from another.

10. For, you must know, the efflorescence that exhaled out of the movement God induced, was not like to itself. For that its first florescence was greater, fuller, every way more pure, than was its second; its second was far second to the first, but greater far than was its third.[2] And thus the total number of degrees reached up to sixty.[3] In spite of this, in laying down the law, He ordered it that all should be eternal, as though from out one essence, the forms of which Himself alone could bring to their completion.

11. Moreover, He appointed for them limits and reservations in the height of upper Nature,[4]

---

[1] *Cf.* Plato, *Tim.*, 41: "He divided the whole mixture into souls equal in number to the stars, and assigned each soul to a star." So also Philo, who speaks of the souls as "equal in number to the stars"—*De Som.*, i. § 22 ; M. 642, P. 586 (Ri. iii. 244).

[2] *Cf.* Plato, *ibid.*: "They [the souls] were not, however, pure as before, but diluted to the second and third degrees.

[3] See § 56 below.

[4] Of the Nature Above (τῆς ἄνω φύσεως); *cf.* the "Jerusalem Above" of the "Gnostics." *Cf.* also *Tim.*, 41 D: "And having there [that is, among the stars] placed them as in a chariot, he showed them the nature of the universe, and declared to them the laws of destiny, according to which their first birth should be one and the same for all,—no one should suffer a disadvantage at his hands; they were to be sown in the instruments of time

that they might keep the cylinder[1] a-whirl in proper order and economy and [thus] might please their Sire. And so in that all-fairest station of the Æther He summoned unto Him the natures of all things that had as yet been made, and spake these words:

"O Souls, ye children fair of Mine own Breath and My solicitude, whom I have now with My own Hands[2] brought to successful birth and consecrate to My own world, give ear unto these words of Mine as unto laws, and meddle not with any other space but that which is appointed for you by My will.

"For you, if ye keep steadfast, the Heaven, with the star-order, and thrones I have ordained full-filled with virtue, shall stay as now they are for you; but if ye shall in any way attempt some innovation contrary to My decrees, I swear to you by My most holy Breath, and by this mixture out of which I brought you into being, and by these Hands of Mine which gave you life,[3] that I will speedily devise for you a bond and punishments."

12. And having said these words, the God,

---

severally adapted to them, and to come forth the most religious of animals; and as human nature was of two kinds, the superior race would hereafter be called man." With the last sentence, *cf* also § 12 below.

[1] *Cf. P. S. A.*, xix. [2] *Cf.* § 31 below.
[3] *Cf.* Hermes-Prayer, iii. 3, and note.

who is my Lord, mixed the remaining cognate elements (Water and Earth [1]) together, and, as before, invoking on them certain occult words, words of great power though not so potent as the first, He set them moving rapidly, and breathed into the mixture power of life; and taking the coagulate (which like the other floated to the top), when it had been well steeped and had become consistent, He modelled out of it those of the [sacred] animals [2] possessing forms like unto men's.

The mixtures' residue He gave unto those souls that had gone in advance and had been summoned to the lands of Gods, to regions near the Stars, and to the [choir of] holy daimones. He said:

13. "My sons, ye children of My Nature, fashion things! Take ye the residue of what My art hath made, and let each fashion something which shall bear resemblance to his own nature. These will I further give to you as models."

He took and set in order fair and fine, agreeably to the motions of the souls, the world of sacred animals, appending as it were to those resembling men those which came next in order, and on these types of lives He did bestow

[1] We have had previous mention of fire, (æther) and air,—the psychōsis being the quintessence.

[2] These are presumably the types of life in the upper world, symbolized by the zodiac.

the all-devising powers and all-contriving pro-creative breath of all the things which were for ever generally to be.

And He withdrew, with promises to join unto the visible productions of their hands breath that cannot be seen,[1] and essence of engendering its like to each, so that they might give birth to others like themselves. And these are under no necessity to do aught else than what they did at first.

14. [And Horus asked :]

What did the souls do, mother, then ?

And Isis said :

Taking the blend of matter, Horus, son, they first looked at the Father's mixture and adored it, and tried to find out whence it was composed ; but this was not an easy thing for them to know.

They then began to fear lest they should fall beneath the Father's wrath for trying to find out, and so they set to work to do what they were bid.

Thereon, out of the upper stuff which had its topmost layer superfluously light, they formed the race of birds ; while they were doing this the mixture had become half-hardened, and by this time had taken on a firm consistency—thereon they fashioned out the race of things

[1] So Meineke in notes, following Cantor,—instead of the traditional "visible."

which have four feet; [next they did fashion forth] the race of fish—less light and needing a moist substance of a different kind to swim in; and as the residue was of a cold and heavy nature, from it the Souls devised the race of creeping things.

15. They then, my son, as though they had done something grand, with over-busy daring armed themselves, and acted contrary to the commands they had received; and forthwith they began to overstep their proper limits and their reservations, and would no longer stay in the same place, but were for ever moving, and thought that being ever stationed in one place was death.

That they would do this thing, however, O my son (as Hermes says when he speaks unto me), had not escaped the Eye of Him who is the God and Lord of universal things; and He searched out a punishment and bond, the which they now in misery endure.

Thus was it that the Sovereign King of all resolved to fabricate with art the human frame, in order that in it the race of Souls throughout might be chastised.

16. "Then sending for me," Hermes says, " He spake: 'Soul of My Soul, and holy mind of My own Mind,[1] up to what point, the nature of the

[1] *Cf.* Cyril, *C. J.*, i. 15 (Frag. xvi.).

things beneath, shall it be seen in gloom? How long shall what has up to now been made remain inactive and be destitute of praise? Bring hither to Me now, My son, all of the Gods in Heaven,' said God"—as Hermes saith.

And when they came obedient to His command,—"Look down," said He, "upon the Earth, and all beneath." And they forthwith both looked and understood the Sovereign's will. And when He spake to them on human kind's behalf, they [all] agreed to furnish those who were to be, with whatsoever thing they each could best provide.

17. Sun said: "I'll shine unto my full."

Moon promised to pour light upon the after-the-sun course, and said she had already given birth to Fear, and Silence, and also Sleep, and Memory—a thing that would turn out to be most useful for them.[1]

Cronus announced himself already sire of Justice and Necessity.

Zeus said: "So that the race which is to be may not for ever fight, already for them have I made Fortune, and Hope, and Peace."

Ares declared he had become already sire of Struggle, Wrath, and Strife.

Nor yet did Aphrodite hesitate; she also said: "I'll join to them Desire, my Lord, and Bliss,

[1] *Cf.* Plat. *Crit.*, 108.

and Laughter [too], so that our kindred souls, in working out their very grievous condemnation, may not exhaust their punishment unto the full."

Full pleased were all, my son, at Aphrodite's words.

"And for my part," said Hermes, "I will make men's nature well endowed; I will devote to them Prudence and Wisdom, Persuasiveness and Truth, and never will I cease from congress with Invention, but ever will I benefit the mortal life of men born underneath my types of life.[1] For that the types our Father and Creator hath set apart for me, are types of wisdom and intelligence, and more than ever [is this so] what time the motion of the Stars set over them doth have the natural power of each consonant with itself."

18. And God, the Master of the universe, rejoiced on hearing this, and ordered that the race of men should be.

"I," Hermes says, "was seeking for the stuff which had to be employed, and calling on the Monarch for His aid. And He gave order to the Souls to give the mixture's residue; and taking it I found it utterly dried up.

"Thereon, in mixing it, I used more water far than was required to bring the matter back unto

[1] *Sc.* "signs of the zodiac," so-called.

its former state, so that the plasm was in every way relaxable, and weak and powerless, in order that it might not, in addition to its natural sagacity, be full of power as well.

"I moulded it, and it was fair; and I rejoiced at seeing mine own work, and from below I called upon the Monarch to behold. And He did look on it, and was rejoiced, and ordered that the Souls should be enfleshed.

"Then were they first plunged in deep gloom, and, learning that they were condemned, began to wail.[1] I was myself amazed at the Souls' utterances."

19. Now give good heed, son Horus, for thou art being told the Mystic Spectacle which Kaměphis, our forefather, was privileged to hear from Hermes, record-writer of all deeds, and I from Kaměphis, most ancient of [us] all, when he did honour me with the Black [Rite] that gives perfection; hear thou it now from me!

For when, O wondrous son of mighty fame, they were about to be shut in their prisons, some simply uttered wails and groans—in just the self-same way as beasts that once have been at liberty, when torn from their accustomed haunts they love so well, will be bad slaves, will fight

[1] There is a lacuna in the text, which I have thus conjecturally completed.

and make revolt, and be in no agreement with their masters; nay more, if circumstance should serve, will even do to death those that oppress them.[1]

Others with louder outcry hissed like snakes; another one shrieked shrilly, and ere he spake shed many tears, and, turning up and down what things served him as eyes, he said:

20. "O Heaven, thou source of our begetting, O Æther, Air, O Hands and holy Breath of God our Monarch, O ye most brilliant Stars, eyes of the Gods, O tireless light of Sun and Moon, co-nurslings of our origin,—reft from [you] all we suffer piteously.

"And this the more, in that from spacious realms of light, from out [thy] holy envelope and wealthy dome, and from the blessed government we shared with Gods, we shall be thus shut down into these honourless and lowly quarters.

"What is the so unseemly thing we miserables have done? What [crime] deserves these punishments? How many sins await us wretched ones? How many are the things we have to do in this our hopeless plight, necessities to furnish for this watery frame that is so soon dissolved?

21. "For that no longer shall our eyes behold

[1] The reading of this sentence has not yet been properly emended, so that its translation is somewhat conjectural.

the souls of God; when through such watery spheres as these we see our own forefather Heaven grown small and tiny, we shall dissolve in sighs, —nay, there'll be times we shall not see at all,[1] for sentence hath been passed on us poor things; the gift of real sight hath not been given to us, in that it hath not been permitted us to see without the light. Windows they are, not eyes![2]

"How wretchedly shall we endure to hear our kindred breaths breathe in the air, when we no longer shall be breathing with them! For home, instead of this great world high in the air, a heart's small mass awaits us. Set Thou us free from bonds so base as these to which we have sunk down, and end our grief!

"O Lord, and Father, and our Maker, if so it be Thou hast thus quickly grown indifferent unto the works of Thine own Hands, appoint for us some limits! Still deem us worthy of some words, though they be few, while yet we can see through the whole world-order bright on every side!"

22. Thus speaking, Horus, son, the Souls gained their request; for that the Monarch came, and sitting on the Throne of Truth made answer to their prayers.

[1] An Orphic verse has here crept into the text from the margin. It runs: "By light it is we see; by eyes we naught behold." *Fragm. Monad.*, x., p. 504, Herm.

[2] *Cf.* Plat., *Men.*, 76; Seneca, *Quæst. Nat.*, iv. 9.

"O Souls, Love and Necessity shall be your lords,[1] they who are lords and marshals after Me of all.[2] Know, all of you who are set under My unageing rule, that as long as ye keep you free of sin, ye shall dwell in the fields of Heaven ; but if some cause of blame for aught attach itself to you, ye shall dwell in the place that Destiny allots, condemned to mortal wombs.

"If, then, the things imputed to your charge be slight, leaving the bond of fleshly frames subject to death, ye shall again embrace your [father] Heaven, and sigh no more; but if ye shall commit some greater sins, and with the end appointed of your frames be not advanced, no longer shall ye dwell in Heaven, nor even in the bodies of mankind, but shall continue after that to wander round in lives irrational."[3]

---

[1] *Cf. Tim.* 42 A : "When they should be implanted in bodies by necessity . . . they should have . . . sensation . . . and love."

[2] *Cf.* Frag. xxiii.

[3] *Cf. Tim.*, 42 B: "He who lived well during his appointed time was to return and dwell in his native star, and there he would have a blessed and congenial existence. But if he failed in attaining this, at the second birth, he would pass into a woman, and if, when in that state of being, he did not desist from evil, he would be continually changed into some brute who resembled him in the evil nature which he had acquired, and would not cease from his toils and transformations until he followed the revolution of the 'same' and the 'like' within him, and overcame by the help of reason the turbulent and irrational mob of later accretions, made up of fire and air and water and earth, and returned to the form of his first and better state." Notice the omission of any reference to the inferior status of woman in the Egyptian tradition.

23. Thus speaking, Horus mine, He gave to all the gift of breath,[1] and thus continued :

"It is not without purpose or by chance I have laid down the law of your transformings[2]; but as [it will be] for the worse if ye do aught unseemly, so for the better, if ye shall will what's worthy of your birth.

"For I, and no one else, will be the Witness and the Watcher. Know, then, it is for what ye have done heretofore, ye do endure this being shut in bodies as a punishment.

"The difference in your rebirths, accordingly, for you, shall be as I have said, a difference of bodies, and their [final] dissolution [shall be] a benefit and a [return to] the fair happiness of former days.

"But if ye think to do aught else unworthy of Me, your mind shall lose its sight so as to think the contrary [of what is true], and take the punishment for benefit; the change to better things for infamous despite.

"But the more righteous of you, who stand upon the threshold of the change to the diviner state, shall among men be righteous kings, and genuine philosophers, founders of states, and lawgivers, and real seers, and true herb-knowers,

[1] Lit. "their spirits"—which apparently link the souls with their bodies.

[2] Reading μεταβολάς.

and prophets of the Gods most excellent, skilful musicians, skilled astronomers, and augurs wise, consummate sacrificers,—as many of you as are worthy of things fair and good.

24. "Among winged tribes [they shall be] eagles, for these will neither scare away their kind nor feed on them; nay more, when they are by, no other weaker beast will be allowed by them to suffer wrong, for what will be the eagles' nature is too just [to suffer it].

"Among four-footed things [they will be] lions,—a life of strength and of a kind which in a measure needs no sleep, in mortal body practising the exercises of immortal life—for they nor weary grow nor sleep.[1]

"And among creeping things [they will be] dragons, in that this animal will have great strength and live for long, will do no harm, and in a way be friends with man, and let itself be tamed; it will possess no poison and will cast its skin,[2] as is the nature of the Gods.

---

[1] *Cf.* Manetho, cited in the *Orthography* of Chœroboscus (Cramer, *Anecd. Ox.*, ii. 235, 32; Ælian, *H. A.*, v. 39, who follows Apion; R. 145, n. 3). But indeed this queer belief is a commonplace of the Mediæval *Bestiaries*, which all go back to their second century Alexandrian prototype, the famous *Physiologus*, which was doubtless in part based on Aristotle's *History of Animals* and Pliny's *Natural History*.

[2] ἰάσει δὲ καὶ γηράσαν. The reading is corrupt. But if we read γῆρας for γηράσαν, we have in the writer's ornate and somewhat strained style ἐᾶν γῆρας for the usual γῆρας ἐκδύνειν found in Aristotle (*H. V.*, 5. 7. 10; 8. 17. 11) for the changing of a serpent's

"Among the things that swim [they will be] dolphins; for dolphins will take pity upon those who fall into the sea, and if they are still breathing bear them to the land, while if they're dead they will not ever even touch them, though they will be the most voracious tribe that in the water dwells."

25. Thus speaking God became imperishable Mind.[1] Thereon, son Horus, from the Earth uprose a very Mighty Spirit which no mass of body could contain, whose strength consisted in his intellect. And though he knew full well the things on which he questioned—the body with which man was clothed according to his type, a body fair and dignified, yet savage overmuch and full of fear—immediately he saw the souls were entering the plasms, he cried out:

"What are these called, O Hermes, Writer of the Records of the Gods?"

And when he answered "Men!"—"Hermes," he said, "it is a daring work, this making man, with eyes inquisitive, and talkative of tongue, with power henceforth to hear things even which

skin. The phrase "as is the nature of the Gods" may then be explained as referring to the parallel between the anciently supposed rejuvenescence of the serpent and the perpetual growing young of the Gods.

[1] *Cf. C. H.*, i. 27: "This when he'd said, the Shepherd mingled with the powers." *Cf. Tim.*, 42 E: "When the Creator had made all these ordinances He remained in His own accustomed nature."

are no concern of his, dainty of smell, who will use to its full his power of touch on every thing.

"Hast thou, his generator, judged it good to leave him free from care, who in the future daringly will gaze upon the fairest mysteries which Nature hath? Wouldst thou leave him without a grief, who in the days to come will make his thoughts reach unto mysteries beyond the Earth?

26. "Men will dig up the roots of plants, and will find out their juices' qualities. Men will observe the nature of the stones. Men will dissect not only animals irrational, but they'll dissect themselves, desiring to find out how they were made. They will stretch out their daring hands e'en to the sea, and cutting self-grown forests down will ferry one another o'er to lands beyond. [Men] will seek out as well the inner nature of the holy spaces which no foot may tread, and will chase after them into the height, desiring to observe the nature of the motion of the Heaven.

"These are yet moderate things [which they will do]. For nothing more remains than Earth's remotest realms; nay, in their daring they will track out Night, the farthest Night of all.

27. "Naught have they, then, to stop them from receiving their initiation in the good of

freedom from all pain, and, unconstrained by terror's grievous goads, from living softly out a life free from all care.

"Then will they not gird on the armour of an over-busy daring up to Heaven? Will they not, then, reach out their souls freed from all care unto the [primal] elements themselves?

"Teach them henceforth to long to plan out something, where they have as well to fear the danger of its ill-success, in order that they may be tamed by the sharp tooth of pain in failure of their hopes.

"Let the too busy nature of their souls be balanced by desires, and fears, and griefs, and empty hopes.

"Let loves in quick succession sway their souls, hopes, manifold desires, sometimes fulfilled, and sometimes unfulfilled, that the sweet bait of their success may draw them into struggle amid direr ills.

"Let fever lay its heavy hand on them, that losing heart they may submit desire to discipline."

28. Thou grievest, dost thou, Horus, son, to hear thy mother put these things in words? Art thou not struck with wonder, art thou not terror-struck at how poor man was grievously oppressed? Hear what is sadder still!

When Momos said these things Hermes was pleased, for what he said was said out of affection for him; and so he did all that he recommended, speaking thus:

"Momos, the Nature of the Breath Divine which doth surround [all things] shall not become inert. The Master of the universe appointed me as steward and as manager.

"Wherefore the overseer of His command will be the keen-eyed Goddess of the all, Adrasteia[1]; and I will skilfully devise an instrument, mysterious, possessed of power of sight that cannot err, and cannot be escaped, whereto all things on earth shall of necessity be subject, from birth to final dissolution,—an instrument which binds together all that's done. This instrument shall rule all other things on Earth as well [as man]."

29. These words, said Hermes, did I speak to Momos, and forthwith the instrument was set a-going.

When this was done, and when the souls had entered in the bodies, and [Hermes] had himself been praised for what was done, again the Monarch did convoke the Gods in session. The Gods assembled, and once more did He make proclamation, saying:

"Ye Gods, all ye who have been made of chiefest Nature, free from all decay, who have

---

[1] Nemesis, the kārmic deity, "she from whom none can escape, according to the generally accepted derivation of the name.

received as your appointed lot for ever more to order out the mighty Æon, through whom all universal things will never weary grow surrendering themselves in turn the one to other,—how long shall we be rulers of this sovereignty that none can ever know? How long these things, shall they transcend the power of sight of Sun and Moon?

"Let each of us bring forth according to his power. Let us by our own energy wipe out this inert state of things; let chaos seem to be a myth incredible to future days. Set hand to mighty work; and I myself will first begin."

30. He spake; straightway in cosmic order there began the differentiation of the up-to-then black unity [of things]. And Heaven shone forth above tricked out with all his mysteries; Earth, still a-tremble, as the Sun shone forth grew harder, and appeared with all the fair adornments that bedeck her round on every side. For beautiful to God are even things which men think mean, in that in truth they have been made to serve the laws of God.

And God rejoiced when now He saw His works a-moving; and filling full His Hands, which held as much as all surrounding space, with all that Nature had produced, and squeezing tight the handfuls mightily, He said:

"Take [these], O holy Earth, take those, all-honoured one, who art to be the mother of all things, and henceforth lack thou naught!"

31. God spake, and opening His Hands, such Hands as God should have, He poured them all into the composition of the world. And they in the beginnings were unknown in every way; for that the Souls as newly shut in prison, not enduring their disgrace, began to strive in emulation with the Gods in Heaven, in full command of their high birth, and when held back, in that they had the same Creator, made revolt, and using weaker men as instruments, began to make them set upon each other, and range themselves in conflict, and make war among themselves.

Thus strength did mightily prevail o'er weakness, so that the strong did burn and massacre the weak, and from the holy places down they cast the living and the dead down from the holy shrines, until the Elements in their distress resolved to go to God their Monarch [to complain] about the savage state in which men lived.

The evil now being very great, the Elements approached the God who made them, and formulated their complaint in some such words as these:

32. It was moreover Fire who first received authority to speak. He said:

"O Lord, Artificer of this new World, thou

Name mysterious among the Gods, and up to now revered by all mankind, how long hast Thou, O Daimon, judged it right to leave the life of mortals without God?

"Show now Thyself unto Thy World consulting[1] Thee; initiate the savagery of life with peace; give laws to life; to right give oracles; fill with fair hopes all things; and let men fear the vengeance of the Gods, and none will sin.

"Should they receive due retribution for their sins, they will refrain henceforth from doing wrong; they will respect their oaths, and no one any more will ponder sacrilege.

"Let them be taught to render thanks for benefits received, that I, the Fire, may joyfully do service in the sacrificial rites, that they may from the altar send sweet-smelling vapours forth.

"For up to now I am polluted, Lord; and by the godless daring of these men I am compelled to burn up flesh. They will not let me be for what I was brought forth; but they adulterate with all indecency my undecaying state."

33. And Air too said:

"I also, Master, am made turbid by the vapours which the bodies of the dead exhale, and I am pestilential, and, no longer filled with health, I gaze down from above on things I ought not to behold."

[1] *Sc.* as supplicants consulting an oracle.

Next Water, O my son of mighty soul, received authority to speak, and spake and said:

"O Father, O wonderful Creator of all things, Daimon self-born, and Nature's Maker, who through Thee doth conceive all things, now at this last, command the rivers' streams for ever to be pure, for that the rivers and the seas or wash the murderers' hands or else receive the murdered."

34. After came Earth in bitter grief, and taking up the tale, O son of high renown, thus she began to speak:

"O sovereign Lord, Chief of the Heavenly Ones, and Master of the Wheels,[1] Thou Ruler of us Elements, O Sire of them who stand beside Thee, from whom all things have the beginning of their increase and of their decrease, and into whom they cease again and have the end that is their due according to Necessity's decree, O greatly honoured One, the godless rout of men doth dance upon my bosom.

"I hold in my embrace as well the nature of all things; for I, as Thou didst give command, not only bear them all, but I receive them also when they're killed. But now am I dishonoured. The world upon the Earth though filled with all things [else] hath not a God.

[1] Or disks, presumably the world-wheels.

"For having naught to fear they sin in everything, and from my heights, O Lord, down [dead] they fall by every evil art. And soaking with the juices of their carcases I'm all corrupt. Hence am I, Lord, compelled to hold in me those of no worth. With all I bear I would hold God as well.

"Bestow on Earth, if not Thyself, for I could not contain Thee, yet some holy Emanation [1] of Thyself. Make Thou the Earth more honoured than the rest of Elements; for it is right that she should boast of gifts from Thee, in that she giveth all."

35. Thus spake the Elements; and God, fulfilling all things with the sound of His [most] holy Voice, spake thus:

"Depart, ye Holy Ones, ye Children worthy of a mighty Sire, nor yet in any way attempt to innovate, nor leave the whole of [this] My World without your active service.

"For now another Efflux of My Nature is among you, and he shall be a pious supervisor of all deeds—judge incorruptible of living men and monarch absolute of those beneath the earth, not only striking terror [into them] but taking vengeance on them. And by his class of birth the fate he hath deserved shall follow every man."

And so the Elements did cease from their com-

[1] τινὰ ἱερὰν ἀπόρροιαν.

plaint, upon the Master's order, and they held their peace; and each of them continued in the exercise of his authority and in his rule.

36. And Horus thereon said:

How was it, mother, then, that Earth received God's Efflux?

And Isis said:

I may not tell the story of [this] birth[1]; for it is not permitted to describe the origin of thy descent, O Horus, [son] of mighty power, lest afterwards the way-of-birth of the immortal Gods should be known unto men,—except so far that God the Monarch, the universal Orderer and Architect, sent for a little while thy mighty sire Osiris, and the mightiest Goddess Isis, that they might help the world, for all things needed them.

'Tis they who filled life full of life. 'Tis they who caused the savagery of mutual slaughtering of men to cease. 'Tis they who hallowed precincts to the Gods their ancestors and spots for holy rites. 'Tis they who gave to men laws, food, and shelter.

'Tis they who will, says Hermes, learn to know the secrets of my records all, and will make separation of them; and some they will keep for themselves, while those that are best suited for the benefit of mortal men, they will engrave on tablet and on obelisk.

[1] *Cf. C. H.*, xiii. (xiv.) 3 (Com.).

'Tis they who were the first to set up courts of law; and filled the world with justice and fair rule. 'Tis they who were the authors of good pledges and of faith, and brought the mighty witness of an oath into men's lives.

'Tis they who taught men how to wrap up those who ceased to live, as they should be.[1]

'Tis they who searched into the cruelty of death, and learned that though the spirit which goes out longs to return into men's bodies, yet if it ever fail to have the power of getting back again, then loss of life results.

'Tis they who learned from Hermes that surrounding space was filled with daimons, and graved on hidden stones [the hidden teaching].

'Tis they alone who, taught by Hermes in God's hidden codes, became the authors of the arts, and sciences, and all pursuits which men do practise, and givers of their laws.

'Tis they who, taught by Hermes that the things below have been disposed by God to be in sympathy with things above, established on the earth the sacred rites o'er which the mysteries in Heaven preside.

'Tis they who, knowing the destructibility of [mortal] frames, devised the grade of prophets, in all things perfected, in order that no prophet who stretched forth his hands unto the Gods,

[1] *Sc.* mummification.

should be in ignorance of anything, that magic and philosophy should feed the soul, and medicine preserve the body when it suffered pain.

38. And having done all this, my son, Osiris and myself perceiving that the world was [now] quite full, were thereupon demanded back by those who dwell in Heaven, but could not go above till we had made appeal unto the Monarch, that surrounding space might with this knowledge of the soul[1] be filled as well, and we ourselves succeed in making our ascent acceptable [to Him]. . . . For that God doth in hymns rejoice.

Ay, mother, Horus said. On me as well bestow the knowledge of this hymn, that I may not remain in ignorance.

And Isis said : Give ear, O son ![2]

* * * * *

[1] θεωρία, contemplative science, face to face knowledge.
[2] The Commentary begins at the end of the following excerpt.

EXCERPT XXVI.

THE VIRGIN OF THE WORLD [II.]

(Patrizzi (p. 32b) runs this on to the last without a break. Text: Stob., *Phys.*, xli. 45, under heading: "In the Same"; G. pp. 420-427; M. i. 299-304; W. i. 407-414.

Ménard; Livre III., No. ii. of "Fragment," etc., as above, pp. 201-208.)

39. Now if thou wouldst, O son of mighty soul, know aught beside, ask on!

And Horus said: O mother of great honour, I would know how royal souls are born?

And Isis said: Son Horus, the distinction which marks out the royal souls is somewhat of this kind.

Four regions are there in the universe which fall beneath a law and leadership which cannot be transgressed—Heaven, and the Æther, and the Air, and the most holy Earth.

Above in Heaven, son, the Gods do dwell, o'er whom with all the rest doth rule the Architect of all; and in the Æther [dwell] the Stars, o'er whom the mighty Light-giver the Sun holds sway; but in the Air [live] only souls,[1] o'er whom doth rule the Moon ; and on the Earth [do dwell] men and the rest of living things, o'er whom he who doth happen to be king holds sway.

40. The Gods engender, son, the kings it has deserved, to rule [the race] that lives on Earth. The rulers are the emanations of the king, of whom the nearer to him is more royal than the rest; for that the Sun, in that 'tis nearer than the Moon to God, is far more vast and potent, to whom the Moon comes second both in rank and power.

The king, then, is the last of all the other Gods, but first of men ; and so long as he is upon the Earth, he is divorced from his true godship, but hath something that doth distinguish him from men and which is like to God.

The soul which is sent down to dwell in him, is from that space which is above those regions whence [the souls] descend to other men. Down from that space the souls are sent to rule for those two reasons, son.

41. They who have run a noble, blameless race throughout the cycle of their lives, and are about to be changed into Gods, [are born as kings,] in order that by exercise of kingship they may train themselves to use the power the Gods enjoy ; while certain souls who are already Gods, but

[1] MS. A adds "of daimones."

have in some slight way infringed the rule of life which God inspired, are born as kings, in order that they may not, in being clothed in bodies, undergo the punishment of loss of dignity as well as nature, and that they may not, when they are enfleshed, have the same lot as other men, but have when bound what they enjoyed when free.

42. The differences which are, however, in the dispositions shown by those who play the part of kings, are not determined by distinguishing their souls, for these are all divine, but by the constitution of the angels and the daimons who attend on them. For that such souls as these descending for such purposes do not come down without a guard and escort; for Justice up above knows how to give to each what is its due estate e'en though they be made exiles from their country ever fair.

When, then, my son, the angels and the daimons who bring down the soul are of a warlike kind, it has to keep firm hold of their proclivities, forgetting its own proper deeds, but all the more remembering the doings of the other host attached to it.

When they are peaceful, then the soul as well doth order its own course in peace.

When they love justice, then it too defends the right.

When they are music-lovers, then it also sings.

And when they are truth-lovers, then it also doth philosophize.

For as it were out of necessity these souls keep a firm hold of the proclivities of those that bring them here; for they are falling down to man's estate, forgetting their own nature, and the farther they depart from it, the more they have in memory the disposition of those [powers] which shut them [into bodies].

43. Well hast thou, mother, all explained, said Horus. But noble souls,—how they are born, thou hast not told me yet.

As on the Earth, son Horus, there are states which differ one from other, so also is it in the case of souls. For they have regions whence they start; and that which starts from a more glorious place, hath nobler birth than one which doth not so. For just as among men the free is thought more noble than the slave—(for that which is superior in souls and of a ruling nature of necessity subjects what is inferior)—so also, son, ...[1]

*   *   *   *   *

44. And how are male and female souls produced?

Souls, Horus, son, are of the self-same nature

[1] A lacuna, unfortunately, here occurs in the text, and must be of some extent, for the way of both of these souls is not given.

in themselves, in that they are from one and the same place where the Creator modelled them; nor male nor female are they. Sex is a thing of bodies, not of souls.

That which brings it about that some of them are stouter, some more delicate, is, son, that [cosmic] "air" in which all things are made. "Air" for the soul is nothing but the body which envelopes it, an element which is composed of earth and water, air and fire.[1]

As, then, the composition of the female ones has more of wet and cold, but less of dry and warm, accordingly the soul which is shut in a plasm of this kind, becomes relaxed and delicate, just as the contrary is found to be in case of males.

For in their case there's more of dry and warm, and less of cold and wet; wherefore the souls in bodies such as these are sturdy and more active.

45. And how do souls become intelligent, O mother mine?

And Isis answered:

The organ of the sight, my son, is swathed in wrappings. When these are dense and thick, the eye is dim; but when they're thin and light, then is the sight most keen. So is it also for the soul. For it as well has envelopes incorporal appropriate to it, just as it is itself incorporal.

[1] *Cf.* 45 below.

These envelopes are "airs" which are in us. When these are light and thin and clear, then is the soul intelligent; but, on the contrary, when they are dense and thick and turbid, then [the soul], as in bad weather, sees not at distance but only things which lie about its feet.

46. And Horus said:

What is the reason, mother, that the men outside our holiest land are not so wise of mind as our compatriots?

And Isis said:

The Earth lies in the middle of the universe upon her back, like to a human being, with eyes turned up to heaven, and portioned out into as many regions as there are limbs in man.

She turns her eyes to Heaven as though to her own Sire,[1] that with his changes she may also bring about her own.

She hath her head set to the south of all, right shoulder to south-east, left shoulder to south-west; her feet below the Bear, right foot beneath its tail, left under its head; her thighs beneath those that succeed the Bear; her waist beneath the middle [Stars].

47. A sign of this is that men in the south, who dwell upon her head, are fine about the head and have good hair.

[1] *Cf. P. S. A.*, xxiv. 1.

Those in the east are ready for a fight and archer folk—for this pertains to the right hand.

Those in the west are steadier and for the most part fight with the left hand, and what is done by others with the right, they for their part attribute to the left.

Those underneath the Bear excel in feet and have especially good legs.

Those who come after them a little way, about the zone which is our present Italy and Greece, they all have well-made thighs and backs. . . .

Moreover, all these [northern] parts being whiter than the rest bear whiter men upon them.

But since the holiest land of our forebears lies in the midst of Earth, and that the midst of a man's body serves as the precinct of the heart alone, and heart's the spot from which the soul doth start, the men of it not only have no less the other things which all the rest possess, but as a special thing are gifted with intelligence beyond all men and filled with wisdom, in that they are begotten and brought up above her heart.

48. Further, my son, the south being the receiver of the clouds which mass themselves together from the atmosphere . . .[1]

[1] Something has evidently fallen out here, as the sentence is nowhere completed.

For instance, it is just because there is this concentration of them in the south, that it is said our river doth flow thence, upon the breaking up of the frost there.

For whensoe'er a cloud[1] descends, it turns the air about it into mist, and sends it downward in a kind of fog; and fog or mist is an impediment not only to the eyes, but also to the mind.

Whereas the east, O Horus, great in glory, in that 'tis thrown into confusion and made overhot by the continual risings of the sun, and in like fashion too, the west, its opposite, in that it suffers the same things through its descents,[2] afford the men born in them no conditions for clear observation. And Boreas with his concordant cold, together with their bodies doth congeal the minds of men as well.

Whereas the centre of all these being pure and undisturbed, foreknows both for itself and all that are in it. For, free from trouble, ever it brings forth, adorns and educates, and only with such weapons wars [on men], and wins the victory, and with consummate skill, like a good

---

[1] Reading νεφέλη for νεφέλῃ. The text is very faulty.

[2] These ideas of course spring from the conception of a flat earth and moving sun. The sun was thus thought to be nearer the earth at its rising and setting, and consequently those at the extremes of east and west were thought to be in danger of being burnt up by its heat.

satrap,[1] bestows the fruit of its own victory upon the vanquished.

49. This too expound, O lady, mother mine! For what cause is it that when men still keep alive in long disease, their rational part—their very reason and their very soul—at times becomes disabled?

And Isis answer made:

Of living things, my son, some are made friends with fire, and some with water, some with air, and some with earth, and some with two or three of these, and some with all.

And, on the contrary, again some are made enemies of fire, and some of water, some of earth, and some of air, and some of two of them, and some of three, and some of all.

For instance, son, the locust and all flies flee fire; the eagle and the hawk and all high-flying birds flee water; fish, air and earth; the snake avoids the open air. Whereas snakes and all creeping things love earth; all swimming things [love] water; winged things, air, of which they are the citizens; while those that fly still higher [love] the fire and have their habitat near it. Not that some of the animals as well do not love fire; for instance salamanders, for they even have their homes in it. It is because one or

[1] Some historical allusion may perhaps be suspected in this term; but I can find nothing appropriate to suggest.

another of the elements doth form their bodies outer envelope.

50. Each soul, accordingly, while it is in its body is weighted and constricted by these four. Moreover it is natural it also should be pleased with some of them and pained with others.

For this cause, then, it doth not reach the height of its prosperity; still, as it is divine by nature, e'en while [wrapped up] in them, it struggles and it thinks, though not such thoughts as it would think were it set free from being bound in bodies.

Moreover if these [frames] are swept with storm and stress, or of disease or fear, then is the soul itself tossed on the waves, as man[1] upon the deep with nothing steady under him.

COMMENTARY

ARGUMENT

1. The "Virgin of the World" is a sacred sermon of initiation into the Hermes-lore, the first initiation, in which the tradition of the wisdom is handed on by the hierophant to the neophyte, by word of mouth. The instructor, or revealer, is the representative of Isis-Sophia, and speaks in her name, pouring forth for her beloved son, the new-born Horus, the first draught of

[1] For ἄνθρωπος Meineke reads ἀνθέρικος ("asphodel"), and compares Callimachus, *H. in Del.*, 193 : παλιρροίη ἐπινήχεται ἀνθέρικος ὥς. But I see no necessity for this strained "emendation."

immortality, which is to purge away the poison of the mortal cup of forgetfulness and ignorance, and so raise him from the "dead."

This pouring-forth explains that the divine economy is perfect order, mystery transcending mystery,—each state of being, and each being, a mystery to those below that state.

This order no mortal intellect can ever grasp; nay, in the far-off ages, when as yet there were no men, but only Gods, those essences that know no death, the first creation of the World-creator,—even these Gods, these mysteries to us, were in amazement at the glories of the greater mysteries which decked the Heaven with their unveiled transcendent beauty. Even these Gods did not know God as yet.

2. The Gods were immortal, but unknowing; they were intoxicated with Heaven's beauty, amazed, nay awestruck, at the splendour of the mysteries of Heaven. Then came there forth another outpouring of the Father over all; He poured the Splendour of His Mind into their hearts and they began to know.[1]

With this representation is blended a mythical historical tradition which suggests that all this was brought about for an "earth" on which our humanity had not as yet appeared, in far-off distant days when apparently our earth was not as now, ages ago, the purest Golden Age when there were Gods, not men. In that race of Gods, those of them in whom the ray was no low-burning spark, but a divine flame, were the instructors in the heavenly wisdom.

3. Of these was Hermes, a race or "being" rather

[1] The arising of the knowledge of God among the Gods, and the gradual descent of this knowledge down to man, reminds us somewhat of the method of the descent of the "Gospel" in the system of Basilides.

than an individual; these "Sons of Fire" left the record of their wisdom engraved on "stone" in symbol, in charge of others of the same race but less knowing than themselves; and so they ascended to Heaven.

4. Those that succeeded them had not the flame so bright within their hearts; they were of the same race, but younger souls—the Tat-race. Hermes could not hand on the direct knowledge to them, the "perfect sight" ($\theta\epsilon\omega\rho\iota\alpha$), and so recorded the wisdom in symbol and myth. Still later the Asclepius-race joined themselves to the Tat-souls.

All this, however, took place many many ages ago, long even before the days of the men-gods Osiris and Isis; for the real wisdom of Hermes was so ancient that even Isis herself had had to search out the hidden records, and that too by means of the inner sight, when she herself had won the power to see, and the True Sun had risen for her mind.

5. But the strain of reconstructing the history of this far-distant past, as he conceived it to have been, is too much for the writer. He knows he is dealing with "myths," with what Plutarch would have called the "doings of the daimones;" he knows that in reality these primæval "Books" of Hermes have no longer any physical existence, if indeed they ever had any; he knows that no matter what legends are told, or whatever the general priesthood may believe about ancient physical inscriptions of the primæval Hermes,—all this has passed away, and that the real wisdom of Hermes is engraved on the tablets of the æther, and not hidden in the shrines of earth.

The "Books" are engraved in the "sacred symbols of the cosmic elements," and hidden away hard by the "secrets of Osiris"—the mysteries of creative fire, the light that speaks in the heart. The true Books of

Hermes are hidden away in their own zones, the pure elements of the unseen world—the celestial Egypt.

6. This wisdom was held in safe keeping for the "souls" of men; it was a soul-gnosis, not a physical knowledge. Hereupon the writer begins the recital of his tradition[1] of the creation of the "souls" of men in their unfallen state, all of which is derived from the "Books of Hermes." The soul-creation runs as follows:

The Watchers[2] approach the Creator. The hour has struck for a new Cosmic Dawn, for a new Day. The time has come for Cosmos to awake after the Night.[3] The Creative Mind of the universe turns His attention, His thought, to a new phase of things, a new world-period.

7. God smiled, and His laughter thrilled through space,[4] and with His Word, called forth into the light the new dawn from out the primæval darkness of the new world-space. His first creation, transcendental or intelligible Nature, stood before Him, in all the marvel of her new beauty, the primal plērōma, or potential fullness, of the new universe or system, the ideal cosmos of our world, for there were many others,—the Gods who marvelled at the mystery.

Straightway this Nature fell from one into three, herself and Toil and their fairest child Invention, to

[1] Or rather apocalypse; see § 15: "As Hermes says when he speaks unto me."

[2] *Cf.* the Egregores of *The Book of Enoch*; see Charles' Translation (Oxford; 1893), Index, under "Watchers."

[3] The new Manvantara following a periodical Pralaya, to use the terms of Indo-Aryan tradition.

[4] The creation is figured in one Egyptian tradition as the bursting forth of the Creator into seven peals of laughter,—a sevenfold "Ha!"

whom God gave the gift of being, themselves producing ideal form alone.

The first creation, then, was the bringing forth of potencies and types and ideas, to whom God gave the gift of being; it was as yet the world "above," the primæval Heaven, in ultimate perfection, thus constituting the unchanging boundaries of the new universe that was to be. These things-that-are were filled with "mysteries," not "breaths" or "lives," for these were not as yet.

8. The next stage is the breathing of the spiritual (not the physical) breath of lives into the fairest blend of the primal elements that condition the world-area. This blend or soul-substance is called *psychōsis*. The primal elements were not our mixed earth, water, fire, and air, but "knowing fire" (perhaps "fire in itself," as Hermes elsewhere calls it, or intelligible fire, perchance the "flower of fire" of the so-called "Chaldæan Oracles"[1]) and unknowing air, if we may judge from the phrase (7): "Let heaven be filled with all things full, and air and æther [?=fire] too!" It is Heaven or the ideal world that is so filled; even earth-water was not yet manifested, much less earth and water.

It seems, then, that these souls (souls corresponding above with the subsequent man-stage below) were a blend of the three: spirit, knowing fire, and unknowing air,—triads, yet a unity called *psychōsis*.

9. They were moreover all essentially equal, but differed according to some fixed law of numbering; they were also apparently definite in number, one soul perchance for every star, as with Plato, according to the law of similarity of less and greater, of within and without.

10. These souls, then, were "sacred (or typical) men,"

[1] *Cf.* the "florescence" of § 10.

a creation prior to that of the "sacred animals"; their habitat was in Upper Nature, the "all-fairest station of the æther"—the celestial cosmos.

11. They were appointed to certain stations and to the task of keeping the "wheel revolving,"—that is, as we shall see, they were to fashion forms for birth and death, and so provide means of transmission for the lifecurrents ever circulating in the great sphere. This was their appointed task, the law imposed on them, as obedient children of the Great King, their sire. So long as they kept their appointed stations they were to live for ever in surroundings of bliss and beauty, in full contemplation of the glories of the greater universe, throned amid the stars. But if they disobeyed the law, bonds and punishment await them.

12. We next come to a further creation of souls—a subject somewhat difficult to follow. These souls are of an inferior grade to the preceding, for they are composed of the primal water and earth, of "water in itself" and "earth in itself" we must suppose, and not of the compound elements we now call by these names. These are the souls of certain "sacred animals" or lives, which bear the same relationship to the souls which "keep the wheel revolving" as animals do to man on earth. They are, however, not shaped like the animals on earth, nor possess even typical animal forms, but bear the forms of men, though they are not men.

13. Still was the divine "water-earth" substance unexhausted, and so the residue was handed over to "those souls that had gone in advance and had been summoned to the land of Gods,"—that is to say, those stations near the Gods, in highest æther, of which mention has just been made. These souls are, of course, the man-souls proper.

Out of this residue these Builders were to fashion

animals, after the models the Creator gave them,—certain types of life, below the "man" type proper, ranged in due order corresponding to the "motions of the souls." That is to say, there were various classes of Builders according to the types of animals which were to be copied. The Builders were to fashion the forms, the Creator was to breathe into them the life.

14. Thus these Builders fashioned the etheric doubles of birds, quadrupeds, fish and reptiles, and not their physical bodies, for as yet the earth was not solid.

15. And so the Builder-souls accomplished their task, and fashioned the primæval copies of the celestial types of animals. Proud of their work, they grew restive at the restraints placed upon them by the law of their stations, and overstepped the limits decreed by the Creator.[1]

Whereupon the punishment is pronounced, and the Creator resolves to make the human frame, therein to imprison the disobedient souls.

And here we learn incidentally that all of this

[1] *Cf.* the same idea as expressed by Basilides (*ap.* Hipp., *Philos.*, vii. 27), but in reversed order, when, speaking of the consummation of the world-process, and the final ascension of the "Sonship" with all its experience gained from union with matter, he says of the remaining souls, which have not reached the dignity of the Sonship, that the Great Ignorance shall come upon them for a space.

"Thus all the souls of this state of existence, whose nature is to remain immortal in this state of existence alone, remain without knowledge of anything different from or better than this state; nor shall there be any rumour or knowledge of things superior in higher states, in order that the lower souls may not suffer pain by striving after impossible objects, just as though it were fish longing to feed on the mountains with sheep, for such a desire would end in their destruction. All things are indestructible if they remain in their proper condition, but subject to destruction if they desire to overleap and transgress their natural limits" (*F. F. F.*, p. 270).

psychogenesis which has gone before was the direct teaching of Hermes to the writer; of no physical Hermes, however, but of that Hermes whose "Books" are hidden in the zones (5), of the Hermes whom the writer, as he would have us believe, came to know face to face only after his inner vision was opened, and he had gazed with all-seeing eyes "upon the mysteries of that new dawn" (4).

16. For the new and mysterious fabrication of the man-form, all the seven obedient Gods, to whom the man-souls are kin (17), are summoned by the chief of them, Hermes himself, the beloved son and messenger of the Supreme, "soul of My Soul, and holy mind of My own Mind."[1]

17. All of the seven promise to bestow the best they have on man.

18. The plasm out of which the man-form is to be modelled is the residue of the mixture out of which the Builders had already made the animal doubles. But the Builder of the man-frames was Hermes himself, who mixed the plasm with still more water.

19. Here the writer inserts a further piece of information concerning the source of his tradition. It is no longer as before what Hermes himself reveals to him in vision, but what the writer was told at a certain initiation called the "Black Rite." This rite was presided over by Kamēphis, who is called the "earliest of all," or perhaps more correctly the "most primæval of [us] all." Kamēphis is thus conceived as the representative of a more ancient wisdom than that of Isis, and yet even he but hands on the tradition of Hermes.[2]

20. The souls are "enfleshed," and utter loud complaints. Apparently not all at first can speak articulately; most of them can only groan, or scream,

[1] *Cf.* Cyril, *C. Jul.*, i. 35 ; Frag. xvi.   [2] *Cf.* §§ 29 and 37.

or hiss. The leading class of souls can, however, so far dominate the plasm as to speak articulately, and so one of their number utters a desperate appeal to Heaven.

21. They have now lost their celestial state, and Heaven is shut away from them; no longer can they see "without the light." They are shut down into a "heart's small compass"; the Sun of their being has become a light-spark only, hidden in the heart. This is, of course, the *logos*, the inmost reality in man.

22. The souls pray for some amelioration of their unhappy lot, and the conditions of the moral law are expounded to them. They who do rightly shall, on their body's dissolution, reascend to Heaven and be at rest; they who do ill, shall work out their redemption under the law of metempsychosis, or change from body to body, from prison to prison.

23. Details of this metempsychosis are then given with special reference to the incarnations of the "more righteous," who shall be kings, philosophers and prophets. Such souls apparently, for it is not expressly so stated, shall, in passing round the wheel of rebirth, when out of incarnation in a human body, have some sort of life with the souls of the leading types of animals, which are given as eagles, lions, dragons, and dolphins. Or, if we are unjustified in this speculation, such souls shall in their animal parts have intimate relation with the noblest types of animal essence (24).

25. There now comes upon the scene the mighty Intellect of the Earth, a veritable Erdgeist, in the form of Mōmus, who speaking out of affection for him (28), urges Hermes to increase ills and trials upon the souls of men, so that they shall not dare too much (25–27). And thereon Hermes sets in motion the instrument or engine of unerring fate and mechanical retribution (28, 29).

29. Now all these things took place at the dawn of earth-life, when all as yet was inert, as far as our now solid earth is concerned. We must then suppose that as yet our present phase of existence on earth had not yet been manifested; that all was as yet in a far subtler or more primitive state of existence, when earth was still all "a-tremble," and had not yet hardened to its present state of solidity;—that is to say, that the man-plasm was in an etheric state (30).

31. The earth gradually hardens. Into the now more solid earth, the Creator and His obedient sons, the Gods who had not made revolt, poured forth the blessings of nature. This is described by the beautiful symbol of the hands of blessing, figured in Egypt as the sun-rays, each terminating in a hand for giving light and life.[1]

The imprisoned souls, the kinsmen of the Gods obedient, continue their revolt; they are the leaders of mankind, of a mankind far weaker than themselves, a humanity, apparently evolved normally from the nature of things and as yet in its childhood. Instead of teaching them the lessons of love and wisdom, the Disobedient Ones use them for evil purposes, for war and conflict, for oppression and savagery.

32. Things go from bad to worse; the earth is befouled with the horrors of savage man, until in despair the pure elements complain to God. They pray that He will send a holy emanation of Himself to set things right (32–34).

35. Hereupon God sends forth the mystery of a new birth, a divine descent, or emanation, an *avatāra*, as the Áryan Hindu tradition would call it, a dual manifestation.[2] And so Osiris and Isis are born to help the

---

[1] *Cf.* Hermes-Prayer, iii. 3.

[2] This is of special interest as showing how the Egyptian tradition, in this pre-eminent above all others, did not limit the manifestation to the male sex alone.

world, to recall men from savagery, and restore the moral order (35-37).

It was they who were taught directly by Hermes (37) in all law and science and wisdom. Their mission meets with success, and the "world" is filled with a knowledge of the Path of Return. But before their ascension into Heaven they have a petition to make to the Father, that not only earth but also the surrounding spaces up to Heaven itself may be filled with a knowledge of the truth. Thus then they proceed to hymn the Sire and Monarch of all in a praise-giving which, unfortunately, Stobæus did not think fit to copy.

The original text of the "Virgin of the World" treatise is obviously broken only by the omission of the Hymn of Osiris and Isis, and Excerpt ii. follows otherwise immediately on Excerpt i. The subject is the birth of royal souls, taken up from the instruction given in *K. K.*, 23, 24 above.

39. There are four chief spaces: (i) Invisible Heaven, inhabited by the Gods, with the Invisible Sun as lord of all; (ii) Æther, inhabited by the Stars, of which *for us* the Sun is leader; (iii) Air, in which dwell nonincarnate souls, ruled by the Moon, as watcher o'er the paths of genesis; (iv) Earth, inhabited by men and animals, and over men the immediate ruler is the Divine King of the time.

40. The king-soul is the last of the Gods but the first of men[1]; he is, however, on earth a demigod only, for his true divinity is obscured. His soul, or *ka*, comes from a soul-plane superior to that of the rest of mankind.

The ascending souls of normally evolving humanity are thought of, apparently, as describing ever widening

[1] *Cf. C. H.*, xviii. 8 ff.

circles in their wheelings in and out of incarnation, rising, as they increase in virtue and knowledge, at the zenith of their ascent in the intermediate state, before they turn to descend again into rebirth, ever nearer to the limits of the sensible world and the frontiers of Heaven.

41. But there is also another class of descending royal souls, who have only slightly transgressed, and therefore descend only as far as this grade of humanity.

42. For the royal or ruling soul is not only a warrior monarch; his sovereignty may be also shown in arts of peace. He may be a righteous judge, a musician or poet, a truth-lover or philosopher. The activities of these souls are not determined, as is the case with souls of lower grades,—that is, those souls which have fallen deeper into material existence,—by what Basilides would have called the "appendages" of the animal nature; they are determined by a fairer *taxis*, an escort of angels and daimones, who accompany them into birth.

43. The description of their manner of birth, however, is, unfortunately, lost to us, owing either to the hesitation of Stobæus to make it public, or to its being cut out by some subsequent copyist.

44. We are next told that sex is no essential characteristic of the soul. It is an "accident" of the body, but this body is not the physical, but the "aery" body, which air, however, is not a simple element, but already differentiated into four sub-elements.[1]

45. Moreover the sight, or intelligence, of the soul also depends upon the purity of certain envelopes, which

[1] The "spirituous" or "aery" body, or vehicle, is composed of the sub-elements, but in it is a predominance of the sub-element "air," just as in the physical there is a predominance of "earth." —Philoponus, *Prœm. in Aristot. de Anima*; see my Orpheus (London, 1896), "The Subtle Body," pp. 276–281. *Cf.* also *S. I. H.*, 15, 20.

are called "airs,"—"airs" apparently more subtle even than the aery body (45).[1]

46. Next follows a naïve reason for the excellence of Egypt and the wisdom of the Egyptians (46-48). Here the writer seems to be no longer dependent directly on the Trismegistic tradition, but is inserting and expanding popular notions.

49. The remaining sections of the Excerpt are taken up with speculations as to the cause of delirium (49, 50), and Stobæus brings his extract to a conclusion apparently without allowing the writer to complete his exposition.

Sources ?

The discussion as to the meaning of the title, which has so far been invariably translated "The Virgin of the World," will come more appropriately later on.

How much of the original treatise has been handed on to us by Stobæus we have no external means of deciding. Our two Extracts, however, plainly stand in immediate connection with each other, and the original text is broken only by the unfortunate omission of the Hymn of Osiris and Isis. The first Extract, moreover, is plainly not the beginning of the treatise, since it opens with words referring to what has gone before; while the second Extract ends in a very unsatisfactory manner in the middle of a subject.

What we have, however, gives us some very interesting indications of how the writer regarded his sources,— whether written or oral, whether physical or psychic. He of course would have us take his treatise as a literary unity; and indeed the subject is so worked up that it is very difficult to discover what the literary

[1] Compare this with the *prāṇa's* of Indian theosophy ; see *C. H.*, x. (xi.) 13, Comment.

sources that lay before the writer may have been, for the story runs on straight enough in the same thought-mould and literary form, in spite of the insertion of somewhat contradictory statements concerning the sources of information.

When, however, Reitzenstein (p. 136) expressly states that the creation-story shows indubitable traces of two older forms, and that this is not a matter of surprise, as we find two (or more precisely four) different introductions,—we are not able entirely to follow him. It is true that these introductory statements are apparently at variance, but on further consideration they appear to be not really self-contradictory.

The Direct Voice and the Books of Hermes

The main representation is that the teacher of Isis is Hermes, who saw the world-creation, that is, the creation of our earth-system, and the soul-making, with his own spiritual sight (2). Isis has obtained her knowledge in two ways: either from the sacred Books of Hermes (4, 5); or by the direct spiritual voice of the Master (15). The intention here is plainly to claim the authority of direct revelation, for even the Books are not physical. They have disappeared, if indeed they ever were physical, and can only be recovered from the tablets of unseen nature, by ascending to the zones (5) where they are hidden; and these zones are plainly the same as the soul-spaces mentioned in *S. I. H.*, 8.

At the same time there is mention of another tradition, which, though in later details purporting to be historic and physical, in its beginnings is involved in purely mythological and psychic considerations. When the first and most ancient Hermes ascended to Heaven, he left his Books in the charge of the Gods, his kinsmen, in the zones, and not on earth (3). On earth there succeeded to this wisdom a younger race, beloved of Hermes, and personified as his son Tat. These were souls as yet too young to understand the true science face to face. They were apparently regarded as the Tat (Thoth) priesthood of our humanity, who were subsequently joined by wisdom-lovers of another line of tradition, the Imuth (Asclepius) brotherhood, who had their doctrine originally from Ptah.[1] This seems to hint at some ancient union of two traditions or schools of mystic science, perhaps from the Memphitic and Thebaic priesthoods respectively.[2]

What, however, is clear is that the writer professes to set forth a higher and more direct teaching than either the received tradition of the Isiac mystery-cult or of the Tat-Asclepius school. This he does in the person of Isis as the face to face disciple of the most ancient Hermes,[3] thus showing us that in the Hermes-circles of the Theoretics, or those who had the direct sight, though the Isis mystery-teaching was considered a tradition of the wisdom, it was nevertheless held to be entirely subordinate to the illumination of the direct sight.

[1] *Cf.* Diog. Laert., *Proem.*, i.: "The Egyptians say that Hephæstus (Ptah) was the son of Neilus (the Nile), and that he was the originator of philosophy, of that philosophy whose leaders are priests and prophets"—that is to say, a mystic philosophy of revelation.

[2] Thus Suidas (*s.v.* "Ptah") says that Ptah was the Hephæstus of the Memphite priesthood, and tells us that there was a proverbial saying current among them: "Ptah hath spoken unto thee." This reminds us of our text: "As Hermes says when he speaks unto me."

[3] The type of Isis as utterer of "sacred sermons," describing herself as daughter or disciple of Hermes, is old, and goes back demonstrably to Ptolemaic times. R. 136, n. 4; 137, n. 1.

KAMEPHIS AND THE DARK MYSTERY

In apparent contradiction to all this we have the following statement: "Now give good heed, son Horus, for thou art being told the mystic spectacle which Kamēphis, our forefather, was privileged to hear from Hermes, the record-writer of all deeds, and I from Kamēphis when he did honour me with the Black [Rite] that gives perfection" (19).[1]

Here Reitzenstein (p. 137) professes to discover the conflation of two absolutely distinct traditions of (i) Kamephis, a later god and pupil of Hermes, and (ii) Kamephis, an older god and teacher of Isis; but in this I cannot follow him. It all depends on the meaning assigned to the words παρὰ τοῦ πάντων προγενεστέρου, which Reitzenstein regards as signifying "the most ancient of all [gods]," but which I translate as "the most ancient of [us] all."

I take it to mean simply that, according to the general Isis-tradition, the founder of its mysteries was stated to be Kamephis, but that the Isis-Hermes circles claimed that this Kamephis, though truly the most ancient figure in the Isis tradition proper, was nevertheless in his turn the pupil of the still more ancient Hermes.

The grade of Kamephis was presumably represented in the mystery-cult by the arch-hierophant who presided at the degree called the "Dark Mystery" or "Black Rite." It was a rite performed only for those

[1] ὁπότ' ἐμὲ καὶ τῷ τελείῳ μέλανι ἐτίμησεν. This has hitherto been always supposed by the philological mind simply to refer to the mysteries of *ink* or writing, and that too without any humorous intent, but in all portentous solemnity. We must imagine, then, presumably, that it refers to the schooldays of Isis, when she was first taught the Egyptian equivalents for pothooks and hangers. This absurdity is repeated even by Meineke.

who were judged worthy of it (ἐτίμησεν) after long probation in lower degrees, something of a far more sacred character, apparently, than the instruction in the mysteries enacted in the light.

I would suggest, therefore, that we have here a reference to the most esoteric institution of the Isiac tradition, the more precise nature of which we will consider later on; it is enough for the moment to connect it with certain objects or shows that were apparently made to appear in the dark. As Clement of Alexandria says in his famous commonplace book, called the *Stromateis*[1]:

"It is not without reason that in the mysteries of the Greeks, lustrations hold the first place, analogous to ablutions among the Barbarians [that is, non-Greeks]. After these come the lesser mysteries, which have some foundation of instruction and of preliminary preparation for what is to follow; and then the great mysteries, in which nothing remains to be learned of the universe, but only to contemplate and comprehend nature [herself] and the things [which are mystically shown to the initiated]."[2]

[1] The more correct title of this work should be "Gnostic Jottings (or Notes) according to the True Philosophy," as Clement states himself and as has been well remarked by Hort in his *Ante-Nicene Fathers*, p. 87 (London, 1895).

[2] *Op. cit.*, v. 11. Sopater (*Dist. Quæst.*, p. 123, ed. Walz) speaks of these as "figures" (σχήματα), the same expression which Proclus (*In Plat. Rep.*, p. 380) employs in speaking of the appearances which the Gods assume in their manifestations; Plato (*Phædr.*, p. 250) calls them "blessed apparitions," or beatific visions" (εὐδαίμονα φάσματα); the author of the *Epinomis* (p. 986) describes them as "what is most beautiful to see in the world"; these are the "mystic sights" or "wonders" (μυστικὰ θεάματα) of Dion Chrysostom (*Orat.*, xii., p. 387, ed. Reiske); the "holy appearances" (ἅγια φαντάσματα) and "sacred shows" (ἱερὰ δεικνύμενα) of Plutarch (Wyttenbach, *Fragm.*, vi. 1, t. v., p. 722, and *De Profect. Virtut. Sent.*, p. 81, ed. Reiske); the

Kneph-Kamephis

But who was Kamēphis in the theology of the Egyptians? According to Reitzenstein, Kamephis or Kmephis, that is Kmeph, is equated by Egyptologists with Kneph, who, according to Plutarch,[1] was worshipped in the Thebaid as the ingenerable and immortal God. Kneph, however, as Sethe has shown,[2] is one of the aliases of Ammon, who is the " bull [or husband] of his mother," the "creator who has created himself." Kneph is, moreover, the Good Daimon, as Philo of Byblus says.[3] He is the Sun-god and Heaven-god Ammon.

"If he open his eyes, he filleth all with light in his primæval[4] land ; and if he close them all is dark."[5]

Here we have Kneph-Ammon as the giver of light in darkness, and the opener of the eyes.

Moreover, Porphyry[6] tells us that the Egyptians regarded Kneph as the demiurge or creator, and represented him in the form of a man, with skin of a blue-black tint, girt with a girdle, and holding

---

'ineffable apparitions" (ἄρρητα φάσματα) of Aristides (*Orat.*, xix. p. 416, ed. Dindorf); the "divine apparitions" (θεῖα φάσματα) of Himerius (*Eclog.*, xxxii., p. 304, ed. Wernsdorf),—those sublime sights the memory of which was said to accompany the souls of the righteous into the after-life, and when they returned to birth. *Cf.* Lenormant (F.) on "The Eleusinian Mysteries" in *The Contemporary Review* (Sept. 1880), p. 416, who, however, thinks that these famous philosophers and writers bankrupted their adjectives merely for the mechanical figures and stage-devices of the lower degrees. See my "Notes on the Eleusinian Mysteries" in *The Theosophical Review* (April, May, June, 1898), vol. xxii., p. 156.

[1] *De Is. et Os.*, xxi.
[2] *Berl. phil. Wochenschr.* (1896), p. 1528 ; R. 137, n. 3.
[3] R. 133, n. 2.
[4] πρωτογόνῳ—*cf.* the προγενεστέρου πάντων above.
[5] Epeius, *ap.* Eusebius, *Præp. Ev.*, i. 10, p. 41 D.
[6] *Ap.* Euseb., *Præp.*, iii. 11, 45, p. 115.

a sceptre, and wearing a crown of regal wings. This symbolism, says Porphyry, signified that he was the representative of the Logos or Reason, difficult to discover, hidden,[1] not manifest[2]; it is he who gives light and also life[3]; he is the King. The winged crown upon his head, he adds, signifies that he moves or energizes intellectually.

Kamephis, then, stands in the Isis-tradition for the representative of Agathodaimon, the Logos-creator. He is, however, a later holder of this office, and has had it handed on to him by Hermes, or at any rate he is instructed in the Logos-wisdom by Hermes.

HERMES I. AND HERMES II.

In this connection it is instructive to refer to the account which Syncellus[4] tells us he took from the statement of Manetho.

Manetho, says Syncellus, states in his Books, that he based his replies concerning the dynasties of Egypt to King Ptolemy on the monuments.

"[These monuments], he [Manetho] tells us, were engraved in the sacred language, and in the characters of the sacred writing, by Thoth the First Hermes; after the Flood they were translated from the sacred language into the then common tongue, but [still written] in hieroglyphic characters, and stored away in books, by the Good Daimon's son, the Second Hermes, the father of Tat, in the inner shrines of the temples of Egypt."

[1] *Cf.* the epithet "utterly hidden" found in the "Words (*Logoi*) of Ammon," referred to by Justin Martyr, *Cohort.*, xxxviii., and the note thereon in "Fragments from the Fathers."

[2] Typified by the dark-coloured body.

[3] ζωοποιός—typified, presumably, by the girdle (the symbol of the woman) and the staff (the symbol of the man).

[4] *Chron.*, xl. (ed. Dind., i. 72).

THE VIRGIN OF THE WORLD 153

Here we have a tradition, going back as far as Manetho, which I have shown, in Chapter V. of the "Prolegomena" on "Manetho, High Priest of Egypt," cannot be so lightly disposed of as has been previously supposed,—dealing expressly with the Books of Hermes.

This tradition, it is true, differs from the account given in our Sermon (3–5), where the writer says nothing expressly of a flood, but evidently wishes us to believe that the most ancient records of Hermes were magically hidden in the zones of the unseen world, and that the flood, if there was one, was a flood or lapse of time that had utterly removed these records from the earth. For him they no longer existed physically.

Manetho's account deals with another view of the matter. His tradition appears to be as follows. The oldest records were on stone monuments which had survived some great flood in Egypt. These records belonged to the period of the First Hermes, the Good Daimon *par excellence*, the priesthood, therefore, of the earliest antediluvian Egyptian civilization. After the flood they were translated from the most archaic language into ancient Egyptian, and preserved in book-form by the Second Hermes, the priesthood, presumably, of the most ancient civilization after the flood, who were in time succeeded by the Tat priesthood.

That this tradition is elsewhere contradicted by the Isis-tradition proper, which in a somewhat similar genealogy places Isis at the very beginning prior even to Hermes I.,[1] need not detain us, since each tradition would naturally claim the priority of those whom it regarded as its own special founders, and we are for the moment concerned only with the claims of the Hermes-school.

[1] Varro, *De Gente Pop. Rom.*, *ap.* Augustine, *De Civ. Dei*, xviii. 3, 8; R. 139, n. 3.

The main point of interest is that there was a tradition which explained the past on the hypothesis of periods of culture succeeding one another,—the oldest being supposed to have been the wisest and highest; the most archaic hieroglyphic language, which perhaps the priests of Manetho's day could no longer fully understand,[1] was supposed to have been the tongue of the civilization before the Flood of Hermes I. It may even be that the remains of this tongue were preserved only in the magical invocations, as a thing most sacred, the "language of the gods."

The point of view, however, of the circle to which our writer belonged, was that the records of this most ancient civilization were no longer to be read even in the oldest inscriptions; they could only be recovered by spiritual sight. Into close relation with this, we must, I think, bring the statement made in § 37, that Osiris and Isis, though they themselves had learned all the secrets of the records of Hermes, nevertheless kept part of them secret, and engraved on stone only such as were adapted for the intelligence of "mortal men."

The Kamephis of the Isis-tradition, then, apparently stands for Kneph as Agathodaimon, that is for Hermes, but not for our Hermes I.,[2] for he has no physical

[1] It is said that with regard to ancient archaic texts which are still extant, modern Egyptology is able to translate them with greater accuracy than the priests of Manetho's day; but this one may be allowed to question, unless the ancient texts are capable solely of a physical interpretation.

[2] The Hermes, presumably, who was fabled to be the son of the Nile, not the physical Nile, but the Heaven Ocean, the Great Green, the Soul of Cosmos, and whom, we are told, the Egyptians would never speak of publicly, but, presumably, only within the circles of initiation. This Nile may be in one sense the Flood that hid the Books of Hermes in its depths or zones; but equally so the son of Nile may be the first Hermes after the Flood.

THE VIRGIN OF THE WORLD 155

contact with the Isis-tradition, but for Hermes II., who was taught by Hermes I.

THE BLACK RITE

But what is the precise meaning of the "black rite" at which Kamephis presides? I have already suggested the environment in which the general meaning may be sought, though I have not been able to produce any objective evidence of a precise nature. Reitzenstein (pp. 139 ff.), however, thinks he has discovered that evidence. His view is as follows:

The key to the meaning, according to him, is to be found in the following line from a Magic Papyrus [1]:

"I invoke thee, Lady Isis, with whom the Good Daimon doth unite,[2] He who is Lord ἐν τῷ τελείῳ μέλανι."

Reitzenstein thinks that the Good Daimon here stands for Chnum, and works out (p. 140) a learned hypothesis that the "black" refers to a certain territory of black earth, between Syene and Takompso, the Dedocaschœnus, especially famed for its pottery, which was originally in the possession of the Isis priesthood, but was subsequently transferred to the priesthood of Chnum by King Došer. Reitzenstein would thus, presumably, translate the latter half of the sentence as "the Good Daimon who is Lord in the perfect black [country]," and so make it refer to Chnum, though indeed he seems himself to feel the inadequacy of this explanation to cover the word "perfect" (p. 144). But this seems to me to take all the dignified meaning out of both our text and that of the Magic Papyrus, and to introduce

[1] Wessley, *Denkschr. d. k. Akad.* (1893), p. 37, l. 500.

[2] So R., though this is a meaning to which the lexicons give no support; the verb generally meaning "to defer" or "assent to."

local geographical considerations which are plainly out of keeping with the context.

It is far more natural to make the Agathodaimon of the Papyrus refer to Osiris; for indeed it is one of his most frequent designations. Moreover, it is precisely Osiris who is pre-eminently connected with the so-called "under world," the unseen world, the "mysterious dark." He is lord there, while Isis remains on earth; it is he who would most fitly give instructions on such matters, and indeed one of the ancient mystery-sayings was precisely, "Osiris is a dark God."[1]

"He who is Lord in the perfecting black," might thus mean that Osiris, the masculine potency[2] of the soul, purified and perfected the man on the mysterious dark side of things, and completed the work which Isis, the feminine potency of the soul, had begun on him.

That, in the highest mystery-circles, this was some stage of union of the man with the higher part of himself, may be deduced from the interesting citations made by Reitzenstein (pp. 142-144) from the later Alchemical Hermes-literature; it clearly refers to the mystic "sacred marriage,"[3] the intimate union of the soul with the *logos*, or divine ray. Much could be written on this subject, but it will be sufficient to append two passages of more than ordinary interest. The Jewish over-writer of the Naassene Document contends that the chief mystery of the Gnosis was but the consummation of the instruction given in the various mystery-institutions of the nations. The

[1] Compare also the mystery ritual in *The Acts of John*: "I am thy God, not that of the betrayer" (*F. F. F.*, p. 434).

[2] As the Gnostic Marcus would have called it.

[3] On this ἱερὸς γάμος or γάμος πνευματικός, see Lobeck (C. A.), *Aglaophamus* (Königsberg, 1829), 608, 649, 651.

Lesser Mysteries, he tells us, commenting on the text of the Pagan commentator, pertained to "fleshly generation," whereas the Greater dealt with the new birth, or second birth, with regeneration, and not with genesis. And speaking of a certain mystery, he says:

"For this is the Gate of Heaven, and this is the House of God, where the Good God [1] dwells alone, into which [House] no impure [man] shall come; but it is kept under watch for the spiritual alone; where when they come they must cast away their garments, and all become bridegrooms obtaining their true manhood through the Virginal Spirit. For such a man is the Virgin big with child, conceiving and bearing a Son, not psychic, not fleshly, but a blessed Æon of Æons." [2]

In the marvellous mystery-ritual of the new-found fragments of *The Acts of John*, lately discovered in a fourteenth century MS. in Vienna, disguised in hymn form, and hiding an almost inexhaustible mine of very early tradition, the "sacred marriage" is plainly suggested as one of the keys to part of the ritual. Compare, for instance, with the "casting away of their garments," in the above-quoted passage of the Naassene writer, the following:

"[*The Disciple.*] I would flee.

[*The Master.*] I would [have thee] stay.

[*The Assistants.*] Amen!

[*The Disciple.*] I would be robed.

[*The Master.*] And I would robe [thee].

[*The Assistants.*] Amen!

[*The Disciple.*] I would be at-oned.

[1] That is, the Agathodaimon.
[2] That is, the "Birth of Horus." Hippolytus, *Philos.*, v. 8 (ed. Dunk. and Schneid, pp. 164, 166, ll. 86-94). see "Myth of Man in the Mysteries," § 28. The last clause is the gloss of the later Christian over-writer.

[*The Master.*] And I would at-one.
[*The Assistants.*] Amen!"[1]

BLACK LAND.

But to return to the "mysterious black." Plutarch tells us: "Moreover, they [the Egyptians] call Egypt, inasmuch as its soil is particularly black, as though it were the black of the eye, Chemia, and compare it with the heart,"[2]—for, he adds, it is hot and moist, and set in the southern part of the inhabitable world, in the same way as the heart in the left side of a man.[3]

Egypt, the "sacred land" *par excellence*, was called Chemia or Chem (Ḥem), Black-land, because of the nature of its dark loamy soil; it was, moreover, in symbolic phraseology the black of the eye, that is, the pupil of the earth-eye, the stars and planets being regarded as the eyes of the gods.[4] Egypt, then, was the eye and heart of the Earth; the Heavenly Nile poured its light-flood of wisdom through this dark of the eye, or made the land throb like a heart with the celestial life-currents.

Nor is the above quotation an unsupported statement of Plutarch's, for in an ancient text from Edfu,[5] we read: "Egypt (lit. the Black), which is so called after the eye of Osiris, for it is his pupil."

Ammon-Kneph, too, as we have seen, is black, or blue-black, signifying his hidden and mysterious

[1] The text is to be found in James (M. R.), *Apocrypha Anecdota*, ii. (Cambridge, 1897), in *Texts and Studies*; F. F. F., pp. 432, 433.

[2] *De Is. et Os.*, xxxiii.

[3] *Cf.* this with K. K., 47, where Egypt is said to occupy the position of the heart of the earth.

[4] *Cf.* K. K., 20: "Ye brilliant stars, eyes of the gods."

[5] Cited by Ebers, "Die Körperteile in Altägyptischen," *Abh. d. k. bayr. Akad.* (1897), p. 111, where other references are given.

character; and in the above-quoted passage he is called "he who holds himself hidden in his eye," or "he who veils himself in his pupil."

This pupil, then, concludes Reitzenstein (p. 145), is the "mysterious black." Is this, then, the origin of this peculiar phrase? If so, it would be connected with seeing, the spiritual sight, the true *Epopteia*.

THE PUPIL OF THE WORLD'S EYE

But Isis, also, is the black earth, and, therefore, the pupil of the eye of Osiris, and, therefore, also of the Chnum or Ammon identified with Osiris at Syene. Isis, therefore, herself is the "Pupil of the World's Eye"—the κόρη κόσμου.[1]

Reitzenstein would, therefore, have it that the original type of our treatise looks back to a tradition which makes the mystery-goddess Isis the disciple and spouse of the mysterious Chnum or Ammon, or Kneph or Kamephis, as Agathodaimon; and, therefore, presumably, that the making of this Kamephis the disciple in his turn of Hermes is a later development of the tradition, when the Hermes-communities gained ascendancy in certain circles of the Isis-tradition.

This is very probable; but dare we, with Reitzenstein, cast aside the "traditional" translation of κόρη κόσμου, as "Virgin of the World," and prefix to our treatise as title the new version, "The Pupil of the Eye of the World"? It certainly sounds strange as a title to unaccustomed ears, and differs widely from any other titles of the Hermetic sermons known to us. But what does the "Virgin of the World" mean in connection with our treatise? Isis as the Virgin Mother is a

[1] Compare also the Naassene document, § 8, in the "Myth of Man" chapter of the Prolegomena, where Isis is called "the seven-robed and *black-mantled* goddess."

familiar idea to students of Egyptology[1]; she is κατ' ἐξοχήν, the "World-Virgin."

THE SON OF THE VIRGIN

And here it will be of interest to turn to a curious statement of Epiphanius[2]; it is missing in all editions of this Father prior to that of Dindorf (Leipzig, 1859), which was based on the very early (tenth century) Codex Marcianus 125, all previous editions being printed from a severely censured and bowdlerized fourteenth century MS.

Epiphanius is stating that the true birthday of the Christ is the Feast of Epiphany, "at a distance of thirteen days from the increase of the light [*i.e.* December 25]; for it needs must have been that this should be a figure of our Lord Jesus Christ Himself and of His twelve disciples, who make up the thirteen days of the increase of the Light." The Feast of the Epiphany was a great day in Egypt, connected with the "Birth of the Æon,"—a phase of the "Birth of Horus." For Epiphanius thus continues:

"How many other things in the past and present support and bear witness to this proposition, I mean the birth of Christ! Indeed, the leaders of the idol-cults,[3] filled with wiles to deceive the idol-worshippers who believe in them, in many places keep highest festival on this same night of Epiphany [= the Manifestation to Light], so that they whose hopes are in error may not seek the truth. For instance, at

[1] *Cf.* "Isis, the Queen of Heaven, whose most ancient and distinctive title was the Virgin Mother." Marsham Adams (F.), *The Book of the Master, or the Egyptian Doctrine of the Light born of the Virgin Mother* (London, 1898), p. 63.

[2] *Hær.*, li. 22.

[3] And pre-eminently, therefore, for Epiphanius, the Egyptians.

THE VIRGIN OF THE WORLD

Alexandria, in the Koreion,[1] as it is called—an immense temple, that is to say the Precinct of the Virgin—after they have kept all-night vigil with songs and music, chanting to their idol, when the vigil is over, at cockcrow, they descend with lights into an underground crypt, and carry up a wooden image lying naked on a litter, with the seal of a cross made in gold on its forehead, and on either hand two similar seals, and on either knee two others, all five seals being similarly made in gold. And they carry round the image itself, circumambulating seven times the innermost temple, to the accompaniment of pipes, tabors and hymns, and with merry-making they carry it down again underground. And if they are asked the meaning of this mystery, they answer: 'To-day at this hour the Maiden (Korē), that is, the Virgin, gave birth to the Æon.'"

He further adds that at Petra, in Arabia, where, among other places, this mystery was also performed, the Son of the Virgin is called by a name meaning the "Alone-begotten of the Lord."[2]

Here, then, at Alexandria, in every probability the very environment of our treatise, we have a famous mystery-rite, solemnized in the Temple of the Virgin, who gives birth to a Son, the Æon. This, we shall not be rash in assuming, signifies not only the birth of the new year, but also still more profound mysteries, when we remember the words of the Naassene Document quoted above: "For such a man is the Virgin, big with child, conceiving and bearing a Son,—not psychic, not fleshly [nor, we may add, temporal], but

[1] That is, the Temple of Korē. This can hardly be the Temple of Persephonē, as Dindorf (iii. 729) suggests, but rather the Temple of Isis.

[2] *Cf. D. J. L.*, pp. 407 ff.

a blessed Æon of Æons"—that is, an Eternity of Eternities, an immortal God.

We should also notice the crowing of the cock, which plays so important a part in the crucifixion-story in the Gospels,[1] and above all things the stigmata on the image, the symbols of a cosmic and human mystery.

The Mystery of the Birth of Horus

In our own treatise the mysterious Birth of Horus is also referred to (35, 36) as follows.

Isis has handed on the tradition of the Coming of Osiris, the Divine emanation, the descent of the efflux of the Supreme, and Horus asks: "How was it, mother, then, that Earth received God's efflux?"—where Earth may well refer to the "Dark Earth," a synonym of Isis herself.

And Isis answers: "I may not tell the story of [this] birth; for it is not permitted to describe the origin of this descent, O Horus, [son] of mighty power, lest afterward the way of birth of the immortal Gods should be known unto men."

Here I think we have a clear reference to the mysterious "Birth of Horus," the birth of the gods,—that is to say, of how a man becomes a god, becomes the most royal of all souls, gains the kingdom, or lordship over himself. This mystery was not yet to be revealed to the neophyte—Horus—and yet this Birth is suggested to Tat by Hermes—*C. H.*, xiii. (xiv.) 2—when he says: "Wisdom that understands in silence [such is the matter and the womb from out which Man is born] and the True Good the Seed."

The womb is the mysterious Silence, the matter is

[1] Though some have conjectured that the "cock" was the popular name for the Temple-watchman who called the hours.

Wisdom, Isis herself, the seed is the Good, the Agathodaimon, Osiris.

But in our treatise Horus has not yet reached to this high state; Isis, as the introductory words tell us, is pouring forth for him "the first draught of immortality" only, "which souls have custom to receive from gods"; he is being raised to the understanding of a daimon, but not as yet to that of a god.

All of this, moreover, seems to have been part and parcel of the Isis mystery-tradition proper, for as Diodorus (i. 25), following Hecatæus, informs us, it was Isis who "discovered the philtre of immortality, by means of which, when her son Horus, who had been plotted against by the Titans, and found dead (νεκρόν) beneath the water, not only raised him to life (ἀναστῆσαι) by giving him life (ψυχήν), but also made him sharer in immortality."

Here we have evidence to show that in the mystery-myth Horus was regarded as the human soul, and that there were two interpretations of the mystery. It referred not only to the "rising from the dead" in another body, or return to life in another enfleshment, but also to a still higher mystery, whereby the consciousness of immortality was restored to the memory of the soul. The soul had been cast by the Titans, or the opposing powers of the subtle universe, into the deep waters of the Great Sea, the Ocean of Generation, or Celestial Nile, for as the mysterious informant of Cleombrotus told him,[1] these stories of Titans concerned daimons or souls proper, not bodies.[2]

[1] See below, where the story is given from Plutarch's *Moralia*.
[2] Compare *The Book of the Dead*, lxxviii. 31, 32; Budge's Trans. (London, 1901), ii. 255: "I shall come forth . . . into the House of Isis, the divine lady. I shall behold sacred things which are hidden, and I shall be led on to the secret and holy things, even as they have granted unto me to see the birth of

From this death in the sea of matter, Isis, the Mother Soul, brings Horus repeatedly back to life, and finally bestows on him the knowledge of immortality, and so raises him from the "dead."[1]

This birth of the "true man" within, the *logos*, was and is for man the chief of all mysteries. In the Chapter on "The Popular Theurgic Hermes-Cult," we have already, in elucidation of the sacramental formula, "Thou art I and I am thou," quoted the *agraphon* from the *Gospel of Eve* concerning the Great Man and the Little Man or Dwarf, and lovers of the Aupaniṣhad literature of Hindu-Aryan theosophy need hardly be

the Great God. Horus hath made me to be a spiritual body through his soul, [and I see what is therein]." Compare the last sentence with *C. H.*, i. 7, and xi. (xii.) 6, where the pupil "sees" by means of the soul of his Master.

[1] This passage, I believe, affords us an objective point of departure for the reconsideration of C. W. Leadbeater's statement, in his *Christian Creed* (London, 1898), p. 45, that "Pontius Pilate" is a pseudo-historical gloss for πόντος πιλητός, the "dense sea" of "matter," into which the soul is plunged. See for a discussion of this hypothesis *D. T. L.*, pp. 423 ff.

In connection with this a colleague has supplied me with an exceedingly interesting note from *Texts and Studies*, iv. 2, *Coptic Apocryphal Gospels*, p. 177, Frag. 4. The Sahidic text is found in *Rendiconti della R. Accademia dei Lincei*, vol. iii., sem. 2, pp. 381-384 (Frammenti Copti, Nota VIa), by Ignazio Guidi (1887). The legend runs that the Devil taking "the form of a fisherman," goes fishing, and is met by Jesus as He was coming down from the Mount with His disciples. The Devil announces that "he who catcheth fish here, he is the Master. It is not a wonder to catch fish in the waters, the wonder is in this desert, to catch fish therein." They then have a trial of skill, but the MS. unfortunately breaks off before the result is told. It is in this Fragment that the following remarkable sentence occurs: "Now as Pilate was saying these things before the authorities of Tiberius, the king, Herod, could not refrain from setting Pilate at naught, saying, '*Thou art a Galilæan foreign Egyptian Pontus.*'" The literal translation from the Coptic runs: "Thou art a Pontus Galilæan foreign Egyptian."

reminded of "the 'man,' of the size of a thumb," within, in the ether of the heart.[1]

"Ishon"

But what is of more immediate interest is that the same idea is to some extent found in the Old Covenant documents, especially in the Prophetical and Wisdom literature, which latter was strongly influenced by Hellenistic ideas.

Ishon, which literally means "little man" or "dwarf,"[2] is in A.V. generally translated "apple of the eye."[3]

Thus we read in a purely literal sense, referring to weeping: "Let not the apple of thine eye cease" (Lam. ii. 18).

It was, however, a common persuasion, that the intelligence or soul itself, not merely the reflection of the image of another person, resided in the eye, and was made manifest chiefly by the eye.

Thus the "apple of the eye" was used as a synonym for a man's most precious possession, the treasure-house as it were of the light of a man.

[1] Compare, for instance, *Kaṭhopaniṣhad*, Sec. ii., Pt. ii., iv. 11, 12 :

"The Man, of the size of a thumb, resides in the midst, within in the self, of the past and the future the lord ; from him a man hath no desire to hide. This verily is That.

"The Man, of the size of a thumb, like flame free from smoke, of past and of future the lord, the same is to-day, to-morrow the same will he be. This verily is That."—Mead and Chaṭṭopādhyāya's Trans. (London, 1896), i. 68, 69.

Here "to-day" and "to-morrow" are said by some to refer to different incarnations ; the "Man" (*puruṣha*) being the potential Self, destined finally to become, or grow into the stature of, the Great Self (*Maha-puruṣha*).

[2] See the article, "Theosophic Light on Bible Shadows," in *The Theosophical Review* (Nov. 1904), xxxv. 230, 231.

[3] The minute image of a person reflected in the pupil of the eye of another may to some extent account for the popular belief underlying this identification.

And so we read: "He [Yahweh] kept him [Israel] as the apple of his eye" (Ps. xvii. 8)—where *ishon* is in the Hebrew further glossed as the "daughter of the eye"; and again: "Thus saith the Lord of Hosts: . . . He that toucheth you toucheth the apple of his eye" (Zech. ii. 8).

The "apple of the eye" (*ishon*) was, then, something of great value, something very precious, and, therefore, we read in the Wisdom-literature that the punishment of the man who curses his father and mother is that "his lamp shall be put out in obscure (*ishon*) darkness" (Prov. xx. 20)—that is, that he shall thus extinguish the lamp of his intelligence, or perhaps spiritual nature, "in the apple of his eye there will be darkness"; and this connects with a passage in the Psalms which shows traces of the same Wisdom-teaching. "In the hidden part[1] [of man] thou shalt make me to know wisdom" (Ps. li. 6).

But the most striking passages are to be found in that pre-eminently Wisdom-chapter in the Proverbs-collection, where the true Israelite is warned to remain faithful to the Law (Torah), and to have no commerce with the "strange woman," the "harlot"—that is, the "false doctrines" of the Gentiles.[2]

"Keep my law as the apple of thine eye" (Prov. vii. 2), says the writer, speaking in the name of Yahweh, for he has seen the young and foolish being led astray by the "strange woman." "He went the way to her house, in the twilight, in the evening; in the black (*ishon*) and dark night" (Prov. vii. 9). That is to say,

[1] The same idea which we found above in connection with Ammon.

[2] To go "a-whoring" after strange gods and strange doctrines was the graphic figure invariably employed by Hebrew orthodoxy; "to commit fornication" not unfrequently echoes the same idea in the New Testament.

his lamp was put out; there was dark night in his eye, in that little man of his, which should be his true light-spark understanding the wisdom of Yahweh.

Here, I think, we have additional evidence, that the idea, that the pupil of the eye was the seat of the spiritual intelligence in man, was widespread in Hellenistic circles.[1] But even so, can we translate κόρη κόσμου as the "Apple of the World-Eye"? It is true that Isis is the instrument or organ of conveying the hidden wisdom to Horus, and that it is eventually Hermes or the Logos who is the true light itself, which shines through her, the pupil of Egypt's eye,[2] out of that mysterious darkness, in which she found herself, when she received illumination at the hands of Kamephis; but is this sufficient justification for rejecting the traditional translation of the title, and adopting a new version?

On the whole I am inclined to think, that though the new rendering may at first sight appear somewhat strained, nevertheless in proportion as we become more familiarized with the idea and remember the thought-environment of the time, we may venture so to translate it. Isis, then, is the "Apple or Pupil of the Eye of Osiris." On earth the "mysterious black" is Egypt

[1] For the latest study on the subject, see Monseur (E.), "L'Âme Pupilline," *Rev. de l'Hist. des Relig.* (Jan. and Feb. 1905), who discusses the significance in primitive religion of the reflected image to be seen in the pupil of the eye. This "little man" of the eye was taken to be its soul, and to control all its functions.

[2] *Cf.*, for the idea in the mind of the ancients, *Tim.* 45 B: "So much of the fire as would not burn, but gave a gentle light, they formed into a substance akin to the light of every-day life; and the pure fire which is within us and related thereto they made to flow through the eyes in a stream smooth and dense, compressing the whole eye, and especially the centre part, so that it kept out everything of a coarser nature, and allowed to pass only this pure element."

herself, the wisdom-land. Isis is the mysterious wisdom of Egypt, but in our treatise she is even more than this, for she is that wisdom but now truly illumined by the direct sight, the new dawn of the Trismegistic discipline of which she speaks (4).

To a Greek, however, the word κόρη would combine and not distinguish the two meanings of the title over which we have been labouring; but even as *logos* meant both "word" and "reason," so *korē* would mean both "virgin" and "pupil of the eye"; but as it is impossible to translate it in English by one word, we have followed the traditional rendering.

THE SIXTY SOUL-REGIONS

We now turn to a few of the most important points which require more detailed treatment than the space of a footnote can accommodate. There are, of course, many other points that could be elaborated, but if that were done, the present work would run into volumes.

The number of degrees into which the soul-stuff (*psychōsis*) is divided, is given as three, and as sixty (10). If this statement stood by itself we should have been somewhat considerably puzzled to have known what to make of it, even when we remembered the mystic statement that 60 is *par excellence* the number of the soul, and that he who can unriddle the enigma will know its nature.

Fortunately, however, if we turn to *S. I. H.*, 6 (Ex. xxvii.), we find that according to this tradition the soul-regions also were divided into 60 spaces, presumably corresponding to the types of souls.

They were in 4 main divisions and 60 special spaces, with no overlapping (7). These spaces were also called zones, firmaments or layers.

We are further told (6) that the lowest division, that

is the one nearest to the earth, consists of 4 spaces; the second, of 8; the third, of 16; and the fourth, of 32.

And still further (7), that there were besides the 4 main divisions 12 intervallic ones. This introduces an element of uncertainty, for, as far as I am aware, we have no objective information which can enable us to determine how the intervallic divisions were located in the mind of the writer; speculation is rash, but a scheme has suggested itself to me, and I append it with all reservation.

First of all we have 4 main divisions or planes, separated from one another by 3 determinations of some sort, for the whole ordering pertains to the Air proper, and perhaps the 4 states of Air were regarded as earthy, watery, aery, and fiery Air. The 3 determinations may perhaps have been regarded as corresponding to the three main grades or florescences of the soul-stuff, which were apparently of a superior substance.

Each division of the 4 may further have been regarded as divided off by three intervallic determinations; so that we should have 3 such intervals in the lowest division, subdividing it into 4 spaces of 1 space each; 3 in the second, subdividing it into 4 spaces of 2 spaces each; 3 in the third, subdividing it into 4 spaces of 4 spaces each; and 3 in the fourth, subdividing it into 4 spaces of 8 spaces each. The sum of these intervals would thus be 12.

PLUTARCH'S YOGIN

In this connection, however, I cannot refrain from appending a pleasant story told by Plutarch.[1]

[1] *De Defectu Oraculorum*, xxi., xxii. (421A–422c), ed. G. N. Bernardakis (Leipzig, 1891), iii. 97–101. See my paper, "Plutarch's Yogī," in *The Theosophical Review* (Dec. 1891), ix. 295–297.

The speaker is Cleombrotus, a Lacedæmonian gentleman and man of means, who was a great traveller, and a greedy collector of information of all sorts to form the basis of a philosophical religion. He had spent much time in Egypt, and had also been a voyage beyond the Red Sea. On his travels Cleombrotus had heard of a philosopher-recluse, who lived in complete retirement, except once a year when he was seen by "the folk round the Red Sea"; then it was that a certain divine inspiration came upon him, and he came forth and "prophesied" to the nobles and royal scribes who used to flock to hear him. With great difficulty, and only after the expenditure of much money, Cleombrotus discovered the hermitage of this recluse, and was granted a courteous reception.

Our old philosopher was the handsomest man Cleombrotus had ever met, deeply versed in the knowledge of plants, and a great linguist. With Cleombrotus, however, he spoke Doric, and almost in verse, and "as he spake perfume filled the place from the sweetness of his breath."

His knowledge of the various mystery-cults was profound, and his intimate acquaintance with the unseen world remarkable; he explained many things to Cleombrotus, and especially the nature of the daimones, and the important part they played as factors in any satisfactory interpretation of ancient mythology, seeing that most of the great myths referred to the doings of the daimones and not of mortals.

Cleombrotus, however, has told his story merely as an introduction to the quotation of a scrap of information let fall by the old philosopher concerning the plurality of worlds[1]; thus, then, he continues:

[1] In this referring to the passage in the *Timæus*, (55 C D), which runs: "Now, he who, duly reflecting on all this, enquires whether

"The Plain of Truth"

"He told me that the number of worlds was neither infinite, nor one, nor five, but that there were 183 of them, arranged in the figure of a triangle of which each side contained 60, and of the remaining 3 one set at each angle. And those on the sides touch each other, revolving steadily as in a choral dance. And the area of the triangle is the Common Hearth of all, and is called the 'Plain of Truth,'[1] in which the *logoi* and ideas and paradigms of all things which have been, and which shall be, lie immovable; and the Æon [or Eternity] being round them [*sc.* the ideas], time flows down upon the worlds like a stream. And the sight and contemplation ($\theta\acute{\epsilon}\alpha\nu$) of these things is possible for the souls of men only once in ten thousand years, should they have lived a virtuous life. And the highest of our initiations here below is only the dream of that true vision and initiation[2]; and the discourses [*sc.* delivered in the mystic rites] have been carefully devised to awaken the memory of the sublime things above, or else are to no purpose."

the worlds are to be regarded as indefinite or definite in number, will be of opinion that the notion of their indefiniteness is characteristic of a sadly indefinite and ignorant mind. He, however, who raises the question whether they are to be truly regarded as one or five, takes up a more reasonable position" (Jowett's Trans., 3rd ed., iii. 475, 476).

[1] *Cf. S. I. H.*, 3 : "Now as I chance myself to be as though initiate into the nature that transcendeth death, and that my feet have crossed the Plain of Truth"; and *K. K.*, 22 : "The Monarch came, and sitting on the Throne of Truth made answer to their prayers." The *locus classicus* is, of course, Plato, *Phædrus*, 248 B.

[2] *Cf. K. K.*, 37 : "'Tis they who, taught by Hermes that the things below have been disposed by God to be in sympathy with things above, established on the earth the sacred rites o'er which the mysteries in heaven preside."

This statement I am inclined to regard as one of the most distinct pronouncements on the nature of the higher mysteries which has been preserved to us from antiquity, and the *locus classicus* and point of departure for any really fruitful discussion of the true nature of the philosophic mysteries, and yet I have never seen it referred to in this connection.

Our old philosopher was well acquainted with the Egyptian mystery-tradition, for Cleombrotus obtained information from him concerning the esoteric significance of Typhon and Osiris, and what I have quoted above falls naturally into place in the scheme of ideas of the tradition preserved in the treatise which we are discussing.[1] It, indeed, pertains to a higher side of the matter, for it purports to be the highest *theoria* of all, and possible for the souls even of the most righteous only at long periods of time.

Of course the representation is symbolical. The triangle is no triangle ; it is the " plain of truth," the " hearth of the universe." The triangle, then, pertained to the plane of Fire proper and not Air. Still, the ordering of the " worlds " is similar to that of our soul spaces. The triangle is shut off from the manifested world by the Æon ; it is out of space and time proper. Time flows down from it. The worlds proper are 3 worlds or cosmoi, each divided into 60 subordinate cosmoi, in choral dance, or orderly harmonious movement of one to the other. Our soul-spaces, then, may have been regarded as some reflection of these supernal conditions.

One is almost tempted to turn the plane triangle

[1] Our difficulty, however, is that Plutarch, in the words of one of his characters, rejects the idea of this numbering being in any way Egyptian, and ascribes it to a certain Petron of Himera in Sicily,—thereby suggesting a probable Pythagorean connection.

THE VIRGIN OF THE WORLD 173

into a solid figure, a tetrahedron,[1] and imagine the idea of a world or wheel, at each of the four angles, and to speculate on the Wheels of Ezekiel, the prototype of the Mercabah or Heavenly Chariot of Kabalism, the Throne of Truth of the Supreme, but I will not try the patience of my readers any further, for doubtless most of them will have cried already : Hold, enough !

The Boundaries of the Numbers which Pre-exist in the Soul

Perhaps, however, it would be as well, before dismissing the subject, to consider very briefly what Plato, following Pythagoras,[2] has to say concerning the " boundaries " of all numbers which pre-exist in the soul. These soul-numbers are 1, 2, 3, 4, 8, 9, 27 (the combination of the two Pythagorean series 1, 2, 4, 8 and 1, 3, 9, 27), or 1, 2, 3, 2^2, 2^3, 3^2, 3^3. Of these numbers 1, 2, 3 are apportioned to the World-Soul itself, in its intellectual or spiritual aspect, and signify its abiding in (1), its proceeding from (2), and its returning to itself (3); this with regard to primary natures. But in addition, intermediate subtle natures or souls are " providentially " ordered in their evolution and involution, by the World-Soul; they proceed according to the power of the fourth term (4 or 2^2), '' which possesses generative powers," and return according to that of the fifth (9 or 3^2), " which reduces them to one." Finally also solid or gross natures are also " providentially " ordered in their procession according to 8 (2^3), and in their conversion according to 27 (3^3).[3]

[1] See the section, "Some Outlines of Æonology," *F. F. F.*, pp. 311-335.

[2] See my *Orpheus* (London, 1896), pp. 255-262.

[3] *Cf.* Taylor (T.), " Introd. to Timæus," *Works of Plato* (London, 1804), p. 442.

From all of which we get the following scheme of circular progression and conversion of the soul, the various main stages through which it passes:

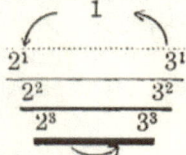

With this compare the "Chaldæan Oracle" (*ap.* Psellus, 19): "Do not soil the spirit, nor turn the plane into the solid"—$\mu\grave{\eta}$ $\pi\nu\epsilon\hat{\upsilon}\mu\alpha$ $\mu o\lambda\acute{\upsilon}\nu\eta s$ $\mu\acute{\eta}\tau\epsilon$ $\beta\alpha\theta\acute{\upsilon}\nu\eta s$ $\tau\grave{o}$ $\epsilon\pi\acute{\iota}\pi\epsilon\delta o\nu$ (ed. Cory, Or. clii., p. 270); where the four stages correspond to the point, line, plane, and solid. It is also to be remembered that since $x^0=1$, $2^0=1$ and $3^0=1$.

That these are the boundary numbers of the soul, according to Pythagoreo-Platonic tradition, is of interest, but how this can in any way be made to agree with the ordering of the soul-spaces in our treatise is a puzzle. That by adding these numbers together $(1+2+3+4+8+9+27)$ we get 54, and by farther adding the numbers of the World-Soul proper $(1+2+3)$ we get 6, and so total out the whole sum of the phases to 60, savours somewhat of "fudging," as we used to call it at school. It is by no means convincing, for we are here combining particulars with universals as though they were of equal dignity; still the ancients frequently resort to such combinations.

That, however, there is something more than learned trifling in these numbers of Plato may be seen by the brilliant study of Adam on the "nuptial number" of Plato,[1] which was based upon the properties of the

[1] *Rep.*, viii. 545c–547A. See Adam (J.), *The Nuptial Number of Plato: Its Solution and Significance* (London, 1891).

"Pythagorean triangle," a right-angled triangle to the containing sides of which the values of 3 and 4 were given, the value of its hypothenuse being consequently 5; and $3 \times 4 \times 5 = 60$. The numbers 3, 4, 5, together with the series 1, 2, 4, 8, and 1, 3, 9, 27, were the numerical sequences which supplied those "canons of proportion" with which the Pythagoreans and Platonists chiefly busied themselves.

Still, as far as I can see, this does not throw any clear light on the ordering of the soul spaces as given in our treatise, and we are therefore tempted to connect it with the tradition of the mysterious 60's of Cleombrotus. But what that choral dance was which ordered the subordinate cosmoi into 60's, and whether they proceeded by stages which might correspond to 3's and 4's and 5's, we have, as far as I am aware, no data on which to base an argument. It may, however, have been connected with Babylonian ideas; the 3 may have been regarded as "falling into" 4, so making 12, and this stage in its turn have been regarded as "falling into" 5, and so making 60.

THE MYSTERIOUS CYLINDER

It is to be noticed, however, that before the souls revolted, the Demiurge "appointed for them limits and reservations[1] in the height of Upper Nature, that they might keep the cylinder a-whirl in proper order and economy" (11).

They were, then, confined to certain orderings and spaces. But what is the mysterious "cylinder" which they were to keep revolving?

So far I have come across nothing that throws any

[1] Which may have been regarded as the prototypes of the soul-spaces.

direct light on the subject. However, Proclus[1] says that Porphyry stated that among the Egyptians the letter χ, surrounded by a circle, symbolized the mundane soul.

It is curious that Porphyry should have referred this idea to the Egyptians, when he must have known that Plato, to whom Porphyry looked as the corypheus of all philosophy, had treated of the significance of the symbol X (in Greek χ) in perhaps the most discussed passage of the *Timæus* (36B).[2] This letter symbolized the mutual relation of the axes and equators of the sphere of the "same" (the "fixed stars") and the sphere of the "other" (the "seven planetary spheres"). Porphyry, however, may have believed that Plato, or Pythagoras, got the idea in the first place from Egypt— the common persuasion of his school.

This enigma of Plato is described as follows by Jowett in his Introduction to the *Timæus*[3]:

"The universe revolves round a centre once in twenty-four hours, but the orbits of the fixed stars take a different direction from that of the planets. The outer and the inner sphere cross one another and meet again at a point opposite to that of their first contact; the first moving in a circle from left to right along the side of a parallelogram which is supposed to be inscribed in it, the second also moving in a circle along the diagonal of the same parallelogram from right to left[4]; or, in

[1] *Comment. in Plat. Tim.*, 216c; ed. C. E. C. Schneider (Vratislaviæ, 1847), p. 250.

[2] A passage which Proclus, *op. cit.*, 213A (ed. Sch., p. 152) further explains by means of the "harmonic canon" or ruler.

[3] Jowett (B.), *Dialogues of Plato* (3rd ed., Oxford, 1892), iii. 403.

[4] *Cf.* text 36c: "The motion of the same he carried round by the side to the right, and the motion of the diverse diagonally to the left,"— that is the side of the rectangular figure supposed to be

other words, the first describing the path of the equator, the second, the path of the ecliptic."

We should thus, just as the Egyptians, according to Porphyry, symbolized it, represent the conception by the figure of a circle with two diameters suggesting respectively the equator and the ecliptic.

But what is the rectangular figure to which Jowett refers, but which he does not further describe? The circles are spheres; and, therefore, the rectangular figure must be a solid figure inscribed in the sphere "of the same." If we now set the circle revolving parallel to the longer sides of the figure, this "parallelogram" will trace out a cylinder, while the seven spheres of the "other," the "souls" of the "planets," moving parallel to one of the diagonals of our figure, and in an opposite direction to the sphere of the "same," will, by their mutual difference of rates of motion, cause their "bodies" (the souls surrounding the bodies) to trace out spiral orbits.

All this in itself, I confess, seems very far-fetched, and I should have thrown my notes on the subject into the waste-paper basket, but for the following consideration:

Basil of Cæsarea, in his *Hexæmeron*, or Homilies on

inscribed in the circle of the "same," and diagonally, across the rectangular figure from corner to corner; and 38D, 39A: "Now, when all the stars which were necessary to the creation of time [*i.e.* the spheres of the sun, moon, and five planets] had attained a motion suitable to them, and had become living creatures, having bodies fastened by vital chains, and learned their appointed task, moving in the motion of the diverse, which is diagonal, and passes through, and is governed by the motion of the same, they revolved, some in a larger and some in a lesser orbit. . . . The motion of the same made them turn all in a spiral." With these instruments of "time," surrounded by the sphere of the same, compare the idea of time flowing down on the worlds, from the Æon, in the story of Cleombrotus.

the Six Days of Creation, declared it "a matter of no interest to us whether the earth is a sphere or a cylinder or a disk, or concave in the middle like a fan."[1]

The cylinder-idea, then, was a favourite theory with regard to the earth-shape in the time of Basil, that is the fourth century.

This cylinder-idea, however, I am inclined to think was very ancient. In the domain of Greek speculation we first meet with it in what little is known of the system of Anaximander of Miletus, the successor of Thales.

Anaximander is reported to have believed that "the earth is a heavenly body, controlled by no other power, and keeping its position because it is the same distance from all things; the form of it is curved, cylindrical, like a stone column; it has two faces; one of these is the ground beneath our feet, and the other is opposite to it."[2]

And again: "That the earth is a cylinder in form, and that its depth is one-third of its breadth."[3]

Now I have never been able to persuade myself that the earliest philosophers of Greece "invented" the ideas ascribed to them. They stood on the borderland of mythology and mysticism, and, in every probability, took their ideas from ancient traditions.

[1] So quoted in Andrew Dickson White's *History of the Warfare of Science with Theology in Christendom* (New York, 1898), i. 92. Dr White, unfortunately, does not give the exact reference. The "fan" is, of course, the winnowing fan, a broad basket into which the corn mixed with chaff was received after threshing, and was then thrown up into the wind, so as to disperse the chaff and leave the grain.

[2] Alexander of Aphrodisias, *Comment. on Aristotle in Meteor.*, 91r (vol. i., 268 I d); Diels, *Doxographi Græci* (Berlin, 1879), p. 478. *Cf.* Aëtius, *De Placitis Reliquiæ*, iii. 10 (Diels, 579).

[3] Plutarch, *Strom.*, 2 (Diels, 579). See Fairbanks (A.), *The First Philosophers of Greece* (London, 1898), pp. 13, 14.

Anaximander himself was in every probability indirectly, for all we know even directly, influenced by Egyptian and Chaldæan notions; indeed, who can any longer doubt in the light of the Cnossus excavations?"[1]

Anaximander is thus said to have regarded the earth-cylinder as fixed, whereas in our treatise the cylinder is not the earth and is not fixed; it is, on the contrary, a celestial cylinder and in constant motion. Can it, then, possibly be that this cylinder notion was associated with some Babylonian idea, and had its source in that country *par excellence* of cylinders? In Babylonia, moreover, the cylinder-shape was frequently used for seals, fashioned like a small roller, so that the characters or symbols engraved on them could be impressed on soft substance, such as wax. Further, the Babylonian and Egyptian civilizations were, as we know, closely associated, and pre-eminently so in the matter of sigils and seals. In the Coptic-Gnostic works, translated from Greek originals, and indubitably mainly of Egyptian origin, the idea of "characters," "seals," and "sigils," as types impressed on matter, is a commonplace.

Can our cylinder, then, have some connection with the circle of animal types, or types of life, of which so much is said in our treatise? The souls of the supernal man class would then have had the task of keeping this cylinder in motion, so that thereby the various types were continually impressed on the plasms in the sphere of generation, or ever-becoming—the wheel of genesis?

This may be so, for in *P. S. A.*, 19, we read: "The air, moreover, is the engine, or machine, through which

[1] Delitzsch also, in his *Babel und Bibel*, states that the great debt of early Greece to Assyria will be made clear in a forthcoming work of German scholarship.

all things are made . . . mortal from mortal things and things like these."

So also in *K. K.*, 28, Hermes says: "And I will skillfully devise an instrument, mysterious, possessed of power of sight that cannot err . . . an instrument that binds together all that's done."

Here again we have the same idea, all connected with the notion of Fate or Heimarmene; the instrument of Hermes is the Kārmic Wheel, by which cause and effect are linked together, and that too with a moral purpose.[1]

Finally, in connection with our cylinder, we may compare the Âryan Hindu myth of the "Churning of the Ocean," in the *Vishṇu Purāṇa*. The churning-staff or Pillar was the heaven-mountain, round which was coiled the cosmic serpent, to serve as rope for twirling it. The rope was held at either end by the Devas and Asuras, or gods and dæmons. There is also a mystic symbol in India which probably connects with a similar range of ideas. It is two superimposed triangles ($\bowtie$), with their apices touching, and round the centre a serpent is twined,—a somewhat curious resemblance to our X and cylinder-idea. And so much for this puzzling symbol.

The Eagle, Lion, Dragon and Dolphin

We now pass to the four leading types of animals, connected with souls of the highest rank—namely, the eagle, lion, dragon, and dolphin (24, 25)—which it may be of interest to compare with the symbolism of some of the degrees of the Mithriac Mysteries [2]

[1] I have also got a stray reference, "$\kappa \upsilon \lambda \iota \nu \delta \rho o s$, Plut., 2, 682 c, Xylander's pages," but I have not been able to verify this.

[2] See Cumont (F.), *Textes et Monuments figurés relat. aux Mystères de Mithra* (Bruxelles, 1899), i. 315.

In one of the preliminary degrees of the rite, we are informed, some of the mystæ imitated the voices of birds, others the roaring of lions.[1] All of this was interpreted by the initiates as having reference to transmigration or metempsychosis. Thus Porphyry[2] tells us that in the Mysteries of Mithras they called the mystæ by the names of different animals, so symbolizing man's common lower nature with that of the irrational animals. Thus, for instance, they called some of the men "lions," and some of the women "lionesses," some were called "ravens," while the "fathers," the highest grade, were called "hawks" and "eagles." The "ravens" were the lowest grade; those of the "lion" grade were apparently previously invested with the disguises and masks of a series of animal forms before they received the lion shape.

Porphyry tells us, further, that Pallas, who had, prior to Porphyry's day, written an excellent treatise on the Mithriaca, now unfortunately lost, asserts that all this was vulgarly believed to refer to the zodiac, but that in truth it symbolized a mystery of the human soul, which is invested with animal natures of various kinds,[3]

[1] Ps. Augustine, *Quæstt. Vet. et Nov. Test.* (Migne, *P. L.*, tom. xxxiv. col. 2214 f.).

[2] *De Abstinentia*, iv. 16 (ed. Nauck, p. 253).

[3] *Cf.* Clement of Alexandria on the Basilidian theory of "appendages," remembering that the School of Basilides was strongly tinctured with Egyptian ideas. "The Basilidians are accustomed to give the name of appendages (or accretions) to the passions. These essences, they say, have a certain substantial existence, and are attached to the rational soul, owing to a certain turmoil and primitive confusion. On to this nucleus other bastard and alien natures of the essence grow, such as those of the wolf, ape, lion, goat, etc. . . . And not only do human souls thus intimately associate themselves with the impulses and impressions of irrational animals, but they even initiate the movements and beauties of plants, because they likewise bear the characteristics

according to the tradition of the Magi. Thus they call the sun (and therefore those corresponding to this nature) a bull, a lion, a dragon, and a hawk.

It is further to be remembered that Appuleius,[1] in describing the robe with which he was invested after his initiation into the Mysteries of Isis, tells us that he was enthroned as the sun, robed in twelve sacramental stoles or garments; these garments were of linen with beautiful paintings upon them, so that from every side "you might see that I was remarkable by the animals which were painted round my vestment in various colours." This dress, he says, was called the "Olympic Stole."

Momus

Finally, it may perhaps be of service to make the reader a little better acquainted with Momus.

Among the Greeks Momus was the personification of the spirit of fault-finding. Hesiod, in his *Theogony* (214), places him among the second generation of the children of Night, together with the Fates. From the *Cypria*[2] of Stasimus,[3] we learn that, when Zeus, in answer to Earth's prayer to relieve her of her overpopulation of impious mankind,[4] first sent the Theban War, and on this proving insufficient, bethought him of annihilating the human race by thunderbolts (fire) and floods (water), Momus advises the Father of gods and men to marry the goddess Thetis to a mortal, so that a beautiful daughter (Aphrodite-Helen) might be born to

of plants appended to them. Nay, there are also certain characteristics [of minerals] shown by habits, such as the hardness of adamant" (*F. F. F.*, p. 276).

[1] *Metamorphoses*, Book xi.
[2] Which Pindar and Herodotus ascribed to Homer himself.
[3] See Frag. I. from the Scholion on Hom., *Il.*, i. 5 ff.
[4] See *K. K.*, 34.

them, and so mankind, Greeks and Barbarians, on her account be involved in internecine strife—namely, the Trojan War. Further, the Scholiast on *Il.*, i. 5, avers that it was Momus whom Homer meant to represent by the " will " or " counsel " of Zeus.

Sophocles, moreover, wrote a Satyric drama called " Momus,"[1] and so also Achæus.[2]

Both Plato[3] and Aristotle[4] refer to Momus. Callimachus, the chief librarian of the Alexandrian Library, from 260-240 B.C., in his *Ætia*,[5] pilloried his critic and former pupil Apollonius Rhodius as Momus.

Momus, moreover, was a favourite figure with the Sophists and Rhetoricians, especially of the second century A.D. In Æl. Aristides,[6] Momus, as he could find no fault with Aphrodite herself, found fault with her shoe.[7] Lucian makes Aphrodite vow to oppose Momus tooth and nail,[8] and makes Momus find fault with even the greatest works of the gods, such as the house of Athene, the bull of Zeus, and the men of Hephæstus,—the last because the god-smith had not put windows in their breasts so that their hearts might be seen.[9]

And, interestingly enough in connection with our treatise, Lucian, in one of his witty sketches,[10] makes

---

[1] Frag. 369-374B (ed. Dind.); the context of which some believe to be found in Lucian's *Hermotimus*, 20.

[2] Frag. 29, from the Scholion on Aristophanes, *Pax*, 357.

[3] *Rep.*, vi. 487A : " Nor would even Momus find fault with this."

[4] *De Partt. Animal.*, iii. 2.

[5] And also at the end of his *Hymn to Apollo*, ii. 112; also *Epigram. Frag.*, 70.

[6] *Or.*, 49; ed. Jebb, p. 497.   [7] *Cf.* Julian, *Ep. ad Dionys.*

[8] *Dial. Deor.*, xx. 2.

[9] *Hermot.*, xx.; *cf. Nig.*, xxxii.; *Dial. Deor.*, ix.; *Ver. Hist.*, ii. 3; *Bab. Fab.*, lix.; and *Jup. Trag.*, xxii.

[10] *Deor. Consil.*, iv.

Momus one of the persons of the dialogue with Zeus and Hermes. Momus finds fault because Bacchus is reckoned among the gods, and is commanded by Zeus to refrain from making ridicule of Hercules and Asclepius.

The popular figure of Momus was that of a feeble old man,[1]—a very different representation from the grandiose Intelligence of our treatise, a true Lucifer.

Some representations give his one sharp tooth, and others wings. The story runs that Zeus finally banished him from Olympus for his fault-finding.[2]

The *Onomastica Vaticana*[3] connects Momus with Mammon; but this side-issue need not detain us.[4]

THE MYSTIC GEOGRAPHY OF SACRED LANDS

With regard to the symbolic figure of the Earth of §§ 46–48 of the second *K. K.* Extract, and the persuasion that Egypt was the heart or centre thereof, we may append two quotations on the subject from widely different standpoints. The first is from Dr Andrew D. White's recent volumes[5]:

"Every great people of antiquity, as a rule, regarded its own central city or most holy place as necessarily the centre of the earth.

"The Chaldeans held that their 'holy house of the gods' was the centre. The Egyptians sketched the world under the form of a human figure, in which Egypt was the heart, and the centre of it Thebes. For the Assyrians, it was Babylon; for the Hindus, it was Mount Meru; for the Greeks, so far as the civilized

[1] Philostratus, *Ep.* 21.
[2] For the above and other references, see Trümpel's art. "Momus," in Roscher's *Lexicon*.
[3] Lug., 194, 59.
[4] See Nestle's art. "Mammon," in Cheyne's *Encyclopædia Biblica*.
[5] *Op. supra cit.*, i. 98, 99.

world was concerned, Olympus or the temple of Delphi; for the modern Mohammedans, it is Mecca and its sacred stone; the Chinese, to this day, speak of their empire as the 'middle kingdom.' It was in accordance, then, with a simple tendency of human thought that the Jews believed the centre of the world to be Jerusalem.

"The book of Ezekiel speaks of Jerusalem as in the middle of the earth, and all other parts of the world as set around the holy city. Throughout the 'ages of faith' this was very generally accepted as a direct revelation from the Almighty regarding the earth's form. St Jerome, the greatest authority of the early Church upon the Bible, declared, on the strength of this utterance of the prophet, that Jerusalem could be nowhere but at the earth's centre; in the ninth century Archbishop Rabanus Maurus reiterated the same argument; in the eleventh century Hugh of St Victor gave to the doctrine another scriptural demonstration; and Pope Urban, in his great sermon at Clermont urging the Franks to the crusade, declared, 'Jerusalem is the middle point of the earth'; in the thirteenth century an ecclesiastical writer much in vogue, the monk Cæsarius of Heisterbach, declared, 'As the heart in the midst of the body, so is Jerusalem situated in the midst of our inhabited earth,'—'so it was that Christ was crucified at the centre of the earth.' Dante accepted this view of Jerusalem as a certainty, wedding it to immortal verse; and in the pious book of travels ascribed to Sir John Mandeville, so widely read in the Middle Ages, it is declared that Jerusalem is at the centre of the world, and that a spear standing erect at the Holy Sepulchre casts no shadow at the equinox.

"Ezekiel's statement thus became the standard of orthodoxy to early map-makers. The map of the world at Hereford Cathedral, the maps of Andrea Bianco,

Marino Sanuto, and a multitude of others fixed this view in men's minds, and doubtless discouraged during many generations any scientific statements tending to unbalance this geographical centre revealed in Scripture."

So much for the righteous indignation of modern physical science; now for cryptology and mysticism. M. W. Blackden, in a recent article on "The Mysteries and the 'Book of the Dead,'" writes as follows [1]:

"One other key there is . . . without which it is useless to approach *The Book of the Dead* with the idea of discussing any of those gems of wisdom for which old Egypt was so famous. . . . The knowledge of its existence is no recent discovery; it is simply that ancient nations such as the Egyptians, Chaldees, and Jews, had a system of symbolic geography. . . .

"The Jewish and Egyptian priestly caste endeavoured to map out their lands in accordance with their symbols of spiritual things, so far as the physical features would permit. This symbolism of mountain, city, plain, desert, and river extended from the various parts and furniture of the Lodge, to use Masonic phraseology, up to the spiritual anatomy, as it were, of both macrocosm and microcosm.

"Thus in the Jewish Scriptures it is not difficult to distinguish, in the prophetic battles of the nations that were to rage round about Jerusalem, the same symbolism as we have more directly expressed in a little old book called *The Siege of Mansoul*, the author of which was the John Bunyan of *The Pilgrim's Progress*, a man who could well grasp the excellence of geographical symbolism.

"I cannot, of course, here enter at length into the geographical symbols of Egypt, it would take too long; but as I have given Jerusalem as a symbol, I may say

[1] *The Theosophical Review* (July, 1902), vol. xxx. pp. 406, 407.

THE VIRGIN OF THE WORLD 187

further that Jerusalem as a symbol corresponds to the Egyptian On, or Heliopolis, and so astronomically to the centre of the world and of the universe, and in the microcosm to the spiritual Heart of Man.[1]

"But there is one difference between the Hebrew and Egyptian city; for whereas the actual Jerusalem corresponds among the Hebrew prophets to that Jerusalem that now is, and is in bondage with her children, Heliopolis corresponded among the Egyptian priesthood to that city which was to come, the Heavenly City, the New Heart, that should be given to redeemed mankind."

Here then we have a thesis that deserves a volume to itself; and so I leave it to him who has a mind to undertake the labour.

[1] "There is an old map of the world in the British Museum which demonstrates both these significations. See also Mappa Mundi, 'Ebsdorf,' 1284, and that in Hereford Cathedral made by Richard of Haldingham, one of the Prebends, 1290-1310."

EXCERPT XXVII.

FROM THE SERMON OF ISIS TO HORUS

(Patrizzi (p. 34b) runs this on to the last without a break.
Text: Stob., *Phys.*, xli. 68, 69, under heading, "Of Hermes: A Sermon of Isis to Horus"; G. pp. 476-481; M. i. 342-352; W. i. 458-472.

Ménard: Livre III., No. iii. of "Fragments," etc., as above, pp. 209-221.)

1.[1] In wondrous fashion—(Horus said)—hast thou explained to me, most mighty mother Isis, the details of God's wondrous soul-making, and I remain in wonder; but not as yet hast thou told me whereto the souls when freed from body go. I would then thank thee for being made initiate by word of mouth[2] into this vision of the soul,[3] O only mother, deathless one!

2. And Isis said:

Give ear, my son; most indispensable is this

[1] I have numbered the paragraphs for convenience of reference.
[2] μύστης. The mystēs, speaking generally, was initiated by word of mouth, the epoptēs by sight or vision.
[3] θεωρία.

research. That which doth hold together, doth also have a place which doth not disappear. For this is what my sermon will set forth.

O wondrous, mighty son of mighty sire Osiris, [the souls] when they go forth from bodies, are not confusedly and in a rush dissolved into the air, and scattered in the rest of boundless Breath, so that they cannot any more as the same [souls] return again to bodies; nor is it possible, again, to turn them back unto that place from which they came at first—no more than water taken from the bottom of a jar can be poured[1] [back again] into the self-same place whence it was taken; nor does the same when taken take a place peculiar to it, but is mixed up with the whole mass of water.[2] Not thus is it [with souls], high-minded Horus!

3. Now as I chance myself to be as though initiate into the nature which transcendeth death, and that my feet have crossed the Plain of Truth, I will explain to thee in detail how it is; and preface this by telling thee that water is a body void of reason condensed from many compound things into a fluid mass, whereas the soul's a thing of individual nature, son, and of a royal kind, a work of God's [own] hands and mind, and of itself led by itself to mind.

[1] Reading ἐπιχεῖν for ἐπέχειν.
[2] The construction of the whole of the above paragraph is exceedingly involved.

What then doth come from "one" and not from "other," cannot be mingled with a different thing; wherefore it needs must be that the soul's congress with the body is a concord wrought by God's necessity.

But that they are not [all] confusedly and [all] at random and by chance sent up again to one and the same place, but each to its own proper region, is clear from what [the soul] doth suffer while still it is in body and in plasm, when it has been made dense against its proper nature.

Now give good heed to the similitude recounted, Horus well-beloved!

4. Suppose in one and the same cage have been shut up both men and eagles, doves and swans, and swallows, hawks and sparrows, flies, and snakes, and lions, leopards, wolves, and dogs, and hares, and kine and sheep, and some amphibious animals, as seals and others, tortoises and our own crocodiles; then, that, my son, at one [and the same] moment they are [all] let out.

They [all] will turn instinctively—man to his gathering spots and roofs; the eagle to the ether, in which its nature is to spend its life; the doves into the neighbouring air; the hawks [to that] above [the doves]; the swallows where men dwell; the sparrows round the fruit-trees; the swans where they may sing; the flies about the earth, [but only] so far from it as they can with [-out their losing] smell of man (for that the fly, my son, is fond of man especially and tends to earth); the lions and the leopards towards the hills; the wolves towards desert spots; the dogs after men's tracks; the kine to stalls and fields; the sheep to pastures; the snakes to earth's recesses; the seals and tortoises, with [all] their kind, unto the deeps and streams, so that they neither should be robbed of the dry land nor taken from their cognate water—each one returning to its proper place by means of its internal means of judgment.

So every soul, both in a human form and otherwise incarnate on the earth, knows where it has to go,—unless some foolish person[1] come and say, my son, that it is possible a bull should live in water and a tortoise up in air!

5. And if this be the case when they are plunged in flesh and blood—that they do nothing contrary to what's appointed them, e'en though they are being punished (for being put in body is a punishment for them)—how much the more [is it the case] when they possess their proper liberty [and are set free] from punishment and being plunged [in body]?

Now the most holy ordering of souls is on this wise. Turn thou thy gaze above, most noble-

[1] τις τῶν τυφωνίων—an interesting phrase as showing that Typhon was regarded as the enemy of Osiris (the Logos or Reason).

natured son, upon their orders. The space from height of heaven to the moon devotes itself unto the gods and stars and to the rest of providence; the space, my son, from moon to us is dwelling place of souls.

This so great air, however, has in it a belt to which it is our use to give the name of wind, a definite expanse in which it is kept moving to refresh the things on earth, and which I will hereafter tell about.

Yet in no manner by its motion on itself does it become an obstacle to souls; for though it keeps on moving, souls can dart up or dart down,[1] just as the case may be, free from all let and hindrance. For they pass through without immixture or adhesion as water flows through oil.

6. Now of this interval, Horus, my son, there are four main divisions and sixty special spaces.

Of these [divisions] the first one upwards from the earth is of four spaces, so that the earth in certain of its mountain heights and peaks extends and comes so far, but beyond these it cannot in its nature go in height.

The second after this is of eight spaces, in which the motions of the winds take place.

Give heed, O son, for thou art hearing

[1] *Cf.* the beginning of the Apocalypse of Thespesius (Aridæus) in Plutarch, *De Sera Num. Vind.*, xxii.

FROM THE SERMON OF ISIS TO HORUS

mysteries that must not be disclosed—of earth and heaven and all the holy air which lies between, in which there is the motion of the wind and flight of birds. For above this the air doth have no motion and sustains no life.

This [moving] air moreover hath of its own nature this authority—that it can circulate in its own spaces and also in the four of earth with all the lives which it contains, while earth cannot ascend into *its* [realm].

The third consists of sixteen spaces filled with subtle air and pure.

The fourth consists of two and thirty [spaces], in which there is the subtlest and the finest air; it is by means of this that [air] shuts from itself the heavens above which are by nature fiery.

7. This ordering is up and down in a straight line and has no overlapping; so that there are four main divisions, twelve intervallic ones and sixty spaces.

And in these sixty spaces dwell the souls, each one according to its nature, for though they are of one and the same substance, they're not of the same dignity. For by so much as any space is higher from the earth than any other, by so much do the souls in them, my son, surpass in eminence the one the other.[1]

What souls, however, go to each of them, I

[1] For a consideration of this ordering, see p. 168 ff. above.

will accordingly begin again to tell thee, Horus, [son] of great renown, taking their order from above down to the earth.

Concerning the Inbreathing and the Transmigration of the Soul[1]

8. The [air] between the earth and heavens, Horus, is spaced out by measure and by harmony.

These spaces have been named by some of our forefathers zones, by others firmaments, by others layers.

And in them dwell both souls which have been set free from their bodies, and also those which have as yet been never shut in body.

And each of them, my son, hath just the place it doth deserve; so that the godly and the kingly ones dwell in the highest space of all, those least in honour and the rest of the decadent ones [dwell] in the lowest space of all, while middling souls dwell in the middle space.

Accordingly, those souls which are sent down to rule, are sent down, Horus, from the upper zones; and when they are set free [again] they go back to the same or even still more lofty ones, unless it be they still have acted contrary

[1] This appears to be a heading inserted by Stobæus (*Phys.*, xli. 64) or some scribe; there seems to be no break in the text.

to their own nature's dignity and the pronouncement of the Law of God.

Such souls as these the Providence above, according to the measure of their sins, doth banish down to lower spaces; just as with those which are inferior in dignity and power, it leads them up from lower [realms] to vaster and more lofty ones.

9. For up above [them all] there are two ministers of universal Providence, of whom one is the warder of the souls, the other their conductor. The warder [watches o'er the souls when out of body], while the conductor is dispatcher and distributor of souls into their bodies. The former keeps them, while the latter sends them forth according to the Will of God.

For this cause (*logos*) then, my son, nature on earth according to the change of deeds above doth model out the vessels and shape out the tents in which the souls are cast.[1] Two energies, experience and memory, assist her.

And this is memory's task, [to see] that nature guards the type of every thing sent down out of its source and keeps its mixture as it is above; while of experience [the work is this, to see] conformably to every one of the descending souls it may have its embodiment, and that the

[1] The text is exceedingly imperfect, and in its present state quite untranslatable.

plasms may be made effective[1]—that for the swift ones of the souls the bodies also may be swift, for slow ones slow, for active active ones, for sluggish sluggish ones, for powerful powerful, and for crafty crafty ones, and in a word for every one of them as it is fit.

10. For not without intention hath she clad winged things with plumage; and tricked out with senses more than ordinary and more exact those which have reason; and some of the four-footed things made strong with horns, some strong with teeth, some strong with claws and hoofs; while creeping things she hath made supple with bodies clad in easy-moving scales, which easily can glide away.

And that the watery nature of their body may not remain entirely weak, she doth provide the sharpened fangs of some of them with power; so that by reason of the fear of death [they cause] they're stronger than the rest.

The swimming things being timorous, she gives to dwell within an element where light can exercise nor one nor other of its powers, for fire in water gives nor light nor heat. But each of them, swimming in water clad in scales or spines, flees from what frightens it where'er it will, using the water as a means of hiding it from sight.

[1] The text is again very imperfect.

11. For souls are shut in each class of these bodies according to their similarity [to them]. Those which have power of judgment go down into men ; and those that lack it into quadrupeds, whose [only] law is force ; the crafty ones [go] into reptiles, for none of them attack a man in front, but lie in wait and strike him down ; and into swimming things the timid ones or those which are not worthy to enjoy the other elements. In every class, however, there are found some which no longer use their proper nature.

How [meanest thou] again, my mother ? Horus said.

And Isis answered :

A man, for instance, son, o'ersteps his power of judgment; a quadruped avoids the use of force ; and reptiles lose their craftiness ; and birds their fear of men. So much [then] for the ordering of [souls] above and their descent, and for the making of their bodies.

12. In every class and kind of the above, my son, there may be found some regal souls ; others also descend with various natures, some fiery, and some cold, some overbearing, and some mild, some skilled, some unskilled, some idle, some industrious, some one thing, some another. And this results from the arrangement of the regions whence the souls leap down to their embodiment.

For from the regal zone they leap down [into birth], the soul of the like nature ruling them [1]; for there are many sovereignties. Some are of souls, and some of bodies, and some of arts, and some of sciences, and some are of ourselves.

How [meanest thou] again, my mother, "of ourselves"?

For instance, son, it is thy sire Osiris who is [the ruler] of the souls of them born after us up to this time [2]; whereas the prince of every race [is ruler] of their bodies; [the king] of counsel is the father and the guide of all, Thrice-greatest Hermes; of medicine Asclepius, Hephæstus' son; of power and might again Osiris, and after him thyself, my son; and of philosophy Arnebeschēnis; of poetry again Asclepius-Imuth.

13. For generally, my son, thou'lt find, if thou inquirest, that there are many ruling many things and many holding sway o'er many. And he who rules them all, my son, is from the highest space; while he who rules some part of them, doth have the rank of that particular realm from which he is.

Those who come from the regal zone, [have] a more ruling [part to play; those from the zone

[1] The text is here very corrupt, and the reading of the last words of the two following sentences very doubtful.

[2] That is presumably since the time when Osiris and Isis lived on earth among men.

of fire [1]] become fire-workers and fire-tenders; those from the watery one live out their life in waters; those from the [zone] of science and of art are occupied with arts and sciences; those from the [zone] of inactivity inactively and heedlessly live out their lives.

For that the sources of all things wrought on the earth by word or deed, are up above, and they dispense for us their essences by weight and measure; and there is naught which hath not come down from above, and will return again to re-descend.

14. What dost thou mean again by this, my mother? Tell me!

And Isis once again did make reply: Most holy Nature hath set in living creatures the clear sign of this return. For that this breath which we breathe from above out of the air, we send out up again, to take it in [once more].

And we have in us organs, son, to do this work, and when they close their mouths whereby the breath's received, then we no longer are as now we are, but we depart.

Moreover, son of high renown, there are some other things which we have added to us outside the weighed-out mixture [of the body].

15. What, then (said Horus), is this mixture, mother?

---

[1] The text is exceedingly defective.

It is a union and a blend of the four elements; and from this blend and union a certain vapour [1] rises, which is enveloped by the soul, but circulates within the body, sharing with each, with body and with soul, its nature. And thus the differences of changes are effected both in soul and body.

For if there be in the corporeal make-up more of fire, thereon the soul, which is by nature hot, taking unto itself another thing that's hot, and [so] being made more fiery, makes the life more energetic and more passionate, and the body quick and active.

If [there be] more of air, thereon the life becomes both light and springy and unsteady both in the soul and body.

And if there's more of water, then the creature also doth become of supple soul and easy disposition, and ready of embrace, and able easily to meet and join with others, through water's power of union and communion with the rest of things; for that it finds a place in all, and when it is abundant, doth dissolve what it surrounds, while if [there's] little [of it], it sinks into and doth become what it is mingled with. As for their bodies, by dampness and by sponginess they are not made compact, but by a slight attack of sickness are dissolved, and fall away by

[1] *Cf.* 17 and 20 below.

little and by little from the bond which holds them severally together.

And if the earthy [element] is in excess, the creature's soul is dull, for it has not its body-texture loosely knit, or space for it to leap through, the organs of sensation being dense; but by itself it stays within, bound down by weight and density. As for its body, it is firm, but heavy and inert, and only moved of choice by [exercise of] strength.

But if there is a balanced state of all [the elements], then is the animal made hot for doing, light for moving, well-mixed for contact, and excellent for holding things together.[1]

16. Accordingly those which have more in them of fire and air, these are made into birds, and have their state above hard by those elements from which they came.

While those which have more fire, less air, and earth and water equal, these are made into men, and for the creature the excess of heat is turned into sagacity; for that the mind in us is a hot thing which knows not how to burn, but has intelligence to penetrate all things.

And those which have in them more water and more earth, but moderate air and little fire,

---

[1] The text is faulty, the language artificial, the analogy strained, and the sense accordingly obscure. Meineke reads: γεννaῖον δὲ εἰς θῆξιν.

these are turned into quadrupeds, and those which have more heat are stronger than the rest. Those which have equal earth and water, are made into reptiles. These through their lack of fire lack courage and straightforwardness; while through their having water in them they are cold; and through their having earth they heavy are and torpid; yet through their having air, they can move easily if they should choose to do so.

Those which have in them more of wet, and less of dry, these are made into fish. These through their lack of heat and air are timorous and try to hide themselves, and through excess of wet and earthy elements, they find their home, through their affinity, in fluid earth and water.

17. It is according to the share [they have] in every element and to the compass of that share, that bodies reach full growth [in man]; according to the smallness of their share the other animals have been proportioned—according to the energy which is in every element.[1]

Moreover, O my well-beloved, I say, that when, out of this state [of things], the blend based on the first commixture [of the elements in any case], and the resultant vapour[2] from it,

[1] The text is utterly corrupt and has not yet been even plausibly emended.
[2] *Cf.* 15 and 20.

so far preserve their own peculiarity, that neither the hot part takes on another heat, nor [does] the aery [take] another air, nor [does] the watery part another wetness, nor [yet] the earthy [take] another density, then doth the animal remain in health.

18. But if they do not, son, remain in the proportions which they had from the beginning, but are too much increased—(I do not mean in energy according to their compass or in the change of sex and body brought about by growth, but in the blend, as we have said before, of the component elements, so that the hot, for instance, is increased too much or too much lessened, and so for all the rest)—then will the animal be sick.

19. And if this [increase] doth take place in both the elements of heat and air, the soul's tent-fellows, then doth the creature fall into symbolic dreams and ecstasies; for that a concentration of the elements whereby the bodies are dissolved has taken place. For 'tis the earthy element itself which is the condensation of the body; the watery element in it as well is a fluidity to make it dense. Whereas the aery element is that in us which has the power of motion, and fire is that which makes an end of all of them.

20. Just then as is the vapour[1] which ariseth

[1] *Cf.* 15 and 17.

from the first conjunction and co-blending of the elements, as though it were a kindling or an exhalation,—whatever it may be, it mingles with the soul and draws it to itself, so that it shares its nature good or bad. And if the soul remains in its original relationship and common life with it, it keeps its rank.

But when there's added from without some larger share than what was first laid down for it, —either to the whole mixture, or to its parts, or to one part of it,—then the resulting change effected in the vapour doth bring about a change or in the disposition of the soul or of the body.

The fire and air, as tending upward, hasten upward to the soul, which dwells in the same regions as themselves ; the watery and the earthy elements, as tending down, sink down upon the body, which doth possess the self-same seat.

*   *   *   *   *

COMMENTARY

ARGUMENT

The Sermon from which this Extract is taken plainly belonged to the same class of literature as the *K. K.* Excerpts. The writer is an initiate of a higher degree, imparting instruction to his pupil by word of mouth.

He himself, however, professes to have "seen," for he has been plunged in the Cup of Immortality, and his feet have crossed the Plain of Truth (3).

1. The subject is the excarnate state of souls (1–3). The instruction is given by an analogy and a similitude (4). Each soul seeks naturally its proper habitat in the unseen world.

5. The ordering of the spaces of the excarnate souls is then described. These spaces are all in the "great air," the sublunary region, extending from the earth surface to the moon.

6. Of this great interval there are 4 main divisions and 60 spaces, the divisions consisting respectively of 4, 8, 16 and 32 sub-spaces. Above the second division from below there is no motion of the "air"; the "wind," or "moving air" belt, belongs properly to this second division, but has also authority over the first or lowest division, which extends from the earth-surface to the tops of the highest mountains.

7. Besides these 4 divisions and 60 spaces, there is a further ordering into 12 "intervallic" divisions.[1]

8. All is arranged by measure and harmony, and after death every soul goes to the space of its desert, ascending and descending according to an unerring law of Providence.

9. To carry out this economy there are two ministers of Providence, the warder and the conductor of souls. The one watches over souls who are out of body, and the other brings them back to suitable bodies. These bodies are made by nature in exact correspondence with their former deeds and characters; in this nature is aided by the energies of experience and memory (9–11).

12. The nature of the soul is conditioned by its habitat in the air-spaces or zones; and this is especially

[1] See Comments on *K. K.*, 10.

the case with those of the regal type. The names of some of these royal souls and their offices are given.

13. In brief all is ordered from above; the source of all is above in the soul-spaces, and as all souls come thence, so will all return thither.

14. How this is effected is explained as being conditioned by a certain link between soul and body, a sort of quintessence, or exhalation, or vapour, of the blend of sub-elements which compose the body (14–20).[1] It is a sort of etheric link between soul and body; it circulates in the body, but also shares with the soul, which is not thought of as being in the body, but as a sphere enveloping the body; or at any rate the body is in the soul, and not the soul in the body. Health is said to depend upon the maintenance of the due proportion of the "vapours"[2] of this "etheric double" (18).

Not only so, but the increase of vitality or intensity in these elements in the "vapour," is the means of remembering symbolic dreams and passing into a state of ecstasy; finally it is the fiery element of this "vapour" which dissolves this "spirituous body" (19).

It is by means of this link that changes are effected from soul to body, and from body to soul (20); and here, unfortunately, Stobæus ends his excerpt.

TITLE AND ORDERING

The "Sermon of Isis to Horus" extract is, in both style and context, so similar to the *K. K.* excerpts that we might almost take it to be part and parcel of the very same treatise; but if this had been the case, Stobæus, following his custom, would have presumably headed it with a simple "from the same." He may,

[1] This bears a curious resemblance to the *prânamaya kosha*, or "vital sheath," of the Vedântins.

[2] Vedântic *prâna's*, of which there are five.

however, have made a mistake, for that the good Joannes sometimes nods, may be seen from the short Excerpt xxi., which he says is also taken from "The [Sermon] of Isis to Horus"[1]; but this cannot be the case, since Isis is here addressing a certain king as her pupil, and not Horus.

Moreover, at the very beginning of our excerpt Horus distinctly states that Isis has already explained to him "the details of God's wondrous soul-making," and thanks her "for being made initiate by word of mouth into the vision of the soul,"—all of which is a precise reference to the contents of the $K. K.$ excerpts. I am, therefore, inclined to think that not only is it a further tractate of instruction following immediately on $K. K.$, but that even if it were supposed to be part and parcel of the same sermon, and that "The [Sermon] of Isis to Horus" was simply a sub-title or alternative title of the "Virgin of the World," the hypothesis could not be easily set aside.[2]

In any case it is quite certain that $S. I. H.$ belongs to precisely the same type as $K. K.$; and that it pertains to the same special class of Trismegistic literature, and to a somewhat similar type as the treatise from which Cyril quotes Fragg. xix., xx., xxi., in which Osiris figures as the disciple of the Good Daimon, Trismegistus.

THE BOOKS OF ISIS AND HORUS

Here also, as in $K. K.$, Isis comes forward as "initiated into the nature that transcendeth death," her "feet

[1] Of which Schow gives the alternative heading: "From the Intercession (or Supplication) of Isis," which Gaisford (in a note) thinks is from the Vienna Codex. This, however, is not the case, for the Vindobonensis preserves the usual reading except that the last word is missing. See R. 134, n. 3.

[2] R. (p. 135, n. 3), however, thinks this impossible.

have crossed the Plain of Truth" (3) that is as we have shown in the Comments on *K. K.*, 10, the writer claims to have reached the degree of illumination which bestows on men the consciousness of the gods. "Isis," then, is not "common to all priests," as Jamblichus says of "Hermes," without the honorific qualification "Thrice-greatest," but rather of a certain grade of initiation; the teacher of that lower grade, or Horus-grade, being Hermes' representative. Isis was commonly regarded as the Lady of all wisdom and teacher of all magic. Already in the earliest Hellenistic period she had attributes similar to those of Thoth-Hermes, and thus comes forward as the Orderer of the world[1]; and not only so, but, like Thoth, she is called Lady of the heart and of the tongue; that is to say, her attributes were those of the Logos.[2]

That there was a secret theosophic and apocalyptic literature ascribed to Isis and Horus may be seen from Lucian, who, in one of his humorous sketches, puts into the mouth of Pythagoras the following sentence:

"I also journeyed to Egypt that I might make the acquaintance of the prophets of wisdom, and I descended into the shrines of the temples and learned the Books of Isis and Horus."[3]

Here again, then, as Manetho tells us, these Books, as the Books of Hermes, were kept secret in the holy of holies of the Temples; and these shrines were evidently

[1] See Reitzenstein, *Zwei religionsgesch. Fragen*, 104 ff.

[2] Plutarch, *De Is. et Os.*, lxviii.: "They say that of the trees in Egypt the persea is especially dedicated to her, and that its fruit resembles a heart, and its leaf a tongue. For nothing that men have is more divine than the word (*logos*), and especially the [word] concerning the gods." The fruit of the persea grew from the stem.

[3] *Gallus*, 18.

underground for Pythagoras is said to have " descended " to them.

This is the Horus who is not only, after Osiris, the lord of power and might, that is, king, but lord of philosophy, as Arnebeschēnis (12). For Arnebeschēnis, that is Har-nebeschēnis, is, as Spiegelberg has shown,[1] an Egyptian proper name, meaning "Horus lord of Letopolis," at one time an important city in the Delta. In the Alchemical literature also we meet with Horus as a writer of books, as for instance in the superscription " Horus the Gold-miner to Cronus who is Ammon." [2]

Here we see that Horus stands to Isis as Asclepius to Hermes; Asclepius wrote books to Ammon, and so Horus wrote books to Ammon; but whereas the Trismegistic tradition proper looked back to Cronus (Ammon) as one of its earliest teachers, the later writings converted Ammon into a king who was taught by Asclepius or by Horus.

THE WATERY SPHERE AND SUBTLE BODY

The writer of *S. I. H.* tells us that the soul in its royal state, that is while lord of itself, is a divine creature, but in incarnation it is united with the watery plasm or subtle body, of *K. K.*, 18, where Hermes says that in making it he "used more water than was required"; and to which the soul in its complaint (§ 21) refers as a "watery sphere." This union makes it dense "against its proper nature" (3), and it is further densified by a certain "vaporous" nature which unites it with the physical frame (15, 17, 20); concerning all of which it is of interest to refer to Philoponus, who tells us that:

[1] *Demotische Studien*, i., "Ägyptische u. griechische Eigennamen," p. 28 (*cf.* also p. 41); R. 135.

[2] Berthelot, p. 103.

"They [the ancients] further add, that there is something of a plantal and plastic life[1] also, exercised by the soul, in those spirituous and airy bodies after death; they being nourished too, though not after the same manner, as these gross earthly bodies of ours are here, but by vapours; and that not by parts or organs, but throughout the whole of them (as sponges),[2] they imbibing everywhere those vapours. For which cause, they who are wise will in this life also take care of using a thinner and dryer diet, that so that spirituous body (which we have also at this present time within our grosser body) may not be clogged and incrassated, but attenuated. Over and above which these ancients made use of catharms, or purgations, to the same end and purpose also: for as this earthly body is washed with water, so is that spirituous body cleansed by cathartic vapours; some of these vapours being nutritive, others purgative. Moreover, these ancients further declared concerning this spirituous body, that it was not organized, but did the whole of it, in every part throughout, exercise all functions of sense, the soul hearing and seeing, and perceivng all sensibles, by it everywhere."[3]

THE HABITAT OF EXCARNATE SOULS

But to return to our treatise; the dwelling-place of excarnate souls is the Air, the sublunary region of four main layers, which are successively subtler and finer as they are more removed from the earth; the uppermost limit of the Air is coterminous with the fiery or ætheric realms (6), the habitat of the gods.

[1] τῆς φυτικῆς ζωῆς,—that is, vegetative.

[2] Endosmosis and exosmosis.

[3] Philoponus, *Proœm. in Aristot. de Anima*, as given in Cudworth's *Intellectual System* (ed. 1820), iii. 506 ff.; see my *Orpheus*, pp. 278, 279.

In the different zones, or firmaments, or layers of this Air, dwell not only excarnate souls, during the period between their incarnations, but also those which have never yet been shut in body—that is, presumably, the daimones (8).

With regard to the manner in which souls are kept in their appropriate spaces after the death of the body, and the way in which they are brought back to appropriate bodies, and the two ministers of Providence (9), it is of value to note that in this we have a simple outline of what is explained at great length and in much detail in the Coptic Gnostic work called *Pistis Sophia*. It would, however, occupy too much space here to deal with the representations of the Egyptian Gnostic work on this subject in a satisfactory manner, and as the text is now accessible in English, it can easily be consulted by the reader.[1]

[1] For Melchizedek, the "Receiver of light and Guide of souls," see *P. S.*, *passim*, and especially 35–37, 292, 327 ; for Zorokothora-Melchizedek and Ieou, see "The Books of the Saviour," *ibid.*, 365 ff. ; and for Gabriel and Michael, *ibid.*, 138.

II

References and Fragments in the Fathers

I.

JUSTIN MARTYR

i. *Cohortatio ad Gentiles*, xxxviii. ; Otto (J. C. T.), ii. 122 (2d ed., Jena, 1849).[1]

THE MOST ANCIENT OF PHILOSOPHERS

Now if any of you should think that he has learnt the doctrine concerning God from those of the philosophers who are mentioned among you as most ancient, let him give ear to Ammon and Hermes. For Ammon in the Words (*Logoi*) concerning himself[2] calls God "utterly hidden"; while Hermes clearly and plainly declares:

To understand God is difficult ; to speak [of Him] impossible, even for one who can understand.[3]

THE "WORDS OF AMMON"

This passage occurs at the very end of the treatise. Justin will have it that the most ancient of all the philosophers are on his side.

[1] The *Exhortation* is considered by most pseudepigraphic, but is supposed by others to be the earliest work of Justin, which may be placed conjecturally about 130 A.D. ; the *First Apology* is generally ascribed to the year 148 A.D.

[2] Taking the reading περὶ ἑαυτοῦ (Otto, n. 13), adopted in R. 138.

[3] Quoted also by Lactantius, *D. I. Epit.*, 4 ; Cyril Alex., *Con. Jul.*, i. 31 ; and Stobæus, *Flor.*, lxxx. [lxxviii.], 94 (Ex. ii. 1).

These are Ammon and Hermes. Justin, moreover, knows of certain Words (Logoi), or Sermons, or Sacred Utterances of Ammon, which must have been circulating in Greek, otherwise it is difficult to see how Justin was acquainted with them. They were evidently of an apocalyptic nature, in the form of a self-revelation of Ammon or God.

These "Words of Ammon" have clearly nothing to do with the Ammonian type of the surviving Trismegistic literature, where Ammon is a hearer and not an instructor, least of all the supreme instructor or Agathodaimon. In them we may see an intermediate stage of direct dependence of Hellenistic theological literature on Egyptian originals, for we have preserved to us certain Hymns from the El-Khargeh Oasis which bear the inscription "'The Secret Words of Ammon' which were found on Tables of Mulberry-wood."[1]

THE INEFFABILITY OF GOD

The sentence from Hermes is from a lost sermon, a fragment of which is preserved in an excerpt by Stobæus. It was probably the opening words of what Stobæus calls "The [Sermon] to Tat,"[2] that is to say, probably one of the "Expository Sermons to Tat," as Lactantius calls them.[3]

The idea in the saying was a common place in

[1] R. 138. The connection between this Ammon and Hermes was probably the same as that which is said to have existed between the king-god Thamus-Ammon and the god of invention Theuth-Hermes. Thamus-Ammon was a king philosopher, to whom Theuth brought all his inventions and discoveries for his (Ammon's) judgment, which was not invariably favourable. See the pleasant story told by Plato, *Phædrus*, 274 c. *Cf.* also the notes on Kneph-Ammon, *K. K.*, 19, Comment.

[2] Stob., *loc. infra cit.*

[3] See Fragg. xi., xii., xiii., xv., xx., xxii., xxiii., xxiv. (?).

Hellenistic theological thought, and need not be always directly referred to the much-quoted words of Plato: "To find the Father and the Maker of this universe is a [great] work, and finding [Him] it is impossible to tell [Him] unto all."[1] Indeed, it is curious to remark that Justin reproduces the text of the Hermetic writer far more faithfully than when he refers directly to the saying of Plato.[2]

ii. *I. Apologia*, xxi. ; Otto, i. 54.

HERMES AND ASCLEPIUS SONS OF GOD

And when we say that the Word (*Logos*) which is the first begetting of God, was begotten without intercourse,—Jesus Christ, our Master,—and that he was crucified, and was dead, and rose again and ascended into heaven, we bring forward no new thing beyond those among you who are called Sons of Zeus. For ye know how many Sons the writers who are held in honour among you ascribe to Zeus:—Hermes, the Word (*Logos*), who was the interpreter and teacher of all; and Asclepius, who was also[3] a healer,[4] and was smitten by the bolt [of his sire] and ascended into heaven . . . [and many others] . . .

iii. *Ibid.*, xxii. ; Otto, i. 58.

HERMES THE WORD WHO BRINGS TIDINGS FROM GOD

But as to the Son of God called Jesus,—even though he were only a man [born] in the common way, [yet] because of [his] wisdom is he worthy to be called Son

---

[1] *Timæus*, 28 c.
[2] See *Cohort.*, xxii. ; *II. Apol.*, x. Clemens Alex., Origen, Minutius Felix, Lactantius, and other of the Fathers also quote this saying of Plato.
[3] That is, like Jesus. [4] θεραπευτὴν (therapeut).

of God; for all writers call God "Father of men and gods." And if we say [further] that he was also in a special way, beyond his common birth, begotten of God [as] Word (*Logos*) of God, let us have this in common with you who call Hermes the Word (*Logos*) who brings tidings [1] from God.

THE SONS OF GOD IN HELLENISTIC THEOLOGY

It is remarkable that Justin heads the list of Sons of God—Dionysus, Hercules, etc.—with Hermes and Asclepius. Moreover, when he returns to the subject he again refers to Hermes and to Hermes alone. This clearly shows that the most telling parallel he could bring forward was that of Hermes, who, in the Hellenistic theological world of his day, was especially thought of under the concept of the Logos.

The immediate association of the name of Asclepius with that of Hermes is also remarkable, and indicates that they were closely associated in Justin's mind; the indication, however, is too vague to permit of any positive deduction as to an Asclepius-element in the Trismegistic literature current in Rome in Justin's time. Justin, in any case, has apparently very little first-hand knowledge of the subject, for he introduces the purely Hellenic myth of Asclepius being struck by a thunderbolt, which, we need hardly say, is entirely foreign to the conception of the Hellenistic Asclepius, the disciple of Hermes.

AN UNVERIFIABLE QUOTATION

To these quotations Chambers (p. 139) adds the following passage from *II. Apologia*, vi.,—which in date may be placed some four or five years after the First.

[1] τὸν παρὰ θεοῦ ἀγγελτικόν. Compare Plutarch, *De Is. et Os.*, xxvi. 5.

"Now to the Father of all no name can be given; seeing that He is ingenerable; for by whatsoever name one may be called, he has as his elder the one who gives the name. But 'Father,' and 'God,' and 'Creator,' and 'Lord,' and 'Master' are not names, but terms of address [derived] from His blessings and His works."

It is quite true that this passage might be taken verbally from a Hermetic tractate, but I can find no authority in the text of Justin for claiming it as a quotation. For the same idea in Hermes compare *C. H.*, v. (vi.) 10, and Lact., *D. I.*, i. 6.

II.

ATHENAGORAS

Libellus pro Christianis,[1] xxviii. ; Schwartz (E.), p. 57, 24 (Leipzig, 1891).[2]

ATHENAGORAS was acquainted with a Greek literature circulated under the name of Hermes Trismegistus, to whom he refers as authority for his euhemeristic contention that the gods were once simply men.[3]

---

[1] Written probably about 176-177 A.D.

[2] In *Texte u. Untersuchungen* (von Gebhardt and Harnack), Bd. iv.

[3] *Cf.* R., pp. 2 and 160.

III.

CLEMENT OF ALEXANDRIA [1]

i. *Protrepticus*, ii. 29 ; Dindorf (G.), i. 29, (Oxford, 1869)
—(24 P., 8 S.).

MANY HERMESES AND ASCLEPIUSES

(AFTER referring to the three Zeuses, five Athenas, and numberless Apollos of complex popular tradition, Clement continues :)

But what were I to mention the many Asclepiuses, or the Hermeses that are reckoned up, or the Hephæstuses of mythology ?

Clement lived in the very centre of Hellenistic theology, and his grouping together of the names of Asclepius, Hermes and Hephæstus, the demiurgic Ptah, whose tradition was incorporated into the Pœmandres doctrine, is therefore not fortuitous, but shows that these three names were closely associated in his mind, and that, therefore, he was acquainted with the Trismegistic literature. This deduction is confirmed by the following passage.

[1] *Fl.*, 175–200 A.D.

ii. *Stromateis*, I. xxi. 134 ; Dindorf, ii. 108 (399 P., 144 S.).

THE APOTHEOSIS OF HERMES AND ASCLEPIUS

Of those, too, who once lived as men among the Egyptians, but who have been made gods by human opinion, [are] Hermes of Thebes and Asclepius of Memphis.

(To this we may appropriately append what Clement has to tell us about the "Books of Hermes," when, writing in the last quarter of the second century, he describes one of the sacred processions of the Egyptians as follows :)

iii. *Ibid.*, VI. iv. 35 ; Dind., iii. 156, 157.

THE BOOKS OF HERMES

First comes the "Singer" bearing some one of the symbols of music. This [priest], they tell us, has to make himself master of two of the "Books of Hermes," one of which contains (1) Hymns [in honour] of the Gods,[1] and the other (2) Reflections[2] on the Kingly Life.

After the "Singer" comes the "Time-watcher" bearing the symbols of the star-science, a dial after a hand and phœnix. He must have the division of the "Books of Hermes" which treats of the stars ever at the tip of his tongue—there being four of such books. The first of these deals with (3) the Ordering of the

[1] I have numbered the books and used capitals for greater clearness.

[2] ἐκλογισμόν ; I do not know what this term means in this connection. The usual translation of "Regulations" seems to me unsatisfactory. Some word such as "Praise" (? read εὐλογισμόν) seems to be required, as may be seen from the title of *C. H.*, (xviii.), "The Encomium of Kings."

apparently Fixed Stars,[1] the next [two] (4 and 5) with the conjunctions and variations of Light of the Sun and Moon, and the last (6) with the Risings [of the Stars].

Next comes the "Scribe of the Mysteries," with wings on his head, having in either hand a book and a ruler[2] in which is the ink and reed pen with which they write. He has to know what they call the sacred characters, and the books about (7) Cosmography, and (8) Geography, (9) the Constitution of the Sun and Moon, and (10) of the Five Planets, (11) the Survey of Egypt, and (12) the Chart of the Nile, (13) the List of the Appurtenances of the Temples and (14) of the Lands consecrated to them, (15) the Measures, and (16) Things used in the Sacred Rites.

After the above-mentioned comes the "Overseer[3] of the Ceremonies," bearing the cubit of justice and the libation cup [as his symbols]. He must know all the books relating to the training [of the conductors of the public cult], and those that they call the victim-sealing[4]

---

[1] τῶν ἀπλανῶν φαινομένων ἄστρων.

κανόνα; this must mean a hollow wooden case shaped like a ruler.

[3] στολιστής, called also ἱερόστολος. This priestly office is usually translated as the "keeper of the vestments," the "one who is over the wardrobe." But such a meaning is entirely foreign to the contents of the books which are assigned to him. He was evidently the organiser of the ceremonies, especially the processions.

[4] μοσχοσφραγιστικά—that is to say, literally, books relating to the art of one who picks out and "seals calves" for sacrifice. The literal meaning originally referred to the selection of the sacred Apis bull-calf, into which the power of the god was supposed to have re-incarnated, in the relic of some primitive magic rite which the conservatism of the Egyptians still retained in the public cult. Its meaning, however, was later on far more general, as we see by the nature of the books assigned to this division. Boulage, in his *Mystères d'Isis* (Paris, 1820, p. 21), says that "the seal of the priests which marked the victims was a man

books. There are ten of these books which deal with the worship which they pay to the gods, and in which the Egyptian cult is contained; namely [those which treat] of (17) Sacrifice, (18) First-fruits, (19) Hymns, (20) Prayers, (21) Processions, (22) Feasts, and (23–26) the like.

After all of these comes the "Prophet" clasping to his breast the water-vase so that all can see it; and after him follow those who carry the bread that is to be distributed.[1] The "Prophet," as chief of the temple, learns by heart the ten books which are called "hieratic"; these contain the volumes (27–36) treating of the Laws, and the Gods, and the whole Discipline of the Priests. For you must know that the "Prophet" among the Egyptians is also the supervisor of the distribution of the [temple] revenues.

Now the books which are absolutely indispensable[2]

kneeling with his hands bound behind his back, and a sword pointed at his throat, for it was in this attitude that the neophyte received the first initiation, signifying that he agreed to perish by the sword if he revealed any of the secrets revealed to him." This he evidently deduced from Plutarch's *De Is. et Os.*, xxxi. 3.

[1] οἱ τὴν ἐκπεμψιν τῶν ἄρτων βαστάζοντες. The "Prophet" belonged to the grade of high priests who had practical knowledge of the inner way. As the flood of the Nile came down and irrigated the fields and brought forth the grain for bread, and so gave food to Egypt, so did the living stream of the Gnosis from the infinite heights of space pour into the Hierophant, and he in his turn became Father Nile for the priests, his disciples, who in their turn distributed the bread of knowledge to the people. A pleasing symbolism, of which the bread and water of the earlier ascetic schools of Christendom, who rejected wine, was perhaps a reminiscence. Nor has even the General Church in its older forms forgotten to sprinkle the people from the water-vase and distribute among them the bread.

[2] This seems to suggest that there were others, the knowledge of which was optional, or rather reserved for the few. There may perhaps have been forty-nine in all.

for Hermes [1] are forty-two in number. Six-and-thirty of them, which contain the whole wisdom-discipline [2] of the Egyptians, are learned by heart by the [grades of priests] already mentioned. The remaining six are learned by the "Shrine-bearers" [3]; these are medical treatises dealing with (37) the Constitution of the Body, with (38) Diseases, (39) Instruments, (40) Drugs, (41) Eyes,[4] and finally (42) with the Maladies of Women.

THE GENERAL CATALOGUE OF THE EGYPTIAN PRIESTLY LIBRARY

This exceedingly interesting passage of Clement gives us the general catalogue of the Egyptian priestly library and the background of the Greek translations and adaptations in our Trismegistic writings.

The whole of these writings fall into this frame, and the oldest deposit or "Pœmandres" type fits in excellently with the content of the hieratic books (the titles of which Clement has unfortunately omitted), or with those that were kept secret. These hieratic books were evidently the more important and were in charge of the "Prophet," that is to say, of those high priests of the temples who were directors of the prophetic discipline, the very subject of our "Pœmandres" treatises.[5]

[1] That is, the priesthood.   [2] Lit. philosophy.

[3] παστοφόροι, those who carried the *pastos* as a symbol; this apparently symbolized the shrine or casket of the soul; in other words, the human body. These Pastophors were the priests who were the physicians of the body, the higher grades being presumably physicians of the soul.

[4] This seems to be an error of the copyist.

[5] As to the hieroglyphic inscription at Edfu, which was thought by Jomasd to contain references to the titles of these forty-two books, see Parthey, *Über Isis und Osiris*, p. 255.

IV.

TERTULLIAN [1]

i. *Contra Valentinianos*, xv.; Œhler (F.), ii. 402 (Leipzig, 1844).

HERMES THE MASTER OF ALL PHYSICS

(WRITING sarcastically of the Gnostic Sophia-myth, Tertullian exclaims:)

Well, then, let the Pythagoreans learn, the Stoics know, [yea,] Plato even, whence matter—which they [*sc.* the Pythagoreans and the rest] would have to be ingenerable—derived its source and substance to [form] this pile of a world,—[a mystery] which not even the famous Thrice-greatest Hermes, the master of all physics, has thought out.

The doctrine of Hermes, and of Hellenistic theology in general, however, is that matter comes from the One God. It is remarkable that Tertullian keeps his final taunt for that school which was evidently thought the foremost of all—that of the "famous Thrice-greatest Hermes."

[1] *Fl.*, c. 200-216 A.D.

ii. *De Anima*, ii.; Œhler, ii. 558.

HERMES THE WRITER OF SCRIPTURE

(Inveighing against the wisdom of the philosophers, Tertullian says:)

She [philosophy] has also been under the impression that she too has drawn from what they [the philosophers] consider "sacred" scriptures; because antiquity thought that most authors were gods (*deos*), and not merely inspired by them (*divos*),—as, for instance, Egyptian Hermes, with whom especially Plato had intercourse,[1] . . . [and others] . . . .

Here again, as with Justin, Hermes heads the list; moreover, in Tertullian's mind, Hermes belongs to antiquity, to a more ancient stratum than Pythagoras and Plato, as the context shows; Plato, of course, depends on Hermes, not Hermes on Plato; of this Tertullian has no doubt. There were also "sacred scriptures" of Hermes, and Hermes was regarded as a god.

iii. *Ibid.*, xxviii.; Œhler, ii. 601.

HERMES THE FIRST TEACHER OF REINCARNATION

What then is the value nowadays of that ancient doctrine mentioned by Plato,[2] about the reciprocal migration of souls; how they remove hence and go thither, and then return hither and pass through life, and then again depart from this life, made quick again from the dead? Some will have it that this is a doctrine of Pythagoras; while Albinus[3] will have it to

[1] *Adsuevit.*
[2] *Cf. Phædo*, p. 70.
[3] A Platonic philosopher, and contemporary of Galen (130–? 200 A.D.).

be a divine pronouncement, perhaps of Egyptian Hermes.

iv. *Ibid.*, xxxiii.; Œhler, ii. 610.

HERMES ON METEMPSYCHOSIS

(Arguing ironically against the belief in metempsychosis, Tertullian writes:)

Even if they [souls] should continue [unchanged] until judgment [is pronounced upon them] . . . a point which was known to Egyptian Hermes, when he says that the soul on leaving the body is not poured back into the soul of the universe, but remains individualized[1]:

FRAGMENT I.

That it may give account unto the Father of those things which it hath done in body.

This exact quotation[2] is to be found nowhere in the existing remains of the Trismegistic literature, but it has every appearance of being genuine.

Œhler (note c) refers to *C. H.*, x. (xi.) 7, but this passage of "The Key" is only a general statement of the main idea of metempsychosis.

A more appropriate parallel is to be found in *P. S. A.*, xxviii. 1: "When, [then,] the soul's departure from the body shall take place,—then shall the judgment and the weighing of its merit pass into its highest daimon's power"— a passage, however, which retains far stronger traces of the Egyptian prototype of the idea than does that quoted by Tertullian.

[1] *Determinatam.*   [2] Tertullian marks it by an "*inquit.*"

V.

CYPRIAN [1]

i. *De Idolorum Vanitate*, vi.; Baluze, p. 220 (Paris, 1726).

GOD IS BEYOND ALL UNDERSTANDING

THRICE-GREATEST Hermes speaks of the One God, and confesses Him beyond all understanding and all appraisement.

This is evidently a reference to the most quoted sentence of Hermes. See Justin Martyr i. below, and other references.

Chambers (p. 140), after this notice in Cyprian, inserts a passage from Eusebius (*c.* 325 A.D.), which he says is "a clear quotation from the 'Pœmandres' of Hermes, whom, however, he [Eusebius] probably confounds with the Shepherd of Hermas."

Eusebius (*Hist. Ecc.*, v. 8), however, quotes Irenæus (iv. 20, 2), who quotes literally *The Shepherd of Hermas* (Mand., i.). Indeed, it is the most famous sentence in that early document. See the list of its quotations by the Fathers in the note to Gebhardt and Harnack's text (Leipzig, 1897), p. 70. Such verbal exactitude is not to be found in the remaining Trismegistic literature; the idea, however, is the basis of the whole Trismegistic theology.

[1] About 200–258 A.D.

VI.

ARNOBIUS[1]

i. *Adversus Nationes*, ii. 13; Hildebrand (G. F.), p. 136 (Halle, 1844).

THE SCHOOL OF HERMES

(ARNOBIUS complains that the followers of the philosophic schools laugh at the Christians, and selects especially the adherents of a certain tradition as follows:)

You, you I single out, who belong to the school of Hermes, or of Plato and Pythagoras, and the rest of you who are of one mind and walk in union in the same paths of doctrine.[2]

---

[1] He was a converted philosopher, and the teacher of Lactantius; flourished about 304 A.D.

[2] Here again, as elsewhere, Hermes comes first; he was evidently regarded as the leader of philosophic theology as contrasted with popular Christian dogmatics. See R. 306.

VII.
LACTANTIUS[1]

i. *Divinæ Institutiones*, i. 6, 1; Brandt, p. 18; Fritzsche, i. 13.[2]

THOYTH-HERMES AND HIS BOOKS ON THE GNOSIS

LET us now pass to divine testimonies; but, first of all, I will bring into court testimony which is like divine [witness], both on account of its exceeding great age, and because he whom I shall name was carried back again from men unto the gods.

In Cicero,[3] Caius Cotta,[4] the Pontifex, arguing against the Stoics about faiths and the diversity of opinions which obtain concerning the gods, in order that, as was the way of the Academics,[5] he might bring all things into doubt, declares that there were five Hermeses; and after enumerating four of them in succession, [he adds] that the fifth was he by whom

[1] A pupil of Arnobius; flourished at the beginning of the fourth century.

[2] Brandt (S.), *L. Caeli Firmiani Lactanti Opera Omnia,—Pars I., Divinae Institutiones et Epitome* (Vienna, 1890). Pars II., to be edited by G. Laubmann, has not yet appeared. Fritzsche (O. F.), *Div. Instit.* (Leipzig, 1842), 2 vols.

[3] *De Natura Deorum*, iii. 22, 56.

[4] C. Aurelius Cotta, 124–76 (?) B.C.

[5] Cicero makes Cotta maintain the cause of this school both here and in the *De Oratore*.

Argus was slain,[1] and for that cause he fled into Egypt, and initiated the Egyptians into laws and letters.

The Egyptians call him Thoyth, and from him the first month of their year (that is, September) has received its name. He also founded a city which even unto this day is called Hermopolis. The people of Pheneüs,[2] indeed, worship him as a god; but, although

---

[1] Argos, according to the many ancient myths concerning him, was all-seeing (πανόπτης), possessed of innumerable eyes, or, in one variant, of an eye at the top of his head. Like Hercules, he was of superhuman strength, and many similar exploits of his powers are recorded. In the Io-legends, Hera made Argos guardian of the cow into which the favourite of Zeus had been metamorphosed. Zeus accordingly sent Hermes to carry off his beloved. Hermes is said to have lulled Argos to sleep by means of his syrinx, or pipe of seven reeds, or by his caduceus, and then to have stoned him or cut off his head. See Roscher's *Ausführ. Lex. d. griech. u. röm. Myth.*, s.v. "Argos." It is to be noticed that instead of *Argum*, four MSS. read *argentum*, which is curious as showing a Medieval Alchemical influence. See n. 4 to *Ciceronis Opera Philosophica* (Delph. et Var. Clas.), vol. ii. (London, 1830).

[2] *Pheneatæ*,—Pheneüs was a town in Arcadia, that country of ancient mysteries. (It is remarkable that Hermas is taken by the "Shepherd" in spirit to a mountain in Arcadia. See *Shepherd of Hermas*, Sim. ix. 1.) Cicero begins his description of the fifth Hermes with this statement, and Lactantius has thus awkwardly misplaced it. Pausanias (viii. 14, 6) tells us that Pheneüs itself was considered as a very ancient city, and that its chief cult was that of Hermes. This cult of Hermes, moreover, was blended with an ancient mystery-tradition, for Pausanias (*ibid.*, 15, 1) tells us that:

"The Pheneatians have also a sanctuary of Demeter surnamed Eleusinian, and they celebrate mysteries in her honour, alleging that rites identical with those performed at Eleusis were instituted in their land. . . . Beside the sanctuary of the Eleusinian goddess is what is called the Petroma, two great stones fitted to each other. Every second year, when they are celebrating what they call the Greater Mysteries, they open these stones, and taking out of them certain writings which bear on the mysteries, they read them in the hearing of the initiated, and put them back in their place that same night. I know, too, that on the weightiest matters

he was [really] a man, still he was of such high antiquity, and so deeply versed in every kind of science, that his knowledge of [so] many things and of the arts gained him the title of "Thrice-greatest."

He wrote books, indeed many [of them], treating of the Gnosis[1] of things divine, in which he asserts the greatness of the Highest and One and Only God, and calls Him by the same names as we [do]—God and Father.[2] And [yet], so that no one should seek after His name, he has declared that He cannot be named, in that He doth not need to have a name, owing, indeed, unto the very [nature of His] unity.[3] His words are these[4]:

FRAGMENT II.

But God [is] one; and He who's one needs not a name, for He [as one] is The-beyond-all-names.

THE HISTORICAL ORIGINS OF THE HERMETIC TRADITION

For Lactantius, then, Hermes was very ancient; moreover, he was one who descended from heaven and had returned thither. When, however, Firmianus attempts the historical origins of the Hermetic tradition, as was invariably the case with the ancients, he can do nothing better than refer us to a complex though

most of the Pheneatians swear by the Petroma." Frazer's Translation, i. 393 (London, 1898).

[1] *Cognitionem.*

[2] *Cf. P. S. A.*, xx. (p. 42, 16, Goldb.) *et pass.*; *C. H.*, v. (vi.) 2.

[3] Compare with *Epitome* 4 below.

[4] Lactantius here quotes in Greek. *Cf. P. S. A.*, xx. (p. 42, 27–43, 3, Goldb.).

interesting myth, and to a legend of it devised to flatter the self-esteem of its Hellenic creators: A Greek god, whose cult, moreover, was known to be intimately connected with an ancient mystery-tradition, was the originator of the wisdom of Egypt. Of course; and so with all nations who had any ancient learning—their special tradition was oldest and best and originator of all others!

For the rest, Lactantius knows nothing historically of the tradition which he esteemed so highly, and the mention of the Latinized name Thoyth[1] and of Hermopolis[2] does but throw the paucity of his knowledge into deeper relief. What Lactantius does know is a large literature in Greek and its general tendency.

The sentence he quotes is not found textually in any of the extant Trismegistic literature.[3]

ii. *Ibid.*, i. 11, 61; Brandt, p. 47; Fritzsche, i. 29, 30.

URANUS, CRONUS AND HERMES, ADEPTS OF THE PERFECT SCIENCE

And so it appears that he [Cronus] was not born from Heaven (which is impossible), but from that man who was called Uranus; and that this is so, Trismegistus bears witness, when, in stating that there have been very few in whom the perfect science has been found,

[1] Was, however, this the spelling found in Cicero, for Firmianus takes it from the text of Tully? It is a pity we have no critical apparatus of the text of Lactantius, for the MSS. of Cicero present us with the following extraordinary list of variants: Then, Ten, Their, Thoyt, Theyt, Theyn, Thetum, Theru, Thernum, Theutatem, Theut, Thoyth, Thoth. See n. 5 to the text of Cicero, cited above. *Cf.* R. 117, n. 2.

[2] Which he probably took from *P. S. A.*, xxxvii. 4: "Whose home is in a place called after him."

[3] Chambers (p. 41, n. 1), in referring it to *C. H.*, v. (vi.) 10, is mistaken.

he mentioned in their number Uranus, Cronus and Hermes, his own kinsfolk.[1]

iii. *Ibid.*, ii. 8, 48; Brandt, p. 138; Fritzsche, i. 89.

DIVINE PROVIDENCE

For the World was made by Divine Providence, not to mention Thrice-greatest, who preaches this.[2]

iv. *Ibid.*, ii. 8, 68; Brandt, p. 141; Fritzsche, i. 91.

ON MORTAL AND IMMORTAL SIGHT

His [God's] works are seen by the eyes; but how He made them, is not seen even by the mind, "in that," as Hermes says:

FRAGMENT III.

Mortal cannot draw nigh[3] to the Immortal, nor temporal to the Eternal, nor the corruptible to That which knoweth no corruption.[4]

And, therefore, hath the earthly animal not yet capacity to see celestial things, in that it is kept shut within the body as in a prison house, lest with freed sense, emancipate, it should see all.

[1] *Cf. C. H.*, x. (xi.) 5; *P. S. A.*, xxxvii. 1. Also Lact., *Epit.*, 14. In my commentary on the first passage I have shown that Lactantius is probably here referring to a lost Hermetic treatise.

[2] *Cf.* Fragg. *ap.* Stob., *Ecl.*, i. 5, 16, 20. It is to be noticed from the context that Lactantius places Trismegistus in a class apart together with the Sibylline Oracles and Prophets, and then proceeds to speak of the philosophers, Pythagoreans, Platonists, etc. He also repeats the same triple combination in iv. 6.

[3] *Propinquare.* L. glosses this as meaning "come close to and follow with the intelligence."

[4] *Cf.* Frag. *ap.* Cyril, *C. I.*, i. (vol. vi., p. 31 c).

The first part of this citation (which Lactantius gives in Latin) is identical in idea with a sentence in Frag. iv.—that favourite source of quotation, which Stobæus, Ex. ii. (*Flor.* lxxx. [lxxviii.] 9), excerpted from "The [Sermon] to Tat."[1] It might, then, be thought that this was simply a paraphrase of Lactantius', or that he was quoting from memory, and that the second sentence was not quotation but his own writing. But the second sentence is so thoroughly Trismegistic that it has every appearance of being genuine.[2]

v. *Ibid.*, ii. 10, 13; Brandt, p. 149; Fritzsche, i. 96.

MAN MADE AFTER THE IMAGE OF GOD

But the making of the truly living man out of clay[3] is of God. And Hermes also hands on the tradition of this fact,—for not only has he said that man was made by God after the Image of God,[4] but also he has attempted to explain with what skilfulness He has formed every single member in the body of man, since there is not one of them which is not admirably suited not only for what it has to do, but also adapted for beauty.[5]

Man made after the Image of God is one of the fundamental doctrines of the Trismegistic tradition. For instance, *P. S. A.*, vii. 2: "The [man] 'essential,' as say the Greeks, but which we call the 'form of the

[1] Compare also Lact., *Epit.*, 4.

[2] It is interesting to note, in the history of the text-tradition, that the received reading σημῆναι ("be expressed") in Stobæus stands in one MS. (A) συμβῆναι, which seems to be a transference from the original of L.'s *propinquare*.

[3] *Limo*,—slime or mud.

[4] Lact. repeats this in vii. 4. *Cf. C. H.*, i. 12.

[5] *Cf. C. H.*, v. (vi.) 6.

Divine Similitude'"; and x. 3: "Giving the greatest
thanks to God, His Image reverencing,—not ignorant
that he [man] is, too, God's image, the second [one]; for
that there are two images of God—Cosmos and man."[1]

vi. *Ibid.*, ii. 12, 4; Brandt, p. 156; Fritzsche, i. 100.

HERMES THE FIRST NATURAL PHILOSOPHER

Empedocles[2] . . . [and others] . . . laid down four
elements, fire, air, water, and earth,—[in this] perchance
following Trismegistus, who said that our bodies were
composed of these four elements by God.

"For that they have in them something of fire, something of air, something of water, and something of earth,
—and yet they are not fire [in itself], nor air, nor water,
nor earth."

———

All this about the elements is, of course, a commonplace
of ancient physics, and we may, therefore, dismiss the
naïve speculation of Lactantius, who evidently thought
he had the very words of the first inventor of the theory
before him; for he renders into Latin word for word
the same text which Stobæus has preserved to us in an
excerpt from "The [Sermons] to Tat"—Ex. iii. 1.[3]

vii. *Ibid.*, ii. 14, 5; Brandt, p. 163; Fritzsche, i. 105.

THE DAIMON-CHIEF

Thus there are two classes of daimons,—the one
celestial, and the other terrestrial. The latter are
impure spirits, the authors of the evils that are done,[4]

[1] *Cf.* also Hermes-Prayer, iii. 11. R. 21, n. 11.
[2] Date *c.* 494–434 B.C.
[3] See also Ex. vii. 3; *C. H.*, ii. (iii.) 11.
[4] *Cf. C. H.*, ix. (x.) 3; *C. H.*, xvi. 10.

of whom the same Diabolus is chief. Whence Trismegistus calls him the " Daimon-chief." [1]

viii. *Ibid.*, ii. 15, 6; Brandt, p. 166; Fritzsche, i. 106.

DEVOTION IS GOD-GNOSIS

In fine, Hermes asserts that those who have known God, not only are safe from the attacks of evil daimons, but also that they are not held even by Fate.[2] He says:

FRAGMENT IV.

The one means of protection is piety. For neither doth an evil daimon nor doth Fate rule o'er the pious man.[3] For God doth save the pious [man] from every ill. The one and only good found in mankind is piety.

And what piety means, he witnesses in another place, saying:

" Devotion is God-Gnosis." [4]

Asclepius, his Hearer, has also explained the same idea at greater length in that " Perfect Sermon " which he wrote to the King.

Both, then, assert that the daimons are the enemies and harriers of men, and for this cause Trismegistus

[1] δαιμονιάρχην. This term is not found in the extant texts; " Diabolus" is, of course, not to be referred to Hermes, but to the disquisition of Lactantius at the beginning of § 14.

[2] *Cf.* Cyril, *C. J.*, iv. (vol. vi. 130 E, Aub.).

[3] For the same idea, see *C. H.*, xii. (xiii.) 9.

[4] ἡ γὰρ εὐσέβεια γνῶσίς ἐστι τοῦ θεοῦ,—which Lactantius in another passage (v. 14) renders into Latin as " *Pietas autem nihil aliud est quam dei notio*,—is given in *C. H.*, ix. (x.) 4 as: εὐσέβεια δέ ἐστι θεοῦ γνῶσις (where Parthey notes no various readings in MSS.).

calls them "evil 'angels',"[1]—so far was he from being ignorant that from celestial beings they had become corrupted, and so earthly.

This passage is given in Greek, and is quoted, but with numerous glosses, also by Cyril (*Contra Julianum*, iv. 130); it is also practically the same as the sentence in *P. S. A.*, xxix.: "The righteous man finds his defence in serving God and deepest piety. For God doth guard such men from every ill."

Now we know that Lactantius had the Greek of this "Perfect Sermon" before him, and we know that our Latin translation is highly rhetorical and paraphrastic.

The only difficulty is that Lactantius' quotation ends with the sentence: "The one and only good found in mankind is piety"; and this does not appear in the Latin translation of *P. S. A.* On the other hand, Firmianus immediately refers by name to a Perfect Sermon, which, however, he says was written by Asclepius, and addressed to the King. Our Fragment is, therefore, probably from the lost ending of *C. H.*, xvi. (see Commentary on the title).

ix. *Ibid.*, iv. 6, 4; Brandt, p. 286; Fritzsche, i. 178.

THE COSMIC SON OF GOD

Hermes, in that book which is entitled the "Perfect Sermon," uses these words:

FRAGMENT V.

The Lord and Master of all things (whom 'tis our custom to call God), when He had made the

[1] ἀγγέλους πονηροὺς,—these words do not occur in our extant Greek texts; but the Lat. trans. of *P. S. A.*, xxv. 4, preserves "*nocentes angeli*."

second God, the Visible and Sensible,[1]—I call Him sensible, not that He hath sensation in Himself (for as to this, whether or no He hath Himself sensation, we will some other time enquire), but that He is object of senses and of mind,—when, then, He'd made Him First, and One and Only,[2] He seemed to Him most fair, and filled quite full of all things good. At Him he marvelled, and loved Him altogether as His Son.[3]

Lactantius here quotes from the lost Greek original of "The Perfect Sermon," viii. 1. We have thus a means of controlling the old Latin translation which has come down to us.

It is, by comparison, very free and often rhetorical; inserting phrases and even changing the original, as, for instance, when in the last clause it says: "He fell in love with him as being part of His Divinity."

It is, however, possible that the translator may have had a different text before him, for there is reason to believe that there were several recensions of the *P. S. A.*[4]

x. *Ibid.*, iv. 6, 9; Brandt, p. 291; Fritzsche, i. 179.

THE DEMIURGE OF GOD

(Speaking of the Son of God and identifying Him with the pre-existent Wisdom spoken of in Proverbs viii. 22, Lactantius adds:)

[1] *Sc.* the Logos as Cosmos. [2] *Cf.* Frag. x.
[3] For last clause, see *C. H.*, i. 12. *Cf.* also Ps. Augustin., *C. Quinque Hæreses*, vol. viii., Append. p. 3 E, Maur.
[4] Lactantius himself also gives a partial translation of this passage in his *Epitome*, 42 (Fritz., ii. 140).

Wherefore also Trismegistus has called Him the "Demiurge of God."[1]

xi. *Ibid.*, iv. 7, 3 ; Brandt, p. 292 ; Fritzsche, i. 179.

THE NAME OF GOD

Even then [when the world shall be consummated],[2] it [God's Name] will not be able to be uttered by the mouth of man, as Hermes teaches, saying:

FRAGMENT VI.

But the Cause of this Cause is the Divine and the Ingenerable Good's Good-will, which[3] first brought forth the God whose Name cannot be spoken by the mouth of man.[4]

xii. *Ibid.*, iv. 7, 3 ; Brandt, p. 293 ; Fritzsche, i. 179, 180.

THE HOLY WORD ABOUT THE LORD OF ALL.

And a little after [he says] to his son :

FRAGMENT VII.

For that there is, [my] son, a Word [*Logos*] of wisdom, that no tongue can tell,—a Holy[5]

[1] δημιουργὸν τοῦ θεοῦ. The exact words do not occur in our extant texts, but the idea is a commonplace of the Trismegistic doctrine ; see especially *P. S. A.*, xxvi. : "The Demiurgus of the first and the one God," and Lact., *ibid.*, vii. 18, 4 : "God of first might, and Guider of the one God." See also *C. H.*, i. 10, 11, xvi. 18 ; Cyril, *C. Jul.*, i. 33 (Frag. xiii.), and vi. 6 (Frag. xxi.) ; and Exx. iii. 6, iv. 2. *Cf.* also Ep. 14 below.

[2] *Cf.* vii. 18 below.

[3] *Sc.* will (βούλησις). *Cf.* especially *P. S. A.*, Commentary.

[4] This is plainly from the same source as the following Fragment.

[5] *Cf. C. H.*, i. 5 ; and Lact. and Cyril, *passim* (*e.g.* Fragg. xxi., xxii.).

[Word] about the only Lord of all, the God before all thought,—whom to declare transcends all human power.[1]

xiii. *Ibid.*, iv. 8, 5; Brandt, p. 296; Fritzsche, i. 181.

HIS OWN FATHER AND OWN MOTHER

But Hermes also was of the same opinion when he says:

"His own father and His own mother."[2]

xiv. *Ibid.*, iv. 9, 3; Brandt, p. 300; Fritzsche, i. 182, 183.

THE POWER AND GREATNESS OF THE WORD

Trismegistus, who has tracked out, I know not how, almost all truth, has often described the power and greatness of the Word (*Logos*), as the above quotation[3] from him shows, in which he confesses the Word to be Ineffable and Holy, and in that its telling forth transcends the power of man.

xv. *Ibid.*, iv. 13, 2; Brandt, p. 316; Fritzsche, i. 190.

THE FATHERLESS AND MOTHERLESS

For God, the Father, and the Source, and Principle of things, in that He hath no parents, is very truly called by Trismegistus "father-less" and "mother-less"[4] in that He is brought forth from none.[5]

---

[1] This passage and the preceding, then, are evidently taken from "The Sermons to Tat." Lactantius quotes in Greek, and again refers to the passage in iv. 9.

[2] αὐτοπάτορα καὶ αὐτομήτορα—not found in the extant texts; but for the idea see *C. H.*, i. 9. See also iv. 13, and Ep. 4 below.

[3] *Ibid.*, iv. 7.

[4] ἀπάτωρ et ἀμήτωρ. *Cf.* Lact., *D. I.*, i. 7, 2 (Brandt).

[5] Terms not found in our extant texts; probably taken from the same source as the terms in iv. 8 above.

xvi. *Ibid.*, v. 14, 11 ; Brandt, p. 446 ; Fritzsche, i. 256.

PIETY THE GNOSIS OF GOD

But "piety is nothing else than Gnosis of God,"[1] as Trismegistus has most truly laid down, as we have said in another place.[2]

xvii. *Ibid.*, vi. 25, 10 ; Brandt, p. 579 ; Fritzsche, ii. 60.

THE ONLY WAY TO WORSHIP GOD

Concerning justice, he [Trismegistus, who in this (namely concerning sacrifice) "agrees substantially and verbally with the prophets"] has thus spoken:

"Unto this Word (*Logos*), my son, thy adoration and thy homage pay. There is one way alone to worship God,—[it is] not to be bad."

Here Lactantius translates literally from *C. H.*, xii. (xiii.) 23, a sermon which now bears the title, "About the Common Mind to Tat." Hermes, however, in the context of the quoted passage, is not writing "about justice," and much less could the whole sermon be so entitled, if indeed Lactantius intended us so to understand it. But see the Commentary, *C. H.*, xii. (xiii.) 6, and Ex. xi., "On Justice."

xviii. *Ibid.*, v. 25, 11 ; Brandt, p. 579 ; Fritzsche, ii. 60.

THE WORTHIEST SACRIFICE TO GOD

Also in that "Perfect Sermon," when he heard Asclepius enquiring of his son,[3] whether it would be pleasing to his[4] father, that incense and other perfumes

[1] *Notio dei.* [2] Namely ii. 15, 6 ; *q.v.* for comment.
[3] That is, Hermes' son Tat.
[4] That is, Tat's father, Hermes.

should be offered in their holy rite to God, [Hermes] exclaimed:

FRAGMENT VIII.

Nay, nay; speak more propitiously, O [my] Asclepius! For very great impiety is it to let come in the mind any such thought about that One and Only Good.

These things, and things like these, are not appropriate to Him. For He is full of all things that exist and least of all stands He in need [of aught].

But let us worship pouring forth our thanks. The [worthiest] sacrifice to Him is blessing, [and blessing] only.

With this compare the passage in *P. S. A.*, xli. 2 (p. 61, 16, Goldb.). Here again we have the means of controlling the old Latin translator, but not with such exactitude as before, for Lactantius has also turned the Greek text into Latin. But not only from the other specimens of Lactantius' Hermes translations, but also from his present close reproduction of the ordinary wording of the Trismegistic treatises, we may be further confident that the Old Latin translation is free, paraphrastic, and rhetorical, as we have already remarked.

xix. *Ibid.*, vii. 4, 3; Brandt, p. 593; Fritzsche, ii. 69.

MAN MADE IN THE IMAGE OF GOD

But Hermes was not ignorant that man was made by God and in the Image of God.[1]

[1] See above, *ibid.*, ii. 10, 13, Comment.

xx. *Ibid.*, vii. 9, 11; Brandt, p. 612; Fritzsche, ii. 82.

CONTEMPLATION

(Speaking of man being the only animal that has his body upright, and face raised to heaven, looking towards his Maker, Lactantius says :)

And this "looking" Hermes has most rightly named contemplation.[1]

xxi. *Ibid.*, vii. 13, 3; Brandt, p. 624; Fritzsche, ii. 90.

THE DUAL NATURE OF MAN

Hermes, in describing the nature of man, in order that he might teach how he was made by God, brings forward the following :

FRAGMENT IX.

From the two natures, the deathless and mortal, He made one nature,—that of man,— one and the self-same thing; and having made the self-same [man] both somehow deathless and somehow mortal, He brought him forth, and set him up betwixt[2] the godlike and immortal

---

[1] θεοπτίαν = θεωρίαν. See, for instance, *C. H.*, xiv. (xv.) 1, and *K. K.*, 1, 38, 51; also Frag. *ap.* Stob., *Flor.*, xi. 23; and also compare *C. H.*, iv. (v.) 2: "For contemplator (θεατής) of God's works did man become." It is also of interest to note that Justin Martyr (*Dial. c. Tryph.*, 218 c) enumerates the Theoretics or Contemplatives, among the most famous sects of Philosophers, naming them in the following order : Platonics, Stoics, Peripatetics, Theoretics, Pythagorics.

[2] Compare the "setting up betwixt" (ἐν μέσῳ . . . ἵδρυσεν) with the "setting up" of the mind "in the midst" (ἐν μέσῳ . . . ἱδρῦσθαι) of *C. H.*, iv. (v.) 3.

nature and the mortal, that seeing all he might wonder at all.

Wonder the Beginning of Philosophy

This idea of "wondering" was, doubtless, a commonplace in Hellenistic philosophical circles and looked back to the Platonic saying: "There is no other beginning of Philosophy than wondering." Compare also one of the newest found "Logoi of Jesus," from the rubbish heaps of Oxyrhynchus, which runs: "Let not him that seeketh . . . cease until he find, and when he finds he shall wonder; wondering he shall reign, and reigning he shall rest."[1]

Wondering is the beginning of Gnosis; this makes a man king of himself, and thus master of gods and men, and so he has peace. The translation of $\beta\alpha\sigma\iota\lambda\epsilon\acute{u}\sigma\epsilon\iota$ by Grenfell and Hunt as "reach the kingdom" seems to me to have no justification.

Lactantius here quotes the Greek text of *P. S. A.*, viii. 3, and so once again we can control the Old Latin version. The Church Father is plainly the more reliable, reproducing as he does familiar Hermetic phrasing and style; and we thus again have an insight into the methods of our rhetorical, truncated, and interpolated Latin Version.

xxii. *Ibid.*, vii. 18, 3; Brandt, p. 640; Fritzsche, ii. 99.

The Cosmic Restoration

And Hermes states this [the destruction of the world][2] plainly. For in that book which bears the title

[1] Grenfell (B. P.) and Hunt (A. S.), *New Sayings of Jesus*, p. 13 (London, 1904).
[2] *Cf.* iv. 7 above.

of "The Perfect Sermon," after an enumeration of the evils of which we have spoken, he adds:

FRAGMENT X.

Now when these things shall be, as I have said, Asclepius, then will [our] Lord and Sire, the God and Maker of the First and the One God,[1] look down on what is done, and, making firm His Will,—that is the Good,—against disorder, recalling error, and purging out the bad, either by washing it away with water-flood, or burning it away with swiftest fire, or forcibly expelling it with war and famine,—He [then] will bring again His Cosmos to its former state, and so achieve its Restoration.[2]

xxiii. *Ibid.*, *Epitome*, 4, 4; Brandt, p 679; Fritzsche, ii. 117.

OF HERMES AND HIS DOCTRINE CONCERNING GOD

Hermes,—who, on account of his virtue and knowledge of many arts, gained the title of Thrice-greatest, who also in the antiquity of his doctrine preceded the philosophers, and who is worshipped as god among the Egyptians,—declaring the greatness of the One and Only God with unending praises, calls Him God and Father, [and says] He has no name, for that He has no need for a distinctive name,[3] inasmuch as He alone is,

[1] *Cf.* Frag. v.
[2] Lactantius quotes the original Greek of *P. S. A.*, xxvi. 1 (p. 48, 24, Goldb.), so that we can thus once more remark the liberties which the Old Latin translation has taken with the text.
[3] *Cf.* Frag. ii.

nor has He any parents, in that He is both from Himself and by Himself.[1]

In writing to his son [Tat] he begins as follows:

"To comprehend God is difficult, to speak [of Him] impossible, even for one who can comprehend; for the Perfect cannot be comprehended by the imperfect, nor the Invisible by the visible."[2]

xxiv. *Ibid.*, *Ep.*, 14; Brandt, p. 685; Fritzsche, ii. 121.

A REPETITION

(Lactantius repeats in almost identical words what he has written in i. 11.)

xxv. *Ibid.*, *Ep.*, 37 (42), 2; Brandt, p. 712; Fritzsche, ii. 140.

PLATO AS PROPHET FOLLOWS TRISMEGISTUS

By means of him [the Logos] as Demiurge,[3] as Hermes says, He [God the Father] hath devised the beautiful and wondrous creation of the world. . . .

Finally Plato has spoken concerning the first and second God, not plainly as a philosopher, but as a prophet, perchance in this following Trismegistus, whose words I have added in translation from the Greek.

(Lactantius then translates verbally from the Greek text he has quoted in iv. 6, 4, omitting, however, the last clause and the parenthesis in the middle.)

[1] See i. 6 and iv. 8 above.

[2] The first clause is a verbatim translation of the text of the Stobæan Extract ii., while the second is a paraphrase even of L.'s own version from the Greek (see ii. 8 above). We learn, however, the new scrap of information that the quotation is from the beginning of the sermon.

[3] The reference to the "Demiurge" looks back to iv. 6, 9.

VIII.

AUGUSTINE

i. *De Civitate Dei*, xxiii.; Hoffmann (E.), i. 392 (Vienna, 1899–1900).[1]

Three Quotations from the Old Latin Version of the "Perfect Sermon"

AUGUSTINE is arguing against the views of Appulcius (first half of the second century) on the cult of the "daimones," and in so doing introduces a long disquisition on the doctrine of "Egyptian Hermes, whom they call Thrice-greatest," concerning image-worship, or the consecrated and "ensouled," or "animated," statues of the gods.

In the course of his remarks the Bishop of Hippo quotes at length from a current Latin version[2] of "The Perfect Sermon" or "Asclepius" (though without himself giving any title), which we see at once must have been the very same text that has come down to us in its entirety. It is precisely the same text, word for word, with ours; the variants being practically of the most minute character.

[1] *Corpus Scriptorum Ecclesiasticorum Latinorum*, vol. xxx. (Imp. Acad. of Vienna). The date of the writing of the treatise, *De Civitate Dei*, is fixed as being about 413–426 A.D.

[2] *Hujus Ægyptii verba, sicut in nostram linguam interpretata sunt.*

First of all Augustine quotes from *P. S. A.*, xxiii. 3, xxiv. 2. This "prophecy" of the downfall of the Egyptian religion Augustine naturally takes as referring to the triumph of Christianity, and so he ridicules Hermes "[*qui*] *tam impudenter dolebat, quam imprudentur sciebat.*"

ii. *Ibid.*, xxiv.; Hoffmann, i. 396.

The Bishop of Hippo begins his next chapter with a quotation from *P. S. A.*, xxxvii. 1, 2, on the same subject, and proceeds scornfully to criticise the statements of the Trismegistic writer.

iii. *Ibid.*, xxvi.; Hoffmann, i. 402.

After quoting the sentence, from *P. S. A.*, xxiv. 3, in which Hermes says that the pure temples of Egypt will all be polluted with tombs and corpses, Augustine proceeds to contend that the gods of Egypt are all dead men, and in support of his contention he quotes *P. S. A.*, xxxvii. 3, 4.

IX.

CYRIL OF ALEXANDRIA [1]

i. *Contra Julianum*, i. 30 ; Migne, col. 548 A.[2]

Cyril's Corpus of XV. Books

(Cyril, after claiming that Pythagoras and Plato obtained their wisdom in Egypt from what, he professes, they had heard of Moses there, proceeds :)

And I think the Egyptian Hermes also should be considered worthy of mention and recollection—he who, they say, bears the title of Thrice-greatest because of the honour paid him by his contemporaries, and, as some think, in comparison with Hermes the fabled son of Zeus and Maia.

This Hermes of Egypt, then, although an initiator into mysteries,[3] and though he never ceased to cleave to the shrines of idols, is [nevertheless] found to have grasped the doctrines of Moses, if not with entire correctness, and beyond all cavil, yet still in part.

---

[1] The date of Cyril's patriarchate is 412–444 A.D.

[2] Migne (J. P.), *Patrologiæ Cursus Completus*, Series Græca, tom. lxxvi. (Paris, 1859). *S. P. N. Cyrilli . . . Pro Christiana Religione adversus Julianum Imperatorem Libri Decem*. The text is also given R. 211, n. 1.

[3] τελεστής.

For both [Hermes] himself has been benefitted [by Moses], and reminder of this [fact] has also been made in his own writings by [the editor] at Athens who put together the fifteen books entitled "Hermaïca." [This editor] writes concerning him [Hermes] in the first book, putting the words into the mouth of one of the priests of the sacred rites:

"In order then that we may come to things of a like nature (?),—have you not heard that our Hermes divided the whole of Egypt into allotments and portions, measuring off the acres with the chain,[1] and cut canals for irrigation purposes, and made nomes,[2] and named the lands [comprised in them] after them, and established the interchange of contracts, and drew up a list of the risings of the stars, and [the proper times [3]] to cut plants; and beyond all this he discovered and bequeathed to posterity numbers, and calculations, and geometry, and astronomy, and astrology, and music, and the whole of grammar?"

This Corpus of XV. Books is evidently the source of Cyril's information, and he takes the above quotation from the Introduction, which purported to be written by an Egyptian priest (as is also the case in the treatise *De Mysteriis*, traditionally ascribed to Jamblichus), but which Cyril says was written at Athens, by presumably some Greek editor.[4]

[1] "Acres," lit. = areas 100 Egyptian cubits square; and "chain," lit. = measuring cord.

[2] Or provinces; Migne's Latin translator gives this as "laws"!

[3] *Sc.* of the moon.

[4] ὁ συντεθεικὼς 'Αθήνησι, a phrase which Chambers (p. 149) erroneously translates by "which he [Hermes] having composed for Athenians"! R. (p. 211, n. 1) thinks this redactor was some Neoplatonist.

ii. *Ibid.*, i. 31; Migne col. 549 B.

THE INCORPOREAL EYE

Thrice-greatest Hermes says somewhat as follows:

(Cyril then quotes, with four slight verbal variants, the first four paragraphs of the passage excerpted by Stobæus, Ex. ii., and then proceeds without a break:)

FRAGMENT XI.

If, then, there be an incorporeal eye,[1] let it go forth from body unto the Vision of the Beautiful; let it fly up and soar aloft, seeking to see not form, nor body, nor [even] types[2] [of things], but rather That which is the Maker of [all] these, —the Quiet and Serene, the Stable and the Changeless One, the Self, the All, the One, the Self of self, the Self in self, the Like to Self [alone], That which is neither like to other, nor [yet] unlike to self, and [yet] again Himself.[3]

Though Cyril runs this passage on to the four paragraphs which in the Stobæan Extract are continued by three other paragraphs, I am quite persuaded that the Archbishop of Alexandria took the above from the same "Sermon to Tat"[4] as the Anthologist.[5]

[1] Sc. the soul.
[2] *Sc.* ideas.
[3] Masc., not neut., as are all the preceding "self's." There is also throughout a play on "self" and "same" which is unreproducible in English.
[4] That is, presumably, the "First Sermon of the Expository [Sermons] to Tat" (see Comment to the Stobæan Excerpt).
[5] See also Fragg. xii., xiii., xv., xx., xxii., xxiii., xxiv. (?).

iii. *Ibid.*, i. 33; Migne, col. 552 D.

THE HEAVENLY WORD PROCEEDING FORTH

And Thrice-greatest Hermes thus delivers himself concerning God:

FRAGMENT XII.

For that His Word (*Logos*) proceeding forth,[1] —all-perfect as he was, and fecund, and creative—in fecund Nature, falling on fecund[2] Water, made Water pregnant.[3]

THE PYRAMID

And the same again [declares]:

FRAGMENT XIII.

The Pyramid, then, is below [both] Nature and the Intellectual World.[4] For that it[5] hath above it ruling it the Creator-Word[6] of the Lord of all,—who, being the First Power after

---

[1] R. (p. 43) glosses this with "out of the mouth of God," but I see no necessity for introducing this symbolism.

[2] The adjective γόνιμος ("fecund") is applied to both Logos and Physis (Nature); it might thus be varied as seedful and fruitful, or spermal and productive. *Cf.* Frag. xiii. Text reproduced R. 43.

[3] Compare *C. H.*, i. 8, 14, 15. This Fragment is also quoted, but plainly reproduced from Cyril, by Suidas (*q.v.*).

[4] That is, the Logos.

[5] *Sc.* the Pyramid, in physics the symbol of fire. See Frag. xxii.

[6] δημιουργὸν λόγον. Compare Lact., *D. I.*, iv. 6, 9.

Him, [both] increate [and] infinite, leaned forth [1] from Him, and has his seat above, and rule o'er all that have been made through him. He is the First-born of the All-perfection, His perfect, fecund and true Son.[2]

The Nature of God's Intellectual Word

And again the same [Hermes], when one of the Temple-folk [3] in Egypt questions him and says:

FRAGMENT XIV.

But why, O most mighty Good Daimon, was he [4] called by this name [5] by the Lord of all?—replies:

Yea, have I told thee in what has gone before, but thou hast not perceived it.

The nature of His Intellectual Word (*Logos*) is a productive and creative Nature. This is as though it were His Power-of-giving-birth,[6] or [His] Nature, or [His] Mode of being, or call it

---

[1] προκύψασα—that is, projected, presumably with the idea of emanation. Compare the hymn: "O Heavenly Word proceeding forth, Yet leaving not the Father's side." Compare the παρέκυψεν of *C. H.*, i. 14, and note.

[2] Compare *C. H.*, i. 6, 9, 10; xiii. (xiv.) 3; xiv. (xv.) 3. For slightly revised text, see R. 243, n. 3. Reitzenstein thinks that the image which the writer had in his mind was the pyramid, or obelisk, with the sun-disk on the top.

[3] τεμενιτῶν. The questioner was undoubtedly Osiris (see Frag. xix. below). Cyril then knows that "Osiris" was understood to stand for a grade of Egyptian priests. *Cf.* R. 131.

[4] Presumably the Logos.   [5] Presumably "Soul" (*Psychē*).

[6] γένεσις.

what you will,—only remembering this: that He is Perfect in the Perfect, and from the Perfect makes, and creates, and makes to live, perfect good things.

Since, then, He hath this nature, rightly is He thus named.[1]

THE WORD OF THE CREATOR

And the same [Hermes], in the First Sermon of the "Expository [Sermons] to Tat,"[2] speaks thus about God:

FRAGMENT XV.

The Word (*Logos*) of the Creator, O [my] son, transcends all sight; He [is] self-moved; He cannot be increased, nor [yet] diminished; Alone is He, and like unto Himself [Alone], equal, identical, perfect in His stability, perfect in order; for that He is the One, after the God alone beyond all knowing.

The first two Fragments (xi. and xii.) seem to be taken from the same sermon, the contents of which resembled the first part of the "Shepherd of Men" treatise; it has all the appearance of a discourse addressed to Tat, and probably came in "The Expository Sermons."

[1] This passage seems to refer to the identity of Soul and Logos. For revised text see R. 131, and the reference there to Plato, *Cratylus*, 400 B, where ψυχή, soul, is explained by the word-play φυσέχη, that is, that which has *physis*, or nature, or the power of production.

[2] τῶν πρὸς τὸν Τὰτ διεξοδικῶν.

The third Fragment (xiii.) belongs to the more frankly Egyptian type, the Agathodaimon literature, in which Hermes, as the Good Spirit, figures as the teacher of the Mystery-god Osiris.[1]

The last Fragment (xv.) is so similar in its phrasing to Fragment xi., already given by Cyril (i. 31), that I am strongly inclined to think the Archbishop took both from the same source. If so, we can reconstruct part of "The First Sermon of the Expository [Sermons] to Tat," the beginning of which (see Lact., *Ep.*, 4) is also given by Stobæus, Ex. ii., with the heading from "The [Book] to Tat," while he heads other extracts "From the [pl.] to Tat."[2]

v. *Ibid.*, ii. 35; Migne, col. 556 A.

MIND OF MIND

And Hermes also says in the Third Sermon of those to Asclepius:

FRAGMENT XVI.

It is not possible such mysteries [as these] should be declared to those who are without initiation in the sacred rites. But ye, lend [me] your ears, [ears] of your mind!

There was One Intellectual Light alone,— nay, Light transcending Intellectual Light. He is for ever Mind of mind[3] who makes [that] Light to shine.

[1] See Frag. xix. below, where Cyril (ii. 56) says that this type was found in the "Sermon to Asclepius," that is, was put with the Asclepius-books in the collection which lay before him.

[2] See also Fragg. xi., xii., xiii., xx., xxii., xxiii., xxiv. (?).

[3] *Cf.* K. K., 16.

There was no other; [naught] save the Oneness of Himself [alone]. For ever in Himself [alone], for ever doth He compass all in His own Mind,—His Light and Spirit.[1]

HE IS ALL

And after some other things he says:

FRAGMENT XVII.

Without Him [2] [is] neither god, nor angel, nor daimon, nor any other being. For He is Lord of all, [their] Father, and [their] God, and Source, and Life, and Power, and Light, and Mind, and Spirit. For all things are in Him and for His sake.[3]

CONCERNING SPIRIT

And again, in the same Third Sermon of those to Asclepius, in reply to one who questions [him] concerning the Divine Spirit, the same [Hermes] says as follows:

FRAGMENT XVIII.

Had there not been some Purpose [4] of the Lord of all, so that I should disclose this word

[1] That is, Light and Life. See *C. H.*, i. 9: "God, the Mind, . . . being Life and Light."

[2] Lit. outside of Him.

[3] For a fuller statement of the idea in this paragraph, see *C. H.*, ii. (iii.) 14. Cyril thinks that the above two Fragments refer to the Father, Son (Mind of mind and Light of light) and Holy Ghost (the Divine supremacy and power), and is thus the source of the statement in Suidas (*s.v.* "Hermes") that Trismegistus spoke concerning the Trinity.

[4] Or Providence, πρόνοια. R. (203, n. 2) refers this to a belief that only when some internal prompting gave permission to the

(*logos*), ye would not have been filled with so great love[1] to question me about it. Now give ye ear unto the rest of the discourse (*logos*).

Of this same Spirit, of which I have already spoken many times, all things have need; for that it raises up all things, each in its own degree, and makes them live, and gives them nourishment, and [finally] removes them from its holy source,[2] aiding the spirit,[3] and for ever giving life to all, the [one] productive One."

THE "TO ASCLEPIUS" OF CYRIL'S CORPUS

From the above statements of Cyril we learn that in addition to "The Expository Sermons to Tat," he had also before him a collection of "Sermons to Asclepius"; of these there were at least three. Was "The Perfect Sermon" one of this collection? It may have been; for the style of it is cast in the same mould as that of these Fragments in Cyril.

Hermes, in the Third Sermon of Cyril's collection, is addressing several hearers, for he uses the plural; so also in *P. S. A.*, i. 2. Hermes addresses Asclepius, Tat, and Ammon.

In the Third Sermon, Hermes also says: "It is not possible such mysteries should be declared to those

master to expand the teaching, could he do so. *Cf.* Appul., *Metam.*, xi. 21, 22; *P. S. A.*, i.

[1] ἔρως τοιοῦτος.

[2] That is, presumably, causing their seeming death.

[3] That is, the individual life-breath, unless the reading ἐπίκουρον πνεύματι is corrupt. The Latin translator in Migne goes hopelessly wrong, as, indeed, is frequently the case. *Cf. C. H.*, x. (xi.) 13, Comment; *P. S. A.*, vi. 4; Exx. iv. 2, xv. 2, xix. 3.

who are without initiation in the sacred rites"; in
P. S. A., i. 2, Hermes declares: "It is a mark of an
impious mind to publish to the knowledge of the
crowd[1] a tractate[2] brimming o'er with the full grandeur
of divinity." The *numinis majestas* (grandeur of
divinity) is precisely the same idea as the Spirit, the
" Divine supremacy and power," as Cyril says referring
to Hermes.

Finally, in the Third Sermon, Hermes makes the
striking remark that the Love ($ἔρως$) of the Gnosis
which urges on the disciples, is inspired by the Providence or Foresight of God—that is, by His Spirit;
P. S. A., i. 28, ends with the words: "To them, sunk
in fit silence reverently, their souls and minds pendent
on Hermes' lips, thus Love ($ἔρως$) Divine[3] began to
speak."

The setting of the mode of exposition is then identical in the two Sermons, and we may thus very well
refer them to the same collection.

v. *Ibid.*, ii. 52; Migne, col. 580 B.

FROM "THE MIND"

To this I will add what Thrice-greatest Hermes wrote
" To his own Mind,"—for thus the Book is called.

(Cyril then quotes, with very slight verbal variants,
the last question and answer in *C. H.*, xi. (xii.) 22.)

In our Corpus the treatise is not written by Hermes
to the Mind, but, on the contrary, it is cast in the mould
of a revelation of "The Mind to Hermes," and is so

[1] That is, the uninitiated, the *profanum vulgus*.
[2] *Tractatus*; presumably *logos* in the original Greek.
[3] *Cf.* also *P. S. A.*, xx. 2 and xxi. 1, 3.

entitled. Cyril thus seems to have been mistaken.[1] It may, then, have been that in the copy which lay before the Church Father, the title read simply: "The Mind."

vi. *Ibid.*, ii. 55 ; Migne, col. 586 D.[2]

OSIRIS AND THRICE-GREATEST AGATHODAIMON

But I will call to mind the words of Hermes the Thrice-greatest; in "The Asclepius"[3] he says:

FRAGMENT XIX.

Osiris said : How, then, O thou Thrice-greatest, [thou] Good Spirit,[4] did Earth in its entirety appear ?

The Great Good Spirit made reply :

By gradual drying up, as I have said ; and when the many Waters got commandment . . .[5] to go into themselves again, the Earth in its entirety appeared, muddy and shaking.

Then, when the Sun shone forth, and without ceasing burned and dried it up, the Earth stood compact in the Waters, with Water all around.[6]

[1] *Cf.* R. 128, n. 1.

[2] Texts of quotations reproduced in R. 127, n. 1.

[3] From the quotations we can see that this could not have been the special heading of the treatise from which Cyril quotes, and which plainly belongs to the Agathodaimon type. Cyril probably means that the treatise, in *his* collection, came under the general title, "The Asclepius."

[4] Ἀγαθὸς δαίμων.

[5] The reading is an untranslatable ἀπὸ τοῦ, where the *lacuna* is probably to be completed with "from the Lord of all."

[6] A distinction is evidently drawn between the (heavenly)

"LET THERE BE EARTH"

Further, in yet another place [he writes]:

FRAGMENT XX.

The Maker and the Lord of all thus spake: Let there be Earth, and let the Firmament appear[1]!

And forthwith the beginning of the [whole] creation, Earth, was brought into existence.[2]

THE GENERATION OF THE SUN

So much about the Earth; as to the Sun, he again says as follows:

FRAGMENT XXI.

Then said Osiris: O thou Thrice-greatest, [thou] Good Spirit, whence came this mighty one?

Would'st thou, Osiris, that we tell to thee the generation of the Sun, whence he appeared?

He came from out the Foresight of the Lord of all; yea, the Sun's birth proceedeth from

Water and water (the companion element of earth). The text is immediately continued in Frag. xxi. below.

[1] See *C. H.*, i. 18, Commentary.

[2] This seems to be taken not from a different place in the "To Asclepius," but from another sermon, or group of sermons, most probably from the "First Expository Sermon to Tat"—as may be seen by comparing its phrasing with Frag. xxii. See also Fragg. xi., xii., xiii., xv., xxii., xxiii., xxiv. (?).

the Lord of all, through His Creative Holy Word.[1]

"LET THE SUN BE!"

In like manner also in the "First Expository Sermon to Tat," he says:

FRAGMENT XXII.

Straightway the Lord of all spake unto His own Holy and Intelligible — to His Creative Word (*Logos*) : Let the Sun be!

And straightway with His word (*logos*), the Fire that hath its nature tending upward,[2]—I mean pure [Fire], that which gives greatest light, has the most energy, and fecundates the most,—Nature embraced[3] with her own Spirit, and raised it up aloft out of the Water.[4]

(After referring to Genesis i. 6: "And God said, Let there be a firmament in the midst of the waters, and let it divide the waters from the waters,"—Cyril proceeds:)

vii. *Ibid.*, ii. 57 ; Migne, col. 588 c.

THE FIRMAMENT

Moreover the Hermes who is with them[5] Thrice-

[1] This is evidently an immediate continuation of Frag. xix. above. *Cf.* R. 126, n. 1, where the texts are reproduced.

[2] See Frag. xiii. below, concerning the pyramid.

[3] Embraced the Fire.

[4] *Sc.* the Water-Earth, one element, not yet separated, according to *C. H.*, i. 5. For other probable quotations from this "First Expository Sermon to Tat," see Fragg. xi., xii., xiii., xv., xx., xxiii., xxiv. (?).

[5] *Sc.* the philosophers.

greatest mentions this [that is, the firmament] again. For he describes God as saying to His creations:

FRAGMENT XXIII.

I will encompass you with this Necessity, you who are disobedient to me,[1] which hath been laid on you as a Command through My own Word (*Logos*); for him ye have as Law.

This quotation also is probably taken from the same source as the previous passage—that is, from the "First Expository Sermon to Tat." The idea and setting, however, should also be compared with the parallel in the *K. K.* Excerpt (Stob., *Phys.*, xli. 44; Gaisf., p. 408): "O Souls, Love and Necessity shall be your lords, they who are lords and marshals after me of all,"—where the "after me" ($\mu\epsilon\tau$' $\dot{\epsilon}\mu\dot{\epsilon}$) might perhaps confirm the "up to me" in the preceding note as the more correct rendering.

viii. *Ibid.*, ii. 64 ; Migne, col. 598 D.

FROM THE "TO ASCLEPIUS"

For Hermes, who is called Thrice-greatest, writes thus to Asclepius about the nature of the universe:

(Here follows with a few slight verbal variants the text of *C. H.*, xiv. (xv.) 6, 7, beginning: "If, then, all things have been admitted to be two.")

[1] $\tau o \hat{i} s$ $\dot{\epsilon}\pi$' $\dot{\epsilon}\mu\epsilon$,—lit. "against me," or it may perhaps be "up to me." Migne's Latin translator gives "*qui in mea potestatis estis*," and Chambers (p. 153), "those from me"; neither of which can be correct.

And some lines after he proceeds in warmer language, setting forth a striking argument, and says:

(Then follows §§ 8, 9 of the same sermon, except the third sentence, and § 10 omitting the last sentence.)[1]

The same treatise must have lain before Cyril as that contained in our Corpus in the form of a letter with the heading, "Unto Asclepius good health of soul!"—for the Archbishop says that Hermes "writes thus to Asclepius."[2]

ix. *Ibid.*, iv. 130; Migne, col. 702.

THE SOLE PROTECTION

(After quoting Porphyry as warning against participation in blood-rites for fear of contamination from evil daimons, Cyril proceeds:)

And their Thrice-greatest Hermes seems also to be of the same opinion; for he, too, writes as follows, in the [sermon] "To Asclepius," concerning those unholy daimons against whom we ought to protect ourselves, and flee from them with all the speed we can:

"The sole protection—and this we must have—is piety. For neither evil daimon, yea nor Fate, can ever overcome or dominate a man who pious is, and pure, and holy. For God doth save the truly pious man from every ill."[3]

[1] Cyril also twice omits the words "ignorance and jealousy" after "arrogance and impotence" in § 8, and also the words "and yet the other things" in § 9.

[2] *Cf.* Frag. iv., Comment.

[3] *Cf. P. S. A.*, xxix. 1. A comparison of this with Frag. iv., quoted by Lactantius (ii. 15), and the Commentary thereon, shows clearly that Cyril has strengthened the original text by interpola-

x. *Ibid.*, viii. 274 ; Migne, col. 920 D.

THE SUPREME ARTIST

Moreover, their Thrice-greatest Hermes has said somewhere about God, the Supreme Artist[1] of all things:

FRAGMENT XXIV.

Moreover, as perfectly wise He established Order and its opposite[2]; in order that things intellectual, as being older and better, might have the government of things and the chief place, and that things sensible, as being second, might be subject to these.

Accordingly that which tends downward, and is heavier than the intellectual, has in itself the wise Creative Word (*Logos*).[3]

xi. *Ibid.* (?).

AN UNREFERENCED QUOTATION

(Chambers (p. 154) gives the following, "*Cyrill. Contra Julian., citing Hermes*," but without any reference, and I can find it nowhere in the text:)

FRAGMENT XXV.

If thou understandest that One and Sole God, thou wilt find nothing impossible; for It is all virtue.

tions. Cyril's quotation (v. 176) from Julian, in which the Emperor refers to Hermes, is given under "Julian."

[1] ἀριστοτεχνοῦ,—an epithet applied by Pindar (Fr. 29) to Zeus.
[2] ἀταξίαν.
[3] This seems somewhat of a piece with the contents of the "First Expository Sermon to Tat." See Fragg. xi., xii., xiii., xv, xx., xxii., xxiii.

Think not that It may be in some one; say not that it is out of some one.

It is without termination; it is the termination of all.

Nothing contains It; for It contains all in Itself.

What difference is there then between the body and the Incorporeal, the created and the Uncreated; that which is subject to necessity, and what is Free; between the things terrestrial and things Celestial, the things corruptible and things Eternal?

Is it not that the One exists freely and that the others are subject to necessity?

X.

SUIDAS [1]

Lexicon, s.v. Ἑρμῆς ὁ τρισμέγιστος ; Im. Bekker (Berlin 1854).

HERMES SPEAKS OF THE TRINITY

Hermes the Thrice-greatest.—He was an Egyptian sage, and flourished before Pharaoh. He was called Thrice-greatest because he spoke of the Trinity, declaring that in the Trinity there is One Godhead, as follows:

"Before Intellectual Light was Light Intellectual; Mind of mind, too, was there eternally, Light-giving. There was naught else except the Oneness of this [Mind] and Spirit all-embracing.

"Without this is nor god, nor angel, nor any other being. For He is Lord and Father, and the God of all; and all things are beneath Him, [all things are] in Him.[2]

(The source of Suidas, or of his editor, is manifestly

---

[1] Date uncertain; some indications point to as late as the twelfth century; if these, however, are due to later redaction, others point to the tenth century.

[2] He is above them as Lord and Father, as Mind and Light; and they are in Him as Lady and Mother, as Spirit and Life.

Cyril, *C. J.*, i. 35 (Fragg. xvi., xvii.), of which a very garbled edition is reproduced. The same statement and passage is also quoted by Cedrenus, John Malalas, and the author of the *Chronicum Alexandrinum*. See Bernhardy's edition of Suidas (Halle, 1853), i. 527, notes.) Suidas then continues without a break:)

"His Word (*Logos*), all-perfect as he was, and fecund, and creative, falling in fecund Nature, yea in fecund Water, made Water pregnant."[1]

After saying this he has the following prayer:

AN ORPHIC HYMN

"Thee, Heaven, I adjure, wise work of mighty God; thee I adjure, Word[2] of the Father which He spake first, when He established all the world!

"Thee I adjure, [O Heaven], by the alone-begotten Word (*Logos*) himself, and by the Father of the Word alone-begotten, yea, by the Father who surroundeth all,—be gracious, be gracious!"

This is not a prayer from Hermes, but three verses (the last somewhat altered) of an Orphic hymn excerpted from Cyril, *ibid.*, i. 33 (Migne, col. 552 c),—lines also attributed to "Orpheus" by Justin Martyr. The last half of the prayer seems to be a pure invention of Suidas, or of his editor, based partially on Cyril's comments.

[1] This is again, and this time almost verbally, taken from Cyril *ibid.*, i. 33 ; Frag. xii.
[2] φωνήν.

XI.

ANONYMOUS

AND here we may conveniently append a reference to the Dialogue of an ancient Christian writer on astrology—a blend of Platonism, Astrology, and Christianity—entitled *Hermippus de Astrologia Dialogus*,[1] from the name of the chief speaker.

This writer was undoubtedly acquainted with our Corpus, for he quotes (p. 9, 3) from *C. H.*, i. 5; (p. 21, 5) from *C. H.*, x. (xi.) 12; (p. 70, 17) from *C. H.*, x. (xi.) 6; in a general fashion (p. 24, 25) from *C. H.*, xvi.; and phrases (p. 12, 21 and p. 14, 13) from *C. H.*, xviii.

[1] Kroll (G.) and Viereck (P.), *Anonymi Christiani de Astrologia Dialogus* (Leipzig, 1895). *Cf.* R. p. 210.

III

References and Fragments in the Philosophers

I.

ZOSIMUS

On the Anthrōpos-Doctrine

(Zosimus flourished somewhere at the end of the third and beginning of the fourth century A.D. He was a member of what Reitzenstein (p. 9) calls the Poimandres-Gemeinde, and, in writing to a certain Theosebeia, a fellow-believer in the Wisdom-tradition, though not as yet initiated into its spiritual mysteries, he urges her to hasten to Poimandres and baptize herself in the Cup.[1] The following quotation is of first importance for the understanding of the Anthrōpos-Doctrine or Myth of Man in the Mysteries.

In one of the Books of his great work distinguished by the letter Omega, and dedicated to Oceanus as the "Genesis and Seed of all the Gods,"—speaking of the uninitiated, those still beneath the sway of the Heimarmenē or Fate, who cannot understand his revelations,—he writes[2]:)

The Processions of Fate.

1. Such men [our] Hermes, in his "Concerning Nature," hath called mind-less,—naught but "processions"[3] of

[1] *Op. sub. cit.*, p. 245.

[2] Berthelot, *Les Alchimistes grecs*, pp. 229 ff. For a revised text, see R. pp. 102–106.

[3] πομπάς,—processions, shows, or pageants. *Cf. C. H.*, iv. (v.) 7: "Just as processions pass by in the middle of the way without

Fate,—in that they have no notion¹ of aught of things incorporal, or even of Fate herself who justly leads them, but they blaspheme her corporal schoolings, and have no notion of aught else but of her favours.

"The Inner Door"

2. But Hermes and Zoroaster have said the Race of Wisdom-lovers is superior to Fate, by their neither rejoicing in her favours, — for they have mastered pleasures,—not by their being struck down by her ills,—for ever living at the "Inner Door,"² and not receiving³ from her her fair gift, in that they look unto the termination of [her] ills.⁴

3. On which account, too, Hesiod doth introduce Prometheus counselling Epimetheus, and doth tell him⁵ not to take the Gift⁶ from Zeus who rules Olympus, but send it back again,—[thus] teaching his own brother through philosophy⁷ to return the Gifts of Zeus,—that is, of Fate.

4. But Zoroaster, boasting in knowledge of all things Above, and in the magic of embodied speech,⁸

being able to do anything but take the road from others, so do such men move in procession through the world led by their bodies' pleasures."

¹ Or "in that they display naught"—φανταζομένους.

² Codd. ἐναυλία. R. reads ἐν ἐναυλίᾳ, which is supported by the title of the Trismegistic treatise mentioned in the next paragraph but one. I feel almost tempted to propose to read ἐν ἀϋλίᾳ (fr. ἄϋλος—"immaterial," the being in a state free from ὕλη or "matter"), and so to translate it "for ever living in the immaterial."

³ Codd. καταδεχόμενοι. R. reads καταδέχεσθαι. I suggest καταδεχομένους.

⁴ Codd. κακῶν, which I prefer to R.'s κακόν.

⁵ *Op. et Dies*, 86.   ⁶ Sc. Pandōra; *cf.* §§ 14 and 19 below.

⁷ Or wisdom-loving.

⁸ Presumably what the Vaidic theurgist would call *mantravidyā*.

professes that all ills of Fate,—both special [ills] and general [ones],—are [thus] averted.

AGAINST MAGIC

5. Hermes, however, in his "About the Inner Door," doth deprecate [this] magic even, declaring that:

The spiritual man, [the man] who knows himself,[1] should not accomplish any thing by means of magic, e'en though he think it a good thing, nor should he force Necessity, but suffer [her to take her course], according to her nature and decree[2]; [he should] progress by seeking only, through the knowledge of himself and God, to gain the Trinity[3] that none can name, and let Fate do whate'er she will to her own clay—that is, the body.

FRAGMENT XXVI.

6. And being so minded (he says), and so ordering his life, he shall behold the Son of God becoming all things for holy souls, that he may draw her[4] forth from out the region of the Fate into the Incorporeal [Man].

7. For having power in all, He becometh all things, whatsoever He will,[5] and, in obedience to the Father['s nod], through the whole Body doth He penetrate, and, pouring forth His Light into the mind of every [soul], He starts it[6]

[1] *Cf. C. H.*, i. 21.　　[2] Or decision or judgment.
[3] τριάδα.　　[4] *Sc.* the soul.
[5] *Cf.* § 15 below. Zosimus is apparently condensing from the original.
[6] *Sc.* the soul or mind.

back unto the Blessed Region,[1] where it was before it had become corporal,—following after Him, yearning and led by Him unto the Light.

THOTH THE FIRST MAN

8. And [there] shall it see the Picture[2] that both Bitos hath described, and thrice-great Plato, and ten-thousand-times-great Hermes, for Thōythos translated[3] it into the first sacred[4] tongue,—Thōth the First Man, the Interpreter of all things which exist, and the Name-maker[5] for all embodied things.[6]

[1] *Cf.* S., § 9 in the Naassene Document.
[2] πίνακα—or tablet. [3] Lit. translates.
[4] Priestly or hieratic. With this compare Syncellus' (*Chron.*, xl.) quotation, from Manetho's *Sothis*, which declares that the first monuments recording the wisdom-mystery of most ancient Egypt "were engraved in the sacred language by Thōth, the first Hermes; after the Flood they were translated from the sacred language into the common tongue." *Cf.* vol. i., ch. v., on "Hermes according to Manetho."
[5] ὀνοματοποιός,—referring specially to the making of names or words corresponding to natural cries and sounds. Compare the Adam of Genesis.
[6] *Cf.* Plato, *Philebus*, 18 B: "Some god, or rather some god-like man, who in Egypt their tradition says was Theuth, observing that sound was infinite, first distinguished in this infinity a certain number of pure sounds [or vowels], and then other letters [or sound elements] which have sound, but are not pure sounds [the semi-vowels]; these two exist [each] in a definite number; and lastly he distinguished a third class of letters, which we now call mutes; and divided these, and likewise the two other classes of vowels and semi-vowels, into their individual elements, and told the number of them, and gave to each and all of them the names of letters." (*Cf.* Jowett's Trans., 3rd ed., iv. 583, 584.)

According to the number-system of the Gnostic Marcus, there are: seven vowels, eight semi-vowels, and nine mutes (*F. F. F.*, p. 368). It is also of interest to notice that these elements of sound are applied to what Marcus calls the "Configuration of *the* Element"—? Sound—(τὸ σχῆμα τοῦ στοιχείου); they constitute the

The Libraries of the Ptolemies

9. The Chaldæans and Parthians and Medes and Hebrews call Him[1] Adam, which is by interpretation virgin Earth, and blood-red[2] Earth, and fiery[3] Earth, and fleshly Earth.

10. And these indications were found in the book-collections[4] of the Ptolemies, which they stored away in every temple, and especially in the Serapeum, when they invited Asenas, the chief priest of Jerusalem, to send a "Hermes,"[5] who translated the whole of the Hebrew into Greek and Egyptian.[6]

11. So the First Man is called by us Thōyth and by them Adam,—not giving His [true] name in the Language of the Angels, but naming Him symbolically according to His Body by the four elements [or letters] out of His whole Sphere,[7] whereas his Inner Man, the

---

Glyph (or Character, or Impression, or Expression) of the Figure (or Diagram) of the Man of Truth. In the phrase "Glyph of the Figure" (ὁ χαρακτὴρ τοῦ γράμματος), the word γράμμα means either (i) a letter of the alphabet, or (ii) a note of music, or (iii) a mathematical figure or diagram (*ibid.*, p. 367). Is there then any connection between the Pinax of Bitos and the Diagram of the Ophites referred to by Celsus?

[1] *Sc.* the First Man.   [2] Or of the nature of blood.

[3] Codd. πυρὰ—? πυρία.

[4] Or libraries.   [5] That is, a learned priest or scribe.

[6] Much translation of this kind was done at that period. Compare the Arabic translation of a "Book of Ostanes" (Berthelot, *La Chimie au Moyen Age*, iii. 121), in which an old inscription on an Egyptian *stēlē* is quoted: "Have you not heard the story that a certain philosopher [*i.e.* Egyptian priest] wrote to the Magi in Persia, saying: 'I have found a copy of a book of the ancient sages; but as the book is written in Persian, I cannot read it. Send me then one of your wise men who can read for me the book I have found'?" R. 363.

[7] Presumably referring to the whole Body of the Heavenly Man, to whose Limbs all the letters were assigned by Marcus.

spiritual, has [also] both an authentic name and one for common use.[1]

NIKOTHEOS

12. His authentic [name], however, I know not, owing to the so long [lapse of time[2]]; for Nikotheos[3] who-is-not-to-be-found alone doth know these things.

---

[1] προσηγορικόν,—this signifies generally the *prænomen* as opposed to the *nomen* proper.

[2] διὰ τὸ τέως,—lit. "because of the so long"; otherwise I cannot translate the phrase. This would, then, presumably refer to the length of time since the physical tradition of the ancient Thōyth initiates had disappeared; or the length of time the soul of Zosimus had been revolving in Genesis.

[3] Lit. God-victor,—symbolizing the victory of the Inner God, or of a man who had raised himself to the status of a god. For Nikotheos, see the Gnostic "Untitled Apocalypse" of the Codex Brucianus (C. Schmidt, *Gnos. Schrift. in kop. Sprach. aus d. C. B.*, p. 285), p. 12a: "Nikotheos hath spoken of Him [namely, the Alone-begotten,—see *ibid.*, p. 601], and seen Him; for he is one [*sc.* of those who have seen Him face to face]. He [N.] said: 'The Father exists exalted above all the perfect.' He [N.] hath revealed the Invisible and the perfect Triple-power."

In the *Life of Plotinus*, by Porphyry (c. xiv.), among the list of "Gnostics" against whose views on Matter the great coryphæus of Later Platonism wrote one of the books of his *Enneads* (II. ix.), there is mention of Nikotheos in close connection with Zoroaster and others (S. 603 ff.). If we now turn to Schmidt's *Plotins Stellung zum Gnosticismus und kirchlichen Christentum* (Leipzig, 1900), in which he has examined at length the matter of the treatise of Plotinus and the passage of Porphyry, we find him returning to the consideration of Nikotheos (pp. 58 ff.). Schmidt (p. 61) takes the "hidden Nikotheos" for a "heavenly being," indeed as identical with the Alone-begotten, and as, therefore, the revealer of Himself. This Alone-begotten is the "Light-Darkness" of p. 13a of the "Untitled Apocalypse" of *C. B.* In other words, Nikotheos seems to be a synonym of the Triumphant Christos. See R. Liechtenhan, *Die Offenbarung in Gnosticismus* (Göttingen, 1901), p. 31. So far for the inner meaning; but is there possibly an outer one? As there was an apocalypse, for the words of Nikotheos are quoted, there was a seer, a prophet, a

But that for common use is Man (*Phōs*),[1] from which it follows that men are called *phōtas*.

FROM THE BOOK OF THE CHALDÆANS

13.[2] "When Light-Man (*Phōs*) was in Paradise, exspiring[3] under the [presence of] Fate, they[4] persuaded Him to clothe himself in the Adam they had made, the [Adam] of Fate, him of the four elements,—as though [they said] being free from [her[5]] ills and free from their[6] activities.

"And He, on account of this 'freedom from ills,' did

Christos, who had seen and handed on. It is somewhat remarkable that one of the by-names given to Jesus (Jeschu) by Rabbinical theological controversy was Balaam (Bileam), meaning "Destroyer of the people." Is there, then, any connection between Nikotheos on the one hand and Niko-laos (the Greek equivalent of Balaam) on the other? There are, at any rate, many other parallels in the Talmud Jeschu-Stories of names of dishonour on the Rabbinical side equating with names of exalted honour on the Gnostic and Christian side. If so—dare we ask the question?—have we in the *logos* of Nikotheos a fragment from an "Apocalypse of Jesus"?

Nay, may not Balaam-Niko-laos,—to take a lesson from the mystic word-play of the time,—"allegorically" have symbolized on the one hand the "victory of the many" (λαός), and on the other the "Victor of the many," for "people" in Philo signifies the "many" as opposed to the "one" "race" (γένος), which sums up all His "limbs" in the Christ?

[1] φώς,—according to the accenting of R., but φῶς would mean "Light."

[2] This is evidently a quotation.

[3] Reading διαπνεόμενος with the Codd., and not διαπνεομένῳ with R. This means "exhaling his light." In the Egypto-Gnostic tradition underlying the *Pistis Sophia*, it is the function of the Rulers of the Fate to "squeeze out" the light from the souls and to devour it, or absorb it into themselves.

[4] The Rulers of the Fate.   [5] *Sc.* Fate's.

[6] *Sc.* the Seven Rulers or Energies of the Fate-sphere,—ἀνενέργητον.

not refuse; but they boasted as though He had been brought into servitude [to them]."[1]

14. For Hesiod said that the outer man was the "bond"[2] by which Zeus bound Prometheus.

Subsequently, in addition to this bond, he sends him another, Pandōra,[3] whom the Hebrews call Eve.

For Prometheus and Epimetheus[4] are one Man, according to the system of allegory,—that is, Soul and Body.

MAN THE MIND

And at one time He[5] bears the likeness of soul, at another of mind, at another of flesh, owing to the imperfect attention which Epimetheus paid to the counsel of Prometheus, his own mind.[6]

15. For our Mind[7] saith:

FRAGMENT XXVII.

For that the Son of God having power in all things, becoming all things that he willeth, appeareth as he willeth to each.[8]

---

[1] This is evidently a quotation from a Greek translation of one of the Books of the Chaldæans (§§ 9, 10) in the Serapeum. It seems to me to be a "source" on which both the Hebrew and non-Hebrew Hellenists commentated in Alexandria. Thus both the commentator in S. and J. in the Naassene Document and the Pœmandrists of the period would use it in common.

[2] *Theog.*, 614.   [3] *Cf.* §§ 3 and 19.

[4] That is, Fore-thought and After-thought.   [5] *Sc.* Man.

[6] I am almost persuaded that § 14 is also a quotation or summary and not the simple exegesis of Zosimus; the original being from the pen of some non-Hebrew Hellenistic allegorizer.

[7] That is, Pœmandrēs, the Shepherd of men.

[8] *Cf.* § 7 above ; evidently a quotation from the "Inner Door." Compare also the *logos* quoted by S. (§ 8) in the Naassene Document from some Hellenistic scripture: "I become what I will, and am what I am." Do Hermes and S. then both depend on

16. Yea, unto the consummation of the cosmos will He come secretly,—nay, openly associating with His own,—counselling them secretly, yea through their minds, to settle their account with their Adam, the blind accuser,[1] in rivalry with the spiritual man of light.[2]

THE COUNTERFEIT DAIMON

17. And these things come to pass until the Counterfeit Daimon[3] come, in rivalry with themselves, and wishing to lead them into error, declaring that he is Son of God, being formless in both soul and body.

But they, becoming wiser from contemplation of

the same scripture, in the form of an apocalypse; that is, does Hermes in his "expository sermon" depend on the direct teaching of the Mind to himself, which would be instruction in the first person?

[1] τυφληγοροῦντος. The lexicons do not contain the word. It is probably a play on κατηγοροῦντος. *Cf.* note on "blind from birth" of C. in the Conclusion of Hippolytus in "Myth of Man" (vol. i, p. 189).

[2] That is, presumably, though in one aspect only, the soul that sees in the Light as opposed to the blind body. This passage reflects the same thought-atmosphere as that which surrounds the saying underlying Matt. v. 25 (=Lk. xii. 57–59): "Agree with thine adversary quickly whiles thou art in the way with him, lest at any time the adversary deliver thee to the judge, and the judge to the officer, and thou be cast into prison. Amēn, I say unto thee, thou shalt not come forth thence till thou hast paid the uttermost farthing." The third Evangelist, instead of the vague "agree," preserves the technical terms ἀπηλλάχθαι, used of the discharge of a debt (*cf.* the technical καταλλαγὴν ἔχειν of our text), and πράκτωρ, an officer charged with the collection of taxes and debts. This Saying was interpreted by the Gnostics as having reference to the reincarnation of the soul into another body in order to discharge its kārmic debts.

[3] ὁ ἀντίμιμος δαίμων. The term "counterfeit spirit" (ἀντίμιμον πνεῦμα) occurs frequently in the *Pistis Sophia*.

Him who is truly Son of God, give unto him [1] his own Adam for death,[2] rescuing their own light spirits for [return to] their own regions where they were even before the cosmos [existed].[3] . . .

18. And [it is] the Hebrews alone and the Sacred Books of Hermes [which tell us] these things about the man of light and his Guide the Son of God, and about the earthy Adam and *his* Guide, the Counterfeit, who doth blasphemously call himself Son of God, for leading men astray.[4]

19. But the Greeks call the earthy Adam Epimetheus, who is counselled by his own mind, that is, his brother, not to receive the gifts of Zeus. Nevertheless being both deceived[5] and repenting,[6] and seeking the Blessed Land. . . .[7]

But Prometheus, that is the mind, interprets all things and gives good counsel in all things to them who have understanding and hearing. But they who have only fleshly hearing are "processions of Fate."

---

[1] The Counterfeit Daimon.   [2] Or execution.

[3] The two last paragraphs are apparently also quoted or summarized from a Hellenistic commentary on a Book of the Hebrews, translated into Greek, and found in the libraries of the Ptolemies. It is remarkable that the contents of this book are precisely similar not only to the contents of the Books from which J. quotes in the Naassene Document, but also to the ideas about the Chaldæans which the commentator of S. sets forth.

[4] If we can rely on this statement of Zosimus, this proves that there was a developed Anthrōpos-doctrine also in the Trismegistic Books, as apart from the Chaldæan Books,—that is, that the Pœmandrists did not take it from the Chaldæan Books, but had it from their own immediate line of tradition, namely, the Egyptian.

[5] *Cf.* § 13 above.   [6] Lit. changing his mind.

[7] A *lacuna* occurs in the text. We could almost persuade ourselves that Zosimus had the text of S. and even the source of J. before him. For "Blessed Land," *cf.* § 7 above.

His Advice to Theosebeia

To the foregoing we may append a version of Zosimus' advice[1] to the lady Theosebeia, to which we have already referred, as offering an instructive counterpart to *C. H.*, xiii. (xiv.). After a sally against the "false prophets," through whom the daimones energize, not only requiring their offerings but also ruining their souls, Zosimus continues:

"But be not thou, O lady, [thus] distracted, as, too, I bade thee in the actualizing [rites], and do not turn thyself about this way and that in seeking after God; but in thy house be still, and God shall come to thee, He who is everywhere and not in some wee spot as are daimonian things.

"And having stilled thyself in body, still thou thyself in passions too—desire, [and] pleasure, rage [and] grief, and the twelve fates[2] of Death.

"And thus set straight and upright, call thou unto thyself Divinity; and truly shall He come, He who is everywhere and [yet] nowhere.

"And [then], without invoking them, perform the sacred rites unto the daimones,—not such as offer things to them and soothe and nourish them, but such as turn them from thee and destroy their power, which Mambres[3] taught to Solomon, King of Jerusalem, and all that Solomon himself wrote down from his own wisdom.

"And if thou shalt effectively perform these rites,

[1] Berth., p. 244; for a revised text see R. 214, n. 1.

[2] The twelve tormenting or avenging daimones of *C. H.*, xiii. (xiv.).

[3] The famous Egyptian Theurgist and Magician who is fabled to have contended with Moses; while others say he was the instructor of Moses.

thou shalt obtain the physical conditions of pure birth. And so continue till thou perfect thy soul completely.

"And when thou knowest surely that thou art perfected in thyself, then spurn . . . from thee [1] the natural things of matter, and make for harbour in P'œmandres' [2] arms, and having dowsed thyself within His Cup,[3] return again unto thy own [true] race." [4]

This was how Zosimus understood the teaching of the Trismegistic tradition, for he had experienced it.

[1] The soul having now found itself wings and become the winged globe.
[2] ἐπὶ τὸν Ποιμένανδρα (sic). [3] Cf. C. H., iv. (v.) 4.
[4] Cf. C. H., i. 26, 29.

II.

JAMBLICHUS

ABAMMON THE TEACHER

THE evidence of Jamblichus[1] is of prime importance seeing that it was he who put the Later Platonic School, previously led by the purely philosophical Ammonius, Plotinus and Porphyry, into conscious touch with those centres of Gnosis into which he had been initiated, and instructed it especially in the Wisdom of Egypt in his remarkable treatise generally known by the title *On the Mysteries*. The authorship of this treatise is usually disputed; but as Proclus, who was in the direct tradition, attributes it to Jamblichus, the probabilities are in favour of its authenticity.

Jamblichus writes with the authority of an accredited exponent of the Egyptian Wisdom as taught in these mysteries, and under the name of "Abammon, the Teacher," proceeds to resolve the doubts and difficulties of the School with regard to the principles of the

[1] The exact date of Jamblichus is very conjectural. In my sketches of the "Lives of the Later Platonists" I have suggested about A.D. 255-330. See *The Theosophical Review* (Aug. 1896), xviii. 462, 463.

sacred science as formulated by Porphyry. Jamblichus begins his task with these significant words [1]:

HERMES THE INSPIRER

"Hermes, the God who is our guide in [sacred] sermons, was rightly held of old as common to all priests. And seeing that it is he who has in charge the real science about the Gods, he is the same in all [our sacred sermons].[2] And so it was to him that our ancestors attributed all the discoveries of their wisdom, attaching the name of Hermes to all the writings which had to do with such subjects.[3] And if we also enjoy that share of this God which has fallen to our lot, according to our ability [to receive him], thou dost well in submitting certain questions on theology to us priests, as thy friends, for their solution. And as I may fairly suppose that the letter sent to my disciple Anebo was written to myself, I will send thee the true answers to the questions thou hast asked. For it would not be proper that Pythagoras and Plato, and Democritus and Eudoxus, and many others of the ancient Greeks,[4] should have obtained fitting instruc-

[1] I translate from the text of Parthey (Berlin, 1857).

[2] The term λόγος is, of course, used technically, as a sacred or inspired sermon or course of instruction.

[3] πάντα τὰ οἰκεῖα συγγράμματα.

[4] Parthey here adds the following interesting note: "The Egyptian teachers of Pythagoras were Œnuphis of On (Plut., *De Is. et Os.*, 10) and Sonchis (Clem. Al., *Strom.*, i. 15, 69); Plato was the pupil of Sechnuphis of On (Clem. *l.c.*), and of Chonuphis (Plut., *De Gen. Socr.*, 578); Democritus was taught by Pammenes of Memphis (Georg. Sync., i. 471 Dind.); Eudoxus by Chonuphis of Memphis (Plut. and Clem. *ll. cc.*)." To this Parthey appends a list of some of the many other famous Greeks who owed their knowledge to Egyptian teachers, viz., Alcæus, Anaxagoras of Clazomenæ, Appuleius, Archimedes, Bias, Chrysippus of Cnidus, Cleobulus, Dædalus, Decæneus, Diodorus Siculus, Ellopion, Euripides, Hecatæus of Abdera, Hecatæus of Miletus, Hellanicus,

tion from the recorders of the sacred science of their times, and that thou, our contemporary, who art of a like mind with these ancients, should lack guidance from the now living bearers of the title 'Common Teachers.'"[1]

From the above important passage we learn that among the Egyptians the books which dealt technically with the science of sacred things, and especially with the science of the Gods, that is to say, with the nature of the hierarchy from man upwards to the Supreme Ruler of our system, were regarded as "inspired." The Ray of the Spiritual Sun which illumined the sacred science was distinguished as a Person, and this Person, because of a partial similarity of attributes, the Greeks had long identified with their God Hermes. He was "common" to the priests of the sacred science, that is to say, it was this special Ray of the Spiritual Sun which illumined their studies. Not, however, that all were equally illumined, for there were many grades in the mysteries, many steps up the holy ascent to union

Herodotus, Homerus, Lycurgus, Melampus, Musæus, Œnopides of Chios, Orpheus, Pausanias, Pherecydes, Polybius, Simmias, Solon, Sphærus, Strabo, Telecles, Thales, Theodorus, Xenophanes of Colophon, Zamolxis. I have quoted this note on purpose to show the overpowering weight of evidence which some modern theorists have to face, in order to maintain their thesis that the philosophy of Greece was solely a native product. The universal testimony of the Greeks themselves is that all their greatest philosophers, geometricians, mathematicians, historians, geographers, and especially their theosophists, were pupils of the Egyptian Wisdom ; the modern theory of the unaided evolution of philosophy on the soil of Greece, which is so universally accepted, is, to my mind, entirely erroneous. The "form" or "manner" of "philosophizing" was of course solely due to Greek genius, but the "matter" of it was of hoary antiquity. *Cf.* Plutarch, *De Is. et Os.*, x.

[1] That is to say, presumably, teachers of all without distinction of race. *Op. cit.*, i. 1.

with Deity. Now the Rays of the Spiritual Sun are really One Light, "polarised" variously by the "spheres" of which we have heard so much in the Trismegistic treatises. These Rays come forth from the Logos, and each illuminates a certain division of the whole hierarchy of beings from the Logos to man, and characterises further the lower kingdoms, animals and plants, and minerals. Hence, for instance, among animals, we get the ibis, the ape and the dog as being especially sacred to Thoth or Hermes.

THOSE OF THE HERMAÏC NATURE

Among men generally, also, there are certain whose characteristics are of a "Hermaïc"[1] nature; the more evolved of these are adapted to certain lines of study and research, while again among those few of these who are beginning to be really conscious of the science of sacred things, that is to say, among the initiated students or priests, the direct influence of this Ray or Person begins to be consciously felt, by each, as Jamblichus says, according to his ability, for there are still many grades.

Now the peculiar unanimity that prevailed in these strictly hierarchical schools of initiation, and the grand doctrine of identification that ran throughout the whole economy—whereby the pupil became identified with the master when he received his next grade of initiation, and whereby his master was to him the living symbol of all that was above that master, that is to say, was Hermes for him, in that he was the messenger to him of the Word, and was the channel whereby the divine inspiration came to him—rendered the ascription to

[1] It is from this region of ideas that the terms "mercurial temperament," and so forth, have reached modern times over the bridge of astrological tradition.

JAMBLICHUS

Hermes of all the sacred scriptures, such as the sermons of initiation, a very natural proceeding. It was not the case of a modern novel-writer taking out a copyright for his own precious productions, but simply of the recorder, scribe or copyist of the sacred science handing on the tradition. As long as this was confined to the disciplined schools of the sacred science it was without danger, but when irresponsible people began to copy a method, to whose discipline they refused to submit, for purposes of edification, and so appended the names of great teachers to their own lucubrations, they paved the way for that chaos of confusion in which we are at present stumbling.

THE BOOKS OF HERMES

Towards the end of his treatise Jamblichus, in treating of the question of the innumerable hierarchies of being and their sub-hierarchies, says that these are so multiplex that they had to be treated by the ancient priests from various aspects, and even among those who were "wise in great things" in his own time the teaching was not one and the same.

"The *main* states of being were completely set forth by Hermes (in the twenty thousand books, as Seleucus[1] writes, or in the thirty-six thousand five hundred and twenty-five as Manetho relates), while the *sub-states* are interpreted in many other writings by the ancients, some of them sub-dividing[2] some of the sub-states and others others."[3]

At first sight it would seem that we are not to sup-

[1] Porphyry (*De Abs.*, ii. c. 55) mentions a Seleucus whom he calls a "theologist"; Suidas says that Seleucus of Alexandria wrote a treatise *On the Gods*, in 100 books or chapters.

[2] Reading διαλαβόντες instead of διαβάλλοντες.

[3] *Ibid.*, viii. 1.

pose that it took 20,000 volumes to set forth the *main outlines* of the cosmic system. Jamblichus would seem to mean that in the library or libraries of the books treating of the sacred science, the general scheme of the cosmos was set forth, and that the details were filled in very variously by many writers, each according to the small portion of the whole he had studied or speculated on. As to the number of books again we should not be dismayed, when we reflect that a book did not mean a large roll or volume but a division or chapter of such a roll. Thus we read of a single man composing no less than 6000 " books " !

But on further reflection this view does not seem satisfactory. The ghost of the very precise number 36,525, which Jamblichus substitutes from Manetho for the vague total 20,000 of Seleucus, refuses to be laid by such a weak-kneed process.

We see at once that 365·25 days is a very close approximation to the length of the solar year. We know further that 36,525 years was the sum of 25 Sothiac cycles ($1461 \times 25 = 36,525$),[1] that most sacred time-period of the Egyptian secret astronomy, which was assigned to the revolution of the zodiac or the Great Year. Now supposing after all that Jamblichus *does* mean that Hermes actually did write the scheme of the cosmos in 36,525 "books" or "chapters"; and supposing further that these "chapters" were not written on papyrus, but in the heavens; and supposing still further that these "chapters" were simply so many great aspects of the real sun, just as the 365·25 days were but aspects of the physical sun—in such case the above favourite passage, which every previous writer has referred to actual books superscribed with the

[1] See Georgius Syncellus, *Chron.*, i. 97, ed. Dindorf. Also Eusebius, *Chron.*, vi.

JAMBLICHUS

name of Hermes, and has dragged into every treatise on the Hermetic writings, will in future have to be removed from the list, and one of the functions of the real Hermes, the Initiator and Recorder, will become apparent to those who are "wise in greater things."

THE MONAD FROM THE ONE

In the next chapter, after first speaking of the God over all, Jamblichus refers to the Logos, the God of our system, whom he calls "God of gods, the Monad from the One, prior to being and the source of being." And then continues:

"For from Him cometh the essence of being and being; wherefore is He called Father of being. For He is prior to being, the source of spiritual existences; wherefore also is He called Source of spiritual things. These latter are the most ancient sources of all things, and Hermes places them before the æthereal and empyrean and celestial gods, bequeathing to us a hundred books on the history of the empyrean, and a like number on that of the æthereal, but a thousand of them concerning the celestial."[1]

I am inclined to think that there is a mistake in the numbers of these books, and that we should have 10 assigned to the first class, 100 to the second, and 1000 to the third. In any case we see that all are multiples of the perfect number 10; and that thus my theory is still supported by the further information that Jamblichus gives us.

THE TRADITION OF THE TRISMEGISTIC LITERATURE

We next come to a passage which deals directly with our Trismegistic literature. Jamblichus tells Porphyry that with the explanations he has already

[1] *Op. cit.*, viii. 2.

given him, he will be able to find his way in the Hermetic writings which have come into his hands.

"For the books in circulation bearing the name of Hermes contain Hermaïc doctrines, although they often use the language of the philosophers, seeing that they were translated from the Egyptian by men well skilled in philosophy."[1]

The information given by Jamblichus is precise; they were translations, but instead of a literal rendering, the translators used the usual phraseology of the Greek philosophical writers.

Jamblichus then goes on to say that physical astronomy and physical research generally were but a very small part of the Hermaïc science, by no means the most important.

For "the Egyptians deny that physics are everything; on the contrary they distinguish both the life of the soul and the life of the mind from nature,[2] not only in the case of the cosmos but also in man. They first posit Mind and Reason (*Logos*) as having a being peculiar to themselves, and then they tell us that the world of becoming [or generation] is created. As Forefather of all beings in generation they place the Creator, and are acquainted with the Life-giving Power which is prior to the celestial spaces and permeates them. Above the universe they place Pure Mind; this for the universe as a whole is one and undivided, but it is variously manifested in the several spheres.[3] And they do not speculate about these things with the unassisted reason, but they announce that by the divine art of their priestly science[4] they reach higher and more

[1] *Ibid.*, viii. 4.

[2] That is, the life of the body.

[3] Lit. distributed to all the spheres as different.

[4] διὰ τῆς ἱερατικῆς θεουργίας,—lit. by the theurgy known to the priests.

universal states [of consciousness] above the [Seven Spheres of] Destiny, ascending to God the Creator,[1] and that too without using any material means, or any other [material] assistance than the observation of a suitable opportunity.

"It was Hermes who first taught this Path.[2] And Bitys, the prophet, translated [his teachings concerning it] for King Ammon,[3] discovering them in the inner temple[4] in an inscription in the sacred characters at Saïs in Egypt. [From these writings it was that Bitys] handed on the tradition of the Name of God, as 'That which pervadeth the whole universe.'"[5]

"As to the Good Itself [the Egyptians] regard It in Its relation to the Divine as the God that transcends all thought, and in Its relation to man as the at-one-ment with Him—a doctrine which Bitys translated from the Hermaïc Books."[6]

From these two passages we learn that the ancient doctrine of Hermes concerning the Path, which is the keynote of our Trismegistic tracts, was to be found either in inscriptions in the sacred script in the secret chambers of the temples, into which no uninitiated person was ever permitted to enter, or in "books," also in the sacred script; that these had never been translated until the reign of King Ammon.[7] But what are we to understand by translated? Into Greek? Not necessarily, but more probably interpreted from the

---

[1] The Mind in its creative aspect.
[2] *Sc.* This Way up to God.
[3] See Commentary on *C. H.* (xvi.).   [4] Or secret shrine.
[5] *Op. cit.*, viii. 5.   [6] *Ibid.*, x. 7.
[7] Identified by some writers with one of the last kings of the Saïtic dynasty (the xxvith), who reigned somewhere about 570 B.C. See Thomas Taylor, *Iamblichus on the Mysteries*, p. 306 n. (2nd ed., London, 1895). But as there is no objective evidence by which this identification can be controlled, we simply record it.

hieroglyphic symbols into the Egyptian vernacular and written in the demotic character. The term used (διερμηνεύειν) clearly bears this sense; whereas if translation from Egyptian into Greek had been intended, we should presumably have had the same word (μεταγράφειν) employed which Jamblichus uses when speaking of the Hermetic books that had been read by Porphyry. Reitzenstein (p. 108), however, has apparently no doubt that the writings of Bitys were in Greek, and that these writings lay before Jamblichus and were the only source of his information. But I cannot be certain that this is the meaning of the Greek.

We have rather, according to my view, probably two strata of " translation "—from hieroglyphic into demotic, from demotic into Greek. As to Bitys, we know nothing more definite than Jamblichus tells us. Perhaps he was the first to translate from the sacred hieroglyphs into the vulgar tongue and script; and by that we mean the first to break the ancient rule and write down in the vulgar characters those holy sermons and treatises which previously had never before been inscribed in any but the most sacred characters. We are not, however, to suppose that Bitys was the only one to do this.

Now in our Trismegistic literature we have a deposit addressed to a King Ammon. Is it then possible that this King, whoever he was, was the initiator of a change of policy in the immemorial practice of the priests? It may be so, but at present we have not sufficient data to decide the point.

Bitys

A further scrap of information concerning Bitys, however, may be gleaned from Zosimus (§ 8), when, speaking of the Logos, the Son of God, pouring His Light into the soul and starting it on its Return Above, to the Blessed Region where it was before it had become corporeal (as described in the Trismegistic tractate, entitled "Concerning the Inner Door")—he writes:

"And there shall it see the Picture ($\pi i \nu a \xi$) that both Bitos hath described, and thrice-greatest Plato, and ten-thousand-times-great Hermes,—for Thōythos translated it into the first sacred tongue,—Thōth the First Man."[1]

The identity of Bitys and Bitos is thus unquestionable.[2] Reitzenstein, however, asserts that neither of these name-forms is Egyptian, and therefore approves of the identification of our Bitys with "Pitys the Thessalian" of the Papyri,[3] as Dieterich has suggested. The headings of the fragments of the writings of Pitys in the Papyri run: "The Way [or Method] of Pitys"; "Pitys to King Ostanes Greeting"; "The Way of Pitys the King"; "Of Pitys the Thessalian."

From this Reitzenstein (n. 2) concludes that already in the second and third centuries (? A.D.) Pitys is included among the prophetical theologi and Magians. What the precise date of these Papyri may be it is not easy to determine, but, whether or not they belong to the second and third centuries, it is evident that Pitys was regarded as ancient and a contemporary of the Magian Sage Ostanes.

King,[4] referring to a passage of the Elder Pliny (*Nat. Hist.*, xxx. 4), which remarks on the similarity of the

[1] See notes appended to the extract from Zosimus.

[2] As has already been supposed by Hoffmann and Riess in Pauly-Wissowa's *Realencyklopädie*, i. 1347. R. 108.

[3] Dieterich, *Jahr. f. Phil.*, Suppl., xvi. 753; Wessely, *Denkschr. d. K. K. Akad.* (1888), pp. 92, 95, 98.

[4] King (C. W.), *The Gnostics and their Remains*, 2nd ed. (London, 1887), p. 421, who, however, does not document his statement.

Magian Gnosis with the Druidical Gnosis of Gaul and Britain, says: " Pliny by his 'Magica' understands the rites instituted by Zoroaster, and first promulgated by Osthanes to the outer world, this Osthanes having been ' military chaplain ' to Xerxes during his expedition to Greece."

This date, if we can rely upon it, would take us back to the Persian Conquest of Egypt, but what has a Thessalian Pitys to do with that?

Curiously enough also Pliny in his xxviiith Book makes use of the writings of a certain Bithus of Dyrrachium, a city on the coast of Illyricum in the Ionic Gulf, known in Grecian history as Epidamnus.

All of this is puzzling enough; but whatever conclusions may be drawn from the evidence, the clearest indication is that Bitys was ancient, and therefore that whatever translating or rather "interpreting" there may have been, it was probably from hieroglyphic into demotic, and the latter was subsequently further "interpreted" into Greek.

OSTANES-ASCLEPIUS

But is Ostanes the Magian Sage of tradition, or may we adopt the brilliant conclusion of Maspero, and equate Ostanes with Asclepius, and so place him in the same circle with Bitys, or rather see in Bitys an "Asclepius"?

At any rate the following interesting paragraph of Granger[1] deserves our closest attention in this connection, when he writes:

" Maspero, following Goodwin, has shown that Ostanes is the name of a deity who belongs to the cycle of

[1] Granger (F.), "The Poemander of Hermes Trismegistus," in *The Journal of Theological Studies*, vol. v., no. 19, ap. 1904 (London), p. 398.

Thoth.¹ His name, Ysdnw, was derived by the Egyptians themselves from a verb meaning 'to distinguish,' and he was a patron of intellectual perception. As time went on, he gained in importance. Under the Ptolemies he was often represented upon the Temple walls (*l.c.*). In Pliny he appears as an early writer upon medicine.² Some of the prescriptions quoted as from him are quite in the Egyptian style.³ Philo Byblius, on whom, to be sure, not much reliance can be placed,⁴ mentions a book of Ostanes—the *Octateuch*.⁵ It is tempting to identify this with some such collection as the six medical books which occupy the last place in Clement's list.⁶ Now Pliny, as appears from his list of authorities, does not quote Ostanes directly. If we note that Democritus is mentioned by Pliny in the same context, and that Ostanes is the legendary teacher of Democritus upon his journey to Egypt, we shall consider it at least probable that Pliny depends upon Democritus for his mention of Ostanes. The Philosopher, whose visit to Egypt may be regarded as a historical fact, would in that case be dealing with a medical collection which passes under the name of Ostanes. Asclepius, who appears in the *Pœmander*, will be the Greek equivalent of Ostanes. Thus the collocation of Hermes and Asclepius is analogous to the kinship of the Egyptian deities, Thoth and Ysdnw."

From the Hermaïc Writings

That these Bitys-books contained the same doctrines as our Trismegistic writings is evident from the whole

[1] *Proc. Soc. Bibl. Arch.*, xx. 142.
[2] *Nat. Hist.*, xxviii. 6.   [3] *P. S. B. A., ibid.*, 256, 261.
[4] He, however, was very well placed to have accurate knowledge on such a point.—[G. R. S. M.]
[5] Eus., *Præp. Ev.*, I. x. 52.   [6] *Strom.*, VI. iv. 37.

treatise of Jamblichus. Jamblichus throughout bases himself upon the doctrines of Hermes,[1] and clearly suggests that he does not owe his information to translations only, as was the case with Porphyry, but to records in Egyptian; but whether to the demotic treatises of the Bitys-school or to the heiroglyphic records themselves he does not say. That these doctrines were identical with the teachings in our Trismegistic literature requires no proof to any one who has read our treatises and the exposition of Jamblichus; for the benefit, however, of those who have not read Jamblichus,[2] we append a passage to show the striking similarity of ideas. Treating of the question of freewill and necessity raised by Porphyry, and replying to the objection that the Egyptians taught an astrological fatalism, Jamblichus writes:

"We must explain to you how the question stands by some further conceptions drawn from the Hermaïc writings. Man has two souls, as these writings say. The one is from the First Mind, and partakes also of the Power of the Creator,[3] while the other, the soul under constraint, comes from the revolution of the celestial [Spheres][4]; into the latter the former, the soul that is the Seer of God, insinuates itself at a later period. This then being so, the soul that descends into us from the worlds[5] keeps time with the circuits of these worlds, while the soul from the Mind, existing in us in a spiritual fashion, is free from the whirl of

[1] Especially in Book VIII., which is entirely devoted to an exposition of Hermaïc doctrine, and ought perhaps to be here translated in full. I have, however, preferred to select the passages definitely characterized by Jamblichus as Hermaïc.

[2] Who must be read in the original and not in the inelegant and puzzling version of Taylor, the only English translation.

[3] The Second Mind according to "The Shepherd."

[4] The Seven Spheres of the Harmony.   [5] The Seven Spheres.

Generation; by this the bonds of Destiny are burst asunder; by this the Path up to the spiritual Gods is brought to birth; by such a life as this is that Great Art Divine, which leads us up to That beyond the Spheres of Genesis,[1] brought to its consummation."[2]

THE COSMIC SPHERES

With regard to the nature of these Spheres, Jamblichus shows very clearly that they are not the physical planets, as may be seen from the following passages of his *De Mysteriis*:

"With regard to partial existences, then, I mean in the case of the soul in partial manifestation,[3] we must admit something of the kind we have above. For just such a life as the [human] soul emanated before it entered into a human body, and just such a type as it made ready for itself, just such a body, to use as an instrument, does it have attached to it, and just such a corresponding nature accompanies [this body] and receives the more perfect life the soul pours into it. But with regard to superior existences and those that surround the Source of All as perfect existences, the inferior are set within the superior, bodies in bodiless existences, things made in their makers; and the former are kept in position by the latter enclosing them in a sphere.

"The revolutions of the heavenly *Bodies*,[4] therefore, being from the first set in the celestial revolutions of the æthereal *Soul*,[5] for ever continue in this relationship; while the *Souls* of the [invisible] Worlds,[6] extending to their [common] *Mind*, are completely

[1] πρὸς τὸ ἀγέννητον. [2] *Op. cit.*, viii. 6.
[3] That is, as an individual soul and not as the world-soul.
[4] *Physical* planets. [5] Of all of our *visible* system ?
[6] That is to say, the seven spheres.

surrounded by it, and from the beginning have their birth *in* it. And *Mind* in like manner, both partially and as a whole, is also contained in superior states of existence."[1]

And again in another passage Jamblichus writes:

"We say that [the Spiritual Sun and Moon, and the rest] are so far from being contained within their Bodies, that on the contrary, it is they who contain these Bodies of theirs within the Spheres of their own vitality and energy. And so far are they from tending towards their Bodies, that the tendency of these very Bodies is towards their Divine Cause. Moreover, their Bodies do not impede the perfection of their Spiritual and Incorporeal Nature or disturb it by being situated in it."[2]

To this we may add what Proclus writes in his Commentary on the *Timæus* of Plato:

"Each of the [Seven] Planetary Spheres is a complete World containing a number of divine offspring, which are invisible to us, and over all of these Spheres the Star[3] we see is the Ruler. Now Fixed Stars differ from those[4] in the Planetary Spheres in that the former have but one Monad, namely, their system as a whole[5]; while the latter, namely the invisible globes in each of the Planetary Spheres, which globes have an orbit of their own determined by the revolution of their respective Spheres, have a double Monad—namely, their system as a whole,[6] and that dominant characteristic which has been evolved by selection in the several spheres of the system. For since globes are secondary to Fixed Stars they require a double order of govern-

[1] *Op. cit.*, i. 8.
[2] *Ibid.*, i. 17.
[3] That is, visible planet.
[4] That is, perhaps, the invisible globes.
[5] Lit. their wholeness.
[6] In our case the whole solar system.

JAMBLICHUS

ment, first subordination to their system as a whole, and then subordination to their respective spheres.[1] And that in each of these spheres there is a host [2] on the same level [3] with each, you may infer from the extremes.[4] For if the Fixed Sphere [5] has a host on the same level as itself, and Earth has a host of earthy animals,[6] just as the former a host of heavenly animals,[7] it is necessary that every whole [8] should have a number of animals on the same level with itself; indeed it is because of the latter fact that they are called wholes. The intermediate levels, however, are outside the range of our senses, the extremes only being visible, the one through the transcendent brilliance of its nature, the other through its kinship with ourselves."[9]

It is evident that we are here dealing with what are known to Theosophical students as the "planetary chains" of our system, and that therefore these Spheres are not the physical planets; the visible planets are

---

[1] Or, as one would say in modern Theosophical terms, to their planetary chains.

[2] Hierarchy.   [3] σύστοιχον.

[4] That is to say, we may infer from the fixed stars (or suns) and from the globes which we can see (*i.e.* the visible planets), the manner of those we cannot see.

[5] The sphere of fixed stars or suns.

[6] That is to say, all the visible globes (*vulgo* planets) of our system as a whole. An "animal" means a "*living* thing"; so that here "earthy animals" mean the living vehicles of the heavenly beings which we so erroneously call "heavenly bodies."

[7] That is to say, suns or solar systems.

[8] Here whole means plane.

[9] That is to say, the brilliant light of the suns in space, and the reflected light of the physical globes of the planetary spheres of our system. See Proclus, *Commentarius in Platonis Timæum*, Bk. iv., p. 279 D, E, p. 676, ed. Schneider (Vratislaviæ, 1847). The passage is very difficult to translate because of its technical nature. Taylor, in his translation (London, 1820, ii. 281, 282), misses nearly every point.

but a very small portion of the globes of these chains, of some of which there are no globes at all visible. The ascription therefore of the "influence" of these Spheres to the sun, moon, and five of the visible planets is at best a makeshift, a "correspondence," or a "symbolism."

III.

JULIAN THE EMPEROR [1]

Text: *ap.* Cyril, *Contra Julianum*, v. 176; Migne, col. 770 A. See also Neumann (C. I.), *Juliani Imperatoris Librorum contra Christianos quæ supersunt* (Leipzig, 1880), p. 193.[2]

THE DISCIPLES OF WISDOM

That God, however, has not cared for the Hebrews only, [but rather] that in His love for all nations He hath bestowed on them [*sc.* the Hebrews] nothing worth very serious attention, whereas He has given us far greater and superior gifts, consider from what will follow. The Egyptians, counting up of their own race the names of not a few sages, can also say they have had many who have followed in the steps[3] of Hermes. I mean of the Third Hermes who used to come down[4] [to them] in Egypt. The Chaldæans [also can tell of] the [disciples] of Oannes and of Belus;

[1] Julian the Emperor reigned 360-363 A.D. It was during the last year of his reign that he wrote *Contra Christianos*.

[2] Also Taylor (Thomas), *The Arguments of the Emperor Julian against the Christians* (London, 1809), p. 36.

[3] Lit. "from the succession" (διαδοχῆς).

[4] ἐπιφοιτήσαντος,—"to come habitually to"; ἐπιφοίτησις is used of the "coming upon one," or inspiration of a God.

303

and the Greeks of tens of thousands [who have the Wisdom] from Cheiron.¹ For it is from him that they derived their initiation into the mysteries of nature, and their knowledge of divine things; so that indeed [in comparison] the Hebrews seem only to give themselves airs about their own [attainments].

Here we learn from Julian that the Third Hermes, the Hermes presumably of our Sermons, was known, by those initiated into the Gnosis, to be no physical historical Teacher, but a Teaching Power or Person, who taught from within spiritually.

[1] Partially quoted by Reitzenstein (p. 175, n. 1).

IV.

FULGENTIUS THE MYTHO-GRAPHER[1]

An intermediate of the parent copy of our Corpus in every probability lay before Fulgentius. Thus we find him (p. 26, 18 H[2]) referring to the first sermon, though barbarously enough, in the phrase: "*Hermes in Opinandre libro*," and quoting from the introductory words; he also quotes (p. 88, 3) some words from *C. H.*, xii. (xiii.), stupidly referring them to Plato, adding in Greek:

FRAGMENT XXVIII.

The human mind is god; if it be good, God [then] doth shower His benefits [upon us].

And twice (p. 85, 21, and p. 74, 11) Fulgentius refers in all probability to the lost ending of "The Definitions of Asclepius," in the latter passage telling us, "as Hermes Trismegistus says," that there were three kinds of music,—namely "*adomenon, psallomenon, aulumenon*," —that is, singing, harping, and piping.

[1] The date of this Afro-Latin writer cannot be later than the sixth century.
[2] Helm (R.), *Fabii Planciadis Fulgentii V. C. Opera* (Leipzig, 1898).

IV

Conclusion

AN ATTEMPT AT CLASSIFYING THE EXTANT LITERATURE

Before we proceed to append our concluding remarks, it will be as well to set down some attempt at classifying our extant sermons and fragments. Unfortunately, however, this cannot be done in any scientific manner, owing to the fact that the literature, even were it fully before us, would be found to be too chaotic. Indeed, even with our fragmentary information concerning it, we are acquainted with no less than four unrelated Corpora—those that lay before Lactantius, Cyril, and Stobæus, and our own imperfect Corpus of Byzantine tradition. There must also have been other Corpora or collections, as, for instance, the books that Jamblichus used, not to mention the ancient body of MSS. which lay before Petosiris and Nechepso.

Of Hermes

First and foremost, standing in a class by itself, must be placed:

C. H. i.—" The Pœmandres."

This is the fundamental Gospel of the School, the Self-instruction of the Hermes- or Master-grade.

With it, as based upon it in general type, though not in form, must be taken:

C. H. xi. (xii.).—" Mind unto Hermes."

This is of later date, but still it must have been comparatively early, for it introduces the Æon-doctrine, which must be early, and is the esoteric instruction on the doctrines laid down in C. H. iv. (v.)—"The Cup"—which was perhaps regarded as the most important sermon after "The Pœmandres."

Of the lost early literature we can get no clear indication; it may, however, be mentioned that the "Sayings of Agathodaimon" referred to in the Tat Sermon, C. H. xii. (xiii.), probably belonged to the most archaic deposit of the Trismegistic literature, and may be compared with the "Sayings of Ammon" mentioned by Justin Martyr. These belonged, presumably, originally solely to the Hermes-grade.

With the same type as the conclusion of the "Pœmandres" in its present form, that is to say with a later development, we must classify:

C. H. iii. (iv.).—"The Sacred Sermon"; and
C. H. vii. (viii.).—"Whither stumble ye."

Here also, for lack of a more satisfactory heading, we must place:

Ex. xxii.—"An Apophthegm of Hermes."
Ex. xxiv.—"A Hymn of the Gods."
Frag. xxvi.—From "The Inner Door."
Frag. xxvii.—"For Our Mind saith."

The last being probably from one of the oldest deposits of the literature.

The next most convenient heading for classification is that under which we can place the greatest number of pieces, namely:

To Tat

We know that the Tat-instruction was divided into

(a) "The General Sermons," of which C. H. x. (xi.)—"The Key"—is said to be the epitome or rather summation; and (b) "The Expository Sermons," of which C. H. xiii. (xiv.)—"The Secret Sermon on the Mountain"—was the consummation.

It is, of course, not certain whether the Tat Sermons were divided simply into these two classes, for though we are certain in a number of instances that we are dealing with an extract from an Expository Sermon, we are often in doubt when the heading is only "From the Sermon," or "Sermons to Tat," how to classify it. We do not know how many General Sermons there may have been, or whether they were divided into Books as were the Expository Sermons and the "To Asclepius," at anyrate in the Corpus of Cyril. For convenience of classification, however, we may consider, though perfectly arbitrarily, that all the sermons and fragments which cannot fall under the heading of "Expository" may be treated as "General."

The General Sermons

C. H. (ii.).—"The General Sermon."[1]
C. H. viii. (ix.).—"That No One of Existing Things do Perish."
Ex. x.—"Concerning the Rule of Providence."[2]
Ex. xi.—"Of Justice."[3]
Ex. xx.—"The Power of Choice."
Fragg. vi. and vii.
C. H. x. (xi.).—"The Key."

[1] The text has bodily fallen out of our Corpus with one of the quires.

[2] This seems to be a complete sermon, and to be presupposed in C. H. xii. (xiii.); as also Ex. xi.

[3] Exx. x.-xiii. probably go here as being part of the "Sermons on Fate to Tat"; but they are assigned otherwise by Stobæus.

312   THRICE-GREATEST HERMES

This last is stated to be the epitome or summation of "The General Sermons." It is addressed to both Asclepius and Tat, and is to be taken in connection with "The Perfect Sermon."

The Expository Sermons

Of these there were in the Corpus of Cyril three Books—to the First of which are assigned:

> Fragg. xx. (?), xxii., xxiii., xxiv.
> Ex. ii. and Fragg. iii., xi., xii., xv.[1]

To be assigned to "The Expository Sermons" in general without any clearer indications:

> Exx. iii. (?).—"Of Truth."[2]
> Ex. iv.[3]
> Exx. v., vi., vii., viii., ix.[4]
> Ex. i.—"Of Piety and True Philosophy."[5]

From the Corpus Hermeticum we may conjecturally assign the following to this class:

> C. H. iv. (v.).—"The Cup."[6]
> C. H. v. (vi.).—"Though Manifest."
> C. H. vii. (viii.).—"About the Common Mind."[7]

---

[1] These all seem to go together from the same Sermon or Book, which in the case of Frag. xv. is definitely assigned by Cyril to the "First of the Expository Sermons." The beginning of the Sermon is given in Lact. xxiv., and a reference in Lact. xiii.

[2] Seems to be a complete tractate.

[3] By comparison with Ex. vii.

[4] Ex. ix. is characterised as "the most authoritative and chiefest of them all," and therefore came, presumably, at the end of one of the Books of these Sermons.

[5] A complete tractate, containing heads or summaries of previous sermons, and probably one towards the end of this collection.

[6] The esoteric counterpart of which is C. H. xi. (xii.).

[7] These three sermons are too advanced to be classed among

CONCLUSION

Finally, the whole course of these "Expository Sermons" is consummated by what we may call "The Initiation of Tat":

> C. H. xiii. (xiv.).—"The Secret Sermon on the Mountain."

We next pass on to what Cyril calls the "To Asclepius," of which, as of "The Expository Sermons, there were in his Corpus at least Three Books.

To Asclepius

In our Corpus Hermeticum the following are assigned to Asclepius:

> C. H. ii. (iii.).—"An Introduction to the Gnosis of the Nature of All Things."
>
> C. H. vi. (vii.).—"In God Alone is Good."
>
> C. H. ix. (x.).—"About Sense."[1]
>
> C. H. xiv. (xv.).—"A Letter to Asclepius."[2]

From the "To Asclepius" in Cyril's collection we have:

Frag. xxv. (?).

And definitely from the Third "To Asclepius":

"The General Sermons," and in the case of the last, Tat is a questioner and not a hearer as he indubitably was in the introductory instruction.

[1] This is said to follow on "The Perfect Sermon," which was not included in our Corpus among the selections of the Pœmandrist apologist who redacted it.

[2] This is said by the editor to be an expansion of an instruction already given to Tat, in Asclepius' absence, and the doctrine is very similar to that contained in C. H. xi. (xii.)—"Mind unto Hermes." It also stood in Cyril's (viii.) "To Asclepius."

Fragg. xvi.–xviii.

In this Third Book it is probable that "The Perfect Sermon" was included in Cyril's Corpus. This sermon, which is the longest we possess, was evidently originally addressed to Asclepius alone, for its alternative title is *par excellence* "The Asclepius," and my conjecture that the introduction of the "holy three"—Asclepius, Tat and Ammon—is due to a later editor, is amply borne out by all the evidence. We may thus well conclude our list with:

"The Perfect Sermon."

For the fragments of the lost Greek original of this important tractate, see Lactantius:

Fragg. v., viii., ix., x.

This Sermon is to be taken in close connection with "The Key" which sums up "The General Sermons" to Tat.

To Ammon

Stobæus ascribes eight of his extracts to a Book or Books of his collection entitled "To Ammon." These excerpts, however, would seem to be more appropriately classified under "Sermons to Tat." As, however, Johannes distinctly so describes them, we will append them here.

Exx. xii., xiii.
Exx. xiv.–xix.—" Of Soul," i.–vi.

Exx. xvi.–xix. follow one another in the text of the Excerpts by Stobæus; as Ex. xviii., however, refers to "The General Sermons," it therefore would make us suppose that either we are here dealing with "The Expository Sermons" to Tat, or that the Ammon-grade had already had communicated to them "The General Sermons."

The above are the four types of Trismegistic Sermons

proper, and we next turn to the writings of the Disciples of Hermes.

Of Asclepius

It is remarkable that Asclepius, the most learned of the Three, writes his treatises and letters, not to philosophers or priests, or students, nor yet to his younger brother Tat—but invariably to the King or to Kings. He invariably writes to "Ammon"; and the once existing literature of this class was a very rich one, if we can believe the writer or redactor of C. H. (xvi.). The fragments that remain, however, are by no means numerous, and include:

> C. H. (xvi.).—"The Definitions of Asclepius."[1]
> Frag. iv.—Probably from the lost ending of above.
> C. H. (xvii.).—"Of Asclepius to the King."[2]
> Ex. xxi. (?)—which may, perhaps, be more correctly headed "Of Asclepius to the King" instead of with Stobæus "Of Isis to Horus."

To neither Tat nor Ammon are tractates assigned; for when Tat is perfected he becomes in his turn Hermes, and so writes as Hermes, while Ammon is the man of action and affairs who does not teach. May we further from these phenomena conclude that "Asclepius" was the man who was skilled in theory and intellectual grasp, but was not capable of direct illumination as was Tat?

The next class of literature falls under the heading:

Of Isis

Whether or not the forms of this literature which we possess are contemporaneous with or later than

[1] The end is lost.
[2] A fragment only from the end of the sermon is preserved.

the Tat and Asclepius Sermons, we cannot say; but in any case they are based on ancient types—the "Books of Isis to Horus." To this type we assign:

Ex. xxi.—" Of Isis to Horus."

Though, as we have suggested above, this is an error of Johannes, and should be rather " Of Asclepius to the King."

Ex. xxiii.—" From Aphrodite."

Where Aphrodite probably equates with Isis.

Exx. xxv., xxvi.—" The Virgin of the World."
Ex. xxvii.—" From the Sermon of Isis to Horus."

The remaining class of literature is connected with the name of Osiris as the Disciple of Agathodaimon, the Thrice-greatest, and may be headed as:

From the Agathodaimon Literature

Our fragments are all taken from Cyril's Corpus, and are referred to by him under the heading "To Asclepius." We have, however, not included them under this heading in our tentative classification, because they are plainly not addressed to Asclepius, but belong to a quite different form of literature, most probably throwing back to an ancient type of the same nature as the "Books of Isis." To this class are to be assigned:

Fragg. xiii., xiv., xix., xxi.

This form may be perhaps more appropriately taken with the "Sayings of Agathodaimon" and the "Sayings of Ammon" as Agathodaimon; both of which pertain to the oldest types of the Trismegistic literature.

Finally, we add the appendix to our Corpus written by a Pœmandrist rhetor and apologist:

C. H. (xviii.).—" The Encomium of Kings."

This may be taken with the quotation from the editor of Cyril's Corpus of XV. Books.

And so we come to the end of our tentative classification; with the full conviction, however, that as no one at the time when the literature was extant in a number of Corpora and collections of all sorts attempted to classify it, so now that we have only the flotsam and jetsam of this once abundantly rich cargo before us, no inventory can be made that is of the slightest scientific value, and we can at best offer the reader a few sorted heaps of *disjecta membra* of varying dates.

OF JUDGMENTS OF VALUE

We now approach the conclusion of our task, but with the feeling that the whole matter should be put aside for years before any attempt be made to set down any judgments of value. We are as yet too much involved in a maze of details to be able to extricate ourselves into the clear space in which we can walk at ease round the labyrinth and view it from a general and detached point of view.

Nevertheless, we will endeavour to set down some general impressions of our experiences in the labyrinth— of the many windings we have had to traverse, and the many places with no way out into which we have been led by following the paths of history and criticism; out of which there has been time and again no egress, even when holding fast to the thread of light woven out of the illuminating rays of the doctrines of the tradition.

It is indeed a difficult task to stand with the feet of the mind set firm on the surface of objectivity, and with the head and heart of it in the heights and depths of the subjective and unmanifest. And yet this almost superhuman task is the Great Work set before every scholar of the Gnosis—the man who would think truly and judge justly, viewing the matter from all standpoints, and appraising it from without and within, from above and below, endeavouring to unite centre and circumference in a blended intuitional sense that transcends our divided senses and intellect.

The Trismegistic literature is scripture, and to its understanding we must bring all and every faculty that the best minds of to-day are bringing to bear upon the special scripture which each one may believe to be the most precious legacy from the Past to the Present.

Now the application of what is called "criticism" to scripture is the wielding of a two-edged sword; this sword is not only two-edged, but it is fiery. If it is rightly used, it will disperse the hosts of error and hew a path into the Paradise of Truth; but if it is wrongly used, it will react on the daring soul that attempts to grasp it, and he will find in it the flaming brand in the hands of the Angel-Warden that keeps him from the Gate of Heaven.

Criticism, which is regarded with such fear and trembling by some, and is sneered at and despised by others, is the sword that the Christ has brought on earth in these latter days. There is now war in the members of the faithful, war within them, such war as they cannot escape, if God has given them a mind with which to reason. Every man of intelligence who loves his own special scripture, is keenly aware of the war within his members—head against heart and heart against head, form against substance and substance against form. This is keenly felt by those who love their own special Bible; but how few can enter into the feelings of another who loves with equal fervour some other Bible? Who can be really fair to any other man's religion? And by this we do not mean an absolutely lifeless indifference, in which the head alone is concerned—for there are not a few men of this type who deal with the comparative science of religion—but a lively sympathy that knows that the other man's religion is the highest thing on earth for him, and the light-giving revelation of God's Wisdom.

THE SONS OF GOD

In treating of the "Religion of the Mind," of the Gnosis of Thrice-greatest Hermes, I have endeavoured to enter into it as I conceive the Disciples of that Way entered into it, with love and reverence. I would do the same with any other of the Great Religions of Humanity (and have done so in some cases), if I desired fervently, all prejudices and predilections apart, I will not say, to understand it—for what mortal mind can grasp the Divine Revelation in any of its Great Forms?—but to share, however imperfectly, in its illumination. Now, this attitude of mind and love of God and man is strongly deprecated by those who fear to stand accused of lack of loyalty to their own particular form of that Great Form of Faith which God has given for their guidance. The one object of their enquiries into other Great Forms of Faith is to "prove" that their own small form of the Great Form to which they give allegiance, is the end of all ends, and the highest of all heights, and that the other countless forms are of the Enemy of their God. My God, or rather God, for He is the Father of all, has no enemies; He has many sons, all brethren, and loves them equally even though they refuse to believe Him. There is but one Religion, its Great Forms are many, the forms of these Forms are innumerable, as many as are the individual minds and hearts of men, and the many hearts and minds of individual man.

And here I would set forth my present all-insufficient notion of the Great Form of Religion known as Christianity, for there will doubtless be some who read these volumes who will accuse me of I know not what attitude other than that of their own to that Faith.

My faith in the Master of Christendom is unbounded; I dare not limit it or qualify it—for that Master is for me the Mind of all master-hood, Pœmandres Himself. For how can any small mind of man dare to limit the Illimitable, the Mystery of all mysteries, that enfolded Jesus the Christ, and Gautama the Buddha, and Zoroaster the Mage, and Lao-tze the Sage, and Orpheus the Bard, and Pythagoras the Philosopher, and Hermes the Gnostic, and all and every Master and Master of masters ? Do I detract from the transcendency of Jesus the Christ, when I mention His Brethren, all Sons of God ? I do not, for the Sons of God are not separate and apart, set over one against the other; they are all one Sonship of the Father, and these apparent differences must be left to those who think themselves wise enough to judge between them—instructed enough to know the within of the matter as well as the without, which in no case has come down to us in any but the most fragmentary and erroneous tradition. I do not know; I dare not judge those who are Judges of the quick and dead. And so I leave this audacity to those who would forget the *logos* of their Saviour: "Judge not."

If, nevertheless, I am still judged as a "calumniator" by some, it is but natural injustice and quite understandable. There is, however, no real Injustice in the universe, and he who would be Justified and rise again with Osiris, must balance mortal seeming justice and injustice to reach the true equilibrium, and so be free of mortal opinion, and stand in the Hall of Truth. It is to the bar of this Judgment Hall that all men in

CONCLUSION

the last resort appeal, whether they be born Christian or Mahommedan, Brāhman or Jew, Buddhist or Taoist, Zoroastrian or Pagan—or whether they be born to a manner of faith that is none of these, or to an ideal of faith that includes them all.

Christianity is the Faith of the Western World—the Faith most suited to it in nature and in form. He who gave that Faith, gave in fullest abundance through many sources; and the greatest sign of His authority, of His *authentia*, was the throwing open of some part of the age-long secret mystery-teaching to the many without distinction of age, sex, class, caste, colour, or nation, or of instruction. The inner doors of the Temple were thrown wide open to the *Amme-ha-aretz*; but the innermost door still remained closed, for it is a door that is not man-made—it opens into the within of things, and not into some inner court of formal instruction. That door still remained naturally closed to the unworthy and unknowing; but no Scribe or Pharisee of the established order of things could any longer keep the key thereof in his selfish hands. The key was given to all, but given still mystically, for it is hidden in the inner nature of each son of man, and if he seek not in himself, searching into the depths of his own nature, he will never find it. That key is the opener of the Gate of the Gnosis, the complement and syzygy and spouse of Faith; the virile husband of the woman-side of the Christ-Religion.

In the early days that Gnosis was given in greatest fullness; Faith there was, Faith in mighty abundance, but there was also Gnosis; and it was because of this Gnosis of not a few that the Faith of the many was so intense. But over these mysterious days, and the inner in-working of the Mystery, a veil has been drawn to hide the holy operations from profane eyes

So that to-day, these many centuries after, the foolish of the Faith deny there was ever a Gnosis; just as their still more foolish predecessors persecuted the Gnostics of Christ and howled them down as Antichrists and First-born Sons of Satan. The natural veil was thus drawn over the too bright light of the Sacred Marriage when Heaven had kissed the Earth once more.

So great, then, is my faith in the *authentia* of the Master, so great my assurance of the wisdom of His Gnosis. If this be thought "calumny" of His transcendency, then we are judged "calumniators" with Hermes, a Knower of the Mystery, and so complimented immeasurably beyond our deserts.

CONCERNING DATES

And now let us turn to the Religion of the Mind, which is also the Religion of the Heart—for is not Thoth Lord of the heart of man?

In the first place we have endeavoured faithfully to investigate every statement or suggestion that can be thought to be indicative of date, and we have not succeeded in any single instance in fixing a precise date for any sermon or fragment. What, however, we have been able to do, is to clear the ground of many false opinions, and to show the insecurity, if not the absurdity, of any attempt at precision. Every hypothesis of precision of date, when that hypothesis has favoured a late date for any sermon, has broken down. Whenever there has been a clearer indication, as, for instance, in the case of the *Shepherd of Hermas*, and the *Pœmandres* of Hermes, it has thrown the time-period backwards and not forwards.

What has been proved, and amply proved, however, is that our literature goes back in an unbroken tradition of type and form and content to the earliest Ptolemaic times. The earliest forms of this literature are lost, but clear records of its nature remain. Of the extant literature there are specimens of varying date, though how they should be ordered is by no means clear; what, however, is clear is that some of our documents are at least contemporaneous with the earliest writings of Christianity.

In the "Prolegomena" we have established an unbroken line of tradition in which Gnosis and Mystery-teaching have been handed down through pre-Christian, Pagan and Jewish, and through Christian hands. We have further shown that the Gnosis of our Trismegistic documents is a simpler form than that of the great doctors of the Christianised Gnosis, Basilides and Valentinus, who flourished in the first quarter of the second century. The earlier of our sermons, therefore, represent one of the main streams, perhaps the main stream, of the Unchristianised Gnosis. We have further shown that, together with many other schools, both our Pœmandrists and the writers of the New Testament documents use a common theological or theosophical nomenclature, and have a common body of ideas.

What is clear from all this is that there is no plagiarism, no deliberate copying, no *logoklopia* of other men's secrets, though there was the freest drawing on a common fund. The condition of affairs and the nature of the problems involved are such, that any theory of plagiarism at once becomes a two-edged sword; he who says that Trismegisticism copied from Christianity, can at once have his argument reversed into the form that Christianity copied from Trismegisticism.

As to date, then, we are dealing with a period when there was as yet no divorcement between Gnosis and Faith even in Christianity itself, and therefore the canons of judgment erected in later times by ecclesiastical self-limitation cannot be made to apply.

THE BLEND OF TRADITIONS

The view of General Christianity, gradually narrowed down by the Church Fathers into dogmatic Nicene Christianity, looked to one tradition only as the schoolmaster of the Faith—the tradition of Israel as the God-favoured Folk. Nevertheless it was the fair Greek tongue and the Greek method of thought that were used in evolving this special dispensation into a world-cult for the many.

The Trismegistic tradition laboured under no such limitation; its sympathies were more catholic. It is true that its main source was in Egypt, but it embraced with whole-hearted affection the wisdom of Hellas and the genius of Greece which were developed under Divine Providence to teach the Western Nations the glory and beauty of the mind. At the same time its sympathies were not divorced from the tradition of the Hebrews, though it refused to set them apart from the rest of humanity, and looked rather to the great river of wisdom in the Books of the Chaldæans, Persians, Medes, and Parthians, than to the single stream shut off in the Books of Israel. The spirit of our Trismegistic writings is the same as that which inspired the Pagan and Jewish and Christian Gnostic scribes of the Naassene Document, all of whom believed that there was but one Mystery which all the mystery-institutions of the world attempted to adumbrate.

If, then, we were to say for the sake of convenience that our Trismegistic writings enshrine the Wisdom of Egypt in Greek tradition, we should not divorce that Wisdom from the Wisdom of the Chaldæans and the rest. The Wisdom was one, the forms were many; and both

CONCLUSION

Egypt and Chaldæa looked back to an Archaic Gnosis that was the common mother of their most ancient forms of Mystery-teaching.

And if we say that this Wisdom has come down to us in Greek tradition, we should ever remember that this Græcising or philosophising has to do with the form and not with the substance. For whence did Thales and Pythagoras and Plato draw the inspiration for their philosophy or love of wisdom; was it not from Egypt? At anyrate so say the Greeks themselves without a single dissentient voice. And can we think that the Greeks, who were always so proud of their own achievements and boasted their own genius so loudly, would have given the palm of wisdom to Egypt had they not been compelled by overwhelming evidence to do so? But this does not mean that we are to deprive Hellas of her just laurels. Hellas was the mother of philosophy in the sense of systematic thinking and the development of the analytic reason This is her great virtue and honour; independent research, and the piercing analysis of the intellect and the beauty of clear thinking in excellent expression, were her gifts to the Western world. It was she beyond the other nations that created for herself a subtler vehicle of thought for the manifestation of the powers of mental analysis. That, however, is not necessarily in itself wisdom, but the perfecting of an instrument whereby wisdom, if it be attained by other means, may be the more clearly expressed for those in whom the analytic faculties are being developed.

Wisdom transcends this mode of mind; for ratiocination is not ecstasis, the practical intelligence is not the contemplative mind. Nor is mind, using it as contrasted with the other faculties and energies and powers in man, the only or even the highest thing in man. This Secret of the Sphinx Egypt had possessed for millennia; so that her priests could say to Solon: "You Greeks are all children"—for the intellect in Greece was young, though destined to grow into a giant; whereas the hoary Gnosis of the heart of man was prior to the æons, and will continue when the æons shall cease.

That Gnosis of Man still awaits decipherment in Egypt; it is hidden in her glyphs and symbols and holy signs. But that Gnosis will never yield its secret to those who persist in interpreting these symbols of the Language of the Gods into their lower forms, forms intended for children and not for men. And indeed our Trismegistic sermons, if they should teach us nothing else, can at least assure us of this, for their writers were still ear to mouth with the Living Voice of that once Great Church of Wisdom. Our Pœmandrists knew what the mystery-tradition inculcated; they knew, for they had been within the holy shrines.

At anyrate for my part I prefer to believe their view of the matter, than to listen to the contemptuous patronage of modern conceit bred of complete ignorance of the manifold natures and powers and energies in man.

OF INITIATION

Indeed the whole of this theosophy of Egypt, as indeed of the theosophy of all climes and times, was intended to lead a man up the stairway of perfectioning, to the portals of the first true natural initiation, whereby he becomes superman, or, as Hermes would say, at last and in truth "man" and not a "procession of Fate." Beyond that stage are many others too sublime for us in any way to understand; and it is just because

CONCLUSION 327

of their sublimity that we do not understand and so we " interpret " things of the height into the lowest notions and opinions of the most limited things of sense. For beyond the superman stage comes the Christ, and then —but who shall speak of that which transcends even perfected master-hood ?

And by initiation, in this sense, we do not mean probationary forms of drama and of instruction, " of things said and done," but a natural thing and process, all that which the Christ of Christendom has laboured to inculcate with so much wisdom even in the blurred record that has come down to us. To this initiation a man may come without a physical guide or the help of any tradition of formal ceremony. Nevertheless, he would indeed be foolish who should say that the greater mystery-institutions which have been established by wise teachers and the Providence of God, have been or are of no effect.

On the contrary, the disciple of wisdom will study every record of such institutions accessible to him, and ponder on their marvellous multiplicity, and marvel at the infinite modes devised to play the pedagogue, that so man may be brought unto his God. Nevertheless, if he has not the love and wit to study such things, he should not despair, for is he not already in the Outer Court of the Temple, if he would but lift up his eyes to see the mysteries of the universe that surround him on every side ?

We all are babes in the Womb of the Great Mother ; how long we continue as babes, as embryos, remains for each of us to decide. For in this Birth the Mother alone cannot bear all the pains of labour; we too must help and strive and struggle and dare to breathe within her holy Womb, so as to accustom our dead lungs to expand, before the Great Birth can be accomplished, and we can at length walk forth into the Inner

World erect upon our feet and draw in at every pore and in every atom its pure air without fear. But this Inner World is no thin shadow of the outer world, as it may appear to us in the dark night of our present ignorance; it is the Inner Cosmos, not the inner earth. Rapts and visions may let us see some mysteries of the inner earth, but not the mysteries of Earth, much less the Divine Mysteries of Cosmos.

Nor is there any need to label these things with precise terms, for now even the most experienced in such vision can know but in part; whereas then we shall know the Fullness, face to face, without a parable. But knowing this, who shall tell the Mystery, who *can* tell the Mystery—for is not the whole of Nature telling us this Mystery now at every moment with infinite voices from infinite mouths, and yet we hear nothing? For is not the whole creation designed with this one purpose to tell every son of man that he *is* of Light and Life and only *happens* to be out of them, as Hermes says?

A Last Word

But it is very possible that some who have done me the honour of reading to the end, will say: "This man is a dreamer, an ecstatic; we have no use for such in the hard world of rigid facts that confront us in our everyday life!"

But indeed I have little time for dreams and ecstasies in the sense in which my supposed critics would use the words, as any one may see who can realise the labour that has been expended on these volumes, nine-tenths of which are filled with translations and commentaries, criticisms and notes, in which dreams and ecstasies have no part, but only strenuous co-labour of mind and soul and body. And that is just the carrying out of what I hold to be the true doctrine of practical

CONCLUSION

mysticism, or if objection be taken by the reader to that much ill-used word, of the Great Work of life. It is true that it is almost impossible to talk of these high or deep things except in language that in every expression and in every word is liable to misconstruction. For even when we call them high things, they are not high in space or place, but rather in the sense that they are of greater intensity than the shows and appearances of opinion that form the surfaces or superficialities of our world of normal conditioning.

Spirit in itself is not superior to mind, or mind to soul, or soul to body; each and all must work together according to their proper dignity, nature, and energy, in perfect equilibrium in the perfect man. They are not descending degrees of some one thing, but are mutually in some mysterious way all aspects of one another.

For should we regard them as quantitatively distinguished solely, then we should be looking at them from the point of view of divided body alone; or should we regard them as qualitatively distinguished, then we should be looking at them from the point of view of separated soul alone; or should we regard them as logically distinguished, then we should be regarding them from the standpoint of the formal reason solely; while if we should look at them as wholes monadically and synthetically, we should be regarding them from an abstract and not a vital view-point.

Nevertheless they are all each of other, the same in difference and different in the same. Their source and middle and their end is Man, and Man alone can reach unto the Gnosis of God.

And therefore we may conclude with the daring counsel given unto Hermes by the Mind—a doctrine fit for Men.

"If, then, thou dost not make thyself like unto God, thou canst not know Him. For like is knowable to like alone.

"Make thou thyself to grow to the same stature as the Greatness which transcends all measure; leap forth from every Body; transcend all Time; become Eternity; and then shalt thou know God.

"Conceiving nothing is impossible unto thyself, think thyself deathless and able to know all—all arts, all sciences, the way of every life.

"Become more lofty than all height, and lower than all depth. Collect into thyself all senses of all creatures—of fire and water, dry and moist. Think that thou art at the same time in every place—in earth, in sea, in sky; not yet begotten, in the womb, young, old, and dead, in after-death conditions.

"And if thou knowest all these things at once—times, places, doings, qualities, and quantities; thou canst know God."

This is the Straight Way, the Good's Own Path, the Ancient Road.

"If thou but sett'st thy foot thereon, 'twill meet thee everywhere, 'twill anywhere be seen, both where and when thou dost expect it not—waking, sleeping, sailing, journeying, by night, by day, speaking, and saying naught. For there is naught that is not image of the Good."

And so for the present writing we bid farewell to Thrice-greatest Hermes and the teachings of his Mind, the Shepherd of all men—with heart-felt thanks that by the Mercy of God the echo of his voice has come to us across the ages and bidden us once more remember.

Index

Āāh-Tehuti, i. 66.
Aahlu, Territory of Illumination, i. 70.
Aall, i. 33.
Āān, i. 55.
Ab, i. 89.
Abammon, the Teacher, iii. 285.
Abbot Olympius, Story of, i. 384.
Abercius, ii. 55.
Abortion, i. 335, ii. 366.
Abraham, i. 253.
Abraxas, i. 82, 402.
Abraxoid, i. 82.
Abydos, i. 292.
Abyss, i. 408, ii. 27, 80, 81, 269.
Accuser, blind, iii. 281.
Achaab, the Husbandman, ii. 265.
Achæa, i. 350.
Acharantus, the Husbandman, ii. 265.
Achemides, i. 400.
Active Principle, the, i. 225.
Acts of John, i. 236, ii. 55, 238, iii. 157; mystery ritual in, i. 182, 183, ii. 243, iii. 156.
Acts of Philip, i. 147.
Adam, i. 115, 149, iii. 277, 281; body of, i. 281; celestial, i. 146.
Adam (J.), i. 336.
Adam Kadmon, i. 146.
Adamant, i. 392.
Adamas, i. 146, 159, 161.
Adams (see Marsham).
Adomenon, iii. 305.
Adonis, i. 151, 156, 294.
Adoration of images, ii. 286.
Adrasteia, i. 430, iii. 116.
Advent, ii. 171.
Adversary, Agree with thine, iii. 281.

Æacus, i. 303.
Ælian, i. 103.
Æon, i. 66, 92, ii. 128, 175, 232, 370, iii. 117, 161; become, ii. 190; birth of the, iii. 160; circle of infinitude, i. 399; communities of the, in Phœnicia, i. 403; demiurgic, i. 410; eternity or, iii. 91; feast of the, i. 403; in Theurgic literature, i. 410; Logos, i. 406; Mithriac, i. 399; in Plato, i. 404; song of praise to the, i. 408; is not time, i. 405; boundary of all universes, i. 392; wealth-giving, i. 402.
Æon or Æons, i. 182, ii. 240.
Æon-doctrine, the, i. 387, ii. 190.
Æonian Essence Above, i. 152.
Æonic Consciousness, ii. 244; Immensities of Egypt, i. 407.
Æonology, ii. 32, 192, 248; Hellenistic origin of, i. 401, 405.
Æons, ii. 373; father of the, i. 411; hymn of the, ii. 43; Great Silence, Mother of, ii. 241; of Pleroma, i. 408, ii. 245; "rootage" of, ii. 317; type of the, ii. 282.
Aerolites, iii. 53.
Æsculapius, cult of, i. 468.
Æther, i. 84, 101, iii. 50, 98, 101, 125; the height of the, i. 233; quintessence or, ii. 92; Mighty Whirlpool, i. 451.
Æthiopia (see Ethiopia), i. 188, 281.
Æthiopian queen, i. 316.
Again-becoming, ii. 76, 83.
Agamemnon, i. 446.
Agathodaimon, i. 85, 98, 105, 109, 479, ii. 213, iii. 156, 157, 163;

Osiris disciple of, i. 478, iii. 261; literature, iii. 257, 316; sayings of, iii. 310, 316; type, iii. 261.
Age, Golden, iii. 135; of seven years, iii. 37.
Agree with thine adversary, iii. 281.
Agrippa (Cornelius), i. 13.
Ahriman, i. 325, 326, 400.
Ahura Mazda (see Ormuzd), i. 326.
Aion, Reitzenstein's monograph on, i. 387.
Aipolos, i. 175, 177.
Air, ii. 342, iii. 66, 129, 210.
Air very air, iii. 17.
Air-spaces, iii. 205.
Ākāshā-Gaṅgā, i. 110.
Akhmîm, i. 282.
Akron, i. 364.
Ajax, i. 446.
Alalkomeneus, i. 148, 286.
Alaric, ii. 401.
Albinus, iii. 227.
Alchemist, the true, ii. 139.
Alethophilus, i. 13.
Alexander, brother of Philo, i. 204; Cornelius (Polyhistor), i. 164.
Alexandria, i. 99, 301; Jewish colony of, i. 204; Library of, i. 197.
Alexandrian religio-philosophy, i. 200.
Alexandrine Gnostics and fourth gospel, i. 38.
Alexarchus, i. 314.
Alkyoneus, i. 149.
All, ii. 310; in all, ii. 221; calumniators of the, ii. 228; genesis of the, i. 406; and Good, ii. 175; master of the, i. 409; and one, ii. 118; is one, ii. 213, 268, 308, 309; one and, i. 136, ii. 230, 344; threefold divided, i. 165; perfected, ii. 255.
All-Father Mind, ii. 8.
All-form, ii. 185, 194.
All-god, Hymn to, ii. 108.
All-goodness, ii. 344.
All-perfection, iii. 255.
All-receiving, i. 333.
All-seed Potency, ii. 30.
All-seeing Light, ii. 253.
All-sense, ii. 364, 396.
All-soul, ii. 145.
Allegory, i. 200.

Almond-tree, i. 182.
Alone Good Father, ii. 283.
Alone-begotten, i. 403, iii. 278.
Alter-egos, ii. 43.
Amasis, i. 465.
Ambrosia, i. 161.
Amélineau, i. 50.
Amen, i. 74, 274, 337.
Amen-Rā, Hymn to, i. 131.
Amenhotep, i. 467.
Amenhotep-Asclepius, i. 473.
Amentet, i. 304.
Amenthē, i. 304.
Amenti, i. 379; Place of Union with Unseen Father, i. 70.
American Encyclopædia, i. 24.
Amme-ha-Aretz, iii. 321.
Ammianus Marcellinus, ii. 113.
Ammon, i. 100, 101, 149, 273, 471, ii. 308; King, iii. 293; Kronos that is, ii. 279; sayings of, iii. 307, 313; words of, iii. 152, 215, 216; temples of, ii. 279; (Zeus), i. 318.
Ammon-Kneph, iii. 158.
Ammonius, iii. 285.
Amoun, i. 274, iii. 61; meaning of, i. 273.
Amphithemis, i. 149.
Amphitrite, i. 359.
Amsu, i. 327.
Amulet, i. 346, 349.
Amygdalos, i. 182.
Amyxai, i. 183.
Anacreon, cup of, i. 167, 193, 455.
Anaktoreion, i. 180, ii. 171.
Anaximander, iii. 178, 179.
Anebo, iii. 286.
Angel, recording, i. 64; sovereign, i. 371.
Angel-chief, i. 234.
Angels, the, i. 240; of Darkness, i. 424; eldest of all, i. 198; evil, ii. 355, iii. 239; of Light, i. 424; paternal, i. 159; tongue of, ii. 32; "words," i. 243.
Anger, ii. 224.
Animal, hylic, ii. 63; soul, ii. 246; spirits, i. 363.
Animal-soul of cosmos, i. 353.
Animals, burials of, i. 295; celestial, ii. 282; circle of, iii. 46, 51; earthy, iii. 301; sacred, ii. 52, 383, iii. 102, 288; worship of, i. 353.
Ankh-tie, i. 61.

INDEX

Ankhnes-Ra-Neferab, i. 73.
Announcement, Great, ii. 170, 317.
Annu, i. 74.
Annuals (winds), i. 316.
Ånpu, i. 342.
Anthropos, Myth of, i. 143; Prototype of humanity, i. 139.
Anthropos-doctrine, i. 193, iii. 273, 282; Zosimus on, i. 196.
Anticleides, i. 314.
Antigonus the Elder, i. 298.
Antilegomena, i. 370.
Antoninus Pius, i. 464.
Ants, iii. 35, 36.
Anubis, i. 88, 100, 283, 284, 315, 322, 342.
Ape, i. 87, 95, 446, 449.
Ape-form, i. 95.
Ape-Thoth, i. 462.
Apelles, i. 298.
Aphrodite, i. 61, 151, 181, 280, 305, 327, 350, 352, 359, ii. 345, iii. 89, 316.
Aphrodite-Helen, iii. 182.
Apion, i. 307, 387, ii. 5.
Apis, i. 267, 268, 277, 292, 303, 304, 307, 309, 311, 322, 337, 355; = Epaphos, i. 314; animated image of Osiris, i. 321.
Apocalypse of Jesus, iii. 279; of Thespesius, iii. 192; Untitled, ii. 107, 282.
Apocalypsis, Vision and, ii. 20 ff.
Apocrypha, i. 365.
Apocryphal, ii. 234, 236.
Apogeneses of souls, ii. 260.
Apokatastasis, ii. 128.
Apollo, i. 279, 298, 334, 342, 352, 359; golden curls of, i. 352; monad, i. 275.
Apollonius of Tyana, i. 374, ii. 197, 252.
Apology of a Pœmandrist, ii. 298.
Apophis, i. 313.
Apophthegm of Hermes, iii. 88.
Apostles, Memoirs of, i. 195.
Apotheosis, ii. 163; of Hermes, iii. 222.
Appendages, iii. 145, 181.
Appetite, iii. 75; and heart, iii. 78.
Apple, of the eye, iii. 165; of the World-Eye, iii. 167.
Appuleius, ii. 307.
Apu, i. 282.
Arabs, i. 272.

Aratus, i. 314.
Arbiter (Thoth), i. 58.
Arcadia, i. 376; Mount of, ii. 238.
Archangelic Book of Moses, i. 197.
Archemachus, i. 301.
Archetypal, Form, ii. 6, 8, 9, 29; Model, i. 236, 241; Pattern, i. 235; Seal, i. 235.
Archetype, ii. 66; of every other light, i. 241; of Soul, ii. 71; Time's, i. 229, ii. 193.
Archi-charila, i. 310.
Architect, iii. 122, 125, 235.
Archontics, i. 424.
Arcturus, i. 288.
Ares, i. 305, 327.
Argives, i. 299, 311.
Argo, i. 296.
Argus, iii. 232.
Aridæus, Vision of, i. 438, 452.
Ariouth, i. 88.
Aristagoras, i. 267.
Aristarchus, i. 100.
Ariston, i. 314.
Aristotle, i. 62, 327, 340, 362; on perfumes, i. 364.
Ark, tables of the laws in the, i. 238.
Arms of the Sun, i. 331.
Arnebeschenis, iii. 198, 209.
Aroueris, i. 279, 280.
Arrival of Isis from Phœnicia, i. 330.
Arsaphes, i. 314.
Art-prose, ii. 300.
Artaud, i. 27.
Artemidorus, i. 158.
Artemis, i. 352; dyad, i. 275.
Artificer of Time, ii. 192; of this new World, iii. 118.
Artist, ii. 290; Supreme, iii. 266.
Arts, iii. 40, 198; and sciences, iii. 199, 325.
Åsår (Osiris), i. 276; and Ast, i. 367.
Åsår-Hāpi, i. 302.
Ascension of Isaiah, ii. 232.
Ascent of the Soul, ii. 41 ff.; Straight, i. 428.
Asclepieion, i. 460.
Asclepius, i. 127, 469, ii. 391, iii. 184, 198; the Healer, i. 467; the pupil of Taautos, ii. 279.
Asclepius-Imuth, i. 461, iii. 96, 198.
Asclepiuses, many, iii. 221.

Asenas, iii. 277.
Ashes, i. 355.
Ashvaghosha, ii. 44.
Ashvattha, ii. 317.
Aso, i. 281.
Asp, i. 356, 357.
Aspalathus, i. 365.
Asphodel, iii. 134.
Ass, i. 290, 307, 329, 422; bound, i. 305, 330.
Ass-like, i. 305.
Assyrians, initiations of the, i. 151; mysteries of the, i. 155, 426.
Astarte, i. 285.
Astral body, the true, ii. 172; crater, i. 453.
Astronomers, iii. 112.
Asuras, iii. 180.
At-one-ment, ii. 50, 190, 371.
Atalanta, i. 446.
Atem-cult, i. 88.
Atf-crown, i. 71, 77.
Athanasius, ii. 72.
Atheism, i. 278.
Atheists, i. 296.
Athena, i. 62, 273, 286, 308, 343, 352, 359; hebdomad, i. 275; house of, iii. 183.
Athenæum, The, i. 68.
Athenagoras, i. 59, 61, iii. 220.
Athenaïs, i. 285, 286.
Athenians, Colonies of the, i. 314.
Athens, i. 350.
Athlete, i. 446; Therapeut, i. 206.
Athur (Athyr), i. 282, 316, 337, 350.
Atlantic Island, i. 106; names, i. 285.
Atlanticum, i. 108.
Atlantis, Plato's, i. 176; Story of, i. 285.
Atom, ii. 269.
Atomicity, i. 395.
Atoms, permanent, i. 289.
Atonement, Great Day of, i. 306.
Atropos, i. 442.
Attis, i. 152; the, i. 179; will I sing, i. 1-6.
Atum, i. 130, 132, 134, 135.
Atum-Ptah-Thoth, i. 136.
Augoeides, i. 361.
Augurs, ii. 273, iii. 112.
Augustine, i. 110, ii. 352; quotations from the old Latin version of, iii. 249.
Aurelian Sun-God, ii. 281.

Autheutia, iii. 318, 319.
Authentic Name, the, ii. 252.
Autozoon, i. 154, 400.
Avarice, ii. 224.
Avatāra, iii. 143.
Avengers, iii. 50.
Avenging Daimon, i. 91, ii. 15, 40.
Awake thou that sleepest, i. 160.
Azazel, Ritual of, i. 306.
Azoth, 1, 281.

Ba, i. 89.
Baba, i. 329.
Babe, ii. 216.
Babel und Bibel, iii. 179.
Babes, ii. 295; new-born, ii. 296.
Babylonian cultus, i. 379; Talmud, i. 115.
Bacchic caves, i. 453; mysteries, i. 212; initiates, i. 191; orgies, i. 311.
Bacchus, ii. 56; starry cup of, i. 414; infant, i. 303.
Bad, i. 341.
Balaam (Bileam), iii. 279; Jeschu, ii. 80; the Lame Man, i. 335; =Nicolaos, ii. 80, iii. 279.
Balaamites, i. 165, ii. 80.
Balance, i. 55, 64, 72, ii. 95, 118.
Balancer, i. 58, 64; Judge of the two Combatant Gods, i. 56.
Baptism, in the Cup, ii. 191; of light, ii. 255; spiritual, ii. 92.
Baptist, John the, i. 470.
Baptize, ii. 87.
Bardic lore, i. 392.
Barga, Da (P. Angelo), i. 10.
Baris, i. 289.
Barley-water, i. 347.
Basilides, i. 436, ii. 32, 98, 107, 160, 400, iii. 135, 140, 145; *Exegetica* of, ii. 215; Hermes and, ii. 215.
Bastardy, i. 334; charge of, ii. 51.
Bath-kol, i. 101, 279, 285.
Bats (simile), i. 161.
Battle, inner, iii. 6.
Baudissin (Count), i. 123.
Baumgarten-Crusius, i. 13, 24.
Bear, i. 176, 295, 422, ii. 101, iii. 51, 130, 131; Little, iii. 51.
Bears, ii. 62.
Beast, i. 398.
Beasts, Great, i. 424, 425.
Beautiful, the, ii. 113, 114, 118; Vision of the, iii. 15, 53.

INDEX

335

Beauty, ii. 8, 28, iii. 54; of the Gnosis, ii. 123; of the Good, ii. 144, 145, 163; of the Truth, ii. 121.
Bebi, i. 329.
Bebon, i. 329, 343.
Becanus Goropius, i. 20.
Become Æon, ii. 190; all things, ii. 194.
Becoming, i. 333.
Beetle, i. 356.
Beginning, i. 234; of philosophy, i. 274.
Begrudgeth, ii. 108.
Behemoth, i. 423, 424; monster of the south land, i. 427.
Behnesa *logoi* (see Oxyrhynchus), ii. 17, 239.
Belly-lust, ii. 112.
Beloved, the, ii. 35.
Belus, iii. 303.
Benci, i. 9.
Benefactor, i. 320; of men, ii. 213.
Beqesu, i. 60.
Bergk, i. 149.
Bernays, ii. 392.
Bestiaries, iii. 112.
Bestower of the Spirit, ii. 231.
Better, i. 333; the, ii. 89.
Better One, i. 328, 340, ii. 291, 294, 297.
Beyond-same, ii. 62.
Bhakti-Mārga, ii. 119.
Bible of Hellas, the, i. 193; of *logia*, ii. 236; of the Veii, ii. 235.
Bileam (Nico-laus), i. 165.
Biographie Générale, i. 27.
Birds, iii. 103.
Birth, iii. 22; from Above, ii. 239; of the Æon, iii. 160; blind from, i. 189, iii. 281; Chamber of, i. 75; of a Christ, the, ii. 243; conception and, iii. 68; demiurge of, ii. 244; engine of, ii. 39; essential, ii. 228, 250; in God, ii. 226; of Horus, i. 75, 76, 95, ii. 242, iii. 122, 157, 160, 162; of Man, ii. 241; mysteries of a divine, i. 75; new, ii. 239, 240, 250; of Osiris, iii. 122; parent of my bringing-into, ii. 232; second, i. 79; in understanding, ii. 226; virgin, ii. 240; way of this, ii. 244.

Birthday of the Eye of Horus, i. 331; of the Sun's Staff, i. 331.
Birthdays of the Gods, i. 279; of Horus, i. 332.
Bithus of Dyrrachium, iii. 296.
Bitos (see Bitys), i. 197, iii. 276, 295; Pinax of, iii. 277.
Bitter Chaos, i. 92, 192; matter, i. 92; path, ii. 362; awesome and, i. 397; water, i. 92.
Bitterness, i. 92, 153; cup of, ii. 139; of God, i. 92; of Jacob Böhme, i. 92, 397.
Bitys (see Bitos), i. 197, iii. 294; the prophet, ii. 280, iii. 293.
Bitys-books, iii. 297.
Bitys-school, iii. 298.
Black dog-ape, i. 88; rite, iii. 107, 141, 149, 155.
Black-robed, i. 332.
Blackden, iii. 186.
Blasphemers, ii. 140, 244.
Blessed Land, iii. 282; Man Above, i. 159, 164; Nature, i. 155; Nature Above, i. 152; Ones, ii. 206; Region, iii. 276, 295; Space, ii. 98.
Blind, Accuser, i. 189; from birth, i. 189, iii. 281.
Bliss, ii. 226.
Boat, i. 52, 89; Solar, i. 270.
Bocchoris, i. 272.
Böckh, i. 107.
Bodhisattvas, ii. 45.
Bodies, how composed, ii. 133; everlasting, iii. 30; glory of celestial, ii. 165; migration into, ii. 329.
Bodiless, ii. 88, 128; the, ii. 65, iii. 14.
Body, iii. 63; of Adam, i. 281; aery, iii. 145; of bliss, ii. 45; divine, ii. 93; elements of, iii. 200; encompasses all things, iii. 46; fiery, ii. 151, 154, 171; of God, ii. 85; of the Great Man, i. 425; house of, ii. 321; of Jesus, i. 286; the last, ii. 187, 195; of the Law, ii. 44; mixture of, iii. 199; nöetic, ii. 242; soul and, ii. 124, 130; spirituous, iii. 145, 210; subtle, iii. 145, 209; that can never die, ii. 221; times of, iii. 9; of transformation, ii. 44; type of, iii. 49; universal, ii. 125.

336 INDEX

Bodying, iii. 31, 36, 38.
Böhme, Jacob, i. 92.
Boissonade, ii. 38.
Bone of Horus, i. 189, 343 ; of the sea-hawk, i. 189, 343 ; of Typho, i. 189, 343.
Bonnet, ii. 108.
Book of Breathings, i. 65.
Book of the Dead, i. 52, 54, 55, 69, 83, 290 ; flood in the, i. 109 ; mysteries and the, iii. 186.
Book of Elxai, i. 369.
Book of Enoch, i. 126, 424.
Book of God, i. 467.
Book of the Great Logos according to the Mystery, i. 166, ii. 96.
"Book of the Living," i. 367.
Book concerning the Logos, ii. 265.
Book of the Master, i. 68, 77, 78.
Book of Ostanes, iii. 277.
Book, The Sacred, i. 75.
Books, canonical, ii. 235 ; of the Chaldæans, i. 392, ii. 81 ff., iii. 280, 321 ; preserved from flood, i. 113 ; on the Gnosis, iii. 231 ; Hermaïc, iii. 293 ; of Hermes, i. 100, 115, 196, 342, 380, iii. 282, 289 ; of Hermes described by Clem. of A., iii. 222 ; hieratic, iii. 225 ; of Isis, iii. 316 ; of Isis and Horus, i. 481, iii. 208 ; of Isis to Horus, iii. 316 ; Lord of, i. 53 ; of Manetho, i. 104 ; of Moses, i. 456, ii. 158 ; of the Saviour, i. 418 ; of Taautos, ii. 279 ; of Thoth, i. 122, 124 ; Victim-Sealing, iii. 223, 224.
Boötes, i. 288.
Boreas, iii. 132.
Boundary, ii. 9 ; Great, ii. 35 ; Horos or, ii. 366 ; of the Spheres, ii. 195.
Boundless Light, i. 93 ; Point, the, i. 184.
Boutos, i. 288.
Brain, the, i. 162, 169.
Branch, The, i. 227.
Brass, sounding, i. 303.
Bread, distribution of, iii. 224 ; which the Lord hath given you to eat, i. 246 ; super-substantial, i. 86.
Breadth-depth-length-height-ray, i. 94.
Breasted, i. 130, 138.

Breath, iii. 199 ; gift of, iii. 111 ; of God, i. 232, ii. 76.
Brethren, ii. 50 ; the two Horus, i. 66 ; of the Lord, i. 147.
Brick-bat, i. 115.
Brimo, i. 180.
Brimos, i. 180, 314.
Bringer-of-good, i. 158.
Brockhaus, i. 35.
Broiled fish, i. 270.
Brother, of the Lord, James, i. 143 ; of Man, ii. 35.
Brucker, i. 21.
Brugsch, i. 49, 55, 57.
Bubble, i. 390.
Buddha, Gautama the, iii. 320 ; Three Bodies of, ii. 44. ff.
Buddhism, Great Vehicle of, ii. 44.
Buddhist seer, i. 379.
Budge, i. 52, 89, 103, 367.
Builder, mind as, ii. 153.
Builder-Souls, iii. 140.
Builders, iii. 139, 140.
Bull-born, i. 311.
Burials of Animals, i. 293, 295 ; of Osiris, i. 295.
Burn living men, i. 355.
Burns his food publicly, i. 270.
Busiris, i. 293, 305.
Butō, i. 315, 347.
Buys Plato, i. 351.
Byblos, i. 284-286.

Cabiri (Kabiri), i. 127.
Caduceus, i. 61, iii. 232.
Caïnites, i. 142.
Call thou me not Good, ii. 72.
Called, i. 147.
Calumniators, ii. 233, 250, iii. 317.
Cambyses, i. 277, 322.
Cana of Galilee, i. 167.
Cancer, i. 415.
Candalle (Flussas), i. 10.
Canopus (Canobus), i. 296, 301.
Capitoline Zeus, i. 352.
Carapace, cosmic, ii. 321 ; of darkness, ii. 121 ; of selfhood, ii. 42.
Caravanserai, ii. 283.
Cardamum, i. 365.
Carpenter, Estlin, i. 468.
Carriers of holy symbols, i. 264.
Casaubon, i. 21.
Cask, drop from a, i. 190.
Cat, i. 344.
Catalogue of kings, i. 277.
Catharms, iii. 210.

INDEX

Cave, ii. 126, 128.
Cedrenus, iii. 269.
Celsus, i. 147, 423 ; *True Word* of, ii. 50.
Celts, i. 350.
Ceremonies, Overseer of the, iii. 223.
Chalcidius, i. 19, 435, ii. 159.
Chaldæans, i. 196, 327, ii. 53 ; Books of the, i. 392, 465, ii. 81 ff., iii. 280, 324 ; mystery-tradition, i. 138.
Chamber of Birth, i. 75 ; of Flames, i. 75 ; of Gold, i. 75.
Chambers, i. 34, iii. 218, 266 ; opinion of, i. 34 f.
Champollion, i. 27.
Chaos, i. 150, 338, 388, 389, ii. 27, 102 ; the bitter, i. 192; liquid, i. 191.
Character, ii. 244, iii. 179.
Charila, i. 310, 311.
Chariot, celestial, i. 154, iii. 173 ; of the Powers, i. 238.
Charioteer, i. 429, 430, ii. 270.
Charity, ii. 346.
Charops, i. 303.
Cheiron, iii. 304.
Chemia, i. 263, 309, iii. 158.
Chemmis, i. 282.
Cherubim, i. 238.
Cheyne, i. 468.
Child of the Egg, i. 139 ; of God, ii. 255.
Child-making, ii. 68.
Children, likeness of, iii. 89 ; recognition of, iii. 20.
Chnouphis (Chnuphis), i. 92, 477, ii. 265.
Chnubis, i. 477.
Chnum, i. 477, 480, iii. 155, 159.
Chœroboscus, iii. 112.
Choir (choirs) of daimons, ii. 89, 145, 272, 273, iii. 102 ; of Gods, ii. 206.
Chonouphis, i. 274.
Chrism, the Ineffable, i. 154, 190.
Christ, i. 301 ; a, ii. 174 ; the, i. 160, iii. 324 ; the birth of a, ii. 241, 243; disciples of, i. 290 ; garment of, ii. 249 ; of God, ii. 43 ; "scourge" of, ii. 173 ; triumphant, ii. 117.
Christ-baptism, ii. 93.
Christ-mystery, i. 198.
VOL. III.

Christ-stage of manhood, i. 367, 368.
Christ-state, ii. 93, 243.
Christos, descent of the, i. 90.
Chronicum (Eusebius), i. 20.
Chrysippus, i. 298.
Church, ii. 117 ; virgin, i. 377.
Churning the Ocean, iii. 180.
Chwolsohn, ii. 57.
Cicala, song of, ii. 292.
Cicero, ii. 235.
Circle of the All, iii. 47 ; of animals, iii. 46, 51 ; Life-producing, iii. 51 ; of Necessity, i. 428 ; of Sun, iii. 52 ; of types-of-life, ii. 194, 227.
Circles, seven, ii. 76, iii. 47.
Circuit (Eudoxus), i. 269.
Circumambient, i. 300.
Circumterrene, ii. 276.
Cities of Refuge, i. 237.
Citizens, true, i. 221.
City, ii. 109 ; of the Eight, i. 57 ; of God, i. 235, 245, 246, ii. 256 ; the grandest, i. 235 ; the Intelligible, i. 235 ; the Little, i. 293.
Civil Wars, i. 352.
Claudius, i. 119.
Cleanthes, i. 347.
Clement, Second Epistle of, i. 153.
Clement of Alexandria, i. 153, ii. 215, 235, 300 ; on the mysteries, iii. 150 ; on the tradition of the Gnosis, i. 148.
Clementine Homilies, i. 388, ii. 72.
Cleombrotus, iii. 170, 175.
Cloak, hateful, ii. 121.
Closed lips, ye of the, i. 210.
Closet, i. 209.
Clotho, i. 442.
Cnossus, iii. 179.
Cock, iii. 162 ; crowing of, iii. 161, 162.
Cocks, i. 325.
Codex Brucianus, i. 50, 93, ii. 282 ; *Untitled Apocalypse* of, ii. 303.
Coffin, i. 287.
Colberg, i. 22.
Colonies of the Athenians, i. 314.
Colony, ii. 354.
Colour, one, i. 391 ; ray-like, i. 224.
Columns, i. 104 ; of Hermes, i. 112.
Combatant Gods, Judge of, i. 53.
Combatants, Two, i. 66.

22

338 INDEX

Come unto us, ii. 43.
Comets, iii. 52.
Common hearth, iii. 171; reason, i. 346; teachers, iii. 287.
Companions of Horus, i. 270, 290; of Odysseus, i. 270.
Completion-Beginning, i. 74.
Comprehensible, Incomprehensibles, i. 184.
Conception, ii. 390; and birth, iii. 68; Typhon, i. 304.
Concupiscence, ii. 224.
Conductor of Souls, i. 159.
Cone-bearing, i. 266.
Configuration of the Element, iii. 276.
Congress, ii. 240.
Consciousness, Æonic, ii. 244; Nirvānic, i. 51, ii. 45, 46.
Constancy, ii. 390.
Constantine, ii. 55.
Consummation, Supreme, ii. 161.
Contemplation, iii. 94.
Contemplative or Theoretic Life, i. 208.
Contemplator, ii. 93.
Continence, ii. 225.
Continuum, ii. 397.
Conybeare, i. 219, ii. 71; critical text of the *D. V. C.*, i. 200.
Coptic Gnostic *Codex Brucianus*, ii. 282; works, the, ii. 51.
Coptos, i. 335.
Coriander seed, i. 246, 247.
Corporality, ii. 212, 218.
Corpse, sensation's, ii. 121.
Corpus (Hermeticum), original MS. of, i. 6; quires lost from, ii. 69.
Corruption's chain, ii. 121.
Cory, i. 104, 106, 123.
Cosmogony, Chart of Orphic, ii. 162; of Taaut, i. 126.
Cosmoi, Seven, i. 407.
Cosmos, ii. 325, 337, 377, iii. 39; Animal-Soul of, i. 353; beautiful, ii. 147; most wise Breath, ii. 118; of Cosmos, i. 91; course of, ii. 133; divine mysteries of, iii. 325; egg or womb of, i. 451; imitator of eternity, ii. 368; second God, ii. 125; good, ii. 358; great body of, ii. 128; higher, ii. 378; Horus, i. 338; intellect of, ii. 373; intelligible, i. 146, ii. 167, 194, 275; principles of, ii. 207; matter or, ii. 336; gaze through Me upon the, ii. 179; meaning of, ii. 85; order, ii. 134; paradigm of, ii. 196; passions of, ii. 185; re-birth of, ii. 357; sense-and-thought of, ii. 133, 139; sensible or hylic, ii. 167; sensible image of, i. 334; a sphere, ii. 148; this, i. 224.
Cotta, iii. 231.
Counterfeit, iii. 282; of Spirit, iii 68.
Covent Garden theory, i. 258.
Cow, i. 316, 332.
Cow-horns, i. 291.
Cowherd, i. 272.
Cradle, Hall of the Child in his, i. 74, 75.
Crater, ii. 92; astral, i. 453; in Orpheus, Macrobius, and Proclus, i. 151; in Plato, i. 450; sidereal of Father Liber, i. 451; vulcanic, i. 452.
Crates, Visions of, i. 380.
Creation, new, ii. 243; of the world, iii. 117.
Creation-myths, i. 51.
Creator, God the, iii. 293; Word of the, iii. 256.
Creator-Word, iii. 254.
Creatures of Light, i. 51.
Cretan civilisation, i. 149.
Crete, i. 359.
Critias, i. 106.
Criticism, iii. 315.
Crocodile, i. 77, 267, 288, 329, 330, ii. 382; sixty eggs, i. 356, 358; tongue-less, i. 357.
Crocodilopolis, ii. 382.
Cronus (see Kronos), i. 390, ii. 144, 162, iii. 234; Ammon, i. 127; Mithriac, i. 400; mystery deity, i. 400.
Cross, i. 286, ii. 367; seal of a, iii. 161.
Crosswise, iii. 24, 47.
Crown of lives, i. 71.
Crux ansata, i. 61.
Cry (of Nature), ii. 34.
Cudworth, i. 32.
Cult of Æsculapius, i. 468; of Jesus, iii. 138.
Cultores et Cultrices pietatis, i. 208.
Cumont, i. 324, 399, 400, 401.

INDEX 339

Cup, ii. 86, iii. 273; of Anacreon, i. 167, 193, 455; baptism in the, ii. 191; of bitterness, ii. 139; of Dionysus, i. 452; of the divine draught, i. 245; His, iii. 284; which I drink, i. 168; of immortality, iii. 205; of initiation, ii. 94; in which the King drinketh, i. 167; of Living Water bubbling-forth, i. 399; of prudence, i. 454; of Tantalus, ii. 198.
Cupido, ii. 309.
Cure of intellect, ii. 347.
Cutting of wood, i. 293.
Cybele, priests of, i. 169.
Cyclic Gods, ii. 77, 89.
Cyclopædia of Biblical Literature, i. 27.
Cyllene, i. 158, 168.
Cylinder, i. 176, 439, iii. 101, 175, 177, 178.
Cymbal, tinkling, i. 303.
Cynocephalus, i. 55, 56, 120.
Cyperus, i. 364.
Cypress, i. 364.
Cyril's Corpus of XV. Books, iii. 251.
Cytherea, iii. 92.

Daimon, i. 324, 443; avenging, i. 91, ii. 15, 40; Chnum the Good, i. 477; counterfeit, iii. 281; essence of, is activity, ii. 273; evil, i. 355; Good, i. 84, 97, 402, ii. 156, 199, 203, 204, 206, iii. 150, 155, 255; Good Holy, i. 94; mind a, ii. 154, 171; self-born, iii. 120.
Daimon-Chief, iii. 237.
Daimones, ii. 313, 375, iii. 49; choirs of, ii. 89, 272, 273, 277, iii. 102; Concerning the, ii. 282; hierarchy of, ii. 314; Homer on, i. 299; incursions of, ii. 277; in service, ii. 274; Theory of the, i. 298.
Daimonial Energy, ii. 137.
Daimonials, ii. 130.
Daimonic Soul, ii. 229.
Damascius, i. 91, 152, 156, ii. 19, 25, 260.
Damatrios, i. 350.
Dark mist, i. 125; mystery, iii. 149; space, ii. 26; wisdom, i. 87, 91.

Darkness, i. 91, 325, 451, ii. 4, 13, 79, 80, 81; carapace of, ii. 121; comprehended it not, i. 125; genesis of fire and, i. 197; serpent of, ii. 31; thrice-unknown, ii. 25; torment of, ii. 226, 245.
Dawn, Land of Eternal, i. 80; New, iii. 96.
Day of Light, i. 326.
De Faye, i. 196.
De Horrack, i. 49.
De Mysteriis, iii. 252.
De Sphæra Barbarica, i. 407.
Dead, Book of the, i. 52, 54, 69, 83, 290; judge of the, i. 64; prayers for the, i. 78; things, if ye have eaten, i. 175; raise, i. 373; resurrection of, ii. 165; rising from, i. 173, iii. 163; shall leap forth from graves, the, i. 172; sheeted, i. 161; the, i. 172.
Death, i. 417, ii. 39, 126, 209; living, ii. 121; of the serpent, ii. 300; there is no, ii. 124; twelve fates of, ii. 249; Way of, ii. 18.
Death-genius, i. 88.
Deathless Water, ii. 18.
Deathlessness, ii. 128; Way of, ii. 39.
Decans, i. 100, iii. 45; Egyptian names of, iii. 54; Six-and-thirty, iii. 45, 46.
Deep, Infinite, i. 390.
Deer, form of a, i. 191.
Deinon, i. 307.
Delphi, i. 256, 310; Oracle at, i. 349.
Demagogue (in Plato), i. 431.
Demeter, i. 305, 318, 345, 350, iii. 232; limbs of, i. 347; wanderings of, i. 298.
Demi-Gods, i. 106.
Demiurge, i. 130, 457, ii. 33, iii. 22, 30; of birth, ii. 244; of God, iii. 240; the Sun, ii. 269.
Demiurgic Æon, i. 410; Mind, i. 137, ii. 35; Thought, iii. 56.
Democritus, i. 323, iii. 297.
Denderah, i. 73, 74, 75.
Deo nubere, i. 216.
Depth, i. 409.
Dêr-el-Bahari, i. 120.
Descent of the Christos, the, i. 90; from the Head Above, i. 169; of Kore, i. 350; of Man, ii. 34.

Desert, i. 163.
Desirable, ii. 161 ; One, ii. 254.
Destiny, iii. 69 ; bonds of, iii. 299.
Destruction, Way that leadeth to, i. 182.
Detailed, ii. 237 ; Discourses, ii. 264.
Determination, ii. 357, 358.
Deus Lunus, i. 166.
Devas, iii. 180.
Dévéria, i. 28.
Devil taking form of fisherman, iii. 164.
Devotee of God, ii. 139.
Devotees, race of, ii. 241.
Devotion, iii. 238 ; God-gnosis, ii. 131, 136 ; and Gnosis, ii. 114 ; Way of, ii. 119.
Devourer, i. 289.
Devourers of the Unrighteous, i. 425.
Dharmakāya, ii. 44, 45.
Diabolus, iii. 238.
Diaconic, i. 300.
Diadochi, i. 102.
Dialogues with Tat, ii. 237.
Diaspora, i. 255.
Diaulos, i. 149.
Didymus, ii. 72.
Dieterich, i. 82, 84, 90, 92, 94, 197.
Diktys, i. 271, 286.
Dinarchus, ii. 236.
Diochite, i. 292.
Diocletian, ii. 300.
Dionysiac rites, i. 256.
Dionysian night-rites, i. 311.
Dionysius (the sculptor), i. 352.
Dionysius Ægeensis, i. 62.
Dionysus, i. 281, 298, 301, 302, 305, 310, 313, 345, 347, 416, 453 ; bull-formed, i. 311 ; cup of, i. 452 ; gladsome, i. 312 ; ivy of, i. 314 ; mysteries of, i. 311 ; Osiris and, i. 310 ; relics of, i. 312 ; and Semele, i. 161 ; Spirit is, i. 318.
Disciples of Thrice - Greatest Hermes, i. 481.
Disciples of the Christ, i. 290 ; of God, i. 254 ; of the Logos, i. 243 ; Triad of, i. 476 ; the Twelve, i. 169 ; of Wisdom, iii. 303.
Discipline of the Priests, iii. 224 ; of Souls, ii. 347.

Discourse on Sense, ii. 131, 132.
Discourses, Detailed, ii. 264.
Disobedient Ones, iii. 143.
Dispensation of all things, ii. 158 ; of the Universe, ii. 173.
Divider of all, the, i. 236.
Divining, art of, i. 262.
Divinity, Feminine, ii. 32 ; Greatness of, ii. 309 ; Reason of, ii. 311, 318.
Dodecagon, i. 305.
Dodecaschœnus, iii. 155.
Dog, i. 87, 90, 277, 284, 288, 295, 296, 322, 325, 342, 352, 353, 358, 422.
Dog-days, i. 355.
Dog-headed, i. 355 ; ape, i. 55.
Dog-town, i. 354.
Dolphin, iii. 113, 180.
Door, About the Inner, iii. 275 ; Inner, iii. 274, 280.
Doser, i. 465, iii. 155.
Double, image or, i. 189.
Dove, i. 352.
Dowsing in the Mind, ii. 255.
Dragon, i. 94, 352, 422, iii. 112, 180 ; lower, i. 426.
Dragon-slayer, i. 94.
Drainer of Water, ii. 39.
Draughts, i. 278.
Dream, ii. 222 ; of Scipio, i. 413.
Dream-sight, ii. 130.
Dreams and ecstasies, iii. 203 ; the people of, i. 162.
Drexler, i. 115, 166.
Druidical Gnosis, iii. 296.
Drummond, i. 200.
Dry, iii. 66 ; space, ii. 75, 76.
Du Preau, i. 10.
Dual Soul, ii. 169.
Dualism, ii. 31, 115 ff.
Dualistic, ii. 140.
Dualists, Theory of the, i. 323.
Dümichen, i. 49.
Duncker and Schneidewin, i. 143.
Duration, ii. 211.
Dwarf, iii. 165.
Dwelling of the Golden One, i. 75.
Dyad, i. 275, 414.

Eagle, i. 56, 284, 330, 422, 446, 449, iii. 133, 180.
Earth, ii. 209, iii. 66, 130, 261 ; the black, i. 156 ; blood-red, iii. 277 ; fiery, iii. 277 ; fleshly, iii. 277 ; depths of, i. 413 ; Let there

INDEX 341

be, iii. 262 ; primal, i. 310 ; red, i. 150 ; Sons of God on, i. 233 ; very earth, iii. 17 ; virgin, iii. 277.
Earth-and-Water, ii. 5, 8, 37.
Earth-born, ii. 49 ; folk, ii. 122.
Ebers Papyrus, i. 50.
Ebionites, i. 369.
Ebony, i. 87.
Eclipses, i. 321.
Ecliptic, iii. 177.
Economy, ii. 28, iii. 61.
Ecstasis, i. 251, ii. 157, 161, 303.
Eden, i. 159 ; brain, i. 187 ; river of, i. 187.
Edersheim, i. 200.
Efflorescence, iii. 100.
Efflux, God's, iii. 121, 122.
Egg, i. 125, 126, 131, 326, 389, 462, ii. 282 ; Child of, i. 139 ; first, i. 391 ; God from, i. 392 ; skull-like, i. 391 ; sphere or, i. 427 ; throbbing, i. 182.
Egregores, iii. 137 ; Watchers, i. 126.
Egypt, is body, i. 164 ; image of heaven, ii. 351 ; holy land, i. 70 ; sacred language of, ii. 280 ; once sea, i. 317 ; geographical symbols of, iii. 186 ; theosophy of, iii. 323 ; wisdom of, ii. 98.
Egyptian alphabet, i. 337 ; names of Decans, iii. 54 ; emanation doctrine, iii. 95 ; teachers of Greeks, iii. 286 ; mysteries, grades of, i. 50 ; philosophy, i. 28 ; rhetor, ii. 299 ; syncretism 1000 B.C., i. 135 ; translation from, iii. 294.
Egyptians, Gospel according to the, i. 38, 142, 150, 153, 242, ii. 54, 164.
Egyptians, Greek disciples of, i. 274.
Eight, i. 71 ; at the, ii. 228 ; ogdoad or, i. 275 ; spheres, ii. 275 ; wardens, i. 85, 121.
Eight-and-twenty, i. 320.
Eighteen, i. 319.
Eighth, ii. 16 ; sphere, ii. 42 ff.
El-Khargeh Oasis, iii. 216.
El Shaddai, i. 159.
Elder Horus, i. 279, 280, 334, 343, 367.
Eldest of all Angels, i. 198.
Elect, i. 147, ii. 117.

Eleians, i. 311.
Element, Configuration of the, iii. 276 ; the One, ii. 195, 244.
Elements of body, iii. 200 ; complaint of, iii. 118 ; four, ii. 311 ; friendship and enmity with, iii. 133.
Elephantine, i. 320, 477.
Eleusinian *logos*, i. 175 ; mysteries, i. 59, 160.
Eleusis, i. 178, 179, 180, ii. 171.
Elis, i. 359.
Elohim, Sons of, i. 159.
Elxai, i. 71 ; *Book of*, i. 369.
Elysian state, i. 152.
Emanation, holy, iii. 121.
Emanations, i. 84.
Embalmment, Ritual of, i. 460.
Embarking, i. 321.
Embryology, ii. 102.
Embryonic stages of Incarnation (*Pistis Sophia*), iii. 68.
Empedocles, i. 159, 300, 435, ii. 362, iii. 237.
Emptiness, ii. 174.
Enclistra, iii. 93.
Encyclopädie, (Pauly), i. 26, 33.
Encyclopædia Britannica, i. 34.
Encyclopædism, i. 107, 108.
End, i. 315.
Endymion, i. 151.
Energies, ii. 211, 212, iii. 37.
Energy, ii. 259 ; and feeling, iii. 34, 40 ; of God, ii. 160, 178, 180, 203.
Enformation according to Gnosis, ii. 246.
Engine of birth, ii. 39 ; cosmic, ii. 34 ; of Justice, ii. 41 ; of the universe, iii. 50.
Enoch, Book of, i. 126, 424.
Entrance, i. 321 ; of the Golden Heavens, i. 75 ; on Light, i. 79.
Envy, ii. 224.
Epachthe, i. 350.
Epaphos, i. 314.
Epeius, i. 446.
Epicurus, i. 323.
Epimetheus, iii. 274, 280, 282.
Epiphanius, ii. 79.
Epiphany, Feast of, iii. 160.
Epiphi, i. 331.
Epopt, ii. 93, iii. 188.
Epopteia, i. 263, ii. 21, iii. 159.
Epoptic, i. 362 ; mystery, i. 362.
Equator, iii. 177.

Equilateral triangle, i. 305, 359.
Equilibrium, i. 56.
Er, Vision of, i. 413, 426, 428, 437, ii. 15, 40, 187.
Erataoth, i. 422.
Erdmann, i. 32.
Erebus, i. 125.
Eros, i. 125, ii. 309, 345.
Error, ii. 224.
Esaldaios, i. 159, 166.
Eschenbach, i. 62.
Essence, ii. 269, iii. 84 ; first, iii. 55 ; of God, ii. 113, 199 ; intelligible, ii. 276, iii. 57 ; moist, i. 187, 388, 390, 454, ii. 4, 75 ; one, i. 391 ; primal, iii. 56 ; of seed, i. 156.
Essence-chief, ii. 341.
Essences, i. 30, 208, 369, 373, ii. 395.
Essential, iii. 236 ; birth, the, ii. 250 ; man, ii. 116, 251, 321.
Eternity, ii. 325, 366 ; Æon, i. 229, iii. 91 ; become, ii. 188 ; cosmos imitator of, 368 ; of eternity, i. 91 ; moving image of, i. 405 ; illumined by Logos, i. 399 ; maker of, i. 66 ; prince of, i. 132.
Etesian Winds, i. 316.
Ether, i. 125.
Etheric double, iii. 206 ; link, iii. 206.
Ethiopia (see Æthiopia), i. 98.
Ethiopian, i. 88 ; enchanters, i. 119.
Ethiopian History, i. 106.
Eucharist, ii. 94.
Eudoxus, i. 269, 274, 293, 305, 332, 343, 345.
Euhemerus (see Evemerus), ii. 162.
Eunomus the Locrian, ii. 300.
Eunuch, business of, i. 186.
Euphrates, i. 188; waters of the, i. 426.
Euripides, i. 323, 352, 357.
Eusebius, i. 20, 123, 370.
Eustathius, i. 172.
Eve, iii. 280.
Eve, Gospel of, i. 142, ii. 24, 25, 238.
Evemerus (see Euhemerus), i. 257, 296, 297 ; theory of, i. 295.
Everard, i. 12.
Evil angels, ii. 355, iii. 239 ; create, i. 91 ; Daimon, i. 355 ; pleroma of, ii. 113.

Evoï, i. 186.
Excerpts from Theodotus, ii. 251.
Executioner, mind the, ii. 201.
Exegetica of Basilides, ii. 215.
Exhalation, iii. 206.
Existing Non-existences, i. 184.
Experience and memory, iii. 195.
Expository Sermons, ii. 250, 264, iii. 54 ; to Tat, iii. 216, 256, 257, 259, 262, 263, 264, 266.
Eye, altogether all, i. 214 ; apple of, iii. 165; heart's, ii. 121 ; of Horus, i. 336 ; House of, i. 288 ; incorporeal, iii. 253 ; of intellect, ii. 308 ; of mind, ii. 253 ; pupil of, i. 84, 394 ; Pupil of the World's, iii. 159 ; of the soul, iii. 129 ; spiritual, i. 214.
Ezekiel, Hebrew poet, i. 164.
Ezekiel, i. 154, 227, 379 ; Mercabah, or Chariot of, i. 238 ; Wheels of, iii. 173.

Fabricius, i. 5, ii. 263.
Face, i. 433 ; of God, i. 218.
Fairbanks, i. 159.
Famine Years, Inscription of the Seven, i. 466.
Famines, plagues and, iii. 49.
Farrar, ii. 55.
Fast to the world, ii. 239.
Fate (see Heimarmene), ii. 7, 201, 202, 273, iii. 61, 85, 265 ; hebdomad of, ii. 251 ; and necessity, ii. 385 ; procession of, ii. 49, iii. 273, 282, 326 ; providence and, iii. 36, 55, 60 ; Sermons on, ii. 217.
Fate-Sphere, ii. 41, 282, 283.
Fates, i. 439.
Father of the æons, i. 411 ; Alone Good, ii. 283 ; who is in the Hidden, i. 209 ; House of the, i. 224 ; own, iii. 242.
Father-God, ii. 6.
Fatherhood, i. 150 ; of God, i. 73.
Fatherless, iii. 242.
Fawn-skin, i. 191, 311.
Fecund, iii. 254, 269.
Feeling, energy and, iii. 34.
Fellow-rulers of height, ii. 302.
Fence of fire, i. 427 ; of iniquity, i. 427 ; of the teeth, i. 162.
Ferment, i. 125, 396.
Fever, iii. 115.

INDEX

Few, the, i. 207, ii. 346, iii. 11.
Ficinio, Marsiglio, i. 8, 9, 19.
Fiery body, ii. 154, 171 ; ruler, i. 166 ; whirlwinds, i. 409.
Fifth part, a, ii. 318.
Fifty-six-angled, i. 305.
Fig-leaf, i. 312.
Figs, i. 349.
Finger on lips, i. 349.
Fire, ii. 310 ; fence of, i. 427 ; very fire, iii. 17 ; flower of, iii. 138 ; knowing, iii. 98 ; and mind, God of, i. 130 ; ordeal of, i. 79 ; robe of, ii. 152 ; and snow, i. 95 ; sons of, iii. 136 ; sphere of, i. 428 ; voice of, ii. 5, 26 ; and water, iii. 66.
Fire-tenders, iii. 199.
Fire-tree, ii. 317.
Fire-workers, iii. 199.
Firmament, iii. 262, 263, 264 ; water above, i. 188.
Firmaments, iii. 194 ; or layers, iii. 211.
Firmicus Maternus, i. 477.
First, egg, i. 391 ; essence, iii. 55 ; God, i. 339, iii. 85 ; Hermes, ii. 83 ; man, i. 115, 139, ii. 27 ; cube (Poseidon), i. 275 ; woman, i. 139, ii. 27.
First-born God, ii. 203 ; His, i. 227 ; of water, i. 398.
Fish, broiled, i. 270 ; cosmic, ii. 56 ; great, i. 425 ; taboos, i. 269.
Fish-eater (Oannes), i. 149.
Fisher-soul, i. 271.
Fishers, i. 59, 61 ; of men, i. 59, 372.
Fishes, i. 373.
Five, i. 336 ; branched, i. 266, 285 ; Fifths, the, i. 203 ; Mercurii, i. 109.
Five-branched, nor from, i. 265.
Flame, i. 457 ; rite of the, i. 93.
Flame-coloured robe, i. 331.
Flames, Chamber of, i. 75 ; Region of, i. 51.
Flask of clay, i. 190.
Flautists, ii. 289.
Fleas, iii. 51.
Flesh, refraining from, i. 267 ; tongue of, ii. 31.
Fleshless meal, ii. 390.
Flies, iii. 51, 133, 190.
Flock, sacred, i. 226, 238.

Flood, i. 106, ii. 83, iii. 154, 276 ; in *Book of the Dead*, i. 109 ; books preserved from the, i. 113 ; in Egypt, i. 317 ; He who inhabiteth the, i. 169, 170 ; of Nile, ii. 83 ; those of the, i. 154.
Flower of Fire, iii. 138.
Food, twofold form of, ii. 317 ; forms of, ii. 317 ; of Gods, i. 86.
Forebears, ii. 329, 381, 382, iii. 5.
Forefather, iii. 21, 98, 292.
Foreknowledge, iii. 12, 58, 96.
Foresight, iii. 262.
Forethought, ii. 12, 39, iii. 22, 280.
Forgiveness of sins, i. 251.
Form, ii. 9 ; archetypal, ii. 6, 8, 9, 29 ; distinctive, ii. 244 ; of divine similitude, ii. 319 ; one, ii. 35 ; root of, ii. 193 ; servant's, i. 398.
Formless state, ii. 31, 45.
Formlessness, iii. 27.
Fornication, iii. 166.
Fornicator, ii. 202.
Fortune, ii. 341.
Fount of Light, i. 74.
Four, i. 337, ii. 65 ; elements, ii. 311 ; quarters, i. 93 ; sets of, ii. 328 ; winds, i. 60, 61, 84.
Fourteen pieces, i. 288, 320.
Fourth Gospel from Alexandrine Gnostics, i. 38 ; quotations from, i. 194.
Fourth state, i. 152.
Foxes have holes, iii. 35.
Fragrance, force of, i. 394.
Frazer, i. 158.
From Thee to Thee, ii. 231, 254.
Fruit, Perfect, i. 182.
Fruitful, i. 177.
Fulgentius, iii. 305.
Fullness, iii. 325 ; of Godhead, ii. 117.
Furies, i. 327.

Gabriel, i. 422, iii. 211.
Galaxy, i. 416.
Galen, i. 100.
Galilee, Mount of, ii. 238.
Ganges, Heavenly, i. 110.
Garamas, i. 149.
Gardener of Life, ii. 140.
Gardthausen, i. 113.
Garment, celestial, i. 399 ; of the Christ, ii. 249 ; of shame, i. 153, 242, ii. 42.

344   INDEX

Garments, twelve sacramental stoles or, iii. 182.

Garrucci, ii. 56.

Gate, guardian of the, i. 428; of heaven, i. 181, ii. 240; which Jacob saw, i. 171; mystery at third, i. 190; True, i. 190.

Gate-keeper, i. 311.

Gates of Celestial Nile, i. 71; of Gnosis, ii. 123; of Oblivion and Wailing, i. 303; of the Sun, i. 162.

Gautama the Buddha, iii. 317.

Gaze into the Light, i. 93; through Me upon the Cosmos, ii. 179.

Genera, ii. 313 ff.; restorer of all, ii. 310; and species, ii. 378.

General, i. 296; instruction, ii. 236; Sermons, the, ii. 141, 145, 158, 219, 236, 264, iii. 45, 77, 308.

Generated Ingenerables, i. 184.

Generation, i. 333.

Generative Law, the, i. 191.

Geneses of Souls, ii. 260.

Genesis, ii. 148, 177, iii. 26; of the all, i. 406; of fire and darkness, i. 197; ground of, i. 337; matter's becoming or, ii. 177; moist essence of, i. 170; and seed of all the gods, iii. 273; soul is cause of all in, i. 151; vase of, iii. 26; wheel of, i. 426, ii. 274, 283.

Geography, mystic, iii. 130; of sacred lands, iii. 184.

Gephyræans, i. 350.

Geryones, i. 147, 166.

Gibbon, i. 23.

Gift, God's greatest, ii. 95.

Gigantic Passions, i. 298.

Globe, winged, i. 390.

Glories, i. 80, 96.

Glory, ii. 75, 261; of celestial bodies, ii. 165; house of, i. 79; king of, i. 171; robe of, i. 361, ii. 43.

Glossalaly, i. 303.

Glosses, i. 342.

Glow-worms, i. 391.

Gnosis, i. 192, ii. 14, 17, 20, 90, 97, 131, 146, 246, iii. 76; of the all, ii. 296; archaic, iii. 322; beauty of, ii. 123; books on, iii. 231; Christianised, iii. 320; devotion joined with, ii. 114; of things divine, iii. 233; of divinity, ii. 330; Druidical, iii. 296; enformation according to, ii. 246; gate of, iii. 318; gates of, ii. 120, 123; goal of, ii. 139; of God, i. 147, ii. 150, 225, iii. 243, 326; of the Good, ii. 113, 144, 163; of Thrice-greatest Hermes, iii. 316; Introduction to the, ii. 68; of joy, ii. 225; Judæo-Egyptian, i. 31; to Klea concerning the, i. 261; light of, ii. 155; love of, iii. 260; Magian, iii. 296; of Man, i. 147, 178, iii. 323; masters of, ii. 162; mathesis or, ii. 264; of Mind, ii. 88, 96; apotheosis of Mind, ii. 167; Ophite systems of, i. 98; path of, ii. 98, 195; beginning of the Path, ii. 248; prayer for, ii. 49; pupil of, ii. 135; Sabæan, ii. 140; end of science, ii. 147; seers of, ii. 94; Sethian, i. 393; Simonian, ii. 107; of teachings, ii. 257; they who are in, ii. 131, 137, 138; of truth, i. 207; of Trismegistic documents, iii. 323; Unchristianised, iii. 323; virtue of soul, ii. 167; way of, ii. 98.

Gnostic, i. 377; elements in Hermas, i. 376; Few, the, i. 382; Horos, i. 250, ii. 348; Jottings, things seen in the mysteries, iii. 150, 156.

Gnosticism, Hermeticism another name for, ii. 192.

Goal of Gnosis, ii. 139; of piety, iii. 5.

Goat-herd, i. 175.

God, ii. 358; is all, ii. 212; iii. 258; all-pure, ii. 295; apostles of, i. 239; artificer of time, i. 229; beyond all names, ii. 99; birth in, ii. 226; body of, ii. 85; Book of, i. 467; born in, ii. 244; born from rock, i. 95; breath of, i. 232, ii. 76; with bull's foot, i. 311; as cause, ii. 66; celestial Messiah of, i. 226; child of, ii. 255; city of, i. 235, 245, 246, ii. 256; contemplator of works of, iii. 245; cosmos, second, ii. 125; creator, iii. 293; cupbearer of, i. 245; demiurge of, iii. 240; devotee of, ii. 131, 139; disciples of, i. 254; efflux of, iii. 122, 162; from egg, i. 392; energy

INDEX

of, ii. 160, 178, 180, 203; essence of, ii. 113, 199; essentiality of, ii. 199; eye of, i. 247, ii. 312; face of, i. 218; father, ii. 67; fatherhood of, i. 73; of fire and mind, i. 130; first, i. 339, iii. 85; first-born, ii. 203; gift of, ii. 87, 95; gnosis of, i. 147, ii. 150, 225, iii. 243, 329; and Gods, ii. 67; Good, ii. 240; is good, ii. 66; Good is, ii. 110, 112; the Good of, ii. 189; greatness of, ii. 244; herald of, ii. 95; house of, i. 171, 181, ii. 240; ignorance of, ii. 120; image of, i. 232, 236, ii. 91, 92, 100, iii. 236, 244; two images of, ii. 326; ineffability of, iii. 14, 216; inner, ii. 294; knower of true, ii. 97, 196; Laughter, Son of, i. 220; law of, iii. 195; light of, i. 232; likeness with, ii. 132; love of, ii. 323; lyre of, ii. 292; Man of, i. 411; Mind is, iii. 305; imperishable Mind, iii. 113; musician, ii. 288; mysteries of, i. 213; mystery of, Son of, i. 226; name of, i. 198, 234, ii. 344, iii. 293; one, i. 53; one and sole, iii. 266; organ of will of, ii. 133; Osiris, a dark, iii. 156; oracle of, i. 250; place of, i. 233, ii. 71; primal, i. 135; race of, i. 253; race, friend of, i. 233; ray of, ii. 275; rays of, ii. 155; river of, i. 244; from rock, i. 392, 399; sacrifice to, iii. 243; second, i. 230, ii. 127, 170, 320, 365; seeds of, ii. 131, 137; seer of, iii. 298; sense-and-thought of, ii. 135; sensible, ii. 311; servant, i. 251; servants of, i. 212, 220; shadow of, i. 236; shepherd, i. 226; son of, i. 138, 157, 198, 226, ii. 28, 116, 118, 133, 140, 221, 222, 241, iii. 239, 275, 280, 282; song of, ii. 332; sons of, i. 198, 229, iii. 217, 316; sons of, in Hellenistic theology, iii. 218; sons of the one, i. 234; sower, ii. 220; sphere of, ii. 230; spirit of, ii. 81; is spirit, ii. 71; two temples of, i. 228; beyond understanding, iii. 229; unwearied spirit, ii. 290; way of birth in, ii. 223, 244; way up to, ii. 280; way to worship, ii. 212, iii. 243; who lookest behind thee, i. 59; will of, ii. 160, 220, 395, iii. 195; wisdom of, ii. 176.

God-circle, i. 132, 133, 135.

God-gnosis, ii. 88, 93, 138, iii. 238; devotion is, ii. 131, 136.

God-the-Mind, male and female, ii. 7.

God-words, i. 134.

Goddess-of-child-bed-town, i. 355.

Godhead, fullness of, ii. 117.

Godlessness, ii. 200.

Gods, ii. 145; birthdays of, i. 279; choir of, ii. 206; creation of, iii. 105; cyclic, ii. 77, 89; duty of, ii. 272; Egyptians don't mourn if they believe in, i. 351; food of, i. 86; genesis and seed of all, iii. 273; great, i. 127, 347; hymn of, iii. 91; inerrant, ii. 145; intelligible, iii. 25; language of, ii. 279, iii. 323; immortal men, ii. 213; mother of, i. 152, 176; mountain of, i. 244; On the, iii. 289; path up to, ii. 169, 299; proscription of worship of, i. 399; scribe of, i. 53; scribe of the nine, i. 50; six-and-thirty, iii. 49; star-flocks of, i. 373; super-cosmic, ii. 373; way-of-birth of, ii. 242; ye are, i. 163.

Going-forth, the, ii. 246.

Going-home, ii. 98.

Gold, Chamber of, i. 75; heavenly flame of Burning, i. 75.

Golden age, iii. 135; calf, i. 316; hawk, i. 76; heaven of Isis, i. 75; Horus, i. 76; One, Dwelling of, i. 75.

Good, ii. 88, 211; All and, ii. 175; Beauty of, ii. 144, 145, 163; Daimon, i. 84, 92, 94, 97, 402, ii. 156, 199, 203, 204, 206, 213 f., iii. 151, 155, 255; Daimon, Son of, i. 104; efflux of, i. 361; gnosis of, ii. 113, 144, 163; God, ii. 240; is God, ii. 110, 112; of God, ii. 189; good-will of, iii. 241; husbandman, ii. 213, 265; imperfect, i. 320; Itself, iii. 293; law, iii. 8; Logos, i. 333; mind, ii. 127, 155, 156; news, i. 141; path of the, ii. 190; own path of, ii. 189, 196, iii. 330; perfect, i. 205; physician, i. 461, ii. 213;

pleroma of, ii. 117 ; shepherd, i. 37, 373, ii. 52 ff., 213 ; spirit, iii. 261 ; threshold of, ii. 97 ; vision of, ii. 119, 143.
Good-Doer, i. 320.
Goodness, i. 215.
Gordian, ii. 198.
Goropius Becanus, i. 20.
Gospel, iii. 135 ; *According to the Egyptians*, i. 38, 142, 150, 153, 242, ii. 54, 164 ; *of Eve*, ii. 85, 142, ii. 24, 25, 238 ; fragment of a lost, i. 153 ; *According to the Hebrews*, ii. 238 ; of Osiris, i. 367 ; *of Perfection*, i. 142 ; *of Philip*, i. 142 ; proem to the fourth, ii. 371 ; quotations from the fourth, i. 194 ; *According to Thomas*, i. 142, 155, iii. 37.
Gourd-tree, ii. 56.
Grace, ii. 20.
Grand Master, ii. 23.
Granger, i. 36 ff., 260, ii. 50 ; theory of, ii. 51.
Grasshopper, story of Pythic, ii. 300.
Grasshoppers, ii. 292.
Grave, three days in the, i. 71.
Graves, dead shall leap forth from, i. 172.
Great Announcement, i. 184, ii. 70, 170, 317.
Great, art divine, ii. 169, iii. 299 ; beast, i. 425 ; beasts, i. 424 ; body of Cosmos, ii. 128 ; boundary, ii. 29, 35 ; creator, Light, i. 71, 79 ; fish, i. 425 ; Gods, i. 127, 347 ; Green, i. 84, 92, 94, 131, 132, 176, 424, iii. 154 ; heart, i. 131 ; ignorance, iii. 140 ; initiator, ii. 21 ; Jordan, i. 163 ; King's viceroy, i. 226 ; likeness, ii. 164 ; and little man, ii. 23 ; lives, ii. 128 ; Man, i. 60, ii. 40, 56 ; Man from Above, i. 150 ; Man, Body of, i. 425 ; Mind, ii. 213 ; Mother, mysteries of the, i. 186 ; Mysteries, the, i. 185, 217, 362, ii. 240 ; Name, i. 93 ; Ocean, i. 171, ii. 92 ; Power, i. 184 ; Ptah, the, i. 130, 135 ; Pyramid, i. 69 ; saying, ii. 234 ; sea, iii. 163 ; serpent, ii. 27, 35 ; snake, ii. 26 ; Vehicle of Buddhism, ii. 44 ; work, iii. 317, 329 ; year, iii. 290.

Greater deaths, greater lots, i. 180.
Greatness, ii. 187, 222, 244, 344 ; a, i. 185 ; of divinity, ii. 309 ; of God, ii. 244.
Greatnesses, i. 165, ii. 28.
Greek, disciples of Egyptians, i. 274, 286 ; names in foreign languages, i. 342 ; philosophizing, ii. 267, 281 ; wisdom, i. 193.
Greeks, Protrepticus, or Exhortation to the, ii. 300.
Green, Great, i. 92, 94, 132, 176, 424, iii. 154 ; tree, i. 266.
Grenfell and Hunt, i. 93.
Grief, ii. 224, iii. 42.
Griffith, i. 53, 88, 118 ff.
Grihastha Āshrama, ii. 73.
Ground of Genesis, i. 337.
Grudging, ii. 86, 108.
Guardian of the Gate, i. 428.
Guards of the whole, iii. 48.
Guile, ii. 224.
Gymnosophists, i. 208.

Habit, ii. 41.
Habitat of excarnate souls, iii. 210.
Hades, i. 302, 305, 325, 327, 342, 350, 362, 453, ii. 337, 338 ; vision of, i. 223 ; visit to, i. 380 ; way of salvation from, i. 152.
Hadrian, i. 195.
Haf, i. 462.
Haggadist, ii. 239.
Haimos, i. 169.
Hall of the Altar, i. 74 ; of the Child in his Cradle, i. 74, 75 ; of the Golden Rays, i. 75.
Halm, i. 56.
Hands, iii. 101, 117.
Haoma or soma-plant, i. 325.
Harbour of good things, i. 293 ; of salvation, ii. 123.
Hardadaf, i. 467.
Harles, i. 5 ; Fabricius, i. 23.
Harlot, i. 174, iii. 166.
Harmonic canon, iii. 176.
Harmony, i. 323, ii. 9, 10, 15, 16, 39, 41, 89, iii. 63, 64, 66, 67, 74, 80, 86 ; heavenly, ii. 253 ; true, ii. 251 ; of wisdom, i. 237.
Harnack, i. 469, ii. 55.
Harnebeschenis (see Arnebeschenis), i. 76, iii. 209.
Harper, story of, ii. 291.

INDEX

347

Harpocrates, i. 291, 346, 349, ii. 265.
Harpocratians, i. 147.
Harris Papyrus, i. 131.
Harrison (Jane E.), i. 310.
Hatch, i. 179.
Hate fish, i. 308.
Hateful cloak, ii. 121.
Hathor, i. 74, 316.
Hating, ii. 115 ; of body, ii. 95.
Hawk, i. 56, 329, 330, 353, 355, iii. 133, 181 ; golden, i. 76.
Head, i. 429 ; Above, descent from, i. 169.
Head-born, i. 359.
Healer, Asclepius the, i. 467.
Health, iii. 203 ; of soul, ii. 257.
Hearer, i. 185, 292, ii. 255.
Heart, iii. 75 ; appetite and, iii. 78 ; eyes of, ii. 121 ; great, i. 131 ; of Rā, i. 53 ; of silence, i. 73 ; and tongue, i. 136.
Hearth, common, iii. 171 ; of universe, iii. 172.
Heather-bush, i. 284.
Heather-tree, i. 284.
Heaven, beauty of, iii. 94 ; and earth contrasted, iii. 9, 10 ; Egypt image of, ii. 351 ; gate of, i. 181, ii. 240, iii. 157 ; Isis, queen of, iii. 160 ; law of, iii. 62 ; ocean, i. 411, iii. 154 ; pole-lords of, i. 176 ; power to travel through, ii. 197 ; seven fortunes of, i. 176 ; song of, ii. 384 ; sphere-like, i. 390 ; Thee I adjure, iii. 269 ; third, i. 166, 173 ; tongues of, ii. 32 ; voices from, i. 323 ; war in, iii. 118.
Heaven-born, ii. 162.
Heaven-walkers, i. 101.
Heavenly bodies, iii. 301 ; chariot, iii. 173 ; flame of burning gold, i. 75 ; Ganges, i. 110 ; harmony, ii. 253 ; horn, i. 167, 193, 453 ; Jerusalem, i. 74 ; Man, ii. 102, iii. 277 ; Nile, iii. 158 ; Word proceeding forth, iii. 254.
Heavens, Entrance of the Golden, i. 75 ; kingdom of, i. 185 ; kingship of, i. 167, ii. 43 ; overseers of, i. 126 : sound of, i. 161.
Hebdomad, Athena, i. 275 ; celestial, i. 422 ; of Fate, ii. 251 ; Ophite, i. 421.
Hebrew influence, ii. 38, 81.

Hebrews, Gospel according to the, ii. 238.
Hecatæus, i. 268, 274, 472.
Hecate, i. 322, 352.
Hedgehogs, i. 325.
Heh, i. 407.
Height of Cosmos to Depths of Earth, i. 413.
Heimarmene (Fate), ii. 275, 341, 384, iii. 273.
Hekekyan Bey, i. 111.
Helen, i. 147.
Heliopolis, i. 103.
Heliopolitan theology, i. 135.
Helios, i. 278.
Hellanicus, i. 310.
Hellas, Bible of, i. 193 ; wisdom of, 186.
Hellenistic, myth of Anthropos, i. 143 ; theology, i. 200, 202, 218, 255.
Hemisphere, upper, ii. 271.
Hemlock juice, i. 179.
Hep-Tep, i. 74.
Hephæstus, i. 61, 130, 307, 347, iii. 148 ; men of, iii. 183 ; Ptah who is, iii. 96.
Hera, i. 305, 307.
Heracleian stone, i. 189.
Heracleides, i. 301.
Heracleitus, i. 302, 323, 327, 361 ; sayings of, ii. 213.
Heracles, i. 303, 318, 319.
Heracleon, i. 39.
Herald, ii. 86 ; of God, ii. 95.
Herb-knowers, iii. 111.
Herba medica, i. 293.
Hercules, myth of, i. 147 ; noose of, i. 61.
Hermæus, i. 314, 320.
Hermaïca, iii. 252.
Hermaïc, books, iii. 293 ; doctrines, iii. 292 ; writings, ii. 169, iii. 297.
Hermanubis, i. 342.
Hermaphrodites, ii. 37.
Hermas, Apocalyptic, i. 378 ; Gnostic elements in, i. 376 ; higher criticism of, i. 370 : name of, i. 374 ; Old Latin version of, i. 378 ; Pastoral, i. 370 ; *Shepherd of,* i 369, ii. 238, 248, iii. 319 ; shepherd of, ii. 229, 232.
Hermeneutic, i. 300.
Hermes, i. 278, 295, 319, 334, ii. 88, iii. 234 ; (I.), ii. 83, iii. 147,

348 INDEX

152 ; (II.), i. 104, iii. 152 ; (III.), iii. 303 ; Alchemical literature, i. 5 ; all-knowing, iii. 95 ; apophthegm of, iii. 88 ; Arab tradition, i. 5 ; and Asclepius, apotheosis of, iii. 222 ; and Asclepius, sons of God, iii. 217 ; and Basilides, ii. 215 ; beloved son of Zeus, i. 122 ; books of, 115, 196, 342, 380, iii. 282, 289 ; books of described by Clem. of A., iii. 222 ; city of, i. 87 ; columns or pillars of, i. 112 ; first natural philosopher, iii. 237 ; gnosis of, iii. 316 ; the Gnostic, iii. 320 ; grade of, ii. 250 ; great-and-great, i. 117 ; inspirer, iii. 286 ; inventions of, i. 5 ; Kriophoros, ii. 52 ; Logius, ii. 54 ; Logos, i. 158 ; master of all physics, iii. 226 ; mind of, iii. 260 ; monuments of, i. 113 ; prior to Moses, i. 19 ; Paut of, i. 263 ; prayer of, i. 402 ; prayers, i. 82 ; a race or being, iii. 135 ; religion of, i. 82 ; rod of, i. 61, 160, 161 ; scriptures of, iii. 227 ; spell of, iii. 97 ; suppliant of, ii. 236 ; teacher of reincarnation, iii. 227 ; ten-thousand-times-great, iii. 276 ; Thoth the first, i. 104 ; writer of scripture, iii. 227 ; Word who brings tidings from God, iii. 217.

Hermes-city, i. 329.
Hermeses and Asclepiuses, many, iii. 221.
Hermetic tradition, origins of the, iii. 233.
Hermippus de Astrologia Dialogus, iii. 270.
Hermodotus, i. 298.
Hermopolis, i. 56, ii. 382.
Heru-Behutet, i. 57.
Heru-em-Ȧnpu, i. 342.
Heru-p-Khart, i. 346.
Heru-nr, i. 279.
Hesiod, i. 265, 300, 338, 389.
Hestia, i. 305.
Hesychius, i. 100, 269.
Het-Abtit, House of the Net, i. 58.
Hexads, ii. 117.
Hexæmeron, iii. 117.
Hezekiah, ii. 232.
Hibbert Journal, ii. 71.
Hidden mystery in silence, the, i. 167 ; Places, House of the, i. 68.

Hierarchies, ii. 276, 314, 340, 342.
Hieratic, iii. 276 ; books, iii. 225.
Hieroglyphics, i. 134, 276, 277, 312, 330.
Hierophants, i. 210, 211 ; of mysteries, i. 212.
Hierosolymus, i. 307.
Higher Criticism of *Pœmandres*, i. 128 ; of *Shepherd of Hermas*, i. 370.
Hilaria, i. 152.
Hildebrand, ii. 307, 392.
Hilgenfeld, i. 370.
Hilgers, i. 25 ; theory of, i. 369.
Hippocrates, i. 155.
Hippolytus, i. 94 ; Conclusion of, i. 186 ; and the divulging of the Mysteries, i. 140 ; *Philosophumena* of, i. 140.
Hippopotamus, i. 329, 330, 427.
Hoeffer, i. 27.
Hoffmann (G.), i. 33 ; (S. F. W.), i. 9.
Holiness, Song of, ii. 50.
Holy, Holy, Holy, ii. 19.
Homer, i. 309, 318, 327, 330, 388 ; on daimones, i. 299 ; nodding, the good, i. 196.
Homilies, Clementine, i. 388, ii. 72.
Honey, i. 349, 364.
Honey-brew, i. 347.
Honey-clover, i. 284, 315.
Hor, Son of the Negress, i. 88 ; Son of Pa-neshe, i. 119.
Horapollo, i. 48, 55, 56, 408.
Horizon, i. 74, 332 ; of Light, i. 75.
Horizoned, i. 335.
Horn, the, i. 190 ; of Mēn, i. 166 ; of one-horned bull, i. 187.
Horœus, i. 427.
Horos or Boundary, ii. 366 ; Great Boundary, ii. 29 ; Gnostic, i. 250, ii. 348 ; Mighty Power, ii. 33.
Horoscopes, ii. 193, 341.
Horse, i. 290.
Horses, i. 430 ; yoke of, i. 430.
Horus, i. 53, 63, 77, 88, 92, 94, 132, 133, 136, 334, ii. 51 ; bastardy suit against, i. 291 ; birth of, i. 75, 76, 95, iii. 122, 157, 160, 162, 242 ; birthday of Eye of, i. 331 ; *Birthdays of*, i. 332 ; bone of, i. 189, 343 ; how born, i. 315 ; Books of Isis and, iii. 208 ; Books of Isis to, iii. 313 ;

INDEX 349

brethren, i. 66 ; companions of, i. 270, 290 ; is cosmos surrounding earth, i. 321 ; cosmos that is, i. 338 ; cutting up into pieces of, i. 291 ; elder, i. 279, 280, 334, 343, 346, 367 ; eye of, i. 336 ; gold-miner, iii. 209 ; golden, i. 76 ; Isis to, iii. 87 ; questions of Osiris to, i. 290 ; and Set, i. 56, 57 ; white, i. 296 ; worshippers of, i. 147 ; the younger, i. 291.

Hour, i. 72, 266.

House, ii. 117 ; of body, ii. 321 ; of the eye, i. 288 ; of virginity, i. 218 ; of Father, i. 224 ; of glory, i. 79 ; of God, i. 171, 181, ii. 240 ; of Hidden Places, i. 68 ; of Net, i. 58 ; of Osiris, i. 79 ; robber in thy, ii. 121.

Hu-siris, i. 310.

Humanists, i. 17, 18 ; MSS., i. 8.

Husbandman, ii. 263 ; Achaab, ii. 265 ; good, ii. 213, 265.

Hyades, i. 161.

Hye Kye, i. 160.

Hyes (Hues), i. 161, 310.

Hyle, i. 151, 389.

Hylic animal, ii. 63 ; cosmic, ii. 319 ; Mind, i. 452 ; Nous, i. 416.

Hymn of the Æons, ii. 43 ; to All-God, ii. 108 ; to Amen-Rā, i. 131 ; to Attis, ii. 56 ; of the Four, ii. 389 ; of the Gods, iii. 91 ; to Jupiter Ammon, i. 149 ; Naassene, ii. 109 ; Orphic, iii. 269 ; of Osiris and Isis, iii. 124, 146 ; of Praise, ii. 49 ; of Praise "Holy art Thou," ii. 19 ; for morning and for evening prayer, ii. 252 ; of Re-birth, ii. 229 ; to the Sun, ii. 253 ; of Valentinus, ii. 284.

Hymnody, secret, ii. 230 f.

Hymns, Orphic, ii. 235.

Hyparxis, ii. 269.

Hysterema, ii. 239.

I am thou, i. 85, 87, 89, ii. 24.

I-em-Hetep, i. 457.

Ialdabaoth, i. 139, 159, 422.

Iaō, i. 411.

Iaō Zeësar, i. 191.

Iamblichus (see Jamblichus).

Iatromathematici, i. 471.

Ibis, i. 48, 54 ff., 87, 353, 355 ; symbolism of, i. 358.

Ibis-headed moon-god, i. 47.

Icheneumon, i. 356, 436.

Idea, i. 336, ii. 185.

Ieou, First Book of, i. 172.

Iexai, ii. 242.

Ignorance, ii. 146, 246 ; of God, ii. 120 ; great, iii. 140 ; mystery of, ii. 25 ; sea of, ii. 123 ; way out of, ii. 237 ; web of, ii. 121 ; wine of, ii. 120.

Illumination, i. 241, ii. 255 ; degrees of, iii. 208.

Image, ii. 35, 368 ; divine, i. 235 ; or double, i. 89 ; of God, i. 232, ii. 91, 92, 100, iii. 236, 244 ; His, i. 233 ; after His, ii. 125 ; image of, i. 235 ; of the One, ii. 118.

Images, adoration of, ii. 286 ; sacred, ii. 381.

Imhotep, i. 459.

Immisch, i. 169.

Immortality, ii. 210 ; cup of, iii. 205 ; draught of, iii. 163 ; philtre of, iii. 163.

Impression of a seal, i. 215, 395.

Impulses, ii. 204.

Imuth-brotherhood, iii. 148.

Imuth-Asclepius, i. 466.

Inaction, ii. 178.

Inbreathing, iii. 194 ; of universe, ii. 254.

Incantations, i. 88.

Incarnation, iii. 145 ; embryonic stages of (*Pistis Sophia*), iii. 68.

Incarnations of Thoth, i. 463.

Incense, i. 363.

Increase and multiply, i. 37, ii. 12, 38, 82.

India, i. 208, 303, ii. 197 ; British Rāj in, i. 354.

Indian, ii. 353 ; wisdom, ii. 198.

Indians, ii. 401.

Induced Days, i. 279, 280.

Inexpressible man, i. 170.

Inferi, ii. 338.

Initiates, the Bacchic, i. 191 ; of Isis, i. 263 ; Orphic, i. 95, 191.

Initiation, iii. 323 ; "in the black," i. 91 ; Cup of, ii. 94 ; into Divine Mysteries, i. 208 ; doctrines of, i. 73 ; final, ii. 43 ; hall, i. 179 ; Isis a grade of, iii. 208 ; mount of, ii. 238 ; in the sacred rites, iii. 257 ; of Tat, iii. 313 ; temples of, i. 74 ; theurgic rite of, ii. 255.

350 INDEX

Initiations, iii. 171 ; of the Assyrians, i. 151 ; Therapeut, i. 251.
Initiator, iii. 251 ; Great, ii. 21 ; Thoth the, i. 71.
Ink, iii. 149.
Inn or caravanserai, ii. 283.
Inner, doctrine of the mystery-institutions, i. 141 ; Door, i. 157, 270, iii. 274, 280 ; Door, About the, iii. 275, 295 ; man, iii. 277 ; way, i. 101.
Iniquity, Fence of, i. 427.
Insufficiency, ii. 174, 241, 245.
Intef, Stele of, i. 138.
Intellect of Cosmos, ii. 373 ; eye of, ii. 308.
Intellectual Light, iii. 257, 268.
Intelligible cosmos, i. 146, ii. 167, 194, 273, 275, 286 ; essence, ii. 276, iii. 57 ; model, i. 241.
Intemperance, ii. 224.
Interception, i. 319.
Intercourse of souls, ii. 314.
Interpreter, i. 158.
Intf, i. 467.
Intoxication, i. 414.
Invention, iii. 98.
Inventor of philosophy, i. 138.
Invert himself, ii. 243.
Invocation, of the powers, ii. 249 ; theurgic rite of, ii. 245.
Io, i. 314.
Irenæus, i. 139, ii. 27.
Iris, i. 292.
Isaac, i. 217, 220, 221.
Isaiah, ii. 232 ; *The Ascension of*, ii. 232.
Iseion, i. 263.
Ishon, iii. 165.
Isia, i. 341.
Isis, i. 63, 279, 332, 346, 349, 373, ii. 30 ; beheading of, i. 291 ; books of, iii. 316 ; books of Horus and, i. 481 ; feminine principle of Nature, i. 333 ; Golden Heaven of, i. 75 ; hastening, i. 340 ; to Horus, iii. 87 ; house of, iii. 103 ; true initiate of, i. 256, 263 ; grade of initiation, iii. 208 ; Intercession of, iii. 87 ; from "knowledge," i. 341 ; Lady, iii. 155 ; mysteries of, i. 155, iii. 182 ; and Osiris, texts and translations of Plutarch on, i. 259 ; Queen of Heaven, iii. 160 ; robe of, i. 62, 264.

Isis-Righteousness, i. 85.
Isis-Sophia, iii. 134.
Israel, ingathering of, ii. 303 ; the myths of, i. 202 ; seeing, i. 198.
Israëlitismus, i. 124.
Italy, iii. 131.
Ithakesian Island men, i. 270.
Ithyphallus, i. 158.

Jackal, i. 87.
Jacob, i. 217 ; dream of, i. 223.
Jamblichus, i. 112, ii. 169, 280, iii. 285.
James, Brother of the Lord, i. 143, 147 ; the Just, i. 148 ; John, and Peter, i. 475.
Janus, i. 59.
Japanese, the, ii. 302.
Jennings, Hargrave, i. 12.
Jeremiah, i. 178, 217.
Jerusalem, i. 246 ; Above, i. 163, 183, 245, ii. 42, 251, iii. 100 ; Below, i. 178.
Jeschu, i. 335, ii. 239.
Jeschu (Jesus), i. 165.
Jeschu ha-Notzri, i. 270.
Jesus, i. 147 ; body of, i. 286 ; cult of, ii. 138 ; the living one, i. 93 ; logoi of, iii. 246 ; Sisters of, i. 147.
Jesus Christ, spiritual oblations through, ii. 254 ; through, ii. 255.
Jesus (Joshua), i. 164.
Jīvanmukta, ii. 167.
Jñāna-Mārga, ii. 119.
Johannine document, sources of, i. 195.
John, Acts of, ii. 55, 238.
John, the Baptist, i. 470.
Jonah, ii. 56.
Jordan, Great, i. 163.
Joseph, i. 220.
Josephus, i. 103, 113, 114.
Jothōr, i. 164.
Joy, i. 220, ii. 346 ; grief and, iii. 42 ; lord of, i. 74 ; religion of, i. 73.
Judæo-Egyptian gnosis, i. 31.
Judæus and Hierosolymus, i. 307.
Judge, of two combatant Gods, i. 53 ; of the dead, i. 64.
Judges, statues of, i. 276.
Judgment, i. 79 ; scene, i. 55.
Judgments of value, iii. 317.

INDEX 351

Julian, the Emperor, i. 113, iii. 303.
Juniper, i. 364, 365.
Jupiter, i. 416, 418, 419.
Jupiter Ammon, Hymn to, i. 149.
Just, the, i. 70, 79, 156.
Justice, i. 359, iii. 58, 243; engine of, ii. 41.
Justice (Maāt), i. 263.
Justification, i. 79.
Justified, i. 71, iii. 320.

Ka, i. 89, 97, 132, 133, 134, 280, 463, ii. 287.
Kabalah, i. 281.
Kabeiros, i. 149.
Kabiri (Cabiri), Seven, i. 127, ii. 279.
Kakodaimon, i. 448.
Kamephis, iii. 107, 149, 159, 167.
Karma, instrument of, iii. 116.
Kārmic, agents, ii. 282; scales, Teller of the, i. 72; wheel, ii. 83.
Kastor, i. 306.
Kaṭhopanishad, ii. 168, 317.
Kaulakau, i. 165, ii. 80.
Kenyon, i. 82, 86, 117.
Khaibit, i. 76, 89.
Khamuas, Tales of, i. 118, 281, 380.
Khat, i. 89.
Khemennu, i. 53, 56, 58, 65; "the eighth city," i. 120.
Kheperá, i. 357.
Khmûn, i. 119, 120.
Khu, i. 89.
Kid, thou hast fallen into the milk, i. 191.
King, Ambassador of the, i. 250; Ammon, i. 77, ii. 280; Correspondence of Asclepius with the, ii. 278; of glory, i. 171; God as shepherd and, i. 226; the highest, ii. 293; The Perfect Sermon to the, ii. 266, 281; Praising of the, ii. 294; the very statues of the, ii. 298; the true, ii. 302.
King (L. W.). i. 61, 328, 344, 348.
King-soul, iii. 144.
Kingdom of the Heavens, the, i. 185; within man, i. 155.
Kingdoms, downfalls of, iii. 48.
Kings, iii. 111, 126; Catalogue of, i. 277; divine, i. 106; encomium of, ii. 299; eulogy of, ii. 298; glorious fame of, ii. 292; guard and escort of souls of, iii. 127; presidents of common weal and peace, ii. 293; successions of, i. 315.
Kingsford and Maitland, i. 15.
Kingship of Heavens, i. 167, ii. 43.
Klea, i. 260, 264, 310; to, i. 276.
Kneph, i. 295.
Kneph-Kamephis, iii. 151.
Knife, i. 277.
Knowledge, vehicle of, i. 49.
Koptō, i. 283.
Koptos, i. 305.
Kore, i. 59, 151, 318, iii. 161; Descent of, i. 350.
Koreion, i. 403, iii. 161.
Korybantes (see Corybantes), i. 149.
Korybas, i. 169.
Koshas, ii. 168.
Kriophoros, ii. 54.
Kroll, i. 100, 101.
Kronos (see Cronus), i. 151, 278, 298, 307, 322, 350; that is, Ammon, ii. 279; whether blest child of, i. 185; sacred dirge on, i. 30; tears of, i. 308.
Kuphi, i. 332, 364, 366.
Kuretes, i. 149.

Labyrinth of ills, i. 191.
Lachares, i. 352.
Lachesis, i. 442.
Ladder, of Being, ii. 165; of the Words, i. 239.
Lady, of heart and tongue, iii. 208; of all wisdom, iii. 208.
Lagides, i. 99.
Lake Mareotis, ii. 403.
Lame, i. 334.
Lamp-magic, i. 92.
Land, Black, iii. 158; Blessed, iii. 282; of Eternal Dawn, i. 80; flowing with milk and honey, ii. 251; of the Living, i. 50, 51; of the Lord, ii. 251; Seriadic, i. 110 ff., 114.
Lang, Andrew, i. 258.
Language, of Gods, ii. 279; of the Word, i. 54.
Larks, i. 356.
Lauchert, i. 56.
Laughter, i. 221; seven peals of, iii. 137.
Law, body of, ii. 44; generative, i. 191; of God, iii. 195; good, iii. 8.

352 INDEX

Laws, of Lycurgus, ii. 235 ; sacred, ii. 235.
Laya, ii. 260.
Layers, iii. 194.
Laying-on of hands, ii. 242.
Lazarel, Loys, i. 10.
Lazarus, i. 71.
Lead, i. 282.
Leading Forth, i. 164.
Leah, i. 217.
Leaven hid in three measures of flour, i. 167.
Leemans, i. 82, 84, 90.
Lentils, i. 346.
Leo, i. 415.
Léontocéphale, la divinité, i. 399.
Lepsius, i. 49, 69.
Lethe, Plain of, i. 447 ; River of, i. 416, 452.
Leto, i. 315.
Letronne, i. 107, 117.
Leviathan, i. 267, 423, 424.
Liberation, ii. 167.
Library, i. 102 ; Alexandrian, i. 197 ; catalogue of Egyptian priestly, iii. 225 ; of Osymandias, i. 50 ; of priesthood of Rā, i. 103 ; at Thebes, i. 465.
Libya, Mount of, ii. 382.
Libyan Hill, ii. 360, 402.
Life, ii. 184 ; circle of types of, ii. 194 ; gardener of, ii. 133, 140 ; and Light, ii. 13, 14, 20, 226, 231, iii. 325 ; lord of, i. 132 ; place of, ii. 133 ; plastic, iii. 210 ; plenitude of, ii. 208 ; shame of, i. 242 ; theoretic, ii. 163 ; tree of, i. 428 ; types of, ii. 245 ; way of, i. 182, ii. 15, 40, 41 ; well of, i. 79.
Life-giving one, iii. 46 ; power, iii. 292.
Life-producing circle, iii. 51.
Lift up the gates, i. 170.
Light, all-seeing, ii. 253 ; baptism of, ii. 255 ; boundless, i. 93 ; creatures of, i. 51 ; day of, i. 326 ; entrance on, i. 79 ; exhaling his, iii. 279 ; fount of, i. 74 ; gnosis of, ii. 155 ; of God, i. 232 ; the great creator, i. 71, 79 ; horizon of, i. 75 ; hymn, i. 94 ; intellectual, iii. 257, 268 ; and life (see life) ; lily of, i. 77 ; Logos is, i. 231 ; manifestation to, iii. 160 ; moist, i. 391 ; mountain of, ii. 238 ; chamber of, i. 75 ; religion of, i. 73 ; revealer of, i. 375 ; treasure of, i. 246 ; veil, ii. 28, 29, 31.
Light-Darkness, iii. 278.
Light-giver, i. 179.
Light-God, i. 473.
Light-man, iii. 279.
Light-spark, i. 395, ii. 29.
Light-word, ii. 5.
Like, ii. 90 ; and unlike, iii. 11.
Likeness (see Image).
Lily, i. 77.
Limbs, ii. 387, iii. 277.
Linen, i. 71, 265 ; cloth, i. 71.
Linus, i. 293 ; song of, i. 293.
Lion, i. 56, 90, 290, 314, 422, 446, 449, iii. 180.
Lionardo of Pistoja, i. 8.
Lionesses, iii. 181.
Lions, iii. 112 ; months, i. 314.
Lipsius, ii. 108.
Liquid Chaos, i. 191.
Littré, i. 155.
Living, Book of the, i. 367 ; death, ii. 121 ; land of the, i. 50, 51 ; mother of the, i. 163 ; one, i. 93 ; stones, ii. 254, 256 ; water, i. 188, 190.
Locust, iii. 133, 356.
Logia, bible of, ii. 236 ; logoi or, ii. 234 ; Oxyrhynchus (see Behnesa), i. 209, ii. 24, 116, 239, 255.
Logoi, Behnesa, ii. 17, 239 ; and ideas, iii. 171 ; of Jesus, iii. 246 ; or logia, ii. 234.
Logoklopia, iii. 323.
Logos, i. 68, 362 ; Æon the, i. 239, 406 ; Book concerning, ii. 265 ; "cause of activity," ii. 254 ; disciples of, i. 243 ; Eternity illumined by, i. 399 ; Good, i. 333 ; Hermes, i. 158 ; Image of God, i. 232 ; Life and Light, i. 231 ; race of, ii. 18, 241 ; sophia-aspect of, i. 49 ; spermatic essence of, i. 390 ; spiritual sun, i. 241 ; Thoth as, i. 63, 90.
Logos-Demiurge, i. 135.
Logos-doctrine, i. 51.
Logos-Mediator, i. 249.
Longing, ii. 346.
Lord, of books, i. 53 ; Brethren of, i. 147 ; of divine words, i. 53 ; of joy, i. 74 ; of all knowledge, i.

INDEX

55; land of the, ii. 251; of life, i. 132; of moist nature, i. 161; of palingenesis, i. 50; of rebirth, i. 50; of time, i. 76; of two lands, i. 134; of unseen world, i. 73; word of, ii. 6.
Loreto, i. 469.
Lost sheep, the, i. 191.
Lotus, i. 347, 458.
Lourdes, i. 469.
Love, i. 77, 125, 338, ii. 12, 39, iii. 259; birth of, i. 338; of gnosis, iii. 260; divine, ii. 94, 309, 346, iii. 260; Himself, ii. 297; and necessity, iii. 110, 264; pure, ii. 332; single, ii. 330.
Loves, the, iii. 95.
Lowrie, ii. 55.
Lucian, i. 158.
Lychnomancy, i. 92.
Lycopolitans, i. 305.
Lycurgus, i. 274; laws of, ii. 235.
Lydus, i. 403, 404, ii. 342, 361, 385.
Lyre, Pythagoreans used, i. 366; strings, i. 335.
Lysippus, i. 298.

Maasse, i. 418.
Maāt, i. 52, 64, 89, 99, 458.
M'Clintock, i. 27.
M'Lennan, i. 353.
Macrobius on "Descent of the Soul," i. 413.
Macroprosopus, ii. 282.
Madiam, i. 164.
Magi, i. 207, 326, ii. 170, iii. 182, 277.
Magian gnosis, iii. 296.
Magic, iii. 275; formulæ, i. 50; papyri, ii. 252.
Magica, iii. 296.
Magna Mater Mysteries, i. 179.
Magnet, i. 189, ii. 91.
Mahā-vākyam, ii. 234.
Mahābhārata, ii. 235, 242.
Mahāyāna, ii. 44.
Mahāyāna-shraddhotpāda-shāstra, ii. 44.
Maia, iii. 251.
Maitland, Kingsford and, i. 15.
Making-manifest, ii. 99.
Making-new-again, ii. 75, 83, 128.
Malalas, iii. 269.
Male-female, i. 146, 152, ii. 10, 12, 33.

Malice, ii. 224.
Malkander, i. 285.
Mambres, iii. 283.
Mammon, iii. 184.
Man, ii. 9, 127, 157, 321, 325, 326; Above, i. 149, 197; Adamas, i. 148; an appearance, iii. 21; birth of, ii. 241; brother of, ii. 35; celestial, ii. 37; cosmic, ii. 12, 116, 382; daring of, iii. 114; descent of, ii. 34; dual nature of, iii. 245; named East, i. 227; essential, ii. 116, 251, 319, 321; first, i. 115, 139, ii. 27, iii. 295; gnosis of, i. 147, 178, iii. 323; great, ii. 23, 40, 56; heavenly, ii. 102, iii. 277; inexpressible, i. 170; inner, iii. 277; of light, iii. 281; after likeness, ii. 277; material, ii. 132; of mighty names, i. 146, ii. 109, 254; a mighty wonder, ii. 315; the mind, iii. 280; mind-led, ii. 203; mystery of, i. 141; new, ii. 43; one, ii. 222, 244; original, i. 168; Phōs, iii. 279; Plato's definition of, i. 433; principles of, ii. 149; second, i. 139, ii. 27; shall not live by bread alone, i. 248; son of, i. 160, ii. 43, 138; sons of one, i. 197, 234; substantial, ii. 132; size of thumb, iii. 165; Thy, ii. 232; true, i. 228; of truth, figure of, iii. 277; twofold, ii. 319; typal, i. 168.
Man-after-His-Likeness, i. 198, 234.
Man-doctrine, i. 138, 193, 197.
Man-mystery, the, i. 198.
Man-Shepherd, ii. 3, 5, 6, 14, 15, 17, 18, 19, 52.
Mānava Dharma Shāstra, ii. 73.
Maneros, i. 287, 288, 293, 294.
Manes, i. 297.
Manetho, i. 99 ff., 103, 273, iii. 289, 302, 329, 355; Beloved of Thoth, i. 102 ff.; books of, i. 104; *Sothis* of, i. 117, 121; translation activity of, ii. 280.
Mangey, i. 200.
Manhood, christ-stage of, i. 367, 368.
Manic, i. 297.
Manna, i. 246.
Mansoul, Siege of, iii. 187.
Mantra-vidyā, i. 64, iii. 274.
Mantrāḥ, i. 64, 365.

354　INDEX

Manu, i. 112.
Manvantara, iii. 137.
Many, ii. 131, 308 ; Avoid converse with, iii. 11 ; unknowing, ii. 250.
Many-named, i. 184.
Maps of the world, iii. 185, 187.
Marcella, Porphyry's Letter to, i. 260.
Marcellus, i. 106.
Marcion, ii. 72.
Marcus, Gnostic, iii. 276.
Marduk, i. 60.
Mareotis, Lake, ii. 403.
Mariam, the sought-for, i. 164.
Mariamne, i. 143, 147, 301.
Marriage, with right reason, i. 223 ; sacred, i. 182, 216, 224, ii. 96, 137, 173, 240, 241, iii. 156, 157, 319.
Mars, i. 416, 418, 419.
Marsham Adams, i. 68, 81.
Marsiglio Ficino, i. 8, 9 ; opinion of, i. 19.
Martha, i. 71, 147.
Martial, i. 116.
Martyrdom of Peter, ii. 108.
Mary, i. 71 ; Magdalene, i. 147 ; *Concerning the Offspring of*, i. 142 ; *Questions of*, i. 142.
Masdesin, i. 297.
Mason, Master, i. 466.
Maspero, i. 130.
Mass, ii. 269.
Master, of the All, i. 409 ; *Book of the*, i. 68, 77, 78 ; of feast, i. 245 ; grand, ii. 23 ; Mason, i. 466 ; of masters, iii. 317 ; of the wheels, iii. 120.
Master-architect, i. 48.
Masterhood, ii. 47, iii. 324.
Mastery, i. 80.
Mastich, i. 365.
Materiality, ii. 212, 218.
Mathematici, i. 292, 336 ; theory of, i. 318.
Mathesis, i. 262, ii. 264, 372, iii. 5.
Matter, i. 225, 276, 334, 336, 338, 339, 389, 390, 415, 451, ii. 125, 176, 210, 211, 241, 269, 332, 333, 335, 343, iii. 26, 66, 226, 278 ; becoming of, ii. 177 ; blend of, iii. 103 ; cosmos, ii. 336 ; fourfold, i. 389 ; by itself, ii. 181 ; is one, ii. 118 ; pure, ii. 7 ; root of, ii. 26.
Māyā, ii. 106 ff.

Māyin, ii. 107.
Mazdæans, i. 400.
Mazdes, i. 297.
Means, i. 338.
Measure, six-and-fiftieth even, i. 305.
Measurer, the great, i. 53 ; Thoth, the, i. 66.
Medes, i. 196.
Median, i. 197.
Mediator, i. 58, 325.
Medici, Cosimo, i. 8.
Medinet Habu, i. 463.
Megaloi Theoi (see Cabiri), i. 127.
Meinian, i. 273.
Meinis, i. 272.
Melchizedec, i. 127, iii. 211.
Melilote, i. 284.
Members, i. 135.
Memnon, i. 96.
Memnonium, i. 50.
Memoirs of the Apostles, i. 195.
Memory, i. 433, ii. 397 ; experience and, iii. 195 ; restored, ii. 221.
Memphis, ii. 105, 292, 293, 347, 460 ; brazen gates at, i. 303 ; Ptah-priests of, i. 135.
Men, benefactor of, ii. 213 ; first, ii. 37 ; fishers of, i. 59, 372 ; of Hephæstus, iii. 183 ; burn living, i. 355 ; gods, iii. 136 ; nourishment of, i. 133 ; perfect, ii. 87, 97 ; sacred or typical, iii. 138 ; seven, ii. 11 ; Shepherd of, i. 372, 375, ii. 231.
Mēn, i. 166 ; heavenly horn of, i. 167, 455.
Menander acts Menander, i. 351.
Ménard, views of, i. 27 ff.
Mendes, i. 320 ; goat at, i. 356.
Mene, iii. 91.
Menelaos, i. 296.
Mercabah, iii. 173 ; or Chariot of Ezekiel, i. 238 ; vision of, i. 154.
Merciful (Potency), i. 237.
Mercury, i. 417, 418, 419.
Mercy-seat, i. 238.
Merriment, ii. 346.
Mesopotamia, i. 171.
Mesorē, i. 349.
Mesotes, ii. 251.
Messala, i. 403, 407.
Messiah-ites, i. 190.
Metamorphoses, i. 150 ; of soul, ii. 163.

Metempsychosis, ii. 164, 166, iii. 26, 110, 142, 228; concerning, i. 429; Plotinus on, i. 434.
Methyer, i. 337.
Meyer, ii. 300.
Michael, i. 422, iii. 211.
Middle Way, ii. 96.
Midst, ii. 316.
Mighty Power, ii. 29, 33.
Migration into other bodies, ii. 329.
Milky Way, i. 414.
Miller, i. 140.
Million, i. 407.
Min, i. 337.
Mind, ii. 6, 86; All-father, ii. 8; born in, ii. 221; as builder, ii. 153; counterpart of, ii. 40; cup of, ii. 242; a daimon, ii. 154, 171; demiurgic, i. 137, ii. 35; door-keeper, ii. 14; dowsing in, ii. 255; eye of, ii. 228, 230, 253; gnosis of, ii. 88, 95; gnosis apotheosis of, ii. 167; good, ii. 127, 155, 156; imperishable, iii. 113; great, ii. 213; hylic, i. 452; joy of, ii. 230; judge, ii. 201; man, iii. 280; of all masterhood, ii. 3, 4, 229; of mind, iii. 257; of my own mind, iii. 104; pilot, ii. 201; pure, ii. 324, iii. 292; religion of, i. 91, ii. 401, iii. 316; of universals, i. 225.
Mind-consciousness, ii. 239.
Mind-led man, ii. 203.
Minerva Mundi, iii. 93.
Ministers, iii. 50.
Minoïdes Mynas, i. 140.
Minos, i. 149.
Mint, i. 293.
Minutoli, i. 465.
Mirrors, ii. 285.
Mist, dark, i. 125.
Mithras, i. 325, iii. 181.
Mithriac, Æon, i. 399; Cronus, i. 400; mysteries, i. 290, iii. 180; mystery-tradition, i. 95.
Mithriaca, i. 178, 179, 182, ii. 276, iii. 181.
Mixture, iii. 102.
Mnaseas, i. 314.
Mnevis, i. 272, 309.
Möhler, i. 25.
Moirogenesis, i. 465.
Moist, i. 309, iii. 66; essence, i. 170, 187, 388, 390, 454, ii. 4, 75; light, i. 391; nature, i. 151, 310, 312, 313, ii. 4, 5, 13, 26.
Moistened, i. 161.
Moistener, i. 161, 279.
Moisture, i. 313.
Moly, i. 325.
Momos, iii. 115, 116, 142, 182; speech of, iii. 113.
Monad, i. 359, 395, 404, 414, 456, ii. 90; Apollo, i. 275; from the One, iii. 291; pleroma, i. 405; quintessence, i. 403.
Monastery, i. 209, iii. 93.
Montanus, ii. 292.
Montet, i. 387.
Moon, i. 319, 321, 332, 417, 419, ii. 180, 312.
Moon-God Thoth, i. 72.
Morning, Infinite, i. 80.
Moses, ii. 38; *Archangelic Book of*, i. 197; Books of, i. 456, ii. 158; companions of, i. 244; Eighth Book of, i. 197, 411; hierophant and prophet, i. 247.
Mōt (see Mut), i. 125, 126.
Mother, of Gods, i. 152, 176; Holy Spirit, ii. 238; of living, i. 163; own, iii. 242; wisdom, i. 224; womb of great, iii. 324.
Mother-Æon, ii. 163.
Mother-city, best, i. 237.
Motion, ii. 61.
Mount, of Arcadia, ii. 238; Athos, i. 140; of Galilee, ii. 238; holy, i. 375; of initiation, ii. 238; of Olives, ii. 54; Passing o'er the, ii. 171; of perfection, ii. 24; Tabor, ii. 238; way up to, ii. 150, 171; wending up, ii. 219, 237; mountain, i. 377; of light, ii. 238; Secret Sermon on, i. 56, ii. 234; top of, ii. 237.
Mozley, i. 34; on poles, i. 176.
Mukti, ii. 167.
Mulberry-tree, i. 284.
Mulberry-wood, tables of, iii. 216.
Müller, i. 104, 117.
Müller (C.), i. 107, 123.
Mummification, iii. 123.
Mummy, i. 71.
Muratorian Fragment, i. 378.
Murderer, ii. 202.
Muses, i. 280, 287, ii. 323; the nine or ennead, i. 85; prophets of the, ii. 292.
Museum, i. 102.

Music, ii. 324, 331.
Music-maker, ii. 290, 291.
Musician, God, ii. 288 ; the, ii. 291.
Mustard seed, i. 247.
Mut (see Mōt), i. 337.
Myer, *Qabbalah* of, i. 281.
Myriad-eyed, i. 184.
Myrrh, i. 332, 364, 366.
Mysteries, iii. 251 ; Anthropos-theory of, i. 193 ; of Assyrians, i. 155 ; Bacchic or Corybantic, i. 212 ; below, the, iii. 94 ; and *Book of the Dead*, iii. 186 ; of Dionysus, i. 311 ; Eleusinian, i. 59 ; the Great, i. 217, 362, ii. 240 ; of Great Mother, i. 186 ; hierophants of, i. 212 ; Hippolytus and divulging of, i. 140 ; most holy, i. 221 ; ineffable, i. 210 ; of Isis, iii. 182 ; Lesser, i. 180, ii. 159, 214, 240 ; of light and divine birth, i. 75 ; Magna Mater, i. 179 ; Mithriac, i. 290, iii. 180 ; On the, iii. 285 ; punishment for revealing, i. 213 ; of purity, i. 154 ; of regeneration, ii. 240 ; scribe of, iii. 223 ; of solemn life, i. 209 ; of godlike virtues, i. 207.
Mysterious black, iii. 158.
Mystery, of birth from virgin womb, ii. 240 ; of blessed bliss, i. 154 ; *Book of the Great Logos according to*, i. 166 ; dark, iii. 149 ; of deity, i. 225 ; deity, Cronus, i. 400 ; epoptic, i. 178 ; at third gate, i. 190 ; of Heavenly Man, i. 226 ; of ignorance, ii. 25 ; of man, i. 141 ; of repentance, ii. 245 ; ritual in *Acts of John*, i. 182, 183 ; of sameness, ii. 241 ; of Samothracians, i. 168 ; of virgin-birth, i. 211.
Mystery-institutions, iii. 327 ; inner doctrine of, i. 141.
Mystery-myth, the, i. 278 ff.
Mystery-play of all time, i. 377.
Mystes, i. 210, ii. 93, iii. 188.
Mystic, ii. 240, iii. 184 ; enclosure, i. 179 ; eucharist, ii. 94 ; images, i. 207 ; spectacle, iii. 107.
Mystical god-blending, i. 156.
Mysticism, practical, iii. 325, 326.
Myths, of Plato, i. 109 ; treatment of, i. 200 ; under-meaning of, i. 201.

Naas, i. 187, 192.
Naassene Document, i. 92, 390, ii. 54, 91, iii. 280, 282 ; analysis of, i. 142.
Naassene Hymn, ii. 109.
Naassenes, i. 141.
Naasseni, i. 146.
Nai, i. 294.
Nakdimon, Rabbi, ii. 239.
Naked, i. 211, 213, 373, 374.
Name, i. 85, ii. 343 ; authentic, ii. 252 ; of God, i. 198, 234, ii. 344, iii. 293 ; ogdoad, ii. 252.
Name-maker, iii. 276.
Names, i. 352 ; of power, ii. 279 ; energetic speech of, ii. 267.
Naos, i. 187.
Nature, iii. 25 ; Arise ! blessed, i 155 ; by-products of, iii. 52 ; contemplators of, i. 206 ; fairest part of, ii. 348, 350 ; moist, i. 151, 161, 310, 312, 313, ii. 4, 5, 13, 26 ; original, i. 155 ; productive, iii. 66 ; seven-robed, i. 156 ; vaporous, iii. 209.
Naughtiness, superfluity of, i. 451.
Naumann, *History of Music of*, i. 294.
Nazorenes, i. 369.
Nebris, fawn-skin, i. 191.
Necessity, i. 101, ii. 211, iii. 61, 264 ; circle of, i. 428 ; daughters of, i. 442 ; fate and, ii. 385 ; foreknowledge and, iii. 12, 58 ; love and, iii. 110, 264 ; spindle of, i. 440 ; throne of, i. 447 ; utterance of, ii. 362.
Nechepso, i. 100 ff., 464, 472, 477.
Necheus, i. 464.
Nectar, i. 415.
Nefer-Tem, i. 458.
Negress, Hor, son of, i. 88.
Nehe-māut, i. 49.
Neilos, i. 307.
Neilotis, i. 115.
Neïth, i. 108, 273.
Nemanous, i. 285.
Nemesis, iii. 116.
Neophytes, i. 214.
Nephthys, i. 280, 284, 315, 322 337, 340, 344.
Nesert, i. 457.
Net, i. 58 ff., 62 ; house of, i. 58 ; temple of, i. 62 ; of Vulcan, i. 62.
Netting, i. 62.

INDEX 357

Nicolaïtans, i. 165, ii. 79.
Night, i. 91, iii. 94, 114.
Night-stool boy, i. 298.
Nightingale, i. 445, 449.
Nigidius, i. 407.
Nikolaos, iii. 279.
Nikotheos, iii. 278.
Nile, i. 267, 269, 308, 314, 316, 345, 347, 384, ii. 265, iii. 148, 154; celestial, i. 70, 92, 156, iii. 163; father, i. 109; flood of, iii. 224; heavenly, iii. 158; Osiris, i. 308; Osiris' efflux, i. 312.
Nine, ii. 16.
Nineteenth Century, ii. 192.
Nirmānakāya, ii. 44.
Nirvāna, ii. 98.
Nirvānic consciousness, i. 51, ii. 45, 46, 98.
Nitriote nome, i. 384.
Noah, ii. 56.
Nochaïtæ, i. 142.
Noëtic, body, ii. 242; world, iii. 80.
Non-Being, ii. 161.
Noose, of Hercules, i. 61.
Nourishment of gods, i. 133.
Numbers, i. 404; which pre-exist in Soul, iii. 173.
Numinis majestas, iii. 260.
Nuptial number, iii. 174, 336.
Nurse, i. 276, 285, 336; of all, i. 310, ii. 209.
Nut, i. 65.

Oannes, i. 149, 425, iii. 303.
Oblivion (Lethe), Place of, i. 454.
Oblong, i. 319.
Obscuration, ii. 260.
Obscure Philosopher, ii. 215.
Ocean, i. 162; churning the, iii. 180; of divine love, ii. 94; of generation, iii. 163; great, ii. 92; heaven, i. 131, iii. 154; stream of, i. 162, 282.
Oceanus, i. 310, iii. 273.
Ochus, i. 277, 307.
Octateuch, iii. 297.
Odysseus, i. 446; companions of, i. 270.
Œnuphis, i. 274.
Ogdoad, i. 57, 120, 130, 132, 246, 263, 275, ii. 42, 228, 251; name, ii. 252.
Old man of sea, i. 176.
Old old path, ii. 98.

Olympian path, the, ii. 171.
Olympic stole, iii. 182.
Olympus, i. 61, 299.
Omar Khayyām, i. 167.
Omega, iii. 273.
Omniform, ii. 194, 245, 341.
Omphis, i. 320.
One, ii. 100; and all, i. 136, 197, ii. 118, 230, 310, 344; is all, ii. 268, 308, 309; colour, i. 391; element, ii. 195, 244; essence, i. 391; form, ii. 35; image of, ii. 118; man, ii. 222, 244; and only, ii. 258, iii. 22; pleroma, ii. 133; second, ii. 118, 268; sense, ii. 139, 244; sight, ii. 161; source, ii 160.
One-and-Only One, ii. 100.
Oneness, ii. 90, 91, 92, iii. 258.
Onion, i. 271.
Only Son, ii. 196.
Onnofris, i. 294.
Onoel, i. 422.
Onomacritus, i. 392, ii. 235.
Ophianæ, ii. 27.
Ophitæ, ii. 27.
Ophite, hebdomad, i. 421; systems of gnosis, i. 98.
Ophites, i. 142; diagram of, i. 422, 423, 449, iii. 277.
Opinion, i. 430; and sensation, iii. 84.
Oracle, at Delphi, i. 349, ii. 42, 228.
Ordeal of fire, i. 79.
Order, ii. 385; and its opposite, iii. 266.
Orderer of the world, iii. 208.
Orelli, i. 24, 123.
Orgies, i. 149, 155, 211, 350.
Origen, i. 140, 423, ii. 72, iii. 99; Celsus and, i. 423.
Original, man, i. 168; nature, i. 155; seed, i. 155.
Orion, i. 295, 296.
Ormuzd, i. 325, 400; servant of, i. 297.
Orpheus, i. 391, 392, 445, iii. 320.
Orphic, eschatology, i. 439; fragments, i. 265; hymn, iii. 269; hymns, ii. 235; initiates, i. 191; Phanes, ii. 282; or Pythagorean initiate, i. 95; world-egg, i. 387, 388.
Orphicism, i. 392.
Osiriaca, the, i. 256, 311.
Osirian Passion, i. 288.

Osiric and Typhonic Passions, i. 298.
Osirified, i. 65, 71, 120 ; Thoth and the, i. 65.
Osiris, i. 63, 74, 80, 193, 279, 367, iii. 198 ; Apis animated image of, i. 321 ; birth of, iii. 122 ; black, i. 296, 309 ; burials of, i. 293, 320 ; great campaign of, i. 353 ; dark God, iii. 156 ; and Dionysus, i. 310 ; disciple of Agathodaimon, i. 478, iii. 261 ; efflux of, i. 328 ; eye of, iii. 158 ; fourteen parts of, i. 289 ; garment of, i. 71 ; gospel of, i. 367 ; house of, i. 79 ; and Isis, blessings of, iii. 122 ; members of, i. 156 ; mystery-god, iii. 257 ; Nile, i. 308 ; secrets of, iii. 96 ; seeking for, i. 332 ; the sun, i. 332 ; tombs of, i. 289, 292, 293, 312 ; is water, i. 156.
Osiris-myth, i. 130.
Osiris-plant, i. 314.
Ostanes, iii. 295 ; *Book of*, iii. 277, 296.
Osymandias, library of, i. 50.
Outbreathing of universe, ii. 254.
Outline of His Face, ii. 282.
Overseer of ceremonies, iii. 223.
Overseers of heavens, i. 126.
Own-form, ii. 46.
Own-nature of masterhood, ii. 47.
Ox, i. 356, 422.
Oxyrhynchus, i. 269, 354, iii. 246 ; logia, i. 172, 173, 209, ii. 24, 116, 239, 255 ; logion, probable completion of, ii. 122.
Oxyrhynchus-town, i. 354.

Pa-neshe, i. 119.
Pæan, i. 293.
Pain, sharp tooth of, iii. 115.
Paitoni, i. 9.
Palæstinos, i. 287.
Palestine, i. 208.
Palingeneses, i. 311.
Palingenesis, i. 283, ii. 83 ; lord of, i. 50.
Palisade, i. 163.
Palladius, ii. 50.
Pallas, iii. 181.
Pamphilus, i. 100.
Pamphus of Athens, i. 181.
Pamyle, i. 279.
Pamylia, i. 279, 312.

Pan, i. 186, ii. 56.
Panacea, i. 241.
Panathenæa, i. 62.
Panchæa, i. 297.
Pandora, iii. 274, 280.
Panics, i. 283.
Panopolis, i. 282.
Pans, i. 282.
Panthers, i. 436.
Pantomorph, ii. 194, 245, 341.
Panu, i. 294.
Paophi, i. 331.
Papa, i. 172.
Paphie, iii. 91.
Papyrus, i. 284, 289 ; Ebers, i. 50 ; Harris, i. 131 ; Insinger, ii. 244.
Paradigm, of cosmos, ii. 196 ; of time, ii. 196.
Paradigms, iii. 56.
Paradise, i. 173, 187, iii. 279 ; a, i. 244 ; celestial, i. 425 ; planted with trees, i. 189.
Parallelogram, iii. 177.
Paraplex, i. 269.
Parents we are to abandon, ii. 96.
Parmenides, i. 181.
Parthey, i. 14, 26 ; criticism of text of, ii. 64.
Parthians, i. 196, 197.
Passage of Sun, i. 71, 77.
Passing o'er Mount, ii. 171.
Passion, i. 283, ii. 204, 262, 288 , and sensation, iii. 42.
Passions, i. 277, 351, ii. 249, 262 ; Osiric and Typhonic, i. 298 ; Titanic, i. 311.
Passive Principle, i. 225.
Pastophors, iii. 225.
Pastos, iii. 225.
Path, i. 70, 74, ii. 89, 91, 114, 118, iii. 293 ; bitter, ii. 362 ; of gnosis, ii. 98, 195, 248 ; up to Gods, ii. 169, iii. 299 ; Good's own, ii. 189, 190, 196, iii. 327 ; secrets of holy, i. 192 ; old old, ii. 90, 98 ; Olympian, ii. 171 ; of return, iii. 144 ; of salvation, ii. 171 ; of self-knowledge, ii. 40 ; moving on a soundless, i. 357 ; steps of, i. 79 ; to supreme, ii. 197 ; thither, iii. 6 ; to truth, iii. 5.
Patrizzi, i. 11.
Paul, propaganda of, i. 204.
Pauly, i. 26.
Paut, i. 57, 132 ; of Hermes, i. 263.

INDEX 359

Pawnbroking bye law, i. 242.
Paÿni, i. 305.
Peace, author of its, iii. 4; virtue of perfect, i. 218.
Peacock, i. 391.
Pearls, i. 175.
Peisistratidæ, i. 392.
Pelasgos, i. 149.
Pelousios, i. 287.
Penelope, i. 159.
Pentateuch, i. 203.
Perception, iii. 84.
Perfect, i. 434; blessedness, ii. 242; fruit, i. 182; men, ii. 87, 97; one, ii. 91; Sermon, ii. 136, 266; glory of soul, ii. 165; the, iii. 14, 256; vision, iii. 96.
Perfection, beginning of, i. 178; *Gospel of*, i. 142; mount of, ii. 24; perfect, i. 178.
Perfume-makers, i. 365.
Permanence, ii. 271.
Permanent atoms, i. 289.
Perret, ii. 56.
Persea, i. 349, iii. 208.
Persephassa (see Proserpina), i. 301.
Persephonē, i. 151, 181, 347, 350, iii. 161.
Persia, ii. 206.
Persians, i. 207.
Person, i. 136, iii. 287, 288.
Persona, ii. 25.
Persons, of Ptah, i. 132.
Peter, James, John, and, i. 475.
Petosiris, i. 100 ff., 464, 472, 477.
Petra, iii. 161.
Petroma, iii. 232.
Petron, iii. 172.
Phæacians, i. 270.
Phædrus, river, i. 287; soul and her mysteries in the, i. 429.
Phallephoria, i. 279, 313.
Phallus, i. 289, 312.
Phamenoth, i. 321.
Phanes, i. 391, 394.
Phaophi, i. 305, 346.
Pharaoh, rat of, i. 356.
Pharisees, i. 209.
Pharos, i. 318.
Pheidias, i. 359, ii. 290.
Pheison, i. 188.
Pheneatians, iii. 232.
Phenëus, i. 376.
Pherecydes, ii. 260.
Philadelphus, i. 104.
Philæ, i. 460.

Philip, Acts of, i. 147; *Gospel of*, i. 142.
Philo, i. 211, ii. 128, 137; of Alexandria on the Man-Doctrine, i. 197; Byblius, i. 122 ff.; of Byblos, i. 402; *De Legatione* of, ii. 237; two Horoi in, i. 367; inspiration i. 203; his method, i. 199; monotheist, i. 231.
Philonean tractates, i. 199.
Philoponus, ii. 172, iii. 209.
Philosophers, iii. 111; most ancient of, iii. 215; prince of, ii. 38.
Philosophumena, of Hippolytus, i. 140.
Philosophy, beginning of, i. 274, iii. 246; Egyptian, i. 28; inventor of, i. 138; piety and, iii. 3; pure, ii. 331; true, ii. 232; work of, i. 233.
Philostratus, ii. 197.
Philtre, immortal, i. 246.
Philtres, i. 88.
Phosilampes, ii. 107.
Photius, i. 62, 152.
Phrygian writings, i. 303.
Phrygians, i. 350.
Phylarchus, i. 303.
Physician, good, i. 461, ii. 213.
Physicists, theory of, i. 307, 312.
Physiologus, i. 56, 330, 345, 356, 357, iii. 112.
Physis, iii. 256.
Picture, iii. 18, 276, 295.
Pierret, i. 28.
Pietschmann, i. 47 ff., 72, 112, 116, 119.
Piety, iii. 3, 5, 243, 265.
Pig taboos, i. 271.
Pillars of Hermes, i. 112.
Pilot, i. 296, 347; mind as, ii. 201.
Pinax, of Bitos, i. 197, iii. 277.
Pindar, i. 312, 366.
Pine, i. 364.
Pine-resin, i. 364.
Piper, the, i. 183.
Pistis Sophia, i. 84, 92, 94, 326, 371, 418, 426, ii. 43, 96; general title of, i. 142; song of powers in, ii. 241.
Pitra, i. 6.
Pitys the Thessalian, iii. 295.
Pius, Bishop of Rome, i. 378.
Plague, i. 364; great, i. 364.
Plagues and famines, iii. 49.

Plain, of Forgetfulness (Lēthē), i. 447; of Truth, i. 430, ii. 19, 49, 50, 97, iii. 171, 172, 189, 205, 208.
Plane, iii. 174.
Planetary chains, iii. 301.
Planets, five, iii. 46.
Plasm, sealing of the members of the, iii. 70.
Plato, i. 62, 103, 113, 265, 274, 277, 297, 298, 299, 300, 333, 336, 337, 338, 340, 362, 392, 405, 406, 414, ii. 167; Atlantis of, i. 176; buys, i. 351; crater in, i. 450; definition of man by, i. 433; marriage scheme of, i. 336; myths of, i. 109; nuptial number of, i. 336; transformation of soul in, iii. 110; follows Trismegistus, iii. 248.
Pleiades, i. 350.
Plenum, space a, ii. 70.
Pleroma, i. 85, 246, 335, ii. 28, 32, 93, 241; of bad, ii. 115; of evil, ii. 113; common fruit of the, ii. 241; of Good, ii. 117; and hysterema, ii. 239; of ideas, ii. 128; intelligible superspatial, ii. 196; monad, i. 405; one, ii. 133; of virtues, ii. 117.
Pletho, i. 8.
Plew, i. 115.
Pleyte, i. 49.
Pliny, iii. 296.
Plotins Stellung zum Gnosticismus, iii. 278.
Plotinus, ii. 42, 198, 228, 302; *Life of*, iii. 278; on metempsychosis, i. 434; soul of, iii. 32; yoga of, i. 251.
Plucked green wheat-ear, i. 178.
Plumes, i. 337.
Plutarch, i. 84, 103, 223, 255, 453; *Consolation of*, i. 260; Yogin of, iii. 169.
Pluto, i. 301, 362.
Pœmandres, early form of the, i. 374; higher criticism of the, i. 128; variant spellings of, i. 3.
Pœmandrist, Apology of a, ii. 298.
Poimandres, the name, ii. 50.
Pole-lords of heaven, i. 176.
Poleis, i. 177.
Poleitai, i. 177.
Poles, i. 87; seven, i. 95, 402.
Polichne, i. 292.

Pontius (Pontus) Pilate, iii. 164.
Poor, i. 373.
Porphyry, i. 113, 123, 124, ii. 42, 229; *Letter to Marcella*, i. 260.
Portrait, iii. 18.
Poseidon, i. 176, 318; first cube, i. 275; trident of, i. 359.
Poseidonius, i. 102.
Possessions, ii. 327, 330.
Pothos, i. 125.
Poverty, i. 338.
Powers, chariot of the, i. 238; invocation of the, ii. 249; song of the, ii. 42, 43.
Pralaya, ii. 260, iii. 137.
Prāna, i. 363, ii. 168, iii. 146, 206.
Prayer for gnosis, ii. 49.
Prayers, for dead, i. 78; of Essenes, ii. 49; Hermes', i. 82.
Praying-room, i. 209.
Pre-existing, i. 150; Amygdalos the, i. 182.
Presence, the, ii. 24, 47.
Priam, i. 299.
Prima Materia, i. 151.
Prince, of eternity, i. 65, 132; of philosophers, ii. 38.
Principles of man, ii. 149; and cosmos, ii. 207.
Privation, i. 327; of sense, ii. 127.
Probation, three stages of, ii. 236.
Probationers, the, i. 185.
Procession, ii. 89; of fate, ii. 49.
Proclus, i. 101, 106, 435, ii. 169; on descent of souls, i. 435; on spheres, iii. 300.
Proem to fourth gospel, ii. 371.
Prometheus, i. 263, 314, iii. 274, 280, 282.
Promise of silence, the, ii. 219.
Pronoia, ii. 39.
Prophetenpredigt, ii. 122.
Proscription of worship of gods, ii. 399.
Proserpina (Kore), i. 59.
Protection, sole, iii. 265.
Proteus, i. 176.
Prototypes, iii. 56.
Protrepticus, or Exhortation to the Greeks, ii. 300.
Providence, ii. 39, 207, 211, 216, iii. 61, 195, 235, 258, 260; and fate, iii. 36, 55, 60; legislative, i. 237; ministers of, iii. 205, 211.

INDEX 361

Psammetichus, i. 268.
Pselcis, i. 117.
Psellus, i. 7, ii. 38, 58.
Pseudo-Appuleius, ii. 392.
Pseudo-Manetho, i. 110, 115.
Psychagogue and psychopomp, i. 159.
Psychosis, iii. 99, 102, 168.
Ptah, i. 457, iii. 148 ; the great, i. 130, 135 ; Hephæstus, i. 160, 382, iii. 96 ; noose of, i. 61 ; persons of, i. 132 ; hath spoken, i. 138, iii. 148 ; temple of, i. 130 ; workshop of, i. 457.
Ptah-doctrine, i. 130.
Ptah-Hotep, i. 74.
Ptah-priests of Memphis, i. 135.
Ptah-Thoth, i. 132.
Ptolemies, i. 102, 103 ; libraries of the, iii. 277.
Ptolemy, Gnostic, ii. 371 ; the saviour, i. 301 ; (II.), i. 103, 105 ; (IV.), i. 460 ; (IX.), i. 463 ; (X.), i. 466 ; (XI.), i. 466.
Ptolemy Philadelphus, i. 104 ; Letter of Manetho to, i. 103.
Pulse, i. 349.
Pupil of the eye, i. 394.
Pupilla Mundi, iii. 93.
Pupilline, l'Âme, iii. 167.
Pupils of the eyes, i. 84.
Pure, and holy love, ii. 332 ; not lawful for, i. 265 ; matter, ii. 7 ; mind, ii. 320, 324, iii. 292 ; philosophy, ii. 331 ; shepherd, ii. 55.
Purpose, iii. 258.
Purgations, catharms or, iii. 210.
Purity, mysteries of, i. 154 ; wedding garment of, ii. 249.
Purusha, ii. 168.
Pyanepsion, i. 350.
Pyramid, ii. 85 : iii. 254, 255 ; great, i. 69.
Pyriphlegethon, ii. 361, 362.
Pythagoras, i. 113, 274, 298, 392, iii. 317 ; his symbols, i. 274.
Pythagorean, i. 305 ; triangle, iii. 175.
Pythagoreans, i. 359.
Pythagoric, messages, i. 275 ; opposites, i. 327.
Pythagorics, i. 308, 327.
Pythian oracle, ii. 42, 228.
Pytho, ii. 300.
Python, i. 298.

Qabbalah, Myer's, i. 281.
Questions, of Mary, i. 142 ; of Osiris to Horus, i. 290.
Quick, i. 186.
Quiet and Serene, iii. 253.
Quintessence, iii. 102, 206 ; æther, ii. 92 ; and monad, i. 403.

Rā, i. 131 ; and Apep, i. 57 ; heart of, i. 53, 68 ; herald of will of, i. 49 ; library of, i. 103 ; light-god, i. 473 ; tongue of, i. 49, 68.
Race, i. 205, 207, ii. 20, 50, 162, 221, 290 ; of Elxai, ii. 242 ; of God, i. 253 ; without a king, i. 164 ; ineffable, i. 166 ; of Logos, ii. 18, 241 ; self-taught, i. 174, 220, ii. 241 ; within, iii. 5.
Rachel, i. 178, 220.
Raise the dead, i. 273.
Raisins, i. 364.
Ram of perfectioning, the, i. 212.
Ramses III., i. 131.
Raphael, i. 422.
Rashness, ii. 224.
Raven, i. 286, 352, iii. 181.
Ray, iii. 288 ; of God, ii. 275.
Ray-like, i. 224.
Rays, hall of golden, i. 75.
Reason, iii. 84 ; articulation of, ii. 224 ; common, i. 346 ; continuing, i. 247 ; of divinity, ii. 311, 318 ; highest whole, ii. 320 ; marriage with right, i. 223 ; self-perfect, i. 222, iii. 60 ; true, ii. 319.
Rebecca, i. 217.
Rebirth, i. 58, 353, ii. 219 ; author of, ii. 222, 243 ; of cosmos, ii. 357 ; hymn of, ii. 229 ; lord of, i. 50 ; manner of, ii. 221, 224, 226, 233, 264 ; sermon on, ii. 219, 227, 236 ; tradition of, ii. 220 ; way of, ii. 248.
Reborn, ii. 239.
Recitation Ode, i. 192, 193.
Recognition of children, iii. 20.
Recollection, i. 433.
Recording Angel, i. 64.
Red, ass, a, i. 306 ; earth, i. 150 ; Sea, i. 163.
Red-skinned, i. 295, 305, 306.
Regeneration, ii. 239 ; mystery of, ii. 240.
Reincarnation, i. 137, ii. 76, 83 ; Hermes, teacher of, iii. 227.

Reitzenstein, i. 15, 51, 121, 143 ; monograph on "Aion," i. 387 ; general view of, i. 40 ff.
Religion, of Hermes, i. 82 ; of joy, i. 73 ; of light, i. 73 ; of mind, i. 91, ii. 401, iii. 316.
Reminiscence, ii. 241, 372.
Ren, i. 89.
Repentance, mystery of, ii. 245 ; true, ii. 98.
Resin, i. 332, 363, 366.
Restoration, ii. 126, 128, iii. 246.
Resurrection of dead, ii. 165.
Return, the, ii. 246.
Revealer, of hidden, i. 49 ; of light, i. 375.
Revelations, divine, i. 216 ; hierophant of, i. 211.
Revelling-place, i. 84, 97.
Rhea, i. 151, 153, 278, 305, 334, 390, ii. 26 ; womb of, i. 335.
Rib, i. 279.
Richter, i. 200.
Riddle, i. 273.
Riess, i. 100, 101.
Right hand, i. 348.
Righteousness, i. 53, 60, 85, 263, ii. 225, 231.
Ring Pass not, ii. 9.
Rishis, ii. 242.
Rising from dead, i. 173.
Rite, black, iii. 107, 141, 149, 155 ; of flame, i. 93.
Ritual, i. 58, 59, 65, 72, 74, 76, 77, 79, 84 ; of Azazel, i. 306 ; of Embalmment, i. 460 ; of Initiation in *Acts of John*, ii. 243.
River, of Divine Reason, i. 244 ; of God, i. 244 ; of Heedlessness, i. 447 ; of Lethe, i. 416, 452.
Road, Ancient, iii. 327.
Robber in house, ii. 121.
Robe, of fire, ii. 152 ; of glory, i. 361, ii. 43, 249 ; of Isis, i. 62 ; single, i. 373.
Robes, her, i. 340 ; of Isis, i. 264 ; sacred, i. 361.
Rock, God from, i. 95, 392, 399 ; the, i. 161.
Rod of Hermes, i. 61.
Root, of form, ii. 193 ; of matter, ii. 26 ; one, ii. 269 ; of universals, i. 184.
Rootage of æons, ii. 317.
Rosetta stone, i. 117.
Rossel, i. 11.

Round-the-same, ii. 62.
Rulers, seven, ii. 7, 9 ; workmen of, iii. 70.
Rush, i. 312.
Rusta, i. 70.

Sacrificers, iii. 112.
Saffron-coloured, i. 342.
Sages, the seven, i. 207.
Sâh, i. 89.
Sai-an-Sinsin, i. 79.
Saïs, i. 108, 273, ii. 280, iii. 293.
Sakkâra, i. 372 ; step-pyramid of, i. 465.
Salmon, i. 147, 195, 196, 421.
Salome, i. 147, 153 ; mother of St John, i. 38.
Salt, i. 267, 397.
Salvation, harbour of, ii. 120, 123 ; path of, ii. 171 ; port of, ii. 120.
Sambhogakāya, ii. 45.
Same, i. 327, ii. 268, 369.
Sameness, ii. 207, 244.
Samothracians, i. 168.
Sampsæans, i. 369.
Saṁsāra, ii. 167, 283.
Sanchuniathon, i. 24, 112 ff., 113, 122, ii. 279.
Saosis, i. 285.
Sarah, i. 217, 220, 221.
Sarapis, i. 301, 302, 342.
Sassanean, i. 297.
Satan, sons of, iii. 319.
Satrap, iii. 133.
Saturn, i. 416, 418, 419.
Satyrs, i. 282.
Saulasau, i. 165.
Save my alone-begotten from lions, i. 170.
Saving One, i. 340.
Saviour, *Books of the*, i. 418 ; my, i. 241 ; Ptolemy the, i. 301 ; the, i. 224.
Sayings, of Good Daimon, ii. 213 f. ; of Heracleitus, ii. 213.
Scaly-coat, i. 289.
Scape-goat, i. 306.
Scarab, i. 276, 356.
Scarabæus, i. 356.
Scetis, i. 384.
Scherer, i. 36.
Schmidt, Carl, i. 50, 93.
Schmitz, i. 34.
Schneidewin, i. 143.
Sciences, iii. 40, 85, 198 ; arts and, ii. 322, iii. 199.

INDEX

Scipio, Dream of, i. 413.
Scorpion, i. 282.
Scourge of Christ, ii. 173.
Scribe, of Gods, i. 53 ; of the nine Gods, i. 50 ; of the mysteries, iii. 223.
Scripture-making, ii. 22.
Scroll, secret, i. 77, 78.
Scyth, ii. 253, 401.
Sea, Great, iii. 163 ; of ignorance, ii. 123 ; infinite, i. 389 ; old man of, i. 176.
Sea-hawk, bone of, i. 189, 343.
Seal, i. 395, iii. 79 ; mighty type of, i. 395 ; which marked victims, iii. 223.
Sealers, i. 306.
Sealing members of plasm, iii. 70.
Sebennyte, i. 104.
Second, birth, i. 79 ; God, i. 230, ii. 127, 170, 365 ; man, i. 139, ii. 27 ; one, ii. 118, 268.
Seeds of God, ii. 137.
Seeing Israel, i. 198, 234.
Seer, ii. 255, iii. 111 ; of Gnosis, ii. 94 ; of God, iii. 298.
Seething, i. 396.
Seirias, i. 115.
Seirios (see Sirius), i. 111.
Sekhem, i. 89, 131.
Sekhet, i. 457.
Selene, i. 151, 278.
Seleucus, iii. 289.
Self-begotten, i. 150.
Self-taught, ii. 242 ; race, i. 174, ii. 241.
Semele, i. 161, 454.
Semiramis, i. 297.
Semitismus, i. 124.
Semneion, i. 209.
Sempiternity, iii. 9.
Seneca, i. 102.
Sensation, iii. 41 ; corpse of, ii. 121 ; energy and, of, iii. 40 ; opinion and, iii. 84 ; passion and, iii. 42.
Sense, ii. 319 ff., 340, 345 ; cosmic, ii. 371, 372 ; discourse on, ii. 131, 132 ; higher, i. 227, ii. 338 ; one, ii. 139, 244 ; privation of, ii. 127 ; sermon about, ii. 129 ; single, ii. 389 ; whole, ii. 371.
Sense-and-thought, ii. 132, 134, 137 ; of cosmos, ii. 133, 139.
Sensible, ii. 286, 320, 340, 377 ; or hylic cosmos, ii. 167.

Separator or Divider, ii. 70.
Sepphora, i. 164, 217.
Sept, i. 111.
Sepulchres, ye are whited, i. 172.
Serapeum, ii. 399, iii. 277.
Seriadic, country, i. 104 ; land, i. 107, 110 ff. ; monuments, i. 113.
Sermon, Perfect, ii. 136 ; Secret, ii. 250 ; about sense, ii. 129 ; on rebirth, ii. 219, 227, 236.
Sermons, classification of, iii. 306 ; Expository, i. 462, ii. 250, 264, iii. 33, 54, 309 ; of Fate, ii. 217 ; General, i. 462, ii. 141, 145, 236, 264, iii. 45, 77, 308.
Serpent, i. 86, 87, 97, 98, 146, 344, ii. 4, 26, 301 ; of Darkness, ii. 31 ; death of, ii. 300 ; great, ii. 27, 35 ; winged, i. 398 ; of wisdom, i. 194, 480.
Servant of God, i. 251.
Servant-form, i. 398, 399.
Servants of God, i. 212, 220.
Seseli, i. 365.
Sesostris, i. 297.
Sesquioctave, i. 320.
Set, i. 53, 57.
Seth, i. 111, 114, 319, 329, 343, ii. 27 ; sons of, i. 114.
Seth-Hermes, sons of, i. 113.
Sethian, i. 139, 393, ii. 4, 27 ; gnosis, i. 192, 393.
Seti, (I.), i. 50.
Setme, i. 380.
Seven, ii. 341 ; basis, i. 419 ; circles, ii. 76 ; cosmoi, i. 407 ; fortunes of heaven, i. 176 ; halls, i. 380 ; Kabiri, ii. 279 ; men, ii. 11 ; peals of laughter, iii. 137 ; poles, i. 95, 402 ; rulers, ii. 7, 9 ; sages, the, i. 207 ; sons of Sydyk, i. 127 ; spheres, iii. 60 ; times, i. 332 ; virgins, i. 176 ; wise ones, i. 458 ; worlds, the, ii. 179 ; youths, i. 176 ; zones, i. 413, ii. 42.
Seven-robed Nature, i. 156.
Sevenfold " Ha," iii. 137.
Seventeen, i. 319.
Seventy-two, i. 281.
Sex, iii. 129, 145, 203.
Shadow, ii. 9 ; casting, i. 326.
Shakti, i. 52, ii. 107.
Shame, garment of, i. 153, ii. 42.
Sharing-with-all, ii. 225.
Sharp-snout, i. 289, 354.

Shaven, i. 265.
She of ten-thousand names, i. 333.
Sheep, i. 356.
Sheeted dead, the, i. 161.
Shepherd, i. 371, ii. 43, 228, 229, 231; good, i. 373, ii. 213; *of Hermas*, i. 369, ii. 238, 248, iii. 229, 232, 319; of men, i. 375, ii. 231, 372; pure, ii. 55; of bright stars, i. 186, ii. 56; symbolic representation of, i. 372; true, i. 238; who hath his fold in the west, i. 373.
Shore, other, ii. 89.
Short-armed, i. 295.
Shrine-bearers, iii. 225.
Shu, i. 131, 133.
Si-Osiri, i. 380.
Sibylline, literature, ii. 330; oracles, iii. 235; writers, ii. 49.
Sickness, health and, iii. 203.
Siddhis, ii. 197.
Siege of Mansoul, iii. 186.
Sige (Silence), ii. 163.
Sight, mortal and immortal, iii. 235; one, ii. 161; of peace, i. 246.
Sigils, iii. 179.
Signs of zodiac, i. 54, ii. 52.
Silence, ii. 19, 20; heart of, i. 73; holy, ii. 163; promise of, ii. 219, 233; vow of, ii. 250.
Simon, Jules, i. 434.
Simon Magus, ii. 108.
Simonian, gnosis, ii. 107, 317; tradition, i. 184, 188.
Simonides, i. 296.
Sinai, i. 384.
Single, love, ii. 330; sense, ii. 389.
Sinope, i. 302.
Sins, forgiveness of, i. 251.
Siren, i. 442.
Siriad land, i. 114.
Siriadic, i. 111.
Sirius, i. 110, 314, 326.
Sister-wife, i. 147, 301.
Sistrum, i. 303, 344.
Sittl, ii. 54.
Six-and-fiftieth even measure, i. 305.
Sixteen, i. 319.
Sixty, iii. 168; spaces, iii. 192.
Skiff (baris), i. 288.
Skin, red, i. 305.
Slave, i. 91, ii. 10; enharmonised, i. 183.

Sleep, iii. 32.
Slime, i. 125.
Smu, i. 343.
Snake, i. 329, 356, ii. 4, iii. 133; great, ii. 26.
Snow, fire and, i. 95.
Socrates, i. 406; Books on Rites, i. 311.
Solar, boat, i. 270; table, i. 452.
Soldier, ii. 276, iii. 50.
Soli, i. 438.
Solid, iii. 174.
Solomon, iii. 283.
Solon, i. 103, 108, 274.
Son, of God, i. 138, 157, 198, 220, 226, ii. 28, 116, 118, 140, 222, 241, iii. 239, 275, 280, 282; only beloved, i. 224; eldest, i. 227; of man, i. 150, 160, ii. 43, 138; of the One, ii. 228, 251; only, ii. 196; of virgin, iii. 160, 161; younger, ii. 192, 257.
Sonchis, i. 274.
Song, of holiness, ii. 50; of Linus, i. 293; of the powers, ii. 42, 43; of praise to Æon, i. 408.
Sons, of Elohim, i. 159; of Fire, iii. 136; of God, i. 198, 233, iii. 316; of His eternal Likeness, i. 234; of the one God, i. 234; of one man, i. 234; of Satan, iii. 319; of Seth, i. 113, 114.
Sonship, ii. 43, 50, iii. 140; wings of, i. 390.
Sophia, i. 335; Above, i. 74, ii. 76.
Sophia-aspect of Logos, i. 49.
Sophia-mythus, i. 334, 377, ii. 26, 30, 32, iii. 226.
Sophist, i. 431.
Sorrow, ii. 225.
Sosibius, i. 302.
Sothiac, i. 111; cycles, iii. 290.
Sothis, i. 80, 104, 115, 117, 121, 295, 342, iii. 276; a forgery, i. 107 ff.
Sotoles, i. 302.
Soul, i. 150, 414, 417, ii. 145, 182, 309, iii. 63, 194; animal, ii. 246; ascent of, ii. 41 ff.; of becoming, i. 49; and body, ii. 124, 130; cosmic, ii. 151, 216; daimonic, ii. 229; dual, ii. 169; essence of, i. 225; eye of, iii. 129; eyes in, i. 214; cause of all in genesis, i. 151; perfect glory of, ii. 165; gnosis virtue of, ii.

INDEX

167 ; group, i. 425 ; health of, ii. 257, iii. 265 ; rational impress in, i. 230 ; infant's, ii. 150, 216 ; Macrobius on descent of, i. 413 ; masculine power of, i. 152 ; metamorphoses of, ii. 163 ; mysteries of, in *Phædrus*, i. 429 ; numbers which pre-exist in, iii. 173 ; parts of, ii. 274, iii. 5 ; passions of, i. 177 ; transformation of, in Plato, iii. 110 ; progression of, iii. 174 ; sluggish, ii. 157 ; transfiguration of, ii. 164 ; vehicles of, ii. 167 ; vision of, iii. 188 ; (II.), of, iii. 65 ; (III.), of, iii. 72 ; (IV.), of, iii. 75 ; (V.), of, iii. 77 ; (VI.), of, iii. 80.

Soul-gnosis, iii. 137.

Soul-making, iii. 188.

Soul-regions, the sixty, iii. 168.

Souls, colours of, i. 223 ; conductor, i. 159 ; discipline of, ii. 347 ; fountain of, i. 452 ; habitat of excarnate, iii. 210 ; intercourse of, ii. 155, 314 ; kinds of, iii. 78 ; of kings, iii. 127 ; lamenting of, iii. 108 ; equal to stars, iii. 100 ; ordering of, iii. 191 ; power of sight of, i. 214 ; Proclus on descent of, i. 435 ; royal, iii. 125 ; simile of animals in a cage and, iii. 190 ; two, iii. 298 ; warder of, iii. 195.

Sound of heavens, i. 161.

Sounding brass, i. 303.

Source, i. 234, ii. 90, 176 ; one, ii. 150 ; of stars, i. 232.

Sovereign, angel, i. 371 ; potency, i. 237.

Sovereignties, iii. 198.

Sower, the, i. 174.

Space, ii. 60, 71, 212, 334, 376, iii. 63 ; dark, ii. 26 ; dry, ii. 75, 76 ; a plenum, ii. 70.

Spaces, sixty, iii. 192.

Species, ii. 313 ; genera and, ii. 378.

Speech, ii. 206.

Spermatic essence of Logos, i. 390.

Sphere, ii. 126, 337 ; cosmos a, ii. 148 ; egg, i. 427 ; eighth, ii. 42 ff. ; of fire, i. 428 ; God's deathless, ii. 230 ; watery, iii. 209.

Spheres, boundary of the, ii. 195 ; cosmic, iii. 299 ; of destiny, iii. 293 ; eight, ii. 275 ; seven planetary, iii. 60, 300 ; Proclus on, iii. 300 ; six, ii. 276 ; Tartarean, i. 445 ; Servius on seven, i. 418.

Sphericity, law of revolution, ii. 387.

Sphinx, secret of, iii. 323.

Spiegelberg, i. 112, 130, ii. 244.

Spiral, fashion, ii. 271 ; orbits, iii. 177.

Spirit, ii. 33, 168, 318, 332, 336, 390, 396, iii. 66, 81, bestower of, ii. 231 ; part played by, in conception, iii. 66 ; counterfeit, iii. 68, 281 ; Dionysus, i. 318 ; divine, iii. 258 ; Do not soil, iii. 174 ; fragrance of, i. 396 ; of God, ii. 81 ; Good, iii. 261 ; in harmony, i. 183 ; sensible, iii. 82 ; story of the, i. 371 ; virginal, i. 181, 182, ii. 240, 241, iii. 157.

Spirit-air, ii. 34.

Spirit-matter, ii. 332, 334.

Spirit-word, ii. 5.

Spirits, iii. 25, 111 ; animal, i. 363 ; delegate, i. 184.

Spiritual, baptism, ii. 92 ; birth, i. 163 ; crucifixion, ii. 238 ; eyes, i. 214 ; prototype of humanity, i. 139 ; sun, ii. 253, 300 ; way, ii. 240.

Spirituous body, iii. 210.

Spit out and cleanse the mouth, i. 291.

Sponges, iii. 210.

Square, i. 319.

Staff, i. 96, i. 373.

Stähelin, i. 196.

Stands, He who, ii. 170.

Star, native, iii. 110 ; the one, i. 232.

Star-courses, ii. 89.

Star-flocks of gods, i. 327.

Star-groups, iii. 53.

Star-mixture, iii. 74.

Starry cup of Bacchus, i. 414.

Stars, iii. 45 ; fixed, ii. 341 ; groups of, ii. 273 ; long-haired, iii. 52 ; souls equal in number to, iii. 100 ; source of the, i. 322.

Statues, ii. 351 ; of judges, i. 276.

Stending, i. 310.

Steward, ii. 358.

Stewart, i. 429, 439.

Stigmata, iii. 162.

Stock, Logos as, ii. 70.
Stoics, i. 83, 318, 319, 323.
Stone cut without hands, the, i. 162.
Stones, iii. 39 ; ensouled, i. 151.
Storks, i. 356.
Stretchers, iii. 50.
Strife, i. 359, ii. 362.
Strive to know yourselves, ii. 256.
Strivers, iii. 50.
Strong, i. 27, 314.
Subsistence, ii. 161.
Substance, ii. 269, 270.
Substantial, ii. 139.
Successions of Kings, i. 315.
Suchness, ii. 44.
Sudan, i. 55.
Suidas, i. 100, iii. 268.
Suitors, i. 159.
Sulphur, i. 262.
Sumerian, ii. 79.
Summa potestas, ii. 4.
Sun, i. 416, 419, ii. 142, 273, 294, 339, 365, 366, iii. 21, 25, 31, 126 ; arms of, i. 331 ; as charioteer with crown of rays, ii. 281 ; circle of, iii. 52 ; delineation of, ii. 282 ; demiurge, ii. 269, 281 ; gates of, i. 162 ; generation of, iii. 262 ; a "head," ii. 270 ; hymn to, ii. 253 ; Osiris is, i. 332 ; passage of, i. 77 ; ray of spiritual, iii. 287 ; rays of the, iii. 288 ; spiritual, ii. 253 ; birthday of staff of, i. 331.
Sun-god, ii. 391.
Sun-ship, i. 94.
Sunshine, the real, ii. 252.
Super-man, i. 301, ii. 93, iii. 323.
Super-substantial bread, i. 86.
Superfluity, i. 265, 267, 268.
Superior One, ii. 292.
Superstition, i. 278.
Supplanter, i. 220.
Suppliant, i. 376, ii. 219, 237, 238 ; of Hermes, ii. 236.
Suriel, i. 422.
Swallow, i. 286.
Swan, i. 445, 449.
Sweet-flag, i. 365.
Swine, i. 175.
Sydyk, i. 127.
Syene, i. 269, 477.
Syncellus, i. 104, iii. 152.
Syncrasia, i. 193.

Syncretism, i. 135, 136 ; theory of Neoplatonic, i. 26.
Syria, i. 208.
Syriktes, i. 183, 398.
Syrinx, iii. 232.

Ta-urt, i. 290.
Taaut, i. 124, 127 ; cosmogony of, i. 126.
Taautos, Asclepius pupil of, ii. 279 ; Books of, ii. 279.
Tables of mulberry-wood, iii. 216.
Taboos, fish, i. 269 ; pig, i. 271.
Tabor, Mount, ii. 238.
Talmud, i. 115, 425 ; Jeschu-stories, iii. 279.
Tamar, i. 224.
Tamarisk, i. 284.
Tanes, iii. 49.
Tanitic mouth, i. 282.
Tantalus, cup of, ii. 198.
Taphosiris, i. 293.
Targum, i. 194.
Tartarean spheres, i. 445.
Tartarus, i. 152, 338, 439, ii. 361, 362 ; of seven zones, i. 421.
Tat, and Asclepius, distinction between, ii. 264 ; dialogues with, ii. 237 ; Expository Sermons to, iii. 13, 16, 44, 216, 256, 257, 259, 262, 263, 264, 266 ; initiation of, iii. 310 ; priesthood, iii. 148.
Tatenen, i. 131, 134.
Tathāgatas, ii. 44.
Tatian, ii. 72.
Tax-gatherers, i. 174.
Taxis, ii. 43, iii. 145.
Taylor on numbers, i. 432.
Tcheser, i. 465.
Teachers, common, iii. 287.
Technactis, i. 272.
Teephibis, i. 463.
Tefnut, i. 131, 133.
Teh, Tehu, Tehut, variants of Thoth, i. 48.
Tehuti, i. 124 ; derivative of, i. 54 ; variants of, i. 112.
Telescope of Zoroaster, i. 13.
Tem, i. 66, 337 ; Young, i. 458.
Templa, regiones coeli, ii. 273.
Templar Codex of Fourth Gospel, i. 475.
Temple-folk, iii. 255.
Temple-watchman, iii. 162.
Temu, i. 459.

INDEX 367

Ten, the. ii. 16, 226, 245.
Tent, ii. 211, iii. 20, 32; or tabernacle of soul, ii. 227.
Tent-fellows, iii. 203.
Teos, i. 463.
Terebinth, i. 87.
Termaximus, i. 53.
Territory of Illumination, i. 70; of Initiation, i. 70.
Tertullian, i. 71.
Testaments, ii. 235.
Tethys, i. 310.
Tetraktys, i. 360.
Thabion, ii. 279.
Thales, i. 103, 160, 187, 274, 309.
Thamus, i. 472, iii. 216.
Thamyras, i. 445.
That art thou, ii. 234.
Thāth, i. 112, 461, 462.
Thautabaoth, i. 422.
Thebes, i. 50, 272; library at, i. 465.
Thekla, i. 147.
Themistius, ii. 236.
Thenen, i. 460.
Theocritus, i. 373.
Theodoret, i. 139, ii. 27.
Theodorus, i. 348.
Theodotus, Excerpts from, ii. 251.
Theognis, ii. 156.
Theophanies, i. 232.
Theopompus, i. 326, 350.
Theoretic Life, ii. 163.
Theoretics, iii. 148, 245.
Theoria, iii. 172.
Theosebeia, iii. 273; advice to, iii. 283.
Theosophical Review, i. 15, 95, 118, ii. 42.
Therapeut, i. 26, 241, ii. 172; allegorical exercises, i. 177; community, i. 208; initiations, i. 251.
Therapeutrides, i. 208, 219.
Therapeuts, i. 30, 31 f., 200, 208, 212, 243, ii. 252, 311, 330, 402, iii. 59; prayers of the Essenes and, ii. 49.
Thersites, i. 436, 446.
Thesmophoria, i. 350.
Thespesius (Aridæus), i. 223, 453; vision of, ii. 363, iii. 192.
Thessalians, i. 356.
Theurgic rite of initiation, ii. 255; invocation, ii. 245.
Theurgy, i. 83, ii. 163.

Theuth, iii. 276.
Theuth-Hermes, iii. 216.
Thiasos, i. 206, 256.
Third heaven, the, i. 166, 173.
Third-born, i. 359.
Thirty-six, ii. 341, iii. 50.
Thomas, Gospel according to, i. 142, 155, iii. 37.
Those-that-are, i. 80, 137, ii. 42.
Thoth, i. 68, 124, 136, ii. 244; books of, i. 122, 124; eight-times-great, i. 119; his company of eight, i. 57 ff.; *The Great Gnoses of*, i. 50; first Hermes, i. 104; ibis symbol of, i. 48; incarnations of, i. 463; the initiator, i. 71; as Logos, i. 48, 63, 90, 135; first man, iii. 295; the measurer, i. 66; moon-god, i. 72; and the Osirified, i. 65; pre-eminence of, i. 67, 467; shrine of, i. 56; variants of name, iii. 234; the wise, i. 68, 134; the eternal wisdom, i. 71, 72; words of, i. 63.
Thoth (Tehuti), i. 47 ff.
Thoth (Tekh), i. 458.
Thought, iii. 84.
Thought-and-sense, ii. 136.
Thōuth, i. 124.
Thōyth, i. 110, 112, ii. 279, iii. 234, 277, 278.
Thōyth-Hermes, iii. 231.
Thōythos, iii. 276, 295.
Thracians, i. 169.
Thraemer, i. 461.
Threshold of the Good, ii. 97.
Thrice-great, i. 53.
Thrice-greatest, Egyptian equivalent of, i. 119; Hermes, iii. 198; the title, i. 66.
Thrice-unknown Darkness, ii. 25.
Throne, of Necessity, i. 447; of Truth, iii. 109, 173.
Thrones, iii. 101.
Through the Word, ii. 255.
Thueris, i. 290.
Thyestian banquets, i. 444.
Thyiades, i. 310, 311, 312.
Thyrsus, i. 311.
Tiamat, i. 60.
Tiedemann, i. 13, 16, 23.
Tigris, i. 188.
Time, ii. 192, 367, iii. 28, 63; archetype of, i. 229, ii. 193; artificer of, ii. 192; grandson of

God, i. 229 ; instruments of, iii. 100 ; lord of, i. 76 ; paradigm of, ii. 196.
Time-watcher, iii. 222.
Timæus, i. 106, ii. 70, 167.
Tinkling cymbal, i. 303.
Titanic Passions, i. 311.
Titans, i. 268, 303, iii. 50, 163 ; or stretchers, i. 282.
Toil, iii. 98.
Tombs of Osiris, i. 292, 293, 312, ii. 121.
Tongue, of angels, ii. 32 ; of flesh, ii. 31 ; is fortune, i. 349 ; heart and, i. 136, iii. 208.
Tongues of heaven, ii. 32.
Tormentors, ii. 223.
Torments of darkness, ii. 245.
Tortoise, i. 359.
Tosothrus-Asclepius, i. 465.
Totemism, i. 353.
Trajan, i. 145.
Transfiguration, ii. 238 ; of soul, ii. 164.
Transformation, body of, ii. 44.
Transformations, ii. 145, iii. 111.
Transmigration, ii. 166, iii. 194.
Treasure, i. 167 ; of light, i. 246.
Treasure-house, i. 211.
Treasury, ii. 269.
Tree of Gnosis, i. 428.
Triad of disciples, i. 476.
Triangle, iii. 172 ; equilateral, i. 305, 359 ; most perfect, i. 358 ; Pythagorean, iii. 175.
Triangles, fairest of the, i. 336.
Tribes, the twelve, i. 169.
Trikāyam, ii. 44.
Trinity, i. 214, ii. 79, iii. 258, 268, 275.
Triphyllians, i. 297.
Tritons, i. 359.
Triumphant Christ, ii. 117.
Trojan War, i. 324, iii. 183.
Trumpeters, ii. 289.
Truth, ii. 225, 231, iii. 17 ; beauty of, ii. 121 ; gnosis of, i. 207 ; hall of, iii. 277 ; figure of man of, iii. 277 ; path to, iii. 5 ; plain of, i. 430, ii. 19, 49, 50, 97, iii. 171, 172, 189, 205, 208 ; is sweet, i. 349 ; throne of, iii. 109, 173.
Turiya, i. 152.
Turmoil, ii. 167.
Turnebos, Adr., i. 10.
Turning-back, ii. 98.

Twelve, disciples, the, i. 169 ; fates of death, ii. 249 ; maidens, ii. 249 ; stoles, iii. 182 ; the, ii. 226, 245 ; tribes, i. 169 ; women in dark robes, ii. 249.
Twice-great, i. 53.
Twin-gods, i. 131.
Two, combatants, i. 66 ; ways, i. 56.
Tybi, i. 329.
Typal Man, i. 168.
Type, of æons, ii. 282 ; of body, iii. 49.
Types, of life, ii. 227, 245 ; of lives, iii. 102 ; of wisdom and intelligence, iii. 106.
Typhon, bone of, i. 189.
Typhon, i. 279, 295, iii. 191 ; bone of, i. 343 ; concerning, i. 304 ; conspiracy of, i. 315 ; foam of, i. 308 ; pursuing pig, i. 272 ; reddish-yellow body, i. 309 ; virilia of, i. 335.
Tyrant, i. 431.

Under-girdings, i. 440.
Under-meaning of myths, i. 201.
Underworkers, iii. 50.
Unfruitful, i. 175.
Unguent, scent of, i. 393.
Uniter of the earth, i. 59.
Unlike, ii. 90, iii. 11.
Unnu, i. 56.
Unorder, ii. 126.
Unseemliness, i. 154.
Unseen World, i. 86, 223 ; Lord of the, i. 73.
Untitled Apocalypse of the Codex Brucianus, ii. 107, 282, 303.
Upanishads, ii. 163, 168, 234.
Uranus, i. 151, ii. 144, 162, iii. 234.
Urim and Thummin, i. 250.
Ursin, i. 21, 110.
Urtuhet, i. 294.
Usertsen (I.), i. 458.

Vāhan, ii. 96.
Valentinian, i. 94, ii. 32.
Valentinus, i. 38 ; hymn of, ii. 284 ; letters of, ii. 283 ; psalm of, ii. 217, 312.
Vānaprastha āshrama, ii. 73.
Vaporous nature, iii. 209.
Vapour, iii. 66, 200, 202, 203, 206.
Vapours, iii. 206, 210.

INDEX

Varro, i. 110, 407.
Vase of genesis, iii. 26.
Vedānta, ii. 107.
Vedāntavādins, ii. 107.
Vegetative, iii. 210.
Vehicles of the soul, ii. 167.
Veii, bible of the, ii. 235.
Venus (Isis), i. 382.
Vergecius, Angelus, i. 10.
Vestments, keeper of the, iii. 223.
Vestures, ii. 152.
Vettius Valens, i. 101, 102.
Vices, horde of, ii. 245; and virtues, i. 377.
Victim-sealing books, iii. 223, 224.
Virgin, i. 179, 218, 403; birth, ii. 220, 240; church, i. 377; big with child, i. 182, ii. 240; precinct of the, iii. 161; sister, i. 147; son of, iii. 160, 161; womb of, i. 399, ii. 240; of the world, iii. 93, 125.
Virgin-birth, mystery of the, i. 211.
Virgin-mother, i. 74.
Virgin-mothers, i. 220.
Virgins, seven, i. 176.
Virginal Spirit, i. 181, 182, ii. 240, 241, iii. 157.
Virginity, i. 218, 219.
Virtue, kinsmen of, i. 241; of perfect peace, i. 218; silence on their, ii. 250.
Virtue-lovers, i. 244.
Virtues, i. 216, ii. 245; company of, ii. 245; seven, ii. 248; lists of vices and, ii. 246.
Vishṇu Purāṇa, iii. 180.
Vision, and apocalypsis, ii. 20 ff.; of Aridæus (Thespesius), i. 438, 452, ii. 363; of Beautiful, iii. 15, 53, 253; most blessed, i. 102; of Er, i. 413, 426, 428, ii. 15, 40, 187; glorious, ii. 161; power of godly, iii. 19; of Good, ii. 143; of Hades, i. 223; of great and little man, ii. 238; of Mercabah, i. 154; perfect, iii. 96; simple, ii. 221; of soul, iii. 188; of spiritual crucifixion, ii. 238; supreme, ii. 264; visions, ii. 210; of Crates, i. 380; of Zosimus, i. 380.
Vital sheath, iii. 206.
Voice, direct, iii. 147; of fire, ii. 5, 26; heavenly, i. 101; living, iii. 323.

Void, ii. 64, 374.
Vortex, i. 389, 390, 453, ii. 187.
Vow of Silence, ii. 250.
Vulcan, net of, i. 62.
Vulcanic Crater, i. 452.
Vulture, i. 90.
Vyāsa, ii. 235.

Wagenfeld, i. 123, 124.
Wagner, ii. 94.
Wall, i. 90, 163.
Walton, Alice, i. 461.
War, i. 327; in heaven, iii. 118; Trojan, i. 324, iii. 183.
Wardens, eight, i. 85, 121.
Warder of the souls, iii. 195.
Warriors, iii. 50.
Wars, Civil, i. 352.
Watcher, witness and, iii. 111.
Watchers (Egrēgores), i. 126, iii. 137.
Water, iii. 189; awesome, i. 394, 395; deathless, ii. 18; drainer of, ii. 39; fire and, iii. 66; above firmament, i. 188; first-born of, i. 398; living, i. 188, 190, 399; Osiris is, i. 156; sinuous, ii. 4; as source, i. 309; sprite, i. 367; very water, iii. 17.
Water-earth, ii. 33, 34.
Water-rats, i. 325.
Watery sphere, iii. 209.
Way, above, ii. 15, 41; of birth in God, ii. 244; of this birth, ii. 244; of death, ii. 18; of deathlessness, ii. 39; that leadeth to destruction, i. 182; of devotion, ii. 119; of gnosis, ii. 98; up to God, ii. 280; to worship God, ii. 212; out of ignorance, ii. 237; inner, i. 101; of life, i. 182, ii. 15, 40, 41; middle, ii. 96; up to mount, ii. 150, 171; old, old, ii. 98; of rebirth, ii. 248; straight, ii. 189, iii. 327, ii. 40, 287.
Weasel, i. 356.
Weasel-armed, i. 295.
Web of ignorance, ii. 121.
Wedding garment, ii. 42, ii. 249.
Well of Life, i. 79.
Wending up the Mount, ii. 219.
Wessely, i. 82, 86, 93, 97.
Whale, belly of, i. 425.
Wheat-ear, i. 178, 179.
Wheel, kārmic, ii. 83.
Wheels of Ezekiel, iii. 173.

INDEX

Whether blest child of Kronos, i. 185.
Whirlwinds, fiery, i. 409.
White, cock, i. 342 ; rock, i. 162, 163.
Whole, ii. 310 ; sense, ii. 371.
Whoring, iii. 166.
Whorl, i. 441, ii. 187.
Wilamowitz, i. 185, 195, ii. 300.
Will, ii. 142 ; of God, ii. 160, 220, 395.
Wind, i. 396.
Windows, not eyes, iii. 109.
Winds, four, i. 84.
Wine, of ignorance, ii. 120 ; of, i. 268.
Winged globe, i. 390.
Wings, i. 432 ; feathers of their, i. 430 ; of sonship, i. 390.
Wisdom, i. 206, 220, 221, 223, 225, ii. 251, iii. 163 ; mass of archaic, ii. 236 ; brotherhood for sake of, i. 233 ; dark, i 87, 91 ; disciples of, iii. 303 ; of Egypt, i. 44, 69, ii. 98, iii. 321 ; church of, iii. 323 ; Greek, i. 193 ; in harmony, i. 183 ; harmony of, i. 237 ; husband of, i. 218 ; Indian, ii. 198 ; lady of all, iii. 208 ; laws of, i. 120 ; mother, i. 224, 228 ; practisers of, i. 206 ; serpent of, i. 194, 480 ; spark of, i. 206 ; supreme master of, i. 68 ; tradition of, i. 208 ; that understands in silence, iii. 162.
Wisdom-discipline, iii. 225.
Wisdom-lover, i. 431.
Wise, Thoth the, i. 134.
Withdrawn volumes, ii. 236.
Witness, the, ii. 50, 51 ; and watcher, iii. 111.
Wolf, i. 87, 90, 325.
Wolf-town, i. 354.
Wolves, i. 436.
Woman, first, i. 139, ii. 27 ; strange, iii. 166.
Womb, i. 396, ii. 128 ; ever-virgin, i. 222 ; fecund, ii. 390 ; of Great Mother, iii. 324 ; tore asunder His, i. 182 ; impure, i. 398 ; of Rhea, i. 335 ; is Silence, ii. 241 ; of Virgin, i. 399.
Women, band of seven, ii. 248 ; maladies of, iii. 225.
Wonder, ii. 93, iii. 246.

Wood, cutting of, i. 293.
Word, of creator, iii. 256 ; He who soweth the, ii. 18 ; language of the, i. 54 ; the proceeding thought, i. 137 ; spoken, ii. 343 ; by whom all things were made, i. 136 ; through the, ii. 233, 255.
Word-play, ii. 106.
Words, of Ammon, iii. 215 ; whom it is custom to call angels, i. 243 ; ladder of, i. 139 ; of Thoth, i. 63 ; three more-than-mighty, i. 165.
Work, great, iii. 314, 326.
World, old age of, ii. 356 ; end of, ii. 400 ; fast to the, ii. 239 ; inner, iii. 325 ; intelligible, ii. 273, 286, 302 ; map of, iii. 187 ; noëtic, iii. 80 ; orderer of, iii. 208 ; shrine of all, ii. 351 ; stranger to, ii. 220 ; unseen, i. 223 ; virgin of, iii. 93.
World-citizens, i. 206.
World-egg, ii. 33 ; Orphic tradition of, i. 387, 388.
World-eye, apple of the, iii. 167.
World-illusion, ii. 220, 237.
World-soul, i. 414, ii. 36, 70, 184, 260, iii. 173.
World-tree, the, ii. 317.
Worlds, number of, 183, iii. 171 ; plurality of, iii. 170 ; seven subject, ii. 179.
Worm, i. 171.
Worms, iii. 51.
Worse, i. 328.
Worship, ii. 323 ; of animals, i. 353.

Xenocrates, i. 298, 299.
Xenophanes, i. 351.
Xoïs, i. 320.

Yahweh, iii. 166, 167.
Ye are Gods, i. 163.
Ye shall leave your parents, i. 249.
Ye are whited sepulchres, i. 172.
Year, great, iii. 290.
Year-god, i. 402.
Years, thousand, i. 432 ; ten thousand, iii. 171 ; three thousand, i. 326.
Yedidyah ha-Alakhsanderi, i. 200.
Yoga, ii. 163 ; of Plotinus, i. 251.
Yoga-practices, ii. 197.
Yogin, Plutarch's, iii. 169.

Yoke of horses, i. 430.
Yonge, i. 201.
Young Tem, i. 458.
Younger son, ii. 192, 257.
Youths, seven, i. 176.
Ysdnw, iii. 297.

Zeësar, i. 165.
Zeller, i. 32, 36, ii. 392.
Zervan Akarana, i. 400.
Zeus, i. 151, 279, 305, 313, 327, 330, 359; above, ii. 359; below, ii. 359; bull of, iii. 183; cosmic breath, i. 313; date of, i. 149; essence-chief, ii. 341; gifts of, iii. 274; lame, i. 343; Phrygius, i. 172; sons of, iii. 217.

Zion, foundation of, i. 162.
Zodia, iii. 53.
Zodiac, i. 414, 416, ii. 245; signs of the, ii. 52.
Zoëga, i. 400.
Zone, regal, iii. 198.
Zones, ii. 41, iii. 97, 194, 211; seven, i. 413, ii. 42.
Zophasemin, i. 126.
Zoroaster, i. 325, 437, iii. 274, 278, 296; the Mage, i. 324, iii. 317; *The Telescope of*, i. 13.
Zorokothora, iii. 211.
Zosimus, i. 157, 270, ii. 249, 265, iii. 273; and the Anthropos-doctrine, i. 196; visions of, i. 380.

About the Author

George Robert Stowe Mead (22/3/1863 -- 28/9/1933) was an English author, editor, translator, and an influential member of the Theosophical Society as well as the founder of the Quest Society. He was born to Colonel Robert Mead, an Officer in the British Army and to Mary Mead, who had received a traditional education at Rochester Cathedral School. Having shown academic potential he began studying mathematics at St John's College, Cambridge. Eventually shifting his education towards the study of Classics he gained much knowledge of both Greek and Latin.

In 1884 he completed a bachelor of arts degree, and in the same year he began to practice the position of public school master

While still at Cambridge University Mead read *Esoteric Buddhism* by Alfred Percy Sinnett. This comprehensive theosophical account of the eastern religion prompted Mead to contact two theosophists in London named Bertam Keightly and Mohini Chatterji, which eventually led him to join the Theosophical Society.

Mead became a member of Helena Petrovna Blavatsky's Theosophical Society in 1884. He abandoned his teaching profession in 1889 to be Blavatsky's private secretary and also became a joint-secretary of the Esoteric Section of the Theosophical Society.

Mead received Blavatsky's six *Esoteric Instructions* and other teachings at twenty-two meetings headed by Blavatsky which were only attended by the Inner Group of the Theosophical Society. It was because of the intimacy Mead felt with the Inner Group that he married Laura Cooper in 1899.

Contributing intellectually to the Theosophical Society, at first most interested in eastern religions, he quickly became more and more attracted to western esotericism of religion and philosophy, particularly Neoplatonism, Gnosticism and Hermeticism, though his scholarship and publications continued to engage with eastern religion. Making many contributions to the Theosophical Society's *Lucifer* magazine as joint editor, he eventually became the sole editor of *The Theosophical Review* in 1907 (as *Lucifer* was renamed in 1897).

As of February 1909, Mead and some seven-hundred members of the Theosophical Society's British Section resigned in protest of Annie Besant's reinstating of Charles Webster Leadbeater to membership in the society. While this prompted Mead's resignation, his frustration at the dogmatism of the Theosophical Society may also have been a major contributor to his break with the society. He had been a member for twenty-five years.

In March 1909 Mead founded the Quest Society, composed of 150 defectors of the Theosophical Society and 100 other new members. Very intentionally this new society was planned to be an undogmatic approach to the comparative study and investigation of religion, philosophy, and science. The Quest Society had lectures at Kensington Town Hall in central London but its most focused effort was in its publishing of *The Quest: A Quarterly Review* which ran from 1909-1931 with many contributors.

Among notable names influenced by G.R.S. Mead there can be found: Ezra Pound, W.B. Yeats, Hermann Hesse, Kenneth Rexroth, and Robert Duncan. In her celebrated biography of Jung, Deirdre Bair states that Carl Gustav Jung was also influenced by George Mead.

Works:
- Simon Magus (1892)
- Orpheus (1895-6)
- Pistis Sophia (1896, 1921 ed).
- Fragments of a Faith Forgotten (1900).
- Apollonius of Tyana (1905).
- Thrice Greatest Hermes (1906).
- The Hymns of Hermes
- The Gnosis of the Mind
- Gnostic John the Baptizer: Selections from the Mandæan John-Book (1924)
- Did Jesus Live 100 BC?
- Address read at H.P. Blavatsky's cremation
- Concerning H.P. Blavatsky
- Doctrine of the Subtle Body in Western Tradition

www.ingramcontent.com/pod-product-compliance
Lightning Source LLC
Chambersburg PA
CBHW032015230426
43671CB00005B/90